W9-ABP-743

BARBARIAN
VIRTUES

ALSO BY MATTHEW FRYE JACOBSON

Whiteness of a Different Color:
European Immigrants and the Alchemy of Race

Special Sorrows: The Diasporic Imagination of Irish, Polish,
and Jewish Immigrants in the United States

Matthew Frye Jacobson

BARBARIAN VIRTUES

The United States Encounters Foreign

Peoples at Home and Abroad, 1876-1917

HILL AND WANG

A division of Farrar, Straus and Giroux

New York

Hill and Wang
A division of Farrar, Straus and Giroux
19 Union Square West, New York 10003

Copyright © 2000 by Matthew Frye Jacobson
All rights reserved
Distributed in Canada by Douglas & McIntyre Ltd.
Printed in the United States of America
Designed by Lisa Stokes
First edition, 2000

Library of Congress Cataloging-in-Publication Data

Jacobson, Matthew Frye, 1958–
    Barbarian virtues : the United States encounters foreign peoples
at home and abroad, 1876–1917 / Matthew Frye Jacobson. — 1st ed.
        p.   cm.
    Includes bibliographical references and index.
    ISBN 0-8090-2808-5 (alk. paper)
    1. United States—Politics and government—1865–1933.   2. United
States—Foreign relations—1865–1921.   3. United States—Ethnic
relations.   4. United States—Race relations.   5. Nationalism—
United States—History—19th century.   6. Nationalism—United
States—History—20th century.   7. Political culture—United States—
History—19th century.   8. Political culture—United States—
History—20th century.   9. National characteristics, American.
I. Title.
E661.J34   2000
973—dc21   99-40574

To the Memory of Richard M. Jones

contents

Acknowledgments

IT HAD NEVER occurred to me to write a synthetic treatment of immigration and foreign policy until Lizabeth Cohen asked me to consider it a few years ago. Liz's good idea became my good luck. Since our first phone conversation in 1995, I have also been grateful for her long-distance comradeship, her advice, and her criticisms.

In addition to Liz, several people read the manuscript and offered valuable critiques and words of encouragement. Thanks to Amy Kaplan, David Waldstreicher, Kio Stark, and Brian Herrera for their interest in the project and for their efforts to improve it. Amy's work on empire continues to inspire, and she has a special knack for posing the perfect, clarifying question. David is always insightful on the politics of race and nation, and, characteristically, he pushed me to confront the demons of parochialism which haunted my own outlook on the nation. Not least, he has also enlivened my existence at Yale with his ready wit and much good-natured banter. In addition to their keen readings, Kio gave me invaluable assistance with the final essay on sources, and Brian located and secured all but a few of the splendid illustrations. Michael Hunt offered a useful caveat on my treatment of economics and economism in U.S. foreign policy. My editor, Lauren Osborne, has improved the manuscript in a thousand big and small ways by uniquely combining a strong hand with a light touch.

This project has sent me back across the terrain of the Gilded Age and the Progressive Era in ways that have renewed and deepened my sense of indebtedness to the mentors who first introduced me to the period when I was a graduate student. I would be remiss if I didn't pause—yet again—to thank Andy Buni, Howard Chudacoff, Elmer Cornwell, Bob Lee, Seymour Levantman, Rich Meckel, Carol Petillo, and Judy Smith. Their collective influence on this book is greater than even I would have guessed going in.

Nor have I suffered any shortage of wonderful influences in more recent times. The book is no doubt much better than it would have been had I not spent some time here and there with Amy Bass, Gail Bederman, Oscar Campomanes, Peter Connolly-Smith, Carlo Corea, Melinda Gray, Matthew Guterl, Louise Newman, Mae Ngai, Jack Salzman, Nikhil Singh, Werner Sollors, Katy Stewart, Michael Topp, Alys Weinbaum, and Barbara Weinstein. Louise Newman was also generous enough to lend me her fabulous turn-of-the-century postcard collection for the better part of a semester. My colleagues and students at Yale continue to influence and expand my thinking in all sorts of tangible and intangible ways. Special thanks to Jean-Christophe Agnew, Alicia Schmidt Camacho, Hazel Carby, Nancy Cott, Michael Denning, Glenda Gilmore, Jackie Goldsby, Robert Johnston, Patricia Pessar, Steven Pitti, Alan Trachtenberg, David Waldstreicher, Mark Weiner, Laura Wexler, Heather Williams, and Bryan Wolf.

I first presented this work at the University of Michigan's symposium "After the American Century" in the fall of 1998. Many thanks to Frances Aparicio, Rey Ileto, Lem Johnson, Terri Koreck, David Pedersen, Kelvin Santiago-Valles, and other participants at that conference who made many helpful corrections and recommendations. A later test flight at the ASA also yielded much useful commentary. Thanks especially to fellow panelists Zita Nuñez, Nikhil Singh, Michelle Stephens, and Priscilla Wald. Another presentation at the University of Minnesota elicited spirited criticisms and advice; thanks to that audience, too, and especially to Dave Roediger and Rudy Vecoli. Yet another audience at Harvard's Warren Center gave me a rough ride and some very good advice—alas, at the eleventh hour. I am grateful for the revisions they suggested, both those that made it in and those that did not.

Anyone who ventures a synthesis of this kind must be humbled at some point or another—or perhaps continually—by the classics in the field. As I have struggled to fashion a new narrative, I have repeatedly been struck by the remarkable freshness and staying power of John Higham's *Strangers in the Land* (1955), Barbara Miller Solomon's *Ancestors and Immigrants* (1956), William Appleman Williams's *The Tragedy of American Diplomacy* (1959), and Walter LaFeber's *The New Empire* (1963). As far as I can tell, these works will repay *any* number of readings a person could devote to them—and I should know. There is not one thematic vista, panorama, or clearing in *Barbarian Virtues* where a discerning reader will fail to see the signs of these authors' earlier encampments.

My parents, Sarah Frye Jacobson and Jerry Jacobson, once again offered marvelous encouragement and gave the manuscript their customary uncritical review.

Francesca Schwartz continues to charm my work and my life. However bemused she may be by some of the topics I throw myself into ("You're writing about *Tarzan* now?"), she always ends up by taking them seriously and pushing me to do better with them. Her skepticism, her insistence on clarity, her distaste for the rarefied usages of academic historiography, and her own intellectual commitment in matters of narrative and interpretation—all of these qualities have gotten under my skin. I do mean that in both senses (dead-on criticism can be pretty annoying), but mainly in the positive sense that in internalizing some aspects of her critical vision I have doubtless become a better historian. Thanks to our children, Nick and Tess, too, who endured the book's demands on my time, when clearly it would have been more fun for them if I had just forgotten the whole thing and spent every day at the swings. They also kept me too busy and happy and tired—and too often at the swings—ever to get lost in the torments that a project like this can inflict.

Finally, *Barbarian Virtues* is dedicated to the memory of Richard M. Jones, my first and most influential mentor when I was an undergraduate at The Evergreen State College. Richard was not your typical teacher—he was a psychology professor, for one thing, who at the time I knew him was far more interested in talking about *Moby-Dick* or *King Lear* than about Freud, Horney, or Erikson. But his teaching was both profound and lasting. In the classroom he conveyed a wondrous mixture of rigor, gravity, an irreverence for disciplinary boundaries, a boundless intellectual playfulness, and a sheer joy in discovery and argument. And an infectious love of writing. I came to him a psychology major, I studied literature with him, and I somehow came away a history major—an odyssey that has everything to do with the roving paths my thinking still runs along today. I can never repay the debt; but perhaps this book will succeed in communicating some of the passions and the habits of inquiry I first encountered in Richard's classroom twenty-some years ago. I could aspire to nothing better.

BARBARIAN
VIRTUES

Introduction: Barbarism, Virtue, and Modern American Nationalism

> Over-sentimentality, over-softness, in fact washiness and mushiness are the great dangers of this age and of this people. Unless we keep the *barbarian virtues,* gaining the civilized ones will be of little avail.
>
> —*Theodore Roosevelt to psychologist*
> G. *Stanley Hall, 1899*

W HEN THEODORE ROOSEVELT penned these words, he identified a deep irony at the heart of American thinking at the turn of the century: his notions of barbarism and virtue indicate not only a pattern of extraordinary self-certainty and a contempt for national outsiders but also a plaguing—if quieter—sense of self-doubt. On the one hand, the "civilization" embodied by the United States and Western Europe was plainly the state to which the world's peoples ought rightly to aspire. Indeed, the unquestioned superiority of "civilization" itself justified virtually any policy that the "civilized" cared to carry out at the expense of the "savage." In *The Winning of the West* (1889–96), Roosevelt had un-self-consciously identified the world's unindustrialized regions as "waste spaces," and he had scoffed at the notion that "these continents should be reserved for the use of scattered savage tribes, whose life was but a few degrees less meaningless, squalid, and ferocious than that of the wild beasts with whom they held joint ownership." And yet, on the other hand, the "primitive" traits of vigor, manliness, and audacity, in his view, had given way to effete overcivilization among the once-hearty Anglo-Saxon race; America's rightful heirs were now threatened by hordes of inferiors—immigrants at home and savages abroad. Civilized peoples' pronounced social and evolutionary distance from savagery may have recommended their stewardship over the entire world, but a good dose of the "barbarian virtues" would still be required to carry out this grand project of "extending the blessings of civilization."

This book borrows Roosevelt's suggestive lexicon of "barbarism" and "virtue" to examine American conceptions of peoplehood, citizenship, and national identity against the backdrop of escalating economic and military involvement abroad and massive population influxes at home. In the period between the Centennial Exposition in Philadelphia in 1876 (in which the United States announced its power on the international scene) and World War I (in which it demonstrated that power), the dynamics of industrialization rapidly accelerated the rate at which Americans were coming into contact with foreign peoples, both inside and outside U.S. borders. American political culture in these years was characterized by a paradoxical combination of supreme confidence in U.S. superiority and righteousness, with an anxiety driven by fierce parochialism.

As modern American nationalism took shape within an international crucible of immigration and empire-building, some of its harshest strains derived less from a confidence in American virtues than from a disturbing recognition of the *barbarian* virtues. American integration into the world economic system in this period of breathtaking industrialization exposed a rather profound dependence upon foreign peoples as imported workers for American factories and as overseas consumers of American products— including "rat-eyed young men" from the shtetls of Eastern Europe, as the *New York Times* once described them, and grass-skirted natives as far-flung as the South Pacific. In this respect, immigration and expansion constituted two sides of the same coin. Not only were massive population influxes and overseas interventions of various sorts generated by the same economic engines of industrialization, but public discussion of problematic aliens at home was of a piece with national debate over the "fitness for self-government" of problematic peoples abroad. Americans like Roosevelt often bristled at the general failure of the world's peoples to adopt obediently the roles scripted for them by the nation's economic requirements, and so beneath the unrippled surface of spread-eagled confidence was a nagging disquiet regarding these new transnational requirements themselves.

Roosevelt's "barbarism" and "virtue" provide the controlling metaphor for this investigation of U.S. culture, but the investigation itself focuses upon the point in the American political economy where industrialization and republicanism meet. It was the combined imperatives of production (the need for reliable workers and markets) and governance (the need for citizens deemed reliable) that gave the notions of barbarism and virtue their powerful, if multivalent, currency. If Roosevelt and others identified a renewed, "strenuous" barbarism as a salve to the encroachments of modernity, the "barbarism" of national or racial "inferiors" also provided a ready-made rationale for conquest and domination. If the delicate U.S. experiment in democracy required a particularly virtuous polity, then the nation's very destiny as "steward to the backward races of the world" and as "asylum for the world's oppressed" was fraught with peril. American greatness itself, in bringing so many "barbarians" within the nation's compass, was corrosive of national virtue.

This began as a book about transnational encounter; it gradually became a book about many other things besides. It is about the force of rapid industrialization, which brought the United States into increasing contact with foreigners by reorganizing the frontiers of labor migration and of export and distribution. It is about the theories of peoplehood and the visions of collective destiny that attended these vast demographic and economic transformations. It is about adventurer-politicians like Teddy Roosevelt, theorists like Lewis Henry Morgan and John R. Commons, and writers like Edith Wharton and Edgar Rice Burroughs, and the ways in which their careers both fed and fed upon imperial encounters with "barbarism" and "savagery." Ultimately, though, it is a book about the temper of American nationalism between Reconstruction and World War I, and about the peculiar dependence of the nation's trumpeted greatness upon the dollars, the labor, and, not least, the very *image* of the many peoples with whom Americans increasingly came in contact and whom they blithely identified as inferiors.

These years witnessed the birth of modern American nationalism, but by that I do not mean that there was a complete break with the political moods and practices that came before. On the contrary, looking backward across the historic landscape from the late nineteenth century, we find familiar enough antecedents to the American scene of the 1890s—Manifest Destiny, the anti-immigrant crusade of the 1840s and '50s, Andrew Jackson's policy of Indian Removal, even the Puritan dream of establishing a Godly "citty vpon a hill" for all the world to emulate. There was nothing altogether new in this period about the contact among U.S. citizens and agencies on the one hand and foreign powers and peoples on the other. Indeed, it is important to see U.S. foreign policy in this period as an extension of principles and trends long apparent in the conquest of the continent, or in the mid-nineteenth-century agitation for annexing Cuba and Mexico. A broad construction of the term "imperialism," then—encompassing a mere projection of vested interest in foreign climes at one end of the spectrum, and overt practices of political domination at the other—is particularly useful in identifying the underlying similarities among otherwise diverse international encounters. Likewise, the arrival of the "new" immigrants from the 1880s to the 1910s, like their unsettled reception, simply continued the massive demographic movements and attendant unrest that had been apparent since the dislocations of the early nineteenth century.

What was new in this period was *scale*—the sheer volume of materials needed to feed the engines of industrial production and the volume of production itself; the sheer volume of population movements in response to this stage of maturing capitalism; the scale of government bureaucracies and their enhanced ability to survey territories, establish beachheads, wage war, and administer far-flung populations; and the scale of a burgeoning culture industry, which not only narrated these events for mass consumption but served up images of the world and its peoples that at once naturalized "large policies" *and* gave voice to the anxieties engendered by these grand designs. Though the story of encounter is a continuous one in U.S. history, various structural innovations and changes lent a particular cast to this period.

I isolate the period from 1876 to 1917 not to argue its uniqueness to American history, in other words. It is telling that the 1890s, the very decade that began with the "Battle" of Wounded Knee, the last massacre in the "winning of the West," ended with U.S. hegemony in Hawaii, Cuba, Puerto Rico, Guam, and the Philippines. The culture of empire that had previously characterized the United States reached a new level of maturation during these years. The development of a modern military and an administrative state are two of the markers that set this era off from earlier periods of expansion; the degree of the nation's economic integration into fully global labor and export markets is another.

But perhaps most striking was what we might call the *collateral damage* of the imperial project during these years. To the indigenous populations affected by such expansionist policies, the Louisiana Purchase, say, may have differed little from the occupation of the Philippines. The result in both instances was domination or death. But in terms of dominant U.S. ideologies and current notions of national mission and destiny, there was a big difference: in 1803, Americans wanted inhabited lands for the wealth and the resources they held; in 1898 and after, Americans wanted various lands not for the sake of the lands themselves but for the path they laid toward a grandly conceived and devoutly wished China market. Filipino lives and rights, then, were a kind of collateral damage in the U.S. quest for something that had little to do with the Philippines per se. To most expansionists the archipelago was but a stepping stone to something more significant. The safety and concerns of Hawaiians, Cubans, Puerto Ricans, Chamorros, and Panamanians, too, went by the wayside not because their lands held the imagined riches of a Louisiana, but because they were indispensable in the quest for an imperial infrastructure of shipping lanes, naval bases, treaty ports, and coaling stations. This approach to entire peoples as pawns in a vast geopolitical game represented a heightened degree of imperialist vision, which was to become standard fare over the course of the twentieth century. Subsequent interventions in Haiti, Nicaragua, Cuba, and Vietnam all followed from a logic that had been operational in the Philippines in 1899 but not in Louisiana in 1803. The policy universe of today's State Department would be legible to Woodrow Wilson in a way in which it simply would not have been to Rutherford B. Hayes.

It is worth noting, in this connection, that these turn-of-the-century interventions took place against the backdrop of a portentous reunion between the sectional combatants of the American Civil War. As Frederick Douglass put it in 1895, as far as the politics of race were concerned, "the cause lost in the [Civil] War is the cause regained in the peace, and the cause gained in the war is the cause lost in the peace." The Reconstruction era's profound philosophical revisions of the concept of citizenship—both Reconstruction's radical promise and its crushing defeat to the forces of white supremacism—formed the crucial background for later public discussions of the many other peoples of color who were drawn into the political and social orbit of the United States.

In order to rethink the texture of American political life, I have chosen to bridge various topics and scholarly orientations that are most often left separate. I depict immigration and foreign policy as two closely related dimensions in the same realm of economic development and civic discourse, first of all. I also trace connections between the civic discourses on immigration law and empire-building on the one hand and the cultural universe of academic evolutionism and popular exotica on the other, and between white (often "Anglo-Saxon") dominance at home and U.S. national hegemony abroad.

There is a danger, as historian Nicholas Thomas has observed, that, in investigating the Victorian era as a colonizing age *par excellence,* we may conveniently overstate its distance from the "open liberal modernity" that presumably characterizes our own historical moment. We may scoff at the glib chauvinisms of the era's anthropological and political discourses, for example; we may take solace in our having defeated many of the ideas that drove the rapacious projects of an earlier day. My intent here is quite the opposite: the reformation of American nationalism in this cauldron of immigration and imperialism is worth looking at so closely precisely because neither the processes nor their results are safely fossilized in a bygone epoch. Our public language has changed a great deal, it is true; the civilities of public discussion in the post-civil-rights era generally do not allow a frank disparagement of "savages" or "Chinamen," nor do they allow presidents and secretaries of state openly to muse on the fate of the world's "waste spaces." But, setting aside the niceties of public language, it behooves us to ponder the continuities between Roosevelt's day and our own, and to consider the ways in which—in the age of *Border Watch* and the Gulf War no less than in the age of the Immigration Restriction League and the Philippine-American War—dominant notions of national destiny and of proper Americanism draw upon charged encounters with disparaged peoples whose presence is as reviled in the political sphere as it is inevitable in the economic.

part one

Markets

Now, once again—altogether Boys!
Siss! boom!! a-h!!!

The U.S. engagement with foreign peoples as potential consumers also entailed their "uplift" to a state of American "civilization." Popular depictions of foreigners' inferiority had much to suggest about American identity as it was now understood. Postcard, 1907

COURTESY OF LOUISE NEWMAN

A turn-of-the-century advertising card for Singer Sewing Machines depicted a grass-skirted Pacific "native" busily working a modern sewing machine inside a grass hut. Here was the national reverie in its crystalline form: the foreigner as both a reliable consumer and an industrious worker. Throughout the period from the 1870s to World War I, American politicians and manufacturers feared that the engines of industry could not be slowed without undermining the nation's stability, but also that, at its accustomed pace of production, the nation risked outstripping its own capacities to absorb its goods. Enhanced productivity meant saturated markets. This dual anxiety cast foreigners in a corresponding dual role: foreign peoples would keep the American economy afloat as both auxiliary consumers in a vast, worldwide export market, and as auxiliary workers in an ever-expanding domestic labor market. National well-being depended upon the grass-skirted native's willingness both to purchase the sewing machine and to take up the needle trades.

In Part I, I examine American economic thought during the boom and bust years from the 1870s to the 1910s, and particularly the implications of that constant watchword "overproduction." Economic and political historians have routinely referred to the "fabled markets" of the Orient in nineteenth-century American economic thought. Chapter 1, "Export Markets," examines some of these fables—their basis in American economic circumstances, their engagement with pat stereotypes of "civilization," "savagery," and "progress," and their portent for the peoples of Asia and other regions whose economic lives and cultural values were to be hitched to the cart of American industry.

If overproduction posed a danger to economic stability (and thus to domestic tranquillity), among the chief symbols of such peril was the image of the intractable or incendiary foreign worker. Chapter 2, "Labor Markets," locates "the immigrant," as a charged cultural icon with both positive and negative valences, within the economic debates surrounding industrialization. While manufacturers and certain local and state governments sent swarms of agents abroad in an effort to woo a steady supply of cheap labor to the United States, other natives worried over the disruptions these new arrivals would cause both for the security of American workers and for the smooth functioning of the polity.

The two sides of this economic saga—the necessary export of goods and the necessary import of labor—generated a strange, Janus-faced ideology of dependence and scorn that profoundly influenced the temper of American nationalism and indeed the very notion of "Americanness" in this period. Various "natives" and "savages" abroad were blithely tarred as inferiors and identified as prime candidates for a brand of "uplift" that entailed, among other things, a strict lesson in modern modes of desire and habits of consumption. They were also reviled for their failure to need U.S. products—shoes, clothing, textiles, machinery—quite as much as the U.S. economy seemed to need their business. Similarly, the soaring numbers of diverse immigrants at home were welcomed for their labor power and yet resented—even violently assaulted—for the economic competition they presented, or for the element of "difference" they introduced to the society. In both cases, the deep American dependence upon these foreign peoples seems to have fueled the animus against them. Americans may have been wont to hold the Pacific native, the African or Latin American savage, the East European greenhorn, or the Chinese sojourner at arm's length, but emergent economic circumstances had set the nation in a rather tenacious embrace with precisely these unassimilated peoples. Their engagement in U.S. economic growth as theoretical consumers and actual workers had much to do with the kind of industrial society the United States was becoming; their perceived backwardness and inferiority had everything to do with the way American identity had come to be understood.

Export Markets: The World's Peoples as Consumers

> A savage, having nothing, is perfectly contented so long as he wants nothing. The first step toward civilizing him is to create a want. Men rise in the scale of civilization only as their wants rise.
>
> —*Josiah Strong,* Our Country *(1886)*
>
> I am an exporter, I want the world.
>
> —*Charles Lovering, textile manufacturer (1890)*

"WE THANK THEE for national prosperity and progress," intoned Bishop Matthew Simpson in his convocation for Philadelphia's Centennial Exposition in 1876, "for valuable discoveries and multiplied inventions, for labor-saving machinery relieving the toiling masses." If progress had become an article of religious faith by 1876—discovery, invention, and machinery its miraculous manifestations—then the exposition in Philadelphia was its most magnificent temple. Here visitors could see the splendid Corliss engine, "that giant wonder . . . , [propelling] an endless system of belts and wheels," as the centennial commissioner put it; "silent and irresistible," it seemed fully to realize "the fabled powers of genii and afrit in Arabian tales." Here they could thrill to the roar and the hum of all sorts of technical innovations in the processes of production—shingle-cutting machines, quartz mills, sugar mills, harvesting machinery, and printing presses. They could examine great slabs of crude metal, gaze upon the polish of a shiny new railway car, or wonder at the power and the workings of a hydraulic ram. They could look over a cornucopia of new consumer items—cutlery, felt hats, silverware, dentifrice, glassware, mincemeat, tobacco, sewing machines, and "show-cases filled with dresses that were enough to drive an ordinary woman crazy." They could view the new tools of commerce, innovative technologies of communication and shipping, including telegraphic equipment, lighthouse service and weather equipment, and Alexander Graham Bell's telephone. And here at the fair, not incidentally, they could also become acquainted with what would turn out to be among the most important tools of all in the quest for worldwide markets—Gatling guns, projectiles, torpedoes, and twenty-inch Rodman guns.

The idea of the world market was largely the point of this exposition. This national celebration took place, after all, in the midst of a rather severe depression cycle that had begun in 1873. And so, if over the course of 159 days the Centennial Exposition introduced nearly ten million visitors to America's wares, as it was meant to do, discussion all around the exposition also introduced new staples of American economic thought: the fear of domestic "overproduction" and the appetite for foreign markets to absorb the resulting surplus of American goods. "Unquestionably international trade and commerce will be promoted," declared one orator at the exposition's end. "The ingenuity and excellence of our mechanics and inventors will be made better known." Throughout the exposition, Philadelphia newspapers had repeatedly referred to the saturation of domestic markets and the importance of cultivating foreign—particularly Asian—markets for American manufactured goods in order "to prevent continued depression." Asia, as one newspaper had it, represented "an almost unlimited field for disposal of many articles of American manufacture, where up to this very moment, such goods are almost unknown."

In the late eighteenth century, Adam Smith had cautioned against creating a great national empire "for the sole purpose of raising up a nation of customers who should be obliged to buy from the shops of our different producers." By the late nineteenth, Americans seemed to have created precisely such an empire; but even this "nation of customers" did not have the spending power to support its shopkeepers. If the attendant revolution of values had its liberating aspects at home, as Americans harvested the blossoming consumer culture for undreamed-of amusements and conveniences, so did it ironically enslave the United States to social forces abroad, as American producers felt themselves more and more dependent upon the spending habits of little-known consumers in distant lands.

Thus the common perception of the nation's economic needs became entangled with a web of myths and stereotypes regarding the diverse peoples of the new global marketplace. Isolation is the mother of barbarism, wrote Josiah Strong in his popular tract of nationalism and Christianity, *Our Country*. For Strong, as for many of his compatriots, the notion of American grandeur entailed not only establishing a global presence by reaching out to other regions and peoples of the world, but fully transforming the ways in which those peoples lived. The transformation, rather loosely envisioned under the imprecise rubric of "civilization," would be both spiritual and material: conveniently, the export of Christian ideals would go hand in hand with the export of finished textiles and manufactured goods. "The mysteries of Africa are being opened," wrote Strong; "the pulse of her commerce is beginning to beat. South America is being quickened, and the dry bones of Asia are moving; the warm breath of the Nineteenth Century is breathing a living soul under her ribs of death. The world is to be Christianized and civilized." Lest the reader miss the crucial connection between the nation's roles as both spiritual savior and industrial supplier to these benighted nations, Strong went on to ask rhetorically, "What is the process of civilizing but *the creating of more and higher wants?*" Commerce, he concluded, would follow the missionary: "The millions of Africa and Asia are someday to have the wants of a Christian civilization." And "with these vast continents added to our market," surely the United States would become "the mighty workshop of the world, and our people 'the hands of mankind.' "

During this period, as transportation routes and communication lines became more extensive, not only did the nation's regional economies become more thoroughly integrated with one another, but the national economy itself became more thoroughly integrated into a world economic system. The United States went out into the world of international trade and empire-building in a complex ideological position: in terms of racial and cultural allegiances, the United States entered world arenas as a European offshoot with some fancied affinity to the Old World. In terms of nationalist propensities and economic necessities, on the other hand, the United States embarked on this ambitious program as the European powers' most menacing rival. The emergence of the United States on the world stage, then, was marked by both a bitter competition among the European and Euro-identified nations, and an articulated kinship among these same powers in their self-proclaimed civilizing mission among the savages, semisavages, and barbarians of Africa, Asia, and Latin America.

Industrial Production and "Terrible Surplus"

The United States' spectacular economic growth at the turn of the century was attended by an equally spectacular pattern of downturns and failures: nearly half of the years between the 1870s and World War I were depression years—1873–79, 1882–85, 1893–97, 1907–8, and 1913–15. The story of the nation's fantastic accumulation of wealth in this period is also a story of crushing poverty. In this context, social and economic remedies were at a premium; indeed, this was a time of frenetic activity in inventing, proposing, and debating solutions of all sorts—distributive innovations like the single tax; remonetizing plans like greenbacks and free silver; protectionist mechanisms like tariffs on international trade; or political programs like populism, socialism, and anarchism.

One of the mainstays of economic discussion throughout these years was the fevered talk of "overproduction" and the need to secure foreign markets. Economic depression, in this formulation, was a sign not of capitalism's failure, but of its stunning and unabsorbed success: the wheels of industry were simply churning out more goods than Americans could hope to consume themselves, and so other markets would have to be sought and secured. In the 1870s, Commander Robert Shufeldt, long interested in opening the "Hermit Kingdom" of Korea to American interests, had put the matter most starkly: "At least one-third of our mechanical and agricultural products are now in excess of our wants, and we must *export* these products or *deport* the people who are creating them." "Our manufactures have outgrown or are outgrowing the home market," concurred the National Association of Manufacturers in an atmosphere of crisis in the mid-1890s; "expansion of our foreign trade is the only promise of relief."

Not everyone subscribed to the "overproduction" thesis. Advocates of free silver and many labor leaders, notably, felt that the problem was best understood not as a case of overproduction but of "underconsumption": the domestic market could indeed absorb the nation's vast output, if only wage scales and reigning patterns of indebtedness were altered to allow it to do so. Among the sharpest—and funniest—critiques of the overproduction thesis was James Jeffrey Roche's parodic poem, "The Terrible Surplus," written amid vigorous national debate over free trade and tariff policy in the 1890s. Roche was the editor of the *Boston Pilot*, an Irish immigrant journal; and it was perhaps his Irish-nationalist sensibility, in which a keen sense of justice was derived from the mythic precedents of tenancy and famine on the Emerald Isle, that led him to question the premise of so much want amid plenty. His poem is an extreme extension of the logic by which, earlier, Senator John Kasson had warned that, if the United States failed to secure sufficient foreign markets, "our surplus will soon roll back from the Atlantic coast upon the interior, and the wheels of prosperity will be clogged by the very richness of the burden which they carry, but cannot deliver." Such an analysis, for Roche, was the stuff of apocalyptic comedy:

> *Abundance clutched, with ruthless hand,*
> *The nation's throat like an iron band;*
> *Silver rivers with golden sand*
> *Inundated the hapless land*
> *In the year of the Terrible Surplus.*

> *Granaries groaned with weight of grain;*
> *Flocks and herds covered every plain;*
> *Oil wells flowed, and every vein*
> *Of mines and minerals swelled the gain*
> *In the year of the Terrible Surplus.*

> *Other peoples, more blest than we,*
> *Joyed in their happy bankruptcy;*
> *Foreign paupers, whose trade was "free,"*
> *Pitied our plethoric misery,*
> *In the year of the Terrible Surplus. . . .*

But whether or not "overproduction" was the proper frame for understanding the boom and bust of the Gilded Age and Progressive Era economy (many economists today question it), whether or not foreign markets indeed held the key to national prosperity, it was true that this period marked a dramatic shift in the balance of U.S. trade. The years 1876 through 1880 represented the first time in U.S. history when the country had a positive balance of trade for five consecutive years. This was not an aberration, but a watershed: before 1876, there were only fourteen years in which the nation's exports exceeded its imports; between 1876 and the 1970s, there were only *three* years (1888, 1889, and 1893) in which they *did not*. As a quick measure of the rise in U.S. productivity in these years, the nation's Gross National Product for the five-year period 1869–73 was $9 billion; for the five-year period 1897–1901, over $37 billion. Gross farm product, too, nearly tripled between the Civil War and the turn of the century.

Agricultural products and textiles led the way in the United States' significant shift toward becoming an exporting rather than an importing nation. New technologies of cultivation and harvest and the opening of new lands after the 1860s dramatically increased the nation's overall agricultural production. Cotton production nearly doubled between 1870 and 1890, for instance; wheat production increased by over 30 percent in the decade of the 1870s alone. Both crops accounted for a huge proportion of the nation's exports. But by the 1890s, even manufactured goods ran in this direction. In 1880, agricultural items accounted for 84 percent of all U.S. exports; just after the turn of the century, that figure had fallen to about 67 percent, as minerals, ore, and manufactured goods gained ground. Interest in the export market was especially sharp among oil producers: by the mid-1880s, Standard Oil shipped over 90 percent of its kerosene abroad (70 percent to Europe, and another 21 percent to Asia). U.S. exports overall climbed by fits and starts throughout this period, from $526 million in 1876 to over $1 billion per year by the late 1890s; exports continued to climb steadily, reaching $2 billion for the first time in 1911, and jumping to $5, $6, and $7 billion per year during the war years of 1916–19. Although the export market continued to receive only a fraction of the foodstuffs and goods that the domestic market absorbed, the trends were still impressive. As of 1893, only Great Britain's exports exceeded those of the United States.

Earlier in the century, apostles of expansion and progress like William Seward had nourished precisely such a vision of export markets and America's capacity to exploit them. As early as the 1850s, Seward had proclaimed, "Multiply your ships, and send them forth to the east. The nation that draws most materials and provisions from the earth, and fabricates the most, and sells the most of productions and fabrics to foreign nations must be, and will be, the great power of the earth." Seward believed that political supremacy would follow commercial ascendancy; and commercial ascendancy depended, in the end, upon access to and control of foreign markets.

Thus, as secretary of state (1861–69), Seward stressed the importance of international commerce and global reach, and he developed ambitious policies toward those ends: he obtained the Midway Islands and Alaska ("the drawbridge between America and Asia," as one enthusiastic observer put it); he had designs on Hawaii; he advocated construction of an isthmian canal; and he toyed with all manner of blueprints for Caribbean and Latin American expansion. Antiexpansionists were able to block many of Seward's plans in the 1860s; but their counterarguments steadily lost force in the 1870s and 1880s, as development of the interior effectively "closed" the frontier (at least in popular imagination), and as agricultural and industrial production threatened to outstrip the capacities of the nation's domestic market. Seward's expansive vision thus formed an important foundation for the later view, during the cycles of depression in the 1870s and after, that—global supremacy aside—the nation's economic *survival itself* would require an aggressive conquest of foreign markets.

Notwithstanding the dissent of labor leaders or of parodists like Jeffrey Roche, over the latter decades of the nineteenth century a formidable consensus did develop on the overproduction thesis and the need for foreign markets. A series of articles by economist David Wells in 1887 and 1888 (later published under the title *Recent Economic Changes and Their Effects on the Production and Distribution of Wealth and the Well-Being of Society*) presented a cyclical economic theory and analysis whose chief solutions included market penetration abroad. Charles Arthur Conant, too, Washington correspondent for the *New York Journal of Commerce* and a financial editor of *Banker Magazine*, concluded that sustained domestic productivity and global expansion were the only means to maintain both labor's wages and capital's profits. Industrialists like Andrew Carnegie quickly agreed that export to foreign markets was the only feasible way of alleviating the surplus.

The interpretation's popularity and the attendant calls for action on the part of policy-makers became particularly widespread during the harsh depression of 1893 (a year, not incidentally, of trade deficit), and a few years later, when the recovery of 1897–98 rather portentously coincided with a boom in the nation's exports. The domestic setting of the 1890s, and particularly the mounting labor radicalism of the decade, lent still more urgency to the question of markets, as labor disaffection came to be seen as a chief danger in the era of overproduction. "We must have new markets," Senator Henry Cabot Lodge argued, "unless we would be visited by declines in wages and by great industrial disturbances, of which signs have not been lacking."

Business and financial organs and organizations like *Banker Magazine*, *Bradstreet's*, the American Banking Association, and the National Association of Manufacturers all became outspoken advocates of export trade as the new panacea for the nation's woes of overproduction. The constituency that coalesced around the overproduction thesis ultimately included not only business and finance, but the conservative press and importantly placed politicians and State Department figures. President Grover Cleveland emphasized the need to "find markets in every part of the habitable globe"; William Day, assistant secretary of state under McKinley, commented enthusiastically upon the "vast undeveloped fields of Africa and the Far East."

As policy-making way back in the days of William Seward had suggested, a keen interest in foreign markets and a determination to conquer them for the good of the country carried wide-ranging implications for statebuilding and for the conduct of foreign policy. In his *Report upon the Commercial Relations of the United States* (1880), Secretary of State William Evarts articulated what would soon become a driving principle of American foreign policy: "The fostering, the developing, and the directing of our commerce by the government should be laid down as a necessity of the first importance." It was scarcely a leap from here to William Howard Taft's "dollar diplomacy" three decades later. "The diplomacy of the present administration," Taft explained, "has sought to respond to modern ideas of commercial intercourse. . . . It is an effort frankly directed to the increase of American trade upon the axiomatic principle that the government of the United States shall extend all proper support to every legitimate and beneficial American enterprise abroad."

The policy implications of the overproduction thesis were clearly spelled out by military and economic theorists like Alfred Thayer Mahan and Brooks Adams.

In *The Influence of Sea Power upon History* (1890), Mahan linked the nation's growing agricultural and industrial productivity to the need for a modern navy that could protect the commercial fleet and control the waterways. The only choices the United States faced, in his view, were to absorb American products at home through some "socialistic" mechanism, or to find new markets for American goods across the seas. Mahan anticipated Frederick Jackson Turner's notion of a new national order in the post-"frontier" era. The seas now constituted the frontier, a vast safety valve to drain off the nation's surplus production. In Mahan's view, production, shipping, and colonization (in that order) constituted the mainspring of historic activity among powerful, seagoing nations. Control of the seas was the key to controlling the nation's economic fate in a period of overproduction.

Brooks Adams, too, started with the premise of overproduction, and, like Mahan, ended with a dramatic series of policy initiatives. As he put it in *America's Economic Supremacy* (1900), the United States "stands face to face with the gravest conjuncture that can confront a people. She must protect the outlets of her trade, or run the risk of suffocation." Without significant changes in economic and administrative arrangements, the United States could conceivably suffer gluts "more dangerous to her society than many panics such as 1873 and 1893." In a frankly Darwinian discussion under the subhead "The New Struggle for Life among Nations," Adams warned, "On the existence of this surplus hinges the future." He thus advocated a policy of territorial expansion and administrative concentration ("for governments are simply huge corporations in competition"), including the consolidation of the West Indies under U.S. control, vigorously maintaining "Asiatic markets," and building an isthmian canal as a key to traffic and communication within this emergent trade empire. "If America is destined to win this battle for life," he argued, "she must win because she is the fittest to survive under the conditions of the twentieth century."

More pragmatic subscribers to the overproduction thesis were no less sweeping in their proposals for a more vigorous state policy. The National Association of Manufacturers (NAM), founded in 1895 in response to precisely the crisis of markets, advocated a strong, active role for the government in securing and protecting foreign commerce, including a comprehensive network of reciprocity treaties, government subsidies to build a merchant fleet, the construction of a Nicaraguan canal, and the improvement of internal waterways. By the time the NAM emerged in the 1890s, however, the state was already well oriented toward this general aim of securing the requisites of a seagoing commercial power. In the 1870s, the United States had concluded a reciprocity treaty with Hawaii with an eye toward securing "a resting spot in the midocean, between the Pacific coast and the vast domains of Asia," and a treaty with Samoa securing use of the harbor at Pago Pago in exchange for certain political protections. In the 1880s, Congress had set about building a modern navy, authorizing thirty-four steel vessels between 1883 and 1889; during this period, the nation had expanded and improved its consular service as well. The wars of 1898 and 1899 in Cuba and the Philippines, then, would both consolidate this expansive world-view and accelerate the trends in American state-building, as the modern administrative state began to take shape under McKinley and Roosevelt.

The newly energetic quest for markets would not only cast American government in an increasingly active role, but would also have tremendous implications for those regions that represented the target of such economic aspiration. According to Africa enthusiast Henry Sanford, for instance, President Chester A. Arthur was "influenced by the idea of covering those unclad millions [in Africa] with our domestic cottons." In 1883, Sanford cultivated interest in Washington in the notion of an African International Association under the sponsorship of Belgium's King Leopold II, and the United States did participate in the Berlin Conference on the development of the Congo in 1884–85. Finally, the African market proved far less important for American exporters than either Latin America or Asia—or, indeed, than the cherished image of those naked millions might have promised—largely because the flurry of imperialist activity on the part of the European powers in the region left U.S. goods at a decided disadvantage. But, however insignificant the efforts of men like Sanford, Senator John Kasson, and Secretary of State Frederick Frelinghuysen to translate a vague American interest in Africa into active markets and actual trade practices, it is no small matter that, as early as the 1880s, the United States had joined the colonial powers of Europe at the conference table on the topic of "developing" the Congo. Increasingly, whether by informal means of economic penetration or by more overt methods of territorial aggrandizement by conquest or treaty, the American quest for new markets would lead down the road of empire.

If the desired global reach never did extend across the south Atlantic to the "dark continent" of Africa, U.S. designs in other regions did take on a decidedly imperialistic cast, either in aspiration or in the actual conduct of policy. The United States looked with feasting eyes upon two regions in particular. China occupied a central place in American economic fantasies throughout the period, although it never did become an actual outlet for U.S. goods on the scale suggested by its enormous population. And Latin America and the Caribbean, if cutting a somewhat less spectacular figure in the American imagination, in fact became a significant market for U.S. exports and a significant proving-ground for those expeditionary forces associated with empire. One key architect of U.S. policy in the region was James Blaine, secretary of state during the assassination-shortened Garfield administration (1881) and then again under Benjamin Harrison (1889–92). Two principles guided his actions in Latin America, he explained: "to bring about peace" and "to cultivate such friendly commercial relations with all American countries as would lead to a large increase in the export trade of the United States." Bringing about peace, as it happened, surprisingly often meant war; and so Latin America became the site of numerous political and military interventions during this formative period in the cultivation of the export trade.

Taken together, China and Latin America nicely demonstrate two distinct dimensions of the imperial imagination that necessarily attended the "overproduction" thesis of American economic health and stability. The story of the United States in China illumines the realm of imperialist fantasy, as the fondest hopes of exporters reduced the whole of Chinese history and culture to a series of "wants" whose particulars were as easily discerned by the Western eye as they were fulfilled by Western industry. The story of the United States in Latin America, on the other hand, illumines the realm of pure imperial power and its deployment, as policy-makers annexed entire nations, not only as consumers of North American goods but as elements in a strategic infrastructure for an export economy whose requirements included canals, harbors, coaling stations, and naval bases all beyond the proper borders of the nation itself.

The New Far West: China

The China clipper was our Parthenon, wrote historian Samuel Eliot Morison. The idea that China and the China market held some special significance for the United States had a long and varied history. As early as 1791, Alexander Hamilton had declared that India and China together represented an "extensive field for the enterprise of our merchants and mariners [and] an additional outlet for the commodities of the country." In 1882, as he vetoed congressional immigration measures, Chester Arthur noted that, though continued Chinese immigration posed a hazard to the republic, it was linked to American opportunity in the East, "the key to national wealth and influence," and therefore forbearance was required on Americans' part. By the time the United States had annexed Hawaii and was asserting hegemony over the Philippines (the "stepping-stones to China") at the turn of the twentieth century, it had become axiomatic among manufacturers, economic theorists, diplomats, and politicians that China was crucial to America's future. When they spoke of attaining foreign markets as a salve to the crisis of overproduction, that is, it was often China that they had in mind.

Indeed, once continental expansion was complete, the *idea* of China if not the vast country itself became annexed to American dreams of continued territorial "progress." As one cotton manufacturer put it in an 1899 address, the government should protect and extend "our interests in what was once the old Far East or what is now our new Far West." In *Harper's Weekly* that same year, another writer proposed expanding the Monroe Doctrine (which since 1823 had opposed any interventions in South America on the part of the European powers) to cover China.

These intertwining themes of American expansiveness and the China market constituted a powerful formulation. As Brooks Adams observed in 1900, "From the earliest times, China and India seem to have served as the bases of human commerce; the seat of empire having always been the point where their products have been exchanged against the products of the West." If the United States was to embrace its destiny not only as a world power but as the next great empire, then surely China had a significant role to play. For many, China held the key to the disposition of America's terrible surplus; and, insofar as marketing the surplus abroad was crucial to the country's economic well-being, there was simply no overstating the importance of capturing the China trade. "Our geographical position, our wealth, and our energy pre-eminently fit us to enter upon the development of eastern Asia," wrote Adams, "and to reduce it to part of our economic system." The Chinese question was no less than "the great problem of the future," and East Asia, "the prize for which all energetic nations are grasping."

Textiles represented the chief U.S. export to China in this period, particularly as the Southern cotton-goods industry expanded in the 1890s. During the last decade of the nineteenth century, the number of spindles in the South nearly tripled from 1.3 million to nearly four million; and as production increased, so, too, did attention to foreign markets. Between 1887 and 1897, as depression weakened the domestic market, textile exports to China more than doubled. "You can see at once what the importance of the China trade is to us," a group of textile manufacturers wrote to their congressman in 1899. "It is everything."

Second to the textile industry among U.S. exporters to China were oil companies like Standard Oil, whose kerosene exports to Asia represented a growing business. In 1898, of just under $10 million in total U.S. exports to China, textiles and oil accounted for about $8 million ($5.1 million and $2.8 million respectively). Other American businessmen with heavy stakes in the China market included producers of wheat flour, iron and steel, and tobacco; also on the list, though in negligible proportions, were finished manufactured goods such as railway machinery and carriages, electrical equipment, and light machinery such as sewing machines and cash registers. Also in 1898, the American-China Development Company was formed in order to obtain a railroad concession in China (although, amid political turmoil, J. P. Morgan later allowed this concession to be canceled without the railroad's having been completed). Thus the actualities of the China trade were significant enough by the 1890s—the high-water mark of the China fable, in many respects—even if they paled in comparison to the undying dreams attached to China's four hundred million consumers.

The United States had essentially ridden into the region on the coattails of the European powers—notably on those of Great Britain during the Opium War (1839–42). When the British ironclad *Nemesis* made quick work of an entire fleet of Chinese war junks, thus "opening" China to "free trade," the United States stood ready to exploit the Western advantage. Under the most-favored-nation status accorded by treaty in 1844, exports from the United States to China increased from roughly $2 million in the 1840s to almost $9 million in the 1860s. Not coincidentally, it was under the watch of the expansive William Seward that China and the Chinese became annexed to the project of developing the American West: Seward's ambitious vision included not only "modernizing" China and thus finding a field for U.S. goods, but also contracting Chinese labor to help build up the American West. Among the terms of the Burlingame Treaty (1868) between the United States and China was a provision for the unrestricted immigration of Chinese laborers—an article that Seward saw as crucial to the rapid development of the Western infrastructure, particularly the railroad. But although Seward approached foreign affairs with a kind of evangelical zeal for the spread of American influence, in this period the United States still acted in cooperation with the European powers. Seward's primary departure from them was a steadfast insistence upon Chinese territorial integrity, which, for the United States, represented the surest—or only—means of having access to the whole of the China market.

American interest in the boundless China market peaked in the 1890s. This rise owed in part to domestic events and the nation's psychic economy during that decade. The Census Bureau's announcement that the nation's Western frontier had "closed," a demographic interpretation endorsed and popularized by historian Frederick Jackson Turner in "The Significance of the Frontier in American History" (1893), lent new urgency to the decades-old web of concerns regarding overproduction, stagnation, discontent, radicalism, and the cure-all of foreign markets. The severe depression of 1893, moreover, along with the precipitant increase in labor agitation and class violence in places like Homestead, Pennsylvania, heightened anxiety and raised the stakes of discovering an economic salve, which, for many, could only mean finding new markets for American goods of all sorts.

Coxey's Army, a ragtag band of unemployed workers who marched into Washington, D.C., in 1894 to demonstrate to the Cleveland administration the need for public works, seemed to underscore both issues. Their presence in Washington, (before being scattered by federal troops) eloquently argued that, by its incapacity to employ all hands, flagging American industry threatened to generate a revolutionary force. By extension, the demonstration also suggested that a massive trek west on the part of disaffected laborers, to the high hopes and quick fortunes of the "frontier," could no longer be counted on to siphon off discontent. That the members of Coxey's Army hailed largely from the Midwest and the West and made their way *east* to Washington was a fact fraught with symbolic import for a nation reared on myths of frontier adventure and self-made men.

It was in the 1890s, too, that Americans cast an eye nervously to China to keep watch over the increasingly aggressive activity of their economic rivals in the region. If domestic unrest and the symbolic blow of the closing of the frontier seemed to increase the stakes of capturing the China market, the international scene added urgency. In the Sino-Japanese War of 1894, Japan triumphed in its bid to wrest control of Korea from a terribly overmatched and outgunned Chinese army. The German seizure of Kiaochow, and a scramble among Japan, Germany, France, Great Britain, and Russia for railroad and mining concessions in China throughout the latter 1890s—culminating in the Russo-Japanese War in 1904—quickly gave shape to a "spheres of influence" arrangement that threatened vivisection of historic Chinese territories. Though many Americans did not at all regret the modernizing influence this would have over China, they did tend to worry over the prospect of securing their own "sphere."

In this context, organs like the *Journal of Commerce* urged the State Department to devote more energy and resources to the protection of U.S. interests in China. In the wake of German activity in Shantung, a Committee on American Interests in China formed behind the leadership of *Journal of Commerce* editor John Foord. Foord, a Scottish immigrant who had been a reporter and editor for the *New York Times*, the *Brooklyn Eagle*, and *Harper's Weekly* before landing a post at the *Journal of Commerce* in the 1890s, was among the most outspoken advocates of a vigorous U.S. policy in China. Along with Clarence Cary, legal counsel for the American China Development Company, and others, Foord founded the American Asiatic Association (AAA) in 1898. The AAA marked the convergence of diverse U.S. interests in Asia, and the emergence of a clear, unified political voice on questions of policy and an activist state role in the overseas economic endeavors of private citizens. Government initiative in securing and protecting American markets in Asia had in fact stepped up significantly as early as the Cleveland administration, particularly thanks to the energies of the American minister to China, Charles Denby. But from the formation of the AAA on, successive administrations faced mounting pressure from a nascent China lobby not only to secure markets, but actively to provide and secure the accouterments of commercial empire in the Pacific, including far-flung coaling stations, naval protection of shipping lanes, and a reassuring military presence in the theater of imperial rivalries.

Around the same time that the specialized interests of the *Journal of Commerce* and the AAA were making their wishes known, the China question entered popular American consciousness through the back door, as it were, during the Spanish-Cuban-American War and the subsequent U.S. war in the Philippines. In the spring of 1898, few Americans would have guessed that a war with Spain in the Caribbean over the political fate of Cuba would end with a heightened U.S. military presence in the Pacific and East Asia. But when Admiral George Dewey routed the Spanish fleet in the Philippines in what began as a more modest effort to impede its progress to the Caribbean theater, new questions suddenly arose regarding U.S. interests and rights in Asia itself. What would become of Spain's former colonies—not only Cuba and Puerto Rico, but the Philippines, too—in the wake of U.S. victory? What would be the relationship between U.S. "liberators" and members of the Filipino independence movement, who, like their counterparts in Cuba, had been fighting Spain side by side with American forces?

The heady glow of victory in this "splendid little war," as Secretary of State John Hay termed it, and the long-standing interest in capturing Asian markets, sealed the question in American debate. Despite a vocal anti-imperialist movement in the United States, and despite the Filipinos' resolve to drive their American "liberators" from the archipelago by force of arms if necessary, the drift of American opinion and the direction of administration policy favored a continued and powerful U.S. presence in Asia and the Pacific. The United States now annexed Hawaii, too, after decades of raising and dropping the plan. But China and the China market provided motive for all of this: interest in the Philippines themselves was rarely held up in American discussion as the chief motive for Philippine conquest. Rather, the archipelago would serve as a "stepping-stone" to the China market, just as Hawaii would be a critical way station for U.S. naval traffic.

Having upped the ante in Asia, the United States now faced a twofold problem. On the one hand, interest in China among many rival powers was keen, and so the China trade brought the United States into open competition with the likes of Japan, Germany, Russia, France, and Great Britain. German activity in Shantung Province and Russia's maneuvers in Manchuria in particular indicated the possibility of a partition of China that threatened to exclude the United States. For observers like Brooks Adams, the United States needed to check a hostile coalition of rival powers, lest they occupy and organize the interior of China, discriminate against U.S. imports, and "[throw] back a considerable surplus on our hands." Others, like John Hay, were more sanguine: "In the field of trade and commerce we shall be the keen competitors of the richest and greatest powers," he wrote in 1899, "and they need no warning to be assured that in that struggle, we shall bring the sweat to their brows."

The question, though, was *how*? Even with an outpost in the Philippines, the United States lacked the geographical advantages of Japan and Russia. And compared with the colonial powers of France, Germany, and Great Britain, the United States was coming to Asia rather late in the game. The solution to such practical problems was announced in September 1899, in John Hay's "Open Door Notes," an appeal to the powers to end discrimination against foreign commerce in their Chinese leaseholds and spheres of influence. The Open Door Policy was initially devised by a Hay adviser, William Rockhill, whose adherence to the economic and military philosophies of Brooks Adams and Alfred Thayer Mahan had led him to conclude that a sovereign China was crucial to the balance of power in Asia and to U.S. interests there. Rockhill was further influenced by Alfred Hippisley, an Englishman serving in the Chinese Imperial Maritime Customs Service, whose primary concern was the fate of the Chinese state, given foreign powers' arrogant disregard for China's tariff revenues and duties. Hippisley knew how to get the American's attention: the Russification of Manchuria had thus far been "simply wonderful," he cautioned (meaning "impressive," not "good"); Peking and North China would surely follow in quick order. *These are precisely the districts which are the great consumers of American textile fabrics*, and I don't for a moment believe that American manufacturers will sit by with folded hands and see these districts closed."

Together, Hippisley and Rockhill hammered out what would appear under John Hay's hand as the "Open Door Notes": "Earnestly desirous to remove any cause of irritation," the United States here proposed to "the various powers claiming 'spheres of interest' that they shall enjoy perfect equality of treatment for their commerce and navigation within such 'spheres.' " In this spirit, Hay requested formal assurances from the interested powers that they would not interfere in treaty ports or leased territories, that the Chinese government would continue to levy and collect duties in all ports, and that harbor dues and railroad charges would be consistent for all nations operating in the region. The "Open Door Notes" thus represented no mere codification of long-standing U.S. policy in China: in enlisting support for that policy among the other leading powers, Hay sought to turn U.S. foreign policy into *international* policy. The Open Door was particularly well suited to U.S. needs and to the existing balance of power in the area: it precluded a direct confrontation with the other powers, and yet did away with the economic disadvantages the United States might have suffered by lacking a "sphere" to call its own. The notes thus represent an imperialist economics in the guise of anticolonialism. In true colonial fashion, it is worth noting, Hay neglected to consult with China before issuing the notes. In conversation with an adviser some years later, he insisted upon the anticolonial dimension of the Open Door Policy, even as his language and his syntax betrayed its imperialist assumptions: "We have done the Chinks a great service," he declared, "which they don't seem inclined to recognize."

If a potential confrontation with Japan and the European powers was one problem the United States faced in its quest for a piece of the China market—and one that, for the time, Hay was able to finesse—monumental Chinese "ingratitude" was yet a second. Like the other colonizers in Chinese territories, whose missionary activities and scramble for spheres and concessions were exerting great force on Chinese society, the United States confronted powerful currents of antiforeign sentiment among the Chinese themselves, and a stubborn Chinese insistence upon adhering to familiar ways. The greatest single outburst of Chinese antiforeignism in the period was the Boxer Uprising, the dramatic armed rising of a patriotic society devoted to driving unwanted foreigners out of China. Among the symbols of the foreign presence singled out for attack were missionaries and mission properties, foreign legations, and tokens of the Western technological presence like railroads and telegraph lines. The Boxers tore up segments of the Tientsin-Peking Railway, downed communications lines, isolated Peking from outside communications and contact, killed the German minister and a member of the Japanese legation, and held the foreign legations under siege for three weeks in the summer of 1900. An allied force, including several thousand U.S. soldiers, was dispatched to relieve the legations and to put down the rising. The siege ended on August 14, after twenty-five days.

The allied military presence continued in the wake of the uprising, but policy-makers in Washington continued to hope for a viable, independent China so that there would be no renewed fight over spoils among the occupying powers. John Hay issued his second round of "Open Door Notes" in July, during the crisis. The United States' goals, as he enumerated them, were to rescue all American officials and missionaries endangered by the antiforeign riots, to afford protection to American life and property, to guard American interests, and to prevent the spread of disorders. In all of this, the overriding aim was to "preserve Chinese territorial and administrative entity, protect all rights guaranteed to friendly powers by treaty and international law, and safeguard for the world the principle of equal and impartial trade with all parts of the Chinese Empire"—in short, to keep the Open Door ajar, notwithstanding the fierce antiforeignism of some of the Chinese themselves.

The powerful antiforeignism that had erupted in the Boxer Uprising found further outlet in the revolutionary activities of leaders like Sun Yat-sen in the early years of the new century. The growing Chinese-nationalist sensibility was one among many factors that caused American interest in the China market to cool considerably after the turn of the century. Beyond the general xenophobia that the colonial presence had generated within China, moreover, the Chinese bore the United States a highly particular grudge: U.S. immigration legislation, so specific and unforgiving in singling the Chinese out for exclusion from the country in 1882, remained a sticking point in all diplomatic dealing between the two countries, notwithstanding Americans' noble defense of China's "territorial integrity." Like the Boxer Uprising, an anti-American boycott in China in 1905 reminded Americans that the will of the Chinese themselves would have an undeniable influence on any American prospects for capturing the fabled market.

Many businessmen, meanwhile, began to recognize the limitations of the market in other respects—regardless of the hundreds of millions of potential customers involved—because of the actual purchasing power of the Chinese, their inclinations as consumers, and the difficulties presented by the country's weak commercial infrastructure. As Rounseville Wildman, the U.S. consul general in Hong Kong, had written in 1899, "99 percent of China is still closed to the world. When the magazine writer refers in glowing terms to the 400,000,000 inhabitants of China, he forgets that 350,000,000 are a dead letter so far as commerce is concerned." Some American politicians, too, now questioned earlier myths of the China trade. In a 1907 article titled "The Awakening of China," Teddy Roosevelt lauded the strides in modernization and education, and the increased commercial and industrial activity, in China, but in general he was unwilling to challenge Japanese hegemony in the region after the Russo-Japanese War of 1904. Unlike many of his predecessors, Roosevelt concluded that China did not rank as terribly significant among the many foreign interests of the United States.

Despite the Taft administration's far more aggressive approach to Chinese markets, and despite Taft's personal view of China as a rich field for investment, the coalition of American interests in China was never again so active and vocal as it had been in the 1890s. Under Taft, the United States joined a consortium of six imperialist powers in China in order to secure a share of the market, an arrangement that Woodrow Wilson abandoned in 1913 (significantly, without consulting the Chinese themselves). Wilson's decision conceded hegemony in the region to Japan, and attention in the United States increasingly turned toward Latin America and to the war in Europe.

Propaganda as to the vast potential of the China market would not abate altogether in some quarters, to be sure. Although the 1890s may have marked the high-water mark of U.S. interest in and hope for the export trade in China—the myth at its most potent—such interest did not vanish altogether. The NAM retained a vivid interest, as did the AAA, which even in the wake of the Boxer Uprising saw the U.S. thrust in East Asia as being "in obedience to the call of manifest destiny." *Harper's Weekly* could offer the sanguine view in 1907 that, "when a Chinaman of today discovers an automobile darting over his native heath, he does not call it a foreign devil-machine and begin to throw things. Instead he opens his eyes and his mouth in great rings of admiration, and begs to know all about the car which, in spite of no pushee, no pullee, still manages to go—like the wind."

Nor had the myth died by the 1920s. In an advertisement in *Asia: The American Magazine of the Orient* in 1921, long after the Boxer Uprising and the Chinese boycott had dampened American optimism regarding the commercial conversion of China, the Pacific Commercial Company continued to preach the gospel of the wondrous potential of the China market, though now, perhaps, with a dose of chastened realism. The ad seems both an expression of boosterist optimism regarding American ends in Asia, and a vague warning as to American means. "Sales success in the Orient depends upon the same principles which govern selling success in the United States," the ad at once assured and cautioned. "You must know the field, the needs and customs of the people, and you must know how to reach the customer in order that a demand and outlet may be created for the goods which you desire to sell." Demands might be created, but not without great sensitivity on the part of the foreign trader—and sensitivity had been in conspicuously short supply in American ventures in China to date.

Throughout this entire period, from Seward's early vision of ushering China into the "modern" world, to the AAA's tenacious view that the Far East should properly represent the United States' Far West, the magic that the China market worked on the American imagination owed largely to the sheer numbers involved. "In China there are four hundred millions of people," exclaimed one business journal, "more than five times as many as exist in the United States. The wants of these four hundred million people are increasing every year. What a market!" The notion of feeding, clothing, and otherwise outfitting those millions was enough to drive decades-long discussions of China's economic significance, even in the face of the contrary realities of actual trade figures and Chinese people's actual indifference to American habits of consumption and modes of dress. *If only* the Chinese could be converted to wheat instead of rice. *If only* they could be persuaded to adopt middle-class American standards of attire and a civilized sense of the requisites of a proper, well-appointed wardrobe.

But if their numbers were too impressive for American manufacturers and merchants to get out of their minds, the Chinese themselves—with their customs and habits, their way of life, and their apparent pride in "isolation" from the civilized West—posed a real problem as potential customers. Ultimately, the question of the China market would rest not upon the number of zeros in the country's population figures, but upon the people's desires— their "wants," not as the likes of Josiah Strong defined them, but as they themselves defined them. And if missionaries and other Western observers frequently commented on how much the Chinese seemed to need, so did they rather humbly acknowledge how little the Chinese seemed to *want.*

As far back as the early nineteenth century, American traders had complained of Chinese traditionalism and the culture's consequent disregard for Western styles and goods. The Chinese were "hostile to all improvement," merchant Ebenezer Townsend had concluded. "If the world were like the Chinese, we should yet have worn fig-leaves." Among the traits commonly attributed to the Chinese in early merchants' and missionaries' accounts were torpidity, a remarkable fondness for stasis whose underside was an equally re-markable resistance to innovation and change, and a stubborn scientific and technological backwardness. These secular traits corresponded roughly to what missionaries meant by the phrase "children of darkness."

The stereotype had changed but little by the century's end, even when hopes for the economic potential of China were pegged the highest. Among the traits catalogued in the missionary Arthur Smith's chapter-by-chapter summary of *Chinese Characteristics* (1900) were "Economy," "Conservatism," and "Indifference to Comfort and Convenience"—none of which boded par-ticularly well for merchants or manufacturers hoping to entice the Chinese with a cornucopia of modern conveniences. Indeed, it was symptomatic, as far as Smith was concerned, that Chinese clothing had no pockets—no nat-ural place to carry "a pocket-comb, a folding foot-rule, a cork-screw, a boot-buttoner, a pair of tweezers, a minute compass, a folding pair of scissors, a pin-ball, a pocket-mirror, . . . a fountain pen," or other such appointments that any middle-class Victorian would likely require. Elsewhere he noted darkly that the merchandise in Chinese shops seemed never to move. Charac-teristically, here and elsewhere points of mere difference between American and Chinese culture were defined as unmistakable shortcomings of the latter. That the rising culture of consumption could not engulf and colonize China as easily as it could the American hinterland became proof of Chinese inferi-ority and backwardness. That the Chinese could not be assimilated to "higher wants," in Josiah Strong's formulation, demonstrated a lamentably stunted "civilization" on their part. All the more lamentable because Chinese torpidity stood in the way of American progress and profit.

In *The Changing Chinese* (1912), sociologist Edward A. Ross interpreted Chinese conservatism not as a "dread of the unknown, [a] horror of the new," but merely as the logical outcome of precedent. Tradition was tenacious, yes, but it could be overcome. Still, the changes in Chinese society would have to be sweeping indeed before the Chinese were ready to adapt to the material progress that characterized Western life. Ross's catalogue of necessary social and cultural changes—a set of new "precedents" to pattern Chinese behav-ior—included "dropping ancestor worship, dissolving the clan, educating girls, elevating women, postponing marriage, introducing compulsive education, restricting child labor and otherwise individualizing the members of the family." Capturing the China market clearly would not simply mean introducing goods whose superiority was self-evident; it would entail a root-and-branch reordering of the society.

Thus, if U.S. hopes for China were never realized, if U.S. influence in the region was never what diverse actors like William Seward, John Foord, John Hay, or the businessmen of the NAM had dreamed of, the history of the United States in China in this period—and the history of China in the popular American imagination—is still a history of imperialist ideology *par excellence.* It involved the impulse to reform a population to suit U.S. needs (or, short of that, to dismiss that population as inferior); it involved making decisions that affected huge numbers of people on the ground in Asia on the basis of American and European economic and political requirements and in accordance with American and European ideas; and it involved exerting influence over secondary regions like Hawaii and the Philippines, again with less attention to the immediate consequences for those peoples than for the requirements of the distant United States. In popular estimation, China may have represented an ancient but now decadent "civilization," not a "barbarous" or "savage" land. But U.S. designs and conduct in "the new Far West" were not altogether inconsistent with the lessons that Teddy Roosevelt had drawn from the old: the globe was covered with mere "waste spaces" eventually to be overrun by the English-speaking peoples of Europe and North America.

Markets and Might: Latin America

Whereas U.S. attitudes toward China generally combined an awe at the size of the potential market with an arrogant aspiration to move this "decadent" civilization into the modern era, attitudes toward Latin America derived from the twin convictions that, first, Latin Americans were mostly savages, and second, destiny had provided lands south of the border as a mere extension of the North American "frontier." Latin America was, as the Monroe Doctrine had declared in 1823, the United States' backyard—a region that was off-limits to the expansive ambitions of the European powers but was to be held in reserve for the pleasures of the United States.

"The savage is over the border," announced one popular song during the Mexican War of the 1840s, "Ready for fight and mischief, / So frontier men—to arms!" The key elements here are portentous: "savage," "mischief," "frontier," "arms." That the peoples of Central and South America and the Caribbean were so many "savages," that their meager capabilities ran primarily to mischief, and that the stewardship of the more civilized United States would benefit these savages whether or not they recognized it were points of such impressive consensus that, from the mid-nineteenth century onward, the border ceased to have much meaning when it came to determining the national interest and the right to pursue it. "Frontier men," that is, continually and rather routinely answered the call to arms, crossing into one or another of these nations in the North American backyard in order to enforce the North American will. If an occasional gunboat patrolled the Yangtze to protect American traders and missionaries or to back up American wishes with force, military coercion became the very way of life in U.S. dealings south of the U.S. border. If the principle of "territorial integrity" governed American thinking on the China question, its very opposite determined U.S. conduct in our own hemisphere.

Latin America and the Caribbean had long occupied the imagination of expansive American nationalists. Way back in 1823, John Quincy Adams had described Cuba as subject to a kind of political "gravitation" that would bring it—like an apple falling from a tree—ineluctably toward the North American Union. Throughout the 1850s, private filibustering expeditions set sail from U.S. ports to conquer Central American nations for personal gain. The most renowned interventionist, William Walker, actually installed himself and served as the ruler of Nicaragua—and received U.S. diplomatic recognition—from 1855 to 1857. (Significantly, the power that unseated him belonged not to any Nicaraguan counterfaction, or even to any European rivals in the region, but to Cornelius Vanderbilt, whose Nicaraguan steamship line was threatened by Walker's ambitions.) The island of Cuba routinely came up in North American discussions of expanding the slave territories in the antebellum period; and during the Civil War, Confederate nationalists envisioned their breakaway republic as ultimately encompassing the Caribbean and much of Latin America. For many Southern businessmen—and, not incidentally, their Northern associates—the dream died hard, even after Appomattox. Latin American trade "is ours by *natural laws*," argued one Southern journal in the late 1880s.

There was thus a rich fund of precedent in U.S. thinking and conduct for the imperialist designs in the region in the late nineteenth century and after—as when the United States resolved a conflict over the placement of the Venezuelan boundary without bothering to consult with officials of Venezuela itself; or when, by the terms of the Platt Amendment, the Senate retained the United States' "right of intervention" in Cuban affairs in order to protect "life, liberty, and property"; or when, by fiat, the Supreme Court declared Puerto Rico to be "appurtenant and belonging to the United States" without granting Puerto Ricans the status of U.S. citizens; or when, in his corollary to the Monroe Doctrine, Teddy Roosevelt assigned the United States sole responsibility for policing the hemisphere; or when, *twenty times* between 1898 and 1920, U.S. marines landed in Caribbean countries to restore order or to establish "stability" on U.S. terms. (When asked what exactly would constitute "stability" in Cuba, General Leonard Wood replied, "When money can be borrowed at a reasonable rate of interest and when capital is willing to invest in the Island, a condition of stability will have been reached.")

Although this story perhaps ends on the theme of imperialist extraction—extraction of natural resources, of cheap labor, of advantage—it begins with the quest for markets. The problem for many Latin American countries in the twentieth century, that is, has been a fatal dependence upon the United States as a market for an overspecialized agricultural crop. Honduras, the original "banana republic," is the prime example of a nation dominated not only by foreign capital and foreign ownership of arable lands—in this case United Fruit—but by the cultivation of those lands for the sake of a specialized product for a single market. Banana and coffee exports have been the basis of many Latin American nations' neodependency upon the giant to the north, but there was a time when Americans were far more concerned with their ability to capture Latin American markets for *their* goods. Indeed, though the myth of the China market dominated the North American imagination through the last quarter of the nineteenth century, Latin American markets were actually far more important. In 1896, for instance, while only $7 million in exports flowed to China (and only another $19 million to the rest of Asia), $93 million in exports flowed to South and Central America, $19 million to Mexico alone. The Spanish-Cuban-American War was a watershed in the Latin American trade, as the United States not only eliminated one of its European rivals from the field, but took virtual control of Spain's Cuban and Puerto Rican colonies. By 1901, actual exports to mythic China still hovered around the $10-million mark, but the relatively tiny island of Cuba alone absorbed $26 million in U.S. goods. The Cuban figure continued to shoot up, reaching $165 million in 1916, when exports to China still amounted to only $32 million. Puerto Rico, meanwhile, went from being the twenty-seventh-largest market for American products as Congress debated the island's political fate in 1900, to the eleventh by 1910, after ten years of U.S. "tutelage" in the wake of Spain's defeat. Elsewhere in Latin America, a country like Colombia would by 1919 import over 70 percent of its commodities from the United States.

Secretary of State "Jingo" Jim Blaine (1881, 1889–92) was among the most important architects of U.S.–Latin American relations in this period. "While the great powers of Europe are steadily enlarging their colonial domination in Asia and Africa," he asserted, "it is the especial province of this country to improve and expand its trade with the nations of America." Much of Latin America depended upon Europe, not the United States, for manufactured goods—a circumstance that Blaine sought vigorously to overturn. "What we want . . . are the markets of these neighbors of ours that lie to the south of us. We want the $400,000,000 annually which to-day go to England, France, Germany, and other countries. With these markets secured new life would be given to our manufactories, the product of the Western farmer would be in demand, the reasons for and inducements to strikers, with all their attendant evils, would cease."

Tariff policy and reciprocity provisions became the chief instruments in the quest for these markets. Under Blaine's and Harrison's provisions in the McKinley Tariff, the president could punish any country that discriminated against the United States in favor of European goods by tacking prohibitive duties on that country's key exports to the United States, including sugar, molasses, coffee, tea, and hides. Under this regime of trade practices and policies, some Latin American countries, like the islands of the West Indies, slipped more closely into the economic orbit of the United States; others, like Cuba, became ripe for the revolution that would ultimately drive their European colonizers out of the Caribbean. Further, under Blaine's watch the United States turned from its historic *negative* implementation of the Monroe Doctrine, which simply demanded the noninterference of European powers, adopting a more active, interventionist approach whose elements included regular Pan-American conferences and a hemispheric system of arbitration.

In this region as in Asia, the Spanish-Cuban-American War of 1898 constituted a watershed in U.S. policy and its conduct. The motive behind the U.S. intervention in Cuba has been a point of much contention since the moment it occurred. Immediate factors contributing to "war fever" in the United States included a notoriously active yellow press, whose daily revelations about Spanish General "Butcher" Weyler inflamed public opinion even as they boosted circulation; the publication of an indiscreet letter from Spanish Minister Depuy De Lôme insulting President McKinley as a "low politician" who "caters to the rabble"; the hope in some quarters that a wartime economy would usher in the coinage of silver, which had been defeated along with William Jennings Bryan in 1896; a rousing speech on the floor of the Senate by Redfield Proctor, an eyewitness who asserted that the situation in Cuba was every bit as dreadful as the yellow press had painted it; and the explosion aboard the *Maine* in Havana Harbor, which killed 264 Americans.

But all of this occurred within the broader context of a decades-long escalation of U.S. economic interest in Latin America and the Caribbean basin and a protracted national discussion of what was demanded by America's rising status as a world economic power—markets, bases, coaling stations, perchance a canal. As McKinley had mused, "We have good money, we have ample revenues, we have unquestioned national credit, but what we need is new markets, and as trade follows the flag, it looks very much as if we are going to have new markets."

Whatever the precise calculus by which the McKinley administration entered the war between Spain and its colony in revolt, the United States emerged from the war not only with a newly invigorated economic power in the region, but with a military presence and the unmistakable beginnings of an administrative empire. Earlier on, as Cuban rebels struggled against Spain and some had pondered the benefits of an alliance with the United States, rebel leader José Martí had wondered, "Once the United States is in Cuba, who will get her out?" A prescient question. If the "splendid little war" brought the United States a stepping-stone to China in the form of the Philippine archipelago, results in the Caribbean were more dramatic still. Chief legacies of the United States' "humanitarian" intervention on behalf of the Cuban rebels included the Platt Amendment, a unique legislative solution to the dilemma of how to control newly liberated Cuba without going so far as to annex it. After two years of U.S. military occupation of the island without any solid consensus on the proper political disposition of the former Spanish colony (Cuba was partially protected from unbridled U.S. acquisitiveness by the Teller Amendment, by which Congress had denied designs for U.S. sovereignty over the island), Secretary of War Elihu Root sketched out a series of provisions under which, he felt, Cuba could be governed in a kind of limited independence. These provisions, the basis of the Platt Amendment, included the United States' "right of intervention" in Cuban affairs for the sake of protecting property and restoring order; a proscription of Cuba's treaty-making rights as a sovereign nation; and the right of the United States to acquire and maintain naval bases and coaling stations on the island. As tight as the U.S. grip would remain on Cuba under the terms of the Platt Amendment, Root frankly asserted that these provisions represented "the extreme limit of [U.S.] indulgence in the matter of the independence of Cuba." (That self-determination was but an "indulgence" in this case speaks volumes about U.S. views of the region and its peoples.)

A second, similar formula came to define the fate of Spain's other major Caribbean colony, Puerto Rico. By an article of the Treaty of Paris between Spain and the United States, Spain ceded "the island of Puerto Rico and the other islands now under Spanish sovereignty in the West Indies." Significantly, however, the treaty contained no specific language regarding the terms of Puerto Rico's eventual incorporation. Rather, it simply stated, "The civil rights and political status of the territories hereby ceded . . . shall be determined by the Congress." Such determination came initially in the form of the Foraker Act in 1900, a bill whose original provisions included extending the U.S. Constitution to the island and granting American citizenship to its inhabitants. It was a much-watered-down bill that actually passed, however, because the Puerto Ricans' "fitness for self-government" was deeply questioned in some quarters. The gutted version of the bill provided that the island's inhabitants would be "citizens of Puerto Rico," not of the United States (this would be reversed only in 1917, by the Jones Act), and yet important aspects of their political life and fate would be decided in Washington, where a Puerto Rican resident commissioner with neither voice nor voting rights acted as the island's liaison in Congress.

The significant ambiguities of this political limbo were subsequently worked out in the U.S. courts, where a series of contests known as the "insular cases" raised and settled important questions regarding the precise legal relationship between the rising imperial power and its colonies. In *Downes* v. *Bidwell*, the most important of these cases, adjudication in the matter of duties and fees on cargo shipped between the United States and Puerto Rico under Foraker led the Supreme Court into the complexities of constitutionality and the precise status of the island in U.S. law. The key to *Downes*—the key to Puerto Rico's troubled political relationship to the United States ever since—resides in clauses asserting that Puerto Rico is "not a foreign country" in an international sense, being "owned" by the United States; but that it is in fact "foreign to the United States in a domestic sense, because the island has not been incorporated into the United States, but was merely appurtenant thereto as a possession." As one Puerto Rican newspaper remarked at the time, the Foraker Act essentially provided that Puerto Rico was to be "treated as a mere chattel of the United States"; another leader shuddered at what he called this "spectacle of terrible assimilation."

Throughout turn-of-the-century American discussion of the Caribbean and of the fate of these former Spanish colonies, it was clear that Cuba and Puerto Rico represented, above all else in the North American imagination, the Eastern "approach" to a devoutly wished isthmian canal. Once the United States controlled the "approaches," perhaps it was just a matter of time before it would control some portion of the isthmus itself. During 1900 and 1901, John Hay negotiated the Hay-Pauncefote Treaty with Great Britain, abrogating an 1850 agreement and now granting the United States sole right to build, control, and fortify a canal. The terms of the Hay-Herrán Treaty with Colombia in 1903 next gave the United States a six-mile-wide zone across the Colombian province of Panama in exchange for $10 million plus $250,000 per year, but the Congress in Bogotá rejected the treaty amid an atmosphere of anti-Yankee skepticism and distrust. U.S. responses were entirely in keeping with traditional arrogance in the region, including recent American imperialist forays in administration in Cuba and Puerto Rico. In a position paper prepared for the United States in 1903, one international lawyer put the matter quite bluntly: "The United States now holds out to the world a certain prospect of a canal. May Colombia be permitted to stand in the way?" Teddy Roosevelt was blunter still: "I do not think that the Bogota lot of Jackrabbits should be allowed permanently to bar one of the future highways of civilization." Elsewhere he denounced the Colombians as "contemptible little creatures."

As the USS *Nashville* sailed off the coast of Panama (the *Boston*, the *Dixie*, and the *Atlanta* were also in the area), a secessionist movement succeeded in the province, and the United States lost no time at all in granting official recognition to the infant republic. Among the first official acts of the new Panamanian government was a treaty that, in exchange for a U.S. "guarantee" of independence, granted the United States use of a zone of land and underwater land "in perpetuity" for the construction, maintenance, and protection of a transisthmian canal. In language and logic reminiscent of the Platt Amendment, the treaty further stipulated that the United States "shall have the right, at all times and in its discretion, to use its police and its land and naval forces or to establish fortifications" in order to ensure the safety of the canal or of marine traffic.

In the wake of the Colombian secession movement and the ensuing canal treaty with the new Republic of Panama, Roosevelt, in his annual message to Congress, at once codified this action and justified future ones in what became known as his "corollary" to the Monroe Doctrine. The United States felt no "land hunger," he asserted. "All that this country desires is to see the neighboring countries stable, orderly, and prosperous. Any country whose people conduct themselves well can count upon our hearty friendship." But "chronic wrongdoing" or a "loosening of the ties of civilized society"—as defined by the region's arbiter of decency, the United States—may "require the intervention of some civilized nation, and in the Western Hemisphere the adherence of the United States to the Monroe Doctrine may force the United States, however reluctantly, . . . to the exercise of an international police power." Coming in the wake of the Platt Amendment, which Roosevelt cited by name, and the friendly revolution in Panama, Roosevelt's message marked the extent to which Blaine and Harrison's earlier quest for Latin American markets had now become a military and administrative imperative. In this region, as in the Pacific, by the time Taft succeeded McKinley and Roosevelt, an initial effort at informal economic empire had been transformed into a policy whose legal, military, and political trappings resembled more closely the colonial systems of the Old World powers.

Nor did the bedrock consensus on U.S. aims and means in the region break down when, in 1912, Woodrow Wilson became the first Democrat to hold office since Grover Cleveland. The quest for Latin American markets was not a partisan matter, in other words. "Since . . . the manufacturer insists on having the world as a market," Wilson had declared while Roosevelt still occupied the White House in 1907, "the flag of his nation must follow him, and the doors of nations which are closed against him must be battered down. Concessions obtained by financiers must be safeguarded by ministers of state even if the sovereignty of unwilling nations be outraged in the process." A decade later, Wilson demonstrated that his administration would be no stranger to such "outrage," even though his rhetoric and his articulated ideals represented a departure from his Republican predecessors.

Under Wilson, the United States intervened in both Haiti (1915) and the Dominican Republic (1916) in an effort to establish precisely the kind of "stable, orderly, and prosperous" climate that Roosevelt had invoked in his "corollary." But by far the most dramatic intervention in these years was the Wilson administration's engagement in the Mexican Revolution, when a coup against Francisco Madero sparked an armed struggle among disparate Mexican factions behind Victoriano Huerta (Madero's immediate successor), Venustiano Carranza, Emiliano Zapata, and Francisco "Pancho" Villa. Between 1913 and 1916, the United States intervened decisively in the struggle, first shipping arms to Huerta in an effort to prop him up; then, having

become convinced of his inability to pacify the countryside, establishing an
arms embargo against him, invading and occupying the port city of Veracruz, and using this beachhead to transfer weapons to the acceptable "Constitutionalist" faction behind Carranza and Alvaro Obregan Salido. In 1916,
after Carranza had come to power, Wilson also sent General John "Black-
jack" Pershing and twelve thousand troops into the interior of Mexico in
vain pursuit of Pancho Villa, whose harassing raids across the countryside
were meant to expose the weakness and the illegitimacy of the Carranza government.

Throughout these events, Wilson was less direct than he had been in
1907 about the necessity of "having the world as a market." On the contrary,
in his support of Carranza he was more apt to speak of the importance of
"teaching" the Mexicans to elect "good men." But although Wilson did not
necessarily see particular American business interests as identical with the
national interest, "good men" in his formulation turned out to be leaders
who would be better for the many American oil, railroad, financial, mining,
timber, rubber, and agricultural interests in Mexico than would "bad men"
like Zapata and Villa, whose programs entailed the redistribution of Mexican
wealth. Nor did Wilson's reliance upon military intervention represent a departure from the "big stick" of his Republican predecessors. Wilson adviser
Robert Lansing later summed up the Mexican intervention as both an economic and a military necessity: "With the present industrial activity, the
scramble for markets, and the incessant search for new opportunities to produce wealth, commercial expansion and success are closely interwoven with
political domination over the territory."

Latin America occupied a different niche in U.S. economic thinking
than did China, although assessments of white Americans' superiority to
Latin American peoples were not altogether different. Like the Chinese, by
long-standing tradition the peoples south of the border were seen as requir-
ing "uplift" and a proper introduction to "progress," and yet—also like the
Chinese—their prospects for assimilating to modern civilization seemed to
some to be slender indeed. At the heart of white American assessments of
Latin America was the issue of race. "If the United States as compared with
the Spanish American republics has achieved immeasurable advance in all

elements of greatness," the U.S. chargé d'affaires in Central America had remarked in the 1850s, "that result is eminently due to the rigid and inexorable refusal of the dominant Teutonic stock to debase its blood, impair its intellect, lower its moral standards, or peril its institutions by intermixture with the inferior and subordinate races of man. In obedience of Heaven, it has rescued half a continent from savage beasts and still more savage men."

Such logic was still current decades later. In 1889, New England patrician Charles Francis Adams, Jr., lauded a policy of extermination as the only alternative to becoming "a nation of half-breeds." Upon the U.S. invasion of Veracruz, General Hugh Scott judged that "firmness is essential in dealing with inferior races." And as sociologist Edward A. Ross surveyed the region in *South of Panama* (1915), he had to conclude that South America was "the victim of a bad start. It was never settled by whites in the way that they settled the United States." Rather, "the masterful whites" exploited the natives without either assimilating them or winning their allegiance. The result, in his view, was a politically stultifying combination of pride, contempt for labor, social parasitism, caste hierarchy, and pronounced authoritarian strains in both church and state, which, though attributable to historical circumstance rather than to race per se, by now seemed to run in the very blood of these peoples.

The temper of U.S. Latin American policy was best summed up in Roosevelt's annual message to Congress in 1904, his "corollary" to the Monroe Doctrine. "Chronic wrongdoing," he warned, "or an impotence which results in a general loosening of the ties of civilized society, may in America, as elsewhere, ultimately require intervention by some civilized nation. . . . If every country washed by the Caribbean Sea would show the progress in stable and just civilization which with the aid of the Platt Amendment Cuba has shown since our troops left the island, . . . all question of interference by this Nation with their affairs would be at an end."

European powers like Spain may have had their shortcomings, and the European presence in Latin America and the East may have been a source of some discomfort. But "chronic wrongdoers" of the sort who required the administration of Roosevelt's "big stick" were exclusively and always peoples identified in the American imagination as nonwhite. Like Leonard Wood, the governor general of Cuba, Roosevelt implicitly mingled economic notions such as "stability" (the atmosphere that a people was able to create for the safe conduct of trade) and "civilization" (a people's full participation in modern material progress) with ideas of "racial development" (a people's innate capacity for modernization or for "progress" in general). As these overlapping languages applied in the U.S. quest for markets abroad, they gave name to the regions whose "backwardness" seemed to cry out for U.S. goods, *and* they provided justification for whatever action or intervention the United States deemed necessary to exert its will outside its own borders. It was through this portentous marriage of a hierarchic world-view and sheer military might that the nation's destiny would become manifest.

Material Prosperity and the Civilizing Mission

As Americans dreamed of China's markets and exerted force in order to secure those of Latin America, images of "savagery," "barbarism," "semicivilization," "civilization," and "decadence" came to occupy a central place in the discussion. Such conceptions of relative social organization, though clearly founded upon a hierarchy of race, were also firmly rooted in an understanding of *temporality* and human development. In his travelogue of Africa, *Mummies and Moslems* (1876), Charles Dudley Warner gave voice to a common conceit that Africans inhabited not just a distant continent but a distant epoch. A journey down the Nile took one "not only away from Europe, away from Cairo, into Egypt and the confines of mysterious Africa; [but] . . . sailing into the past. . . . We have committed ourselves to a stream that will lead us thousands of years backwards into the ages, into the depths of history." Decades later, in 1916, Theodore Roosevelt, too, mused upon his sojourn among the timeless savages of Africa. "The fierce wild life of parts of Africa to-day has nothing in common with what we now see in Europe and the Americas. Yet in its general aspect, and in many of its most striking details, it reproduces the life that once was . . . in what paleontologists call the Pleistocene age." Many of the "naked or half skin-clad savages" whom he met, Roosevelt concluded, were leading "precisely the life" once led by our own "ages-dead forebears." As Joseph Conrad put it in *Heart of Darkness*, Europeans in Africa were "wanderers on a prehistoric planet."

The logic of this conceit led in two directions: the differences between civilized and savage peoples are so profound as to be thoroughly unbridge-able; or, conversely, if Africans and other "savages" now live in a state once occupied by civilized peoples, then civilization represents the state that "sav-ages" must someday attain themselves. If their present is our past, must not our present be their ineluctable future? These two quite different conclusions ultimately amounted, not to a contradiction, but to a powerful, double-edged imperative: if we know the savages' proper path of development, then surely they should remain under our tutelage and stewardship; and if they are so dramatically "behind" us on that path (the Pleistocene age!), then we are not beholden to treat them as equals—or even as human—in this long process of helping them along. As Secretary of War Lewis Cass had written back in the era of Indian removal, "The Indians are entitled to the enjoyment of all the rights which do not interfere with the obvious designs of Provi-dence."

The notion of "civilization" in American thinking has historically repre-sented a dense weave of ideas and assumptions regarding not only proper comportment, manners, social bearing, and Judeo-Christian belief, but also regarding the fundamental social issues of property relations, the distribu-tion of wealth, modes of production, and patterns of consumption. The dom-inance of the idea of property "as a passion over all the other passions marks the commencement of civilization," wrote Lewis Henry Morgan in *Ancient Society* (1877), his classic synthesis of evolutionist thought. "A critical knowledge of the evolution of the idea of property would embody, in some respects, the most remarkable portion of the mental history of mankind."

Although most often draped in the complementary logics of Christian moralism and white supremacy throughout the turn-of-the-century period, at its core "civilization" was an economic concept. First, that is, the very idea of "civilization" implacably ranked diverse peoples' ways of life according to a hierarchy of evolutionary economic stages (industrial production over hunting and gathering; capitalist individualism over communal or clan own-ership); and second, these assessments themselves had tremendous economic consequences, as the value judgments embedded within the notion of "civi-lization" at once suggested and justified any number of interventions into "savage" society on the part of "civilized" nations, ranging from total extermination on one end of the spectrum to paternalistic assimilation on the other.

It was in precisely this vein, for instance, that Roosevelt could refer to lands held by non-Europeans as "waste spaces." The superiority of civilized society itself justified nearly any action imaginable in relations with less civilized peoples, lest mere savages stand in the way of progress (as the Colombians did in Panama in 1903). And where these peoples were to be suffered at all, their savagery denoted an impoverishment whose only antidote was that brand of enrichment provided by "civilization." Change or begone. In the bargain, the "civilized" nation tended to become further enriched by this process of rooting out savagery, either by gaining access to resources or by appropriating "savages'" lands outright. Not incidentally, as many traders and missionaries noted, the civilizing process could also transform a savage population into a new market for the many material trappings of civilized life.

Whether applied to peoples across the plains or across the seas, "teaching the arts and habits of civilization" was among the key phrases in the American lexicon of progress throughout the nineteenth century, as politicians, traders, missionaries, and diplomats and other government agents discussed the possibility and means of reforming diverse populations. The phrase was laden with economic meaning: "arts," in this formulation, generally had something to do with production; "habits," with patterns of consumption. Fencing and cultivating land were among the "arts" of civilization, for instance; wearing machine-spun clothing was among its "habits." As William Howard Taft rather frankly put the matter in an address at the opening exercises of the National University of Havana in 1906, at the crux of "all modern, successful civilization" lay "the right of property and the motive of accumulation."

U.S. dealings with North American Indians represented the first encounters in this national mission of reforming the savage, and provided a template of sorts for such endeavors in Asia, Latin America, and the Pacific later in the century. As early as 1802, the young government's articulated motives for sending Indian agents to reside among the Indians included "the introduction of the Arts of husbandry, and domestic manufactures, as means of producing, and diffusing the blessings attached to a well regulated civil society." One missionary society in 1823 looked forward to the day "when the hunter shall be transformed into the mechanic; when the farm, the workshop, the School-House, and the Church shall adorn every Indian village." Perhaps the most spectacular rendering of this economic dimension of the civilizing mission was Merrill Gates's address before the Lake Mohonk Conference of Friends of the Indian in 1896. "We have . . . the absolute need," he announced,

> *of awakening in the savage Indian broader desires and ampler wants. To bring him out of savagery into citizenship we must make the Indian more intelligently selfish before we can make him unselfishly intelligent. We need to* awaken in him wants. *In his dull savagery he must be touched by the wings of the divine angel of discontent. . . . Discontent with the teepee and the starving rations of the Indian camp in winter is needed to get the Indian out of the blanket and into trousers,—and trousers with a pocket in them, and with a pocket that aches to be filled with dollars!*

"There is an immense moral training that comes from the use of property," Gates went on. "We have found it necessary, as one of our first steps in developing a stronger personality in the Indian, *to make him responsible for property.*"

This had been exactly the impulse behind the General Allotment Act (the Dawes Act) of 1887, by which tribal lands were broken up and individual Indians were encouraged to turn away from their tribal allegiances and obligations by first abandoning the notion of collectively held property. Under the Dawes Act, holding individual title to private property was the first step toward "adopting the habits of civilization" and becoming a reliable citizen. (Not coincidentally, this experiment in "civilization" also ended in the impoverishment of the "savage" society: privately held lands passed quickly from Indians to whites, so that tribal lands were actually reduced by ninety million acres during the fifty years that the allotment system was in effect.)

The prospect of making good, reliable, civilized citizens of those savages in Africa, Latin America, or Asia never burned as keenly in the American imagination as it did in the case of the Indians within the nation's borders. Still, the prospect of their economic "civilization" did retain considerable interest. Recall missionary Arthur Smith's observation, so laden with significance, that Chinese clothing (like the customary blankets of American Indians) had no pockets. Elsewhere, in *Village Life in China* (1899), Smith meditated at length upon the question "What Can Christianity Do for China?" Significantly, the logic of the piece ultimately came to rest on the subject of property. Indeed, the acceptance of Christianity among the Chinese would fully overturn current property relations—a monumental development, since "there is no single Chinese custom which is the source of a larger variety of mischief than that of keeping large family organizations in a condition of dependence upon one another and upon common property."

The web of ideological associations between "civilization" and material prosperity was complex indeed. The mastery of nature indicated by Western technology and the material splendor that was the fruit of industrialization convinced many Europeans and Euro-Americans of the righteousness of their ultimate stewardship of the world. Would it not benefit humanity, truly, to export the power of scientific insight and to spread the cornucopia of modern conveniences, "the blessings of civilization," before the benighted peoples of darkened lands? Over the course of the late eighteenth and nineteenth centuries, the language of technological supremacy (as against primitive "backwardness") joined the languages of Christian and racial supremacy in the Euro-American lexicon of human hierarchy. The same scientific and technological wherewithal, of course, also gave Europeans and Euro-Americans a decisive military advantage in the case of conflict with these peoples. Technology had thus increasingly become the most dramatic measure of both the relative worth of diverse societies and their relative power; technology at once suggested the superiority of Western ways and granted the West an unarguable advantage in those military struggles that inevitably occurred as "civilized" invaders trampled the lifeways and wrested lands and resources from various regions' "savage" inhabitants. As Scottish missionary David Livingstone remarked with a striking gentility, "Firearms command respect, and lead [African] men to be reasonable who might otherwise feel disposed to be troublesome."

The link between technological advantage and future export markets was irresistible. "Civilization," like water on an uneven surface, would naturally run down into low regions to find its own level. That this was the case owed not only to the imperial ambitions of Western powers, but to the natural awe and interest of their "primitive" counterparts. Throughout the nineteenth century, one of the signatures of European and American travel literature was the obligatory scene in which the Western traveler dazzled the "natives" with some—often thoroughly mundane—display of technological know-how. The literature is rife with caricatured natives of various climes gaping in awe at clocks, compasses, magnets, or photographic equipment. They recoiled from matches. They gathered in huge numbers to examine a reed organ. They wondered at the proximity of the moon when viewed through a telescope; they puzzled over watches and measuring devices and lamps and bilge pumps. And, of course, with wide eyes they took due note of the capabilities of Western weaponry.

The implicit question for those who advocated a "large policy" for the United States or who fretted over the terrible industrial surplus and looked abroad for relief, was, can the native's wonder be transformed into *want?* Many people thought so. Josiah Strong was scarcely alone when, in *Our Country*, he argued, "Men rise in the scale of civilization only as their wants rise." Mere exposure to Western ways and to the fruits of Western industry were bound to light the way. Hence one Episcopal bishop posited a "direct relation between the missionary and commerce," because the missionary alters habits of mind and social customs in a fashion that "makes markets for American goods." Many missionaries may have bristled, but even Charles Denby, the American minister to China under Grover Cleveland, concurred: "Missionaries are the pioneers of trade and commerce," he remarked. "Civilization, learning, instruction breed new wants which commerce supplies."

A series called "The Cannibals at the Movies" that ran in *Asia*, the journal of the American Asiatic Association, in 1921 voiced both the optimism of culture-bearing among savage peoples, and the pessimism evoked by the extent to which the "blessings of civilization" were so lost on these poor souls. Describing a tour among far-flung peoples to show off motion-picture technology, the series did embody the travelogue tradition wherein the traveler bedazzles his uncivilized audience with the miracles of the modern. As one village chieftain examined the wondrous projector, "He . . . Lacked the Power Necessary for Solving the Mysteries of Machinery." And yet the author had to concede that wonder had its limits. "It does not pay to advertise in the New Hebrides," he declared. "We had to bribe the Cannibals with tobacco to come to our show."

By the turn of the century, both the discourse of overproduction and the discourse of civilization had become familiar enough to serve as the stuff of satire. In O. Henry's *Cabbages and Kings* (1904), an American diplomat decides to "jolly" an entrepreneur from his home town who wants to sell shoes to all the barefooted inhabitants of the fictional Latin American land of Anchuria. "There is no place on the habitable globe," he writes with mock enthusiasm, "that presents to the eye stronger evidence of the need of a first-class shoe store than does the town of Coralio. There are 3,000 inhabitants in the place, and not a single shoe store! The situation speaks for itself." Much to his chagrin, the businessman takes the bait and comes to Anchuria, bringing an alarmingly extensive inventory of American-made shoes along with him. The mismatch between the wares and the market in this instance leads to a second plan, this time to import vast quantities of a certain cocklebur that will render shoes a necessity in this tropical city.

Behind O. Henry's parody lurked some significant truths about American economic development and the growth and deployment of state power in this period. By economic "necessity," the United States had indeed become more deeply invested in the internal affairs of foreign lands—in the question, that is, of whether or not they wore shoes. But the widespread acceptance of the overproduction thesis meant that American domestic tranquillity was dependent not only upon the "wants" of various peoples, but also upon the environment for international trade itself—a "stability" that was to be defined on U.S. terms and secured, increasingly, by U.S. military might. Thus did the state amass its power ever more squarely behind the needs of American economic interests—as when the United States reserved the right of military intervention in Cuba, "took" Panama for the sake of an interoceanic trade route, or unilaterally landed troops to "stabilize" Santo Domingo.

Further, dominant American views of these overseas peoples derived from economically invested preconceptions of "progress" and "backwardness" that had the capacity to generate new power relations in their wake. Given the reigning American notion of "civilization," interventions that were advantageous to the United States could conveniently be described as advantageous to the "savages" as well, so in need of uplift were they. Conveniently, too, such engagements were beyond the scope of serious discussion with the natives themselves, for their own abjection proved that they had no rights or wishes that the United States, in its enlightenment, was bound to respect. If the natives' shoelessness suggested that they might profitably be introduced to the concept of shoes, that is, it also suggested that they needed guidance in identifying their own needs. This, in its turn, suggested that the one thing they surely did not need was a voice in determining their own fate.

But the foreigner abroad constituted only half of the sociopolitical equation under this regime of industrial progress and aggressive export; the resettled foreigner here at home was the other. If the exposition in Philadelphia in 1876 represented a grand unveiling of the nation's new wares and its new thinking on the importance of securing a world market, it also hinted at one of the peculiar social dynamics that this global trade would create: in their economic affairs Americans were set on becoming more and more engaged with the world's peoples, but in their social outlook they were not necessarily becoming any less parochial than they had ever been. Foreigners at the fair found themselves very much out of favor among the American throngs. Turks, Egyptians, Spaniards, Japanese, and Chinese, according to one observer, "were followed by large crowds of idle boys and men, who hooted and shouted at them as if they had been animals of a strange species instead of visitors who were entitled to only the most courteous attention." Such strains of xenophobia would become increasingly important in American civic life in the years between 1876 and World War I, as the successful export of American goods to all the world's peoples would also entail a massive *import* of the world's peoples—as workers—to take up places tending the nation's factories and machines. World labor migration was a natural twin to the phenomenon of the world market; and since their own superiority to most of the world's peoples was a powerful current in American thought about illimitable foreign markets, Americans were decidedly uneasy about the growing presence of these inferior foreigners, either within the gates of the American factory or within the bounds of the domestic polity.

Labor Markets: The World's Peoples as American Workers

> We have taken into our body politic the refuse of the Paris Commune, incendiaries from Berlin and from Tipperary, some hundreds of thousands of European agitators, who are always at war with every form of government thus far known among civilized nations.
>
> —New York Tribune, *1877*

> The gates will not be closed; the wheels of industry will not retard; America is in the race for the markets of the world; its call for workers will not cease.
>
> —*Peter Roberts,* The New Immigration *(1912)*

AMONG THE ITEMS on display at Philadelphia's Centennial Exposition in 1876 was a gigantic disembodied arm, upraised, clenching an equally impressive lighted torch. It was the first installment of Frédéric-Auguste Bartholdi's Statue of Liberty, which would finally be erected in New York Harbor ten years later. Its debut in Philadelphia was fitting. The exposition self-consciously trumpeted the United States' arrival as an industrial power whose textiles, sewing machines, railroad cars, and milling equipment were poised to conquer the markets of the world; Bartholdi's Liberty, once inscribed with the exhortation to SEND THESE TO ME, would announce that this rising industrial dynamo was also ready to put the world to work. Whether or not they liked the prospect, one inevitable result of Josiah Strong's and Brooks Adams's economic project of "civilizing" the world's peoples to the higher wants of American consumers would be the transformation of millions of the world's peoples into American workers. When William Seward had negotiated the Burlingame Treaty with China (1868), whose provisions included the unhindered immigration of Chinese workers, it was in recognition of an indisputable economic fact: the rapidly industrializing United States needed cheap labor and needed a lot of it, notwithstanding the possible objections of American nativists.

In an Albanian settlement near Palermo in the early years of the twentieth century, an American journalist inquired what the region's leading industries were. Second only to agriculture, came the answer, was "emigration to America." The dynamic was ineluctable. The same forces that enabled the United States to strike out across the oceans in search of markets drew millions of workers back across the waters in the opposite direction in search of work. As historian David Montgomery has put it, by the 1870s global patterns of industrialization had developed an international industrial core—a vast geographic swath bounded by Chicago and St. Louis in the west; by Toronto, Glasgow, and Berlin in the north; by Warsaw, Łódź and Budapest in the east; and by Milan, Barcelona, and Louisville in the south. This industrialized region and its urban outposts were surrounded by an international agricultural periphery whose economic life, communal fabric, patterns of indebtedness, customs of payment, cultivating and harvesting technologies, scales of production, conceptions of the market, and horizons of opportunity had all been pulled and transformed by the social and economic vortex of the industrializing center.

This vast international hinterland supplied agricultural goods and raw materials to the industrial center, just as it received its manufactures and finished goods from that region. But what the hinterland sent above all else was people. Pulled by new opportunities in distant cities, pushed by changing patterns of land tenure, by the encroachment of a global market for agricultural goods and hence by the imperatives of commercialized production and a cash economy, more and more inhabitants of the international hinterland began to make short-range migrations for work—from Italy to Germany, from the Ukraine to Poland. Increasingly they crossed entire continents and oceans, now trekking from Grinkiskis to Chicago, from Shantung to San

Francisco. Indeed, in the latter half of the nineteenth century, the chief import of the United States came to consist in rather dramatic fashion of Europe's, Asia's, and the Americas' dislocated inhabitants themselves, a new and growing body of international industrial proletarians. Between 1870 and 1920, some twenty-six million immigrants entered the United States.

Did they represent a scourge or a godsend? Befitting the ambivalence that has historically characterized the nation's relationship with its newest arrivals, the AFL's *American Federationist* remarked in 1894, "The sources of our national wealth and greatness are threefold. First—God. Second—Our form of government. Third—Our immigrants." The country had grown in both national and individual wealth "in exact proportion as our immigration increased." This paean to "Our immigrants," however, appeared in an editorial entitled "Close the Ports"—an impassioned plea, ironically enough, to cut off this particular "source of wealth and national greatness" at once. By the 1890s, this writer warned, it had become dangerously sentimental for workers to support an open immigration policy amid the chill winds of economic depression and against the cold imperatives of self-preservation.

By the depression years of the 1890s, many other Americans had found quite different grounds for closing the door on Emma Lazarus's "huddled masses"—Henry Cabot Lodge, for instance, and the newly established Immigration Restriction League, worried less over the fate of the American worker in the face of foreign competition than over the fate of the country's cherished institutions in the face of massive influxes of inferior "stock." A fatal bomb blast at a workers' rally in Haymarket Square in Chicago in 1886 had raised the specter of imported radicalism; and the anti-Chinese agitation and violence of the 1870s and 1880s had given voice to profound misgivings about the prospect of absorbing so many "unassimilable" strangers. Indeed, the entire period from 1876 to the 1920s was marked by a varying—but mostly escalating—doubt about the desirability of continued immigration. The period was characterized by powerful strains of nativist thinking, even if industry's voracious appetite for cheap supplies of unskilled labor never abated, and even though rhapsodic national self-congratulation over the democratic openness that the immigrant so nicely symbolized never died completely away.

Since the immigrant became a national icon charged with awesome positive *and* negative value, this is a history tinged by considerable irony. Immigrants provided the basis for self-flattering portraits of the openness of the nation's democratic order; and yet they bore the brunt of some of the nation's fiercest antidemocratic impulses. Hailing largely from preindustrial regions, immigrants nonetheless came to symbolize for many Americans the encroachments of the modern, because they formed a visible urban proletariat. Feared as agitators by management and despised as competitors by labor, immigrants came to symbolize a number of contradictory threats to the economic order: though they were often disparaged by labor for their presumed docility, immigrants' "un-American," incendiary attitudes became the stuff of American political legend. If their very diversity militated against an easy, class-based alliance among workers, their presence in such huge numbers still signaled the hardening of the American class structure. And the presence of so many who had fled the Old World because its horizons of opportunity seemed so narrow was for some a lamentable sign that America might yet *become* the Old World. "Where Braddock and his men . . . were struck by the painted savages in the primeval woods," sighed Frederick Jackson Turner, "huge furnaces [now] belch forth perpetual fires and Huns and Bulgars, Poles and Sicilians struggle for a chance to earn their daily bread, and live a brutal and degraded life."

For the country's older residents—like Turner—the image of the immigrant in this period inevitably evoked the question, what is America to become? Henry James wrote with palpable anxiety of "the terrible little Ellis Island" and its inconceivable throngs, who made the proper American feel as though he had seen "a ghost in his supposedly safe old house." Elsewhere he described a troubling encounter with a number of Italians in his native Boston, "gross aliens to a man . . . in serene and triumphant possession" of the city. Artist Frederic Remington's response, if unusual in its severity, cut closer to the heart of the issue for a once-frontier nation on the threshold of industrial supremacy: "Jews, Injuns, Chinamen, Italians, Huns—the rubbish of the earth I hate—I've got some Winchesters and when the massacring begins, I can get my share of 'em, and what's more, I will." Remington mourned the passing of the frontier era even as he clung to its codes of honor and brandished its side arms; he expressed a profound sense of American self-hood whose natural boundary, like that of the geographic "frontier" itself, was marked by the discomfiting presence of the degraded outsider. But these versions of Americanism and un-Americanism were as much a product of the ascending industrial era as of the waning days of the frontier. The nation's quest for what Brooks Adams called "economic supremacy" generated an endless, self-renewing throng of migrant worker–barbarians clamoring at the nation's gates.

Wanted: Immigrant Workers

"The ebb and flow of the labor market is like the ebb and flow of the commodity market," wrote labor sociologist John R. Commons in 1919. A whole range of forces—famines, earthquakes, ethnic violence, indebtedness and the vagaries of small farming, unbearable tax burdens—could unsettle people from their homelands, but the labor market and the laws of supply and demand dictated where they were likely to go. Americans then as now liked the pretty story of Emma Lazarus's teeming millions "yearning to breathe free"; and American political mythology has long relied upon the icon of the freshly disembarked immigrant to give a human face to the grand but hazy ideal of "liberty." But the truth is more prosaic: as even the Congressional Commission on Immigration (the Dillingham Commission) concluded in its massive investigation early in the century, "With comparatively few exceptions the emigrant of to-day is essentially a seller of labor seeking a more favorable market." Weekly earnings for laborers in the United States were estimated at $8.82 in 1890, $8.94 in 1900, and $10.68 in 1910. Laborers in Ireland, by contrast, could expect about $2 per week during this period; Italians in the Mezzogiorno most often worked for well under $2 per week; and field hands in the rural areas of turn-of-the-century Hungary could expect roughly $22 *per year.*

Even despite its depressions and downturns, then, and notwithstanding American trade unionists' fears that the labor market had become saturated, the United States represented "a more favorable market" to people from all over the world for a very long time. Immigration from Italy first began to reach appreciable numbers in the 1880s, and nearly four million Italians arrived between 1880 and World War I (though as many as 60 percent may have returned to Italy at one point or another). Migration from Russia—and particularly Jewish migration—mounted in the wake of the czar's anti-Semitic May Laws and a rash of violent pogroms in 1881; by 1915, the U.S. Census had tabulated over three million arrivals from Russian lands. Even despite the passage of the Chinese Exclusion Act in 1882, Asia sent nearly a half-million immigrants between 1880 and 1915, including almost two hundred thousand from Japan. At the Southern border, Mexican immigration began to mount in the first decade of the new century, and the years 1906 to 1915 witnessed 127,000 Mexican arrivals. The same ten-year period saw a total of over 650,000 arrivals from the rest of the Americas, including over a half-million from Canada and another 125,000 from the West Indies. From Northern and Western Europe—the countries that accounted for what was inaccurately called the "old immigration"—Scandinavia sent well over a million and a half between 1876 and 1915; Germany sent over two and a half million; and even Ireland, whose statistical bell-curve had peaked way back in the 1840s and '50s, sent well over a million and a half immigrants during this period, over fifty thousand per year during the 1880s alone. This was an astonishing movement of populations, no matter how one looked at it.

Just as his "frontier thesis" became both impetus and rallying cry for the nation's late-century quest for overseas markets, so Frederick Jackson Turner's writing provided a ready frame for thinking about the portent of this massive immigration. "The free lands are gone," he warned; "the conditions of a settled society are being reached with suddenness and with confusion." What, then, would these teeming millions of new settlers *do?* The question of assimilating these immigrants lay at the very heart of Turner's interest in the frontier and its passing in the first place. The nation's demography and economy were changing dramatically, and they were changing together. From the vantage point of native observers like Turner and his University of Wisconsin colleagues, sociologists Edward A. Ross and John R. Commons, the nation was becoming heavily peopled with a new, problematic element; and this demographic decline was inseparable from the marked changes in the economy that immigrants were entering. "The changing character of immigration is made possible by the changing character of industry," argued Commons; "races wholly incompetent as pioneers and independent proprietors are able to find a place once manufactures, mines, and railroads have sprung into being, with their captains of industry to guide and supervise their semi-intelligent work." To pose the problem in Turner's terms, what hope for a republic whose democratic traditions were said to depend upon free lands and upon the sturdy virtues of a population of independent ("Anglo-Saxon") yeoman farmers?

Indeed, as merchant capitalism yielded to industrial capitalism, the rationalization of the factory system and the advent of mechanization heightened the nation's already voracious appetite for unskilled labor; occupation after occupation fell into the recently created category of mere machine-tending. In 1870, over half of American workers were farmers or farm laborers; by the 1910s, over two-thirds were factory workers. By 1914, fully 95 percent of the workers in Henry Ford's foundry were unskilled, trained to do just one specialized task in the overall operation—each task of the simple sort that, in Ford's words, "the most stupid man can learn in two days." Whereas only 55 percent of the "old" (pre-1870s, primarily North and West European) immigration had consisted of unskilled laborers, such workers accounted for 81 percent of the "new" (post-1880, primarily South and East European) immigration—and, unlike earlier arrivals, the new immigrants found a mechanized economy ready to accommodate their skill level. This was a matter of some portent for those Americans who cared for neither the new arrivals nor the changing nature of American industry. The immigrant symbolized a whole complex of unwanted developments in American life. Political and religious ideals were too scarce among the new immigrants, E. A. Ross felt: "Those who bring anything but their hands are a very small and diminishing contingent." For Ross, the Old Immigration had consisted of "home seekers," the New, merely "job seekers."

The reservations of natives like Turner, Ross, and Commons notwithstanding, clearly some Americans somewhere profited by this massive influx of unskilled workers. Among those who fought recurrent restrictionist proposals most fiercely over the years were business groups like the National Association of Manufacturers and the National Union of Manufacturers, and a Southern coalition of businessmen and congressmen who wanted the influx of cheap labor into the region to continue. Indeed, vast numbers of publicists—in the employ of various industries, companies, shipping lines, or even individual states and towns—peddled seductive images of America abroad in an effort to draw potential settlers and workers across the seas to the New World. Describing Colorado as the "Switzerland of America," for example, one boosterist pamphlet exhorted, "The poor should come to Colorado, because here they can by industry and frugality better their condition. The rich should come here, because they can more advantageously invest their means than in any other region. . . . It is the Mecca for all classes and conditions." Similarly, a state-sponsored pamphlet on Minnesota called out "To Labouring Men, who earn a livelihood by honest toil; to Landless Men, who aspire to the dignity and independence which comes from possession of God's free earth; to All Men of moderate means, and men of wealth, who will accept homes in a beautiful and prosperous country . . . it is well for the hand of labour to bring forth the rich treasures hid in the bosom of the NEW EARTH."

The organizational infrastructure of this massive propaganda effort included government agencies, such as the boards of immigration in states like Wisconsin and Colorado, the Immigration Association of California, or, at the local level, the San Francisco Board of Trade or the Rome, Georgia, Chamber of Commerce (who boasted "the great commercial centre of the finest bodies of agricultural and mineral lands on the continent of America"); it included private boosters, such as the freelance author of *Semi-Tropical California*, and boosters-for-hire, such as the author of *California, the Cornucopia of the World*, distributed by the Southern Pacific Railroad; it included networks of agents working for the Southern Pacific, Northern Pacific, Union Pacific, and Burlington Railroads, who organized lectures, exhibitions, and tours for newspaper editors; and it included ticket agents for the large steamship companies, engaged in "a great hunt for emigrants." At their peak these agents were said to number over thirty-six hundred in the British Isles alone, and by another estimate, between five and six thousand in Galicia. This vast network of professional New World yea-sayers sent out torrents of literature in English, German, Welsh, Dutch, Norwegian, Swedish, Czech, Polish, and Russian; and the agents themselves, as one observer put it, covered certain regions abroad "as the locusts covered Egypt."

The flow of immigrants continued at impressive rates up to World War I, partially managed and directed by various middlemen and labor agents in the sending countries. Labor contractors and agents, known in various local vernaculars as "labor czars," "*padroni*," or "*reganchistas*," steered their compatriots toward specific work in specific regions of the United States—Chinese or Japanese laborers toward the Western railroads, Hungarians toward the Pennsylvania mines, Mexicans toward the Texas smelter industry, Greeks toward the Western copper mines, or Italians toward the city-building projects of the Eastern Seaboard and the Midwest. The Alien Contract Labor Law (the Foran Act) of 1885 forbade the importation of "contract laborers"—that is, anyone who had contracted to do a particular job before immigrating—yet employers routinely circumvented the spirit of the law by drawing not upon contracts per se but upon the existing, informal ethnic networks and family ties of their workers. As the Japanese consul in Tacoma reported in 1898, the continual arrival of impoverished Japanese laborers in the Pacific Northwest could be attributed directly to the railroad contractors who were abetting them.

> *For a small sum, they get some of their workers to send letters to friends at home telling them of the benefits of railroad construction work, thereby persuading many unknowing Japanese to come to this region. Some of these unknowing ones cannot even afford lodging when they reach an open port, and the contractors or their agents advance them money for clothing and travel expenses. In some cases, the contractors or their agents also temporarily loan the thirty dollars people must have at the time they enter the country.*

"The real agents who regulate the immigration movement," another observer thus concluded in 1912, "are the millions of earlier immigrants already in the United States."

Thus certain immigrant groups concentrated not only in certain geographical locales, but also in certain occupational niches. In 1911, the

Dillingham Immigration Commission devoted sixteen volumes of its monumental forty-volume study to *Immigrants in Industries.* The commission's compendium of statistics speaks not only to the immense presence of foreign workers in American industry in general, but also to the clustering of particular groups within particular industries. In American clothing manufacture, to take one of the more striking instances, 72 percent of the workforce was foreign-born, and another 22 percent were children of immigrant fathers (the commission did not record the nativity of workers' mothers). In New York City's garment industry, the figures were even higher: 87 percent and 10 percent respectively—or 97 percent immigrants and children of immigrants. Although Austrians, Germans, Poles, and other groups worked in the industry in significant numbers nationwide, fully three-quarters of the garment workers in New York were either East European Jews or Italians. In Chicago meatpacking, the numbers were nearly as dramatic: 78 percent foreign, and 14 percent children of foreign fathers, or all together 92 percent immigrants and their children. Poles and Lithuanians constituted fully 39 percent of this polyglot workforce. Nor were these industries anomalous. The statistics were remarkably consistent: from coal mining to the cotton factories, immigrants and their children constituted the vast majority of the workforce. Indeed, throughout this period some industries were impossible to conceive without their chief labor imports—Mexicans in Southwestern metalliferous mining, the Chinese in railroad construction, Slavs in meatpacking, or Jews in the needle trades. As one Bureau of Labor report in Maine remarked, in that region "it would be difficult at the present time to build a railroad of any considerable length without Italian labor."

American employers, contracting agents, and government officials thus sized up various populations and watched their movements with great interest. "A laboring population heretofore unknown in Württemberg is becoming now quite numerous," wrote a U.S. State Department official from Germany in 1878. Italians who had migrated north to work German mines and railroads were making a good impression, not only because of their industry, but because they were "so easily satisfied." They lived very cheaply on polenta and cheese, and they raised "no clamor for more 'luncheon' and 'more drink.'"

Not only did immigration help to fill the positions and staff the factories as the nation's economy expanded, but monitoring and tapping the immigrant streams became an important element of workforce management, as employers sought just the right kind of workers and the right combinations of workers to maximize productivity and to minimize labor's stridence and solidarity. Sometimes this meant introducing foreign populations as strikebreakers, perhaps under the protection of local police or Texas Rangers. In 1903 and 1904, for instance, Colorado coal-mining executives recruited Mexican, Italian, Slavic, Greek, and Japanese labor to break a strike of English-speaking miners. Under more ordinary circumstances, it meant using ethnic or racial difference itself in engineering a workforce that was usefully divided against itself: "Last week we employed Slovacks," a Chicago meatpacker told John Commons in 1904. "We change about among various nationalities and languages. It prevents them from getting together. We have the thing systematized. We have a luncheon each week of the employment managers of the large firms of the Chicago district. There we discuss problems and exchange information." Likewise, garment manufacturers deliberately seated Yiddish-speaking women next to Italian speakers in some New York shirtwaist factories as a way of preventing workers' alliances. Some employers actively cultivated ethnic discord by spreading false rumors about one group and attributing them to the other. Indeed, so widespread and effective were such practices that Commons later concluded, "The only device and symptom of originality displayed by American employers in disciplining their labor force has been that of playing one race against the other."

Notions of race and racial difference (which in this period distinguished not only whites, blacks, Asians, and Latinos from one another, but also Hebrews, Celts, Slavs, Finns, Italians, Teutons, Magyars, and Anglo-Saxons) came most forcefully into play around questions of immigrant civic participation—did this or that immigrant group possess the virtues necessary to participate safely in democratic civic life? But the notion of biologically determined, characterologically stable racial types did exert some influence over purely economic discussions of immigration and the immigrants' place in the New World industrial order. Racial language came increasingly to

identify the American workforce and its fluctuations, first of all. An economist could comment offhandedly in 1910 that, in the anthracite coalfields
of Pennsylvania, "the tall, dark-complexioned and dolichocephalic [long-
headed] Anglo-Saxon is largely supplanted by the thick-set, light-haired,
brachycephalic [broad-headed] Slav." But as far as employers were concerned,
there were two other, more important dimensions to such racial typing: the
particular "racial" character of different groups when it came to general questions of workforce management—their inherent tractability, for instance—
and the specific kinds of labor, the precise tasks, for which various groups
were suited because of their particular "racial" makeup.

Captain Jones, a superintendent for the Cambria steelworks in Pennsylvania, wrote with remarkable candor about the racial dimension of shop-floor
management in 1875. "We must steer clear of the West [of Europe] where
men are accustomed to infernal high wages," he cautioned. "We must steer
clear as far as we can of Englishmen who are great sticklers for high wages,
small production and strikes." Jones's personal judgment was that "Germans
and Irish, Swedes and what I denominate 'Buckwheats'—young American
country boys . . . make the most effective and tractable force you can find.
Scotsmen do very well. . . . Welsh can be used in limited numbers."

Such thinking about race and tractability became increasingly intricate
over the course of the later nineteenth century, taking on regional shapes and
shades in response to regional demographics and regional imperatives of productivity. Among cotton planters in Texas, for instance, Mexican workers
were thought to be "easily domineered," and hence more desirable than
white workers or sharecroppers, who felt an equal right with the white boss.
The Mexican worker, according to one planter, "understands that he is to do
what you tell him." Superintendents in the Minnesota mines, on the other
hand, reported to interviewers for the Dillingham Commission that, of all
the "races" employed in the mines, the Finns stood out for their intractabil-
ity: "These people are good laborers but trouble breeders." The Dillingham
Commission itself took the trouble to calculate rates of union membership
both by "race" and by length of residence for the various foreign peoples.
Many employers were no doubt interested to learn that less than 6 percent of
the Slovak bituminous-coal miners who had been in the United States for

less than five years had joined unions; roughly 8 percent of Magyars; 13 percent of Poles; and 19 percent of southern Italians.

After the question of tractability came the question of racial "gifts." Peter Roberts, an early scholar of immigration, was scarcely alone in combining an economic understanding of immigrants' contribution to the United States with a racial theory as to various groups' particular talents. "American industry had a place for the stolid, strong, submissive, and patient Slav and Finn," he wrote in 1912; "it needed the mercurial Italian and Roumanian; there was much coarse, rough, and heavy work to do in mining and construction camps; in tunnel and railroad building; around smelters and furnaces. . . . The new immigrant has admirably supplied the need."

Race not only suggested specialized economic assignments in their broadest contours ("rough" work for "mercurial" peoples, for example), but far more specific assignments as well. One rural-California journal commented in 1886 that, "in the matter of picking and packing fruit," it was difficult to find "any desirable white help who will do this as satisfactorily to the consumer as the trained Chinaman, who, by tact peculiar to themselves mainly, seem to have reduced it to a science." In garment manufacture, the Jewish workers' inborn "dexterity" explained their predominance in the industry; one observer in the early 1920s praised "the peculiar genius of these people for merchandising" and their "artistic perception." According to a turn-of-the-century Industrial Commission report, piecework and high speed had come to characterize garment work because "the Jewish people are peculiarly eager to earn a big day's wages, no matter at what sacrifice." Similarly, as Italians moved into the industry alongside Jews, race provided the explanation: "The Italian, like the Jew, has a very elastic character," noted the Industrial Commission. "He can easily change habits and modes of work and adapt himself to different conditions." The Italian was particularly well suited to "the manufacture of clothing, silk weaving, hat making, and other trades where taste and a fine sense of touch are essential."

Even the Dillingham Commission's *Dictionary of Races and Peoples* (1911), which for the most part fretted over the menacing shift in U.S. immigration toward the problematic races of Southern and Eastern Europe, paused to ponder the economic merits of various new arrivals. The Bohemians, for instance, "excel as miners and craftsmen"; the Serbo-Croatian "is vigorous and well-adapted to hard labor. He makes a good workman in America." Russians are "practical and persevering," though the Slav generally is given to "carelessness as to the business virtues of punctuality and often honesty, [and to] periods of besotted drunkenness." Gypsy men, quite simply, are "pilferers." As late as the 1920s, a company in Pittsburgh worked up an elaborate chart that rated a number of racial groups according to their suitability to specific tasks and to work under specific conditions within the factory. How did Mexicans, Hebrews, or Bohemians rate, for instance, when it came to doing heavy work or light? Oily work or clean? Working the day shift or the night?

This kind of racial logic and the local patterns of employment discrimination that went with it resulted in a highly stratified and segmented labor market in most parts of the country—a "split" market in which women and entire ethnic or racialized populations were funneled into sectors of the economy whose wages were "naturally" lower and whose avenues of advancement led neither to other, more promising sectors, nor even terribly far upward within whatever industries constituted the region's economic "mudsill." When a Yale graduate inquired about a helper's job in the cast house of a steel mill in the early twentieth century, for instance, he was told, "You don't want to work there. Only Hunkies [Slavs] work on those jobs, they're too damn dirty and too hot for a 'white' man." Race and gender, those market forces that have most often remained unnamed in the discourse of the free market, thus spared "white men" and condemned "Hunkies," "Negroes," "Chinamen," adult "girls," or anyone else on the local scene whose natural "needs" were not as advanced. This labor segmentation was no doubt part of what one Slavic priest had in mind when he declared, early in the century, "My people are not in America; they are under it."

If the mechanisms of market segmentation tended to protect many native white workers from the harshest forms of labor exploitation, these workers nevertheless perceived a potential threat to the dignity and the standard of living of all American workers in the superexploitation of nonwhites and immigrants. The overall response to immigrant labor in the United States, then, was fiercely double-edged: if immigration made possible the emergence of the United States as a major—ultimately *the* major—industrial power, so did "the immigrant," as a charged cultural icon, come to symbolize the ugliest features of corporate capitalism amid rapid industrialization—its exploitive wages, its inhuman hours, its physical dangers, its degradations—and, ironically, so did the immigrant become a scapegoat for those very excesses of capital. As E. A. Ross put it in *The Old World in the New*, thanks to the immigrants, "we have bigger outputs, tonnages, trade-balances, fortunes, tips, and alimonies; [but] also bigger slums, red-light districts, breweries, hospitals, and death-rates." Despite the fantastic wealth immigrants created, Americans found no shortage of reasons to despise these new arrivals.

Unwanted Immigrant Workers: Labor Competition

The growing presence of foreigners on American soil raised many questions—among them, the very questions of "civilization," "barbarism," and "virtue" that attended the American quest for markets abroad during the same period. As one congressman complained during a debate over immigration in 1884, the new immigrants from Southern and Eastern Europe "do not know to purchase any of the luxuries which tend to elevate and enlighten people." As with the tribes of the plains or the Chinese in China, then, immigrants' status was not altogether independent of their habits of consumption.

Far more than their habits of consumption, however, their perceived capacity for production determined how various foreign peoples were viewed once upon American shores. And here they have historically posed a considerable array of threats. As recently as 1995, a state labor investigator in New York concluded that "an immigrant community living in fear" was "fertile soil" for the sweatshop system. This is one instance in a long history of blaming immigrants for their own plight, for the plight of their counterparts among American labor, and even for some of the less flattering features of the U.S. industrial landscape—tenements, slums, and sweatshops, for instance.

Again, the triumvirate of John Commons, E. A. Ross, and Frederick Jackson Turner offers a useful portrait of the turn-of-the-century brand of prolabor nativism. In *Races and Immigrants* (1907), Commons most eloquently linked the immigrants' potential menace to American labor with the economic thesis of "overproduction": "Commodities are produced to be sold," he wrote,

> *and if the market falls off, then production comes to a standstill with what is known as "overproduction." Now, wage-earners are the mass of consumers. If their wages do not rise in proportion to prices and profits, they cannot purchase as large a proportion of the country's products as they did before the period of prosperity began. "Overproduction" is mainly "underconsumption" of wage-earners. Immigration intensifies this fatal cycle of "booms" and "depressions."*

But it was not just that immigrants would degrade American labor by the sheer volume of their numbers (though these and other commentators did worry about the vast pool of excess labor). Immigrants would also inevitably degrade American labor, in that they were simply so degraded themselves. "The competition of races is the competition of standards of living," wrote Commons. "The race with the lowest necessities displaces the others." The presence within the U.S. labor market of so many millions whose "necessities" were so low could only bid down the standard of living for all American workers, including those whose inherent "necessities" were "higher." The new immigrants from Europe were the "neediest, meekest laborers to be found within the white race," concurred E. A. Ross. The combination of desperation and docility that characterized workers from "the backward parts of Europe" would "tend to weaken, if not to shatter, labor organizations in the fields they enter."

Many also feared that foreign labor—by its very foreignness—eroded the esteem that American labor had once enjoyed among the capitalist and managerial classes. Not only would laborers become degraded by their competition with workers whose needs and whose lifeways were so barbarous, but in fact labor itself—the process of production in the abstract—would also become degraded to the point of stigma. "With the insweep of the unintelligible bunk-house foreigner," wrote Ross, "there grows up a driving and cursing of labor which no self-respecting American will endure. Nor can he bear to be despised as the foreigner is. It is not the work or the pay that he minds, but the stigma." Noting that the immigration of the single year 1907 was composed of one-quarter of "the Mediterranean race, one-quarter of the Slavic race, one-eighth Jewish, and only one-sixth of the Alpine, and one-sixth of the Teutonic [that is, a total of one-third North or West European]," Frederick Jackson Turner, too, lamented that "the sympathy of employers with labor has been unfavorably affected by the pressure of great numbers of immigrants of alien nationality and of lower standards of life."

Works like Commons's *Races and Immigrants* (1907), Turner's "Social Forces in American History" (1910), and Ross's *The Old World in the New* (1913) did not articulate wholly new or unheard-of concerns but, rather, gave scholarly voice to a set of common prejudices that had circulated at street level and in policy-making circles for some time. The most powerful outburst of working-class nativism had been the anti-Chinese movement. This racially based, vigorously prolabor agitation had escalated in California and other regions of the West in the 1870s, and had captured the federal political machinery in the 1880s, when Congress passed the first bill for Chinese Exclusion. Even as early as the 1850s, when some fifty thousand Chinese immigrants arrived on the West Coast, a Committee of Vigilance had appeared in California to protest the attempts of capital to flood the state with coolies and "degraded Asiatics." Sporadic anti-Chinese violence broke out, and the state legislature passed a Foreign Miners Tax—enforced primarily against the Chinese—as a means of stemming the tide. In 1855, the State Assembly declared, "We want the Chinese *trade*, but we do not want her surplus *population*," a sentiment that aptly summed up the dominant American stance for the balance of the century and beyond. Over the next several decades, the political landscape of California, Oregon, Washington, Idaho, Wyoming, and Colorado became dotted with anticoolie clubs, Leagues of Deliverance, and other anti-Chinese organizations.

Anti-Chinese sentiments among white workers both intensified and became nationalized after 1869, when the completion of the transcontinental railroad stoked the flames of anti-Chinese race hatred in two distinct ways. First, as many mines dried up and as the railroad reached completion, Chinese laborers who had largely worked in these two industries began to drift into other sectors of the economy, particularly manufacturing enterprises that by custom had been "white." The overpopulation of San Francisco and the newly pronounced Chinese presence in occupational niches in cigar manufacture and shoemaking, for instance, heightened white workers' alarm over their own potential displacement by Chinese contract labor. By 1873, Chinese labor was producing over half of California's boots and shoes; Samuel Gompers later recalled the feeling among cigar workers that, "unless protective measures were taken, it was evident the whole industry would soon be 'Chinaized.'" Indeed, the Chinese presence prodded cigar-makers toward a national organization of labor unions, because "the help of all wage earners was needed in support of Chinese exclusion."

Since the completion of the transcontinental railroad nationalized the market for these Western goods, moreover, it also nationalized the perceived threat posed by Chinese labor. Not only did the Chinese presence threaten to depress wages in California's cigarmaking industry, but the opportunities for distribution afforded by the railroad now brought Western and Eastern workers into direct competition with one another. If the Chinese drove wages down in the West, the argument went, they would also drive them down in the East, as California cigar manufacturers made a bid for the national market. The peril was registered more directly still in shoemaking when, in 1870, five hundred striking white workers in the newly formed Knights of St. Crispin were replaced by Chinese strikebreakers in North Adams, Massachusetts. The year 1870 was thus marked not only by an anti-Chinese convention in California, but by anti-Chinese labor rallies in Eastern cities like New York and Boston as well.

The link in white workers' minds between the unsavory practices of monopoly capital on the one hand and the unfair competition of degraded Chinese labor on the other was forged during the early 1870s. At a Boston meeting of the Knights of St. Crispin, shoemakers denounced "Chinamen" as "ignorant tools in the hands of oppressive capitalists." Labor leaders and theorists like Henry George now denounced Chinese immigrants as "long-tailed barbarians," complaining that, "in every case in which Chinese come into fair competition with white labor, the whites must either retire from the field or come down to the Chinese standard of living." Resolutions passed at an anti-Chinese demonstration in New York's Tompkins Square in July 1870 likewise combined antimonopoly rhetoric with a racial logic familiar from the discourses of overproduction and export: capital, by these lights, had imported "the lowest and most degraded of the Chinese barbaric race" to compete with "those whose more advanced intelligence and improved tastes have generated in them a proportionately greater number of wants and desires."

Like employers themselves, these white workers saw something natural in the degraded state of Chinese labor—yet it was a degradation that could ultimately affect even the superior "white" worker unless, as this assembly urged, Congress put an end to "the importation of coolies." "The Chinamen labor for such pitiful wages that they undermine Caucasians," commented *The Atlantic Monthly* in 1871; "no white labor can live with any decency or self-respect" at such wage levels. As E. A. Ross summarized the argument in retrospect years later, whites could compete favorably with the Chinese under normal conditions, but not under bad conditions. His pithy formula: "Reilly can *outdo* Ah San, but Ah San can *underlive* Reilly." (Chinese Viceroy Li Hung-chang turned this reasoning around, cutting an anti-*European* argument from the same cloth: "The Chinese can live cheaper than the Irish," he conceded, but the real reason the laboring classes hated the Chinese was that "they [the Chinese] are possessors of higher virtues than themselves.")

Because so many of the imperiled "white" workers were actually immigrants themselves (hence Ross's use of the Irish "Reilly"), race became increasingly important in this formulation. As A. Oakey Hall argued at the Tompkins Square rally, the American people could not object to immigration per se, only to the capitalist venture to overrun labor with "another kind of tawny slave labor." Another orator, speaking in German, asserted that the country owed its greatness to "the laborers that had come from Europe." The Joint Congressional Committee to Investigate Chinese Immigration in 1877 also drew careful distinctions along the color line separating Asian from European immigrants. Unlike Europeans, "there is not sufficient brain capacity in the Chinese to furnish the motive power for self-government," the committee declared. "Upon the point of morals, there is no Aryan or European race which is not far superior to the Chinese as a class." Just as whiteness

gathered European immigrants into the American fold in the legal framework of naturalization law (whose key phrase in defining eligibility since
1790 was "free white persons"), so whiteness in the cauldron of labor competition naturalized European newcomers as honorary Americans, as against
the *truly* foreign "Mongolian" immigrants—at least for a time.

But whereas racialism provided the venom of the anti-Chinese campaign
(and, indeed, the "free white persons" clause in naturalization law had left
the Chinese ineligible for citizenship and hence uniquely vulnerable), the
driving logic of the movement was economic. Even the Joint Congressional
Committee, whose concern was largely for the safety of American institutions, adopted labor's anti-Chinese argument wholesale. "The Chinese have
reduced wages to what would be starvation prices for white men and
women," ran the report; "this distinctive competition in some branches of labor operates as a continual menace, and inspires fears that . . . these ruinously
low rates will . . . degrade all white working people to the abject condition
of a servile class."

Although a "California thesis" of the anti-Chinese movement rather too
neatly exonerates the rest of the country, it is true that the movement was
nowhere more militant than on the infamous "Sand Lot" in San Francisco,
where labor leader Dennis Kearney spewed anti-Chinese invective, where organized anti-Chinese agitation mounted throughout the latter 1870s, and
where, increasingly, anti-Chinese violence originated. In April 1877, an organization appeared in California calling itself The Order of Caucasians for
the Extermination of the Chinaman; its announced aim was to "drive the
Chinaman out of California" by a regime of harassment that, as spelled out in
the bylaws, included the policy to "pursue and injure" not only Chinese immigrants themselves but also any white persons who "countenance their existence in any way." Members pledged to oppose the Chinese "to annihilation
by every manner and means within the thin gauze of the law."

Misgivings about the Chinese presence on the grounds of their religion
or "civilization" were frequently aired, but the laborite strain of the movement was predominant in the tenor of the anti-Chinese argument. "We declare that the Chinaman must leave our shores," ran one Workingmen's Party
manifesto. "We declare that white men, and women, and boys, and girls,

cannot live as people of the great republic should and compete with the single Chinese coolies in the labor market. . . . To an American, death is preferable to life on par with the Chinamen." And "life on par with the Chinamen" was all that the future of California held for the white working class, unless the swarm of Asian newcomers could be turned away.

Both major political parties in California carried anti-Chinese planks from 1871 onward; and the Workingmen's Party, the first Marxist political party in the United States, garnered roughly a third of the vote in state elections during the decade behind the no-nonsense slogan "The Chinese Must Go!" Thanks largely to the influence of California labor, the state's second Constitution (ratified in 1879) included an article prohibiting any corporation's employing, "directly or indirectly, in any capacity, any Chinese or Mongolian"; prohibiting the employ of Chinese "on any state, county, municipal, or other public work, except in punishment for crime"; and mandating that the legislature "delegate all necessary power to the incorporated cities and towns of this state for the removal of Chinese without the limits of such cities and towns, or for their locations within prescribed portions of those limits, and it shall also provide the necessary legislation to prohibit the introduction into this state of Chinese after the adoption of this Constitution."

In the late 1870s, Western delegations of the U.S. Congress also brought the Chinese question to the national agenda. A congressional report submitted in 1877 (by a committee that happened to be dominated by Californians) urged legislation "to restrain the great influx of Asiatics to this country." Several bills calling for the termination of Chinese immigration were introduced in 1878 and '79, culminating in the Fifteen Passenger Bill (1879), which provided that no ship could take aboard more than fifteen Chinese passengers for transport to the United States. At a time when Chinese immigration was running toward ten thousand per year, such limitations would have a tremendous impact. President Hayes vetoed the bill, however, largely out of sensitivity to diplomatic and commercial relations with China, and to the treaty protections affecting American nationals and interests in Asia.

But by now the talk of Exclusion was not to be quieted. "Every country owes its first duty to its own race and citizens," opined the *San Francisco Ex-*

aminer in 1880. "This duty properly observed on this Coast will cause much riddance of the Chinese pest." In 1882, Senator John F. Miller of California introduced the first bill to suspend Chinese immigration—in this version, for a period of twenty years. The bill won vigorous support among Western and Southern congressmen, passing the Senate by a vote of 29 to 15, and the House by a vote of 167 to 66 (55 abstaining). Like his predecessor, Chester Arthur vetoed this bill, for his part on the grounds that the twenty-year suspension was too long, and that such a draconian law would damage the U.S. image among trading partners in Asia. But in the spring of 1882, he did sign a revised bill that reduced the suspension to ten years (subject to renewal), and the Chinese Exclusion Act became law. So portentous was this triumph for American labor perceived to be that its possible *repeal* became the stuff of science fiction: offering a horrific vision of American life a hundred years hence in *Caesar's Column* (1890), populist Ignatius Donnelly projected that the industrial "underworld" would include, among myriad other races and nations, "even Chinese and Japanese; for the slant eyes of many, and their imperfect, Tartar-like features, reminded me that the laws made by the Republic, in the elder and better days, against the invasion of the Mongolian hordes, had long since become a dead letter."

Still despised (as Donnelly's comments indicate) and now newly vulnerable, the Chinese immigrants who had already entered the United States suffered a series of violent attacks in the long wake of Exclusion. Indeed, historian Shih-Shan Henry Tsai has identified fifty-five anti-Chinese riots in the West during the latter decades of the nineteenth century, including thirty-four in California, nine in Washington, and four in Nevada. Though the residents of Wyoming perpetrated only one anti-Chinese riot, the outrage at Rock Springs (1885) was among the most spectacular in its fury: twenty-eight Chinese miners were killed, fifteen others injured, several hundred driven out of town, and Chinese property estimated at $147,000 was destroyed. Rock Springs stands out only for the scale of violence; the distinction from other anti-Chinese outrages across the West was in degree, not in kind. Like the upheaval in Tacoma in 1885, many of these riots were regarded as serious enough even by an avowedly anti-Chinese federal government to provoke the intervention of federal troops.

Anti-Chinese agitation is unique in the history of American nativism for the consistency of its violence, for its success in capturing the major workers' organizations as well as both national political parties, and, ultimately, for its success in winning legislation that singled out one national group for total exclusion. Indeed, since some of the movement's key participants were immigrants themselves, it is only with major qualification that we can consider this "nativism" at all. But the argument against the foreign worker that began with the Chinese was broadly applied in ensuing years, in both its racialist and its economic dimensions—even to those European newcomers whose perceived "whiteness" initially shielded them during the Sand Lot tumult of the 1870s. By the turn of the century, it was not at all unusual to hear that any number of groups—whether Bohemians, Italians, Japanese, or Jews—were fundamentally "like the Chinese."

The Exclusion Act of 1882 may have been broadly anti-Asian in its spirit, but it was narrowly anti-Chinese in its letter. Hence, even in the wake of Exclusion, immigration from other areas of Asia—particularly Japan—began to mount in the 1890s and after. This migration, too, would gradually be curtailed over the years—by an executive order in 1907, which prohibited immigration through the United States' insular possessions (in this case Hawaii), and by racially based, staunchly anti-Asian legislation in 1917 and 1924, creating a "barred zone" that effectively extended the principle of Exclusion to the whole of the Asian continent. But in the meantime, significant numbers of Japanese immigrants did arrive, and labor-contracting firms like the Oriental Trading Company (Seattle), Ban Shinzaburo (Portland), the Japanese American Industrial Corporation (San Francisco), and the Oriental Contracting Company (Denver) funneled them into the Western railroad, mining, and agricultural industries. By 1909, over thirty-eight thousand Japanese workers were employed as agricultural field hands, primarily in California; another ten thousand worked as section hands on the Western railroads; thirty-six hundred worked the salmon canneries in Alaska, Oregon, and Washington; twenty-two hundred tended the sawmills of the Pacific Northwest; and two thousand worked the mines of Colorado and Wyoming.

It was not long before the influx of laborers from this new Asian source had put figures like Dennis Kearney back in business: "The foreign shylocks are rushing another breed of Asiatic slaves to fill up the gap made vacant by the Chinese who are shut out by our laws," he told a Sacramento audience in 1892. "Japs," he declared, "are being brought here now in countless numbers to demoralize and discourage our domestic labor market." Echoing his earlier campaign of the 1870s, he ended with the slogan "The Japs Must Go!"

The sporadic anti-Japanese agitation and violence of the 1890s had become a full-fledged movement by 1900, when the first truly large-scale demonstration of anti-Japanese sentiment took place in California. Speakers included E. A. Ross (then at Stanford), who compared a prudently restrictionist immigration policy to a prudent tariff policy: "We keep out pauper-made goods but let in the pauper," he objected. "A restrictive policy devised in the true interest of labor would think first of keeping out the foreigner, and then of keeping out his product."

In the 1890s and after, an occasional "white" union did attempt to embrace—even if reluctantly—the newcomers from Asia. In response to a strike of Mexican and Japanese sugar-beet workers in Oxnard, California, in 1903, the Los Angeles County Council of Labor resolved:

> We declare our belief that the most effective method of protecting the American workingman and his standard of living is by the universal organization of the wage-workers regardless of race or national distinction.
>
> Resolved, That while we are utterly opposed to the unrestricted immigration of the various Oriental races, we heartily favor the thorough organization of those now here, and believe that the fact that men are able to do our work when we strike is sufficient reason why they should be organized, regardless of race or color.

But Samuel Gompers voiced the prevailing opinion of American labor when he agreed to issue an AFL charter to the Council of Labor only on the condition that "your union will under no circumstances accept membership of any Chinese or Japanese." For Gompers and others, the Japanese issue melded entirely with the anti-Chinese agitation of decades earlier, particularly as the Exclusion Act came due for renewal in the early years of the new century. "Every incoming coolie means the displacement of an American, and the lowering of the American standard of living," he argued in 1901. That same year, Gompers penned a pamphlet bearing the provocative title *Some Reasons for Chinese Exclusion: Meat vs. Rice, American Manhood Against Asiatic Coolieism, Which Shall Survive?* The *Federationist*, the AFL organ, flatly declared that the Japanese immigrant "can not be *unionized*. He cannot be *Americanized.*"

Yellow Peril hysteria mounted in the early years of the century, particularly as the Japanese victory in the Russo-Japanese War elevated Japan to new heights of perceived menace in the American political imagination: "Once the war with Russia is over," predicted the *San Francisco Chronicle*, "the brown stream of Japanese immigration [will become] a raging torrent." *Chronicle* headlines in this period included: "How Japanese Immigration Companies Override Laws," "Brown Men Are Made Citizens Illegally," "Japanese a Menace to American Women," "The Yellow Peril—How Japanese Crowd Out the White Race," "Brown Peril Assumes National Proportions," and "Brown Artisans Steal Brains of Whites." The journal's editor feared no less than the "complete orientalization of the Pacific coast."

Like the impetus for Chinese Exclusion, anti-Japanese sentiment originated in certain industries but soon spilled across the entire West. "We view with alarm the pouring of cheap Japanese labor into our western States," explained a Wyoming delegate to the United Mine Workers of America in 1904.

> *We believe that Americans today, as in 1776, stand for independence and the noblest manhood; the Japanese laborer, as we find him in our mines and other industries, stands for neither. The Jap, like the Chinaman, works for whatever the company is pleased to pay him, and returns a portion of his earnings regularly to a Japanese agent, who is called a "boss," doubtless to evade technically the law prohibiting contract labor.*

The Japanese immigrant "should be excluded from our shores," he concluded. "Therefore we pray Congress to enact a law excluding the Japanese as well as the Chinese."

Soon enough, such rough calls for workingmen's "justice" crystallized in formal organizations with concrete legislative agendas. Early anti-Japanese organizations like the Boot and Shoemaker's White Labor League were joined soon in the new century by the more ambitious Asiatic Exclusion League and the suggestively named Anti-Jap Laundry League, which frankly opposed "the patronizing or employing of Asiatics in any manner." The California legislature, for its part, began passing anti-Japanese resolutions and legislation, noting in 1905, for instance, that Japanese immigrants "contribute nothing to the growth of the State. They add nothing to its wealth, and they are a blight on the prosperity of it." Further, "the close of the war between Japan and Russia will surely bring to our shores hordes, to be counted only in thousands, of the discharged soldiers of the Japanese Army, who will crowd the State with immoral, intemperate, quarrelsome men, bound to labor for a pittance, and to subsist on a supply with which a white man can hardly sustain life." In 1913, the state legislature passed the Alien Land Law, which forbade land ownership (or even the leasing of land beyond three years) on the part of any "alien ineligible for citizenship"—clearly a proscription intended for Japanese immigrants, who indeed had become active in small farming. As the *Elk Grove Citizen* put it that year in a hateful little jingle, "Ill fares the land, / to hastening ills a prey, / Where Japs accumulate, / day by day."

Or where any Asians accumulate, for that matter. A mob drove a hundred East Indian farm workers out of Live Oak, California, in 1908; and between 1909 and 1915, white residents perpetrated a number of assaults against Koreans in the West, though Korean settlement was quite modest. In 1913, a mob of several hundred unemployed whites ran fifteen Korean fruit pickers out of Hemet, California, under threat of violence. By the 1910s, there was a good deal of enthusiasm for a further-reaching Exclusion Act than that which merely proscribed the Chinese. As Paul Scharrenberg, an AFL officer in California, put it in 1915, "We are anxious to have enacted an exclusion law which will effectively and permanently bar these little brown men from our shores"—by which he meant much more than just "The Chinese Must Go!" Even Woodrow Wilson, who resisted proposals like the literacy test that would have restricted European immigration, was sympathetic to the anti-Asian strains of American labor. "In the matter of Chinese and Japanese coolie immigration," he said, "I stand for the national policy of exclusion." Although the president did voice his concern for the assimilability of a people "who do not blend with the Caucasian race," his adoption of the term "coolie" here was critical: "Their lower standard of living as laborers will crowd out the white agriculturalist and is, in other fields, a serious industrial menace." In 1917, Wilson signed a new immigration law creating a "Barred Zone" east of the Caucasus Mountains, the Ural River, and the Ural Mountains. The new law effectively united Japanese, Korean, and East Indian immigrants with the excluded Chinese as racial pariahs whose continued immigration was not to be countenanced.

Asians, of course, were not the only immigrants to run afoul of American labor and its allies in government. Armenians in California, for instance, though exempted from the prohibitions imposed by the Alien Land Law, did suffer discrimination in housing and in the social organization of cities like Fresno, whose color bars, by local custom, placed them on the nonwhite side of the divide; and Armenian farm workers were sometimes terrorized by violent night-riders in the state's orchard lands. Likewise, in the 1910s members of the AFL decried Mexican immigration as a "torrent of peon poison," and lamented that able-bodied American men were forced to sit idle without work while "slim-legged [Mexican] peons with tortillas in their stomachs" performed construction work in their full view. "Cheap labor," spat the AFL *Advocate* in a 1915 piece on Mexican labor in the Southwest, "—at the cost of every ideal cherished in the heart of every member of the white race, utterly destroyed and buried beneath the greedy ambitions of a few grasping money gluttons, who would not hesitate to sink the balance of society to the lowest levels of animalism, if by so doing they can increase their own bank account." Like the Asians before them, Mexican workers were not seen as potential fellows in common cause, but as dangerous tools in the hands of monopoly capital whose innate racial degradation threatened to degrade even the noblest of American laborers.

Nor, ultimately, were European laborers themselves immune to such objections on the part of American natives, even if in some cases they had comfortably participated in the agitation against Asian or Mexican immigration.

For some natives, in fact, if the anti-Chinese movement had proved anything at all, it proved that the nation's gates ought to be closed against *European* immigrants. The *San Francisco Argonaut* depicted the anti-Chinese rallies of the 1870s as consisting of "the refuse and sweepings of Europe, the ignorant, brutal, idle off-scourings of civilization." In a pamphlet titled *Must the Chinese Go?* (1890), another writer charged: "The immigrant from across the Atlantic desires and intends to command the labor market here; not only to rule in our homes, but in every other department of industry in which he enters; to fix prices of labor, to strike for more, to do or not to do, without fear of competition." Like the Chinese in the eyes of a Dennis Kearney, the anti-Chinese agitators from Europe merely sought unfair control of the labor market.

The perceived crimes of the "new" European immigrants included not only their tendency to drive down wages by their very presence, but their tendency to impede the prospects of workers' organization by their inborn docility. Given the tendency among American conservatives and the managerial elite to pin American radicalism on immigrants from Germany, Russia, or Hungary, it is no small irony that in other quarters immigrant *docility* reached legendary proportions. As W. Jett Lauck wrote in *The Atlantic Monthly* in 1912, the South or East European immigrant has "been inclined, as a rule, to acquiesce in the demand on the part of employers for extra work or longer hours. . . . Where older employees have found unsafe or unsanitary working conditions prevailing, and have protested, the recent immigrant wage-earners . . . have manifested a willingness to accept the alleged unsatisfactory working conditions."

American radicals themselves, moreover, were often far from kind or hospitable to these newly arrived proletarians. "The Dago works for small pay and lives far more like a savage or wild beast, than the Chinese," wrote socialist leader Eugene Debs in 1891. Like the Chinaman and his infernal rice diet, the Italian immigrant "fattens on garbage" and "is able to underbid an American workingman. Italy has millions of them to spare and they are coming." Decades later, in 1911, Milwaukee socialist Victor Berger, too, denounced "Slovenians, Italians, Greeks, Russians, and Armenians" as "modern white coolies." Though Debs himself blunted his anti-immigrant sentiments over time, the Socialist Party as a whole never did entirely abandon a nativist rhetoric and logic. The party's national convention in 1910 adopted a resolution that, though placating Jews in a clause affirming the maintenance of the United States as "a free asylum" for persons persecuted in their homelands on political, religious, or racial grounds, nonetheless endorsed "all legislative measures tending to prevent the immigration of strikebreakers and contract laborers, and the mass importation of workers from foreign countries, brought about by the employing classes for the purpose of weakening the organization of American labor, and of lowering the standard of life of American workers."

However sympathetic American laborers might have been to the plight of workers from the Old World, as one AFL spokesman declared, the United States was now "in the position of any other asylum whose dormitories are full up. . . . We cannot go abroad and hope to lift up the labor of the world. . . . The selfishness that provides for the home and protection of the family from want or danger is the only spirit in which this question may be considered successfully." Thus, though foreign workers in some very real sense actually *constituted* "American labor," they were despised, repulsed, and plotted against politically by congeries of organized groups who recognized the name as applying only to themselves, not to this invasion of degraded foreigners.

In this, native labor leaders in the AFL or even the Socialist Party ironically held something in common with conservative patricians like Elihu Root. "The subject of the exclusion of laborers is acquiring a new interest in my mind," wrote Root to his friend Oliver Wendell Holmes in 1907, the nation's peak year of immigration. "The whole subject of a peaceful invasion by which the people of a country may have their country taken away from them, and the analogy and contrast between the swarming of peaceful immigration and business enterprise and the popular invasions of former times, such, for instance, as those overrunning the Roman Empire, are most interesting." Like Victor Berger, Dennis Kearney, or the riotous members of the Asiatic Exclusion League, Elihu Root feared for the ultimate *possession* of the country. But, like so many among the elite classes who throughout this period grappled with the perils of "overproduction," Root parted ways with the likes of these laborites in the terms by which he defined the problem. If a Kearney or a Berger was most concerned with standards of living and the dignity of labor, Root came to fear laborers themselves. Indeed, for Root and others like him throughout this period of boom and bust, labor's very disquiet was among the most alarming features of the immigrants' "peaceful invasion" of the nation.

Unwanted Immigrant Workers: Labor Radicalism

" 'Barbarians, savages, illiterate Anarchists from Central Europe, men who cannot comprehend the spirit of our free American institutions,'—of these I am one." So begins the brief autobiography of August Spies, written from his jail cell after a bomb had exploded in the midst of a group of Chicago policemen in Haymarket Square during a workers' rally in support of the eight-hour workday. Charged with "general conspiracy to murder" for his advocacy of worker self-defense in the violent days of the eight-hour movement, Spies was hanged on November 11, 1887. The trial itself had been carried out in a frenzied atmosphere of antiradicalism heavily accented by frank nativism. As August Spies knew, he was on trial less for his deeds (which remained unproved) than for his "foreign" ideas and even his foreign birth. "I admit," he wrote, "I ought not to have made the mistake, ought not to have been born a *foreigner*, but little children, particularly unborn children, will make mistakes!"

In its aftermath, "Haymarket" was long an emblem for the dangerous, unpredictable tendencies of America's growing foreign-born population—the *Volcano Under the City*, as one anonymous chronicler phrased it at the time. But this "riot" was only one beat in a much longer litany that extended throughout the period—the nationwide railroad strike along the B&O lines from Baltimore to St. Louis and beyond (1877); the clash of striking steelworkers with Pinkerton Guards in Homestead, Pennsylvania (1892); the dispatch of federal troops to meet striking workers from the Pullman Palace Car Company in Chicago (1894); the three-month strike of U.S. garment workers, known as the Uprising of the Twenty Thousand (1909); the textile workers' strike in Lawrence, Massachusetts, said to be inspired by radical "agitators" from the Industrial Workers of the World (1912); and the five-month silk-workers' strike, also IWW, in Paterson, New Jersey (1913). Each episode conjured images of blood in the streets, an explosive and distinctly *foreign* brand of political chaos—never more "foreign," perhaps, than when the unruly mobs consisted largely of women, as in the 1909 uprising of "our wonderful fervent girls," as the Yiddish press hailed the twenty thousand garment workers, or in the fight "for bread and roses" in Lawrence in 1912. And the ever-lengthening litany as a whole seemed to prove the folly of accepting the rest of the world's "dangerous classes" as a chief import.

In the summer of 1883, when garment workers in several New York shops had struck for better working conditions, area newspapers dubbed it "the emigrants' strike," thus pointing up one of the peculiar ironies of the age: if immigrant workers could be hired for their supposed docility and reviled by native labor for their supposed unwillingness to organize and their consequent degradation of labor, so, nonetheless, could strikers be presumed "emigrants" and striking itself presumed inherently "un-American." "There has appeared in great force," wrote *Nation* editor E. L. Godkin in 1887,

> *and for the first time on American soil, the dependent, State-managed laborer of Europe, who declines to take care of himself in the old American fashion. When he is out of work, or does not like his work, he looks about and asks his fellow-citizens sullenly, if not menacingly, what they are going to do about it. He has brought with him, too, what is called "the labor problem," probably the most un-American of all the problems which American society has to work over today.*

Having walked directly into the fray between American capital and American labor, immigrants now came to symbolize the rising industrial order itself—and its discontents. In 1886, the year of the Haymarket violence, there were 1,572 work stoppages in the United States involving some 610,000 workers. Fifteen years later, in 1901, there were 3,012 stoppages; in 1917, 4,450. These workers' protests reflected at once the growing class-consciousness and the hardening class-lines of the industrializing republic, as well as a collective outrage at the exploitive employment practices at a time when the availability of cheap labor and the doctrines of social Darwinism combined to cheapen the very lives of American workers in the eyes of many employers. Throughout this period, defining radicalism as inherently "un-American" and pinning it exclusively on foreigners became the common sleight of hand by which Americans disowned the social conditions that capitalism had spawned and which radicalism was meant to address.

The tendency to conflate the immigration question and the labor question had become especially pronounced in the wake of the Great Railroad Strike of 1877. Perhaps more forcefully than the Centennial Exposition, this first nationwide strike against the country's premiere nationwide corporation announced the arrival of the United States as a fully industrial civilization. In response to a 10-percent wage reduction in July 1877—the second such cut in a four-year stretch during which cuts totaled up to 37 percent for many workers—railroad workers in Martinsburg, West Virginia, went out on strike against the Baltimore and Ohio Railroad. Sympathetic workers all along the B&O line came to their support, and within a few days crowds were attacking the railroads and waging pitched battles against militiamen in West Virginia, Pennsylvania, and Ohio. Within a few days more, over a hundred thousand workers had gone out in a national strike, from Pittsburgh to Chicago to St. Louis to San Francisco. The battle for Pittsburgh was particularly fierce, ultimately killing nearly fifty workers and militiamen and destroying $5 million worth of property. A call put out by the Workingmen's Party in St. Louis produced a gathering of some twenty thousand workers in that city alone, bearing placards, among others, reading, "Why Does Overproduction Cause Starvation?" Local police, state militias, and three thousand federal troops under the direction of the War Department finally crushed the rebellion after two full weeks of fighting from coast to coast.

This was a portentous moment. After the uprising was crushed, the *Chicago Tribune* heaved a troubled sigh: "We now have the communists on our soil." But where had these radicals come from? Although the consensus at the time was that this was chiefly an uprising of native, not immigrant, workers, evidently the German and Bohemian sections of the Workingmen's Party were conspicuous far beyond their actual numbers, or else the very notion of such an uprising was itself so "foreign" that its perpetration by American natives was impossible to contemplate. In any case, that the Great Railroad Strike was "an emigrants' strike" became a fairly broadly accepted interpretation. The conspirators were "probably an amalgamation of the Molly Maguires and the Commune," supposed one observer. Godkin lamented the "vast additions" to the American population, to whom American ideals "appeal but faintly" and who "carry in their very blood traditions which give universal suffrage an air of menace to many of the things which civilized men hold most dear."

The strikes made an especially vivid impression on John Hay. As he wrote to his father-in-law at the time, "Any hour the mob chooses it can destroy any city in the country—that is the simple truth." Among the more interesting documents of American antiradicalism of the period is his novel, *The Bread-Winners* (1883), a fiercely antilabor melodrama of the 1877 strike. Revolving around Arthur Farnham, an upstanding citizen of one of the city's wealthier wards, and his love interests during the several days bracketing the general strike, the novel is primarily an exercise in dismantling the philosophical and political claims of a hazily defined American (un-American, rather) radicalism. There is no genuine "class struggle" in this cosmos, only self-interested scheming cloaked in high-sounding political phrases. Nor are there "classes," even—only respectable types and their disagreeable brethren, separated to some extent by degrees of prosperity, perhaps, but far more by the content of their characters. The novel does not seriously entertain and rebut socialist assaults on the capitalist order, that is; rather, it portrays such dissent as inherently dishonest—in every case a ruse hiding the agitator's opportunism or his outright thievery, a highly personal plot to win riches, women, or both.

The economic ethos of Hay's world-view, his sense of economic and technological triumph, is nicely expressed in his description of Buffland, a fictional port city on the shores of Lake Erie: "Its air was filled with the smoke and odors of vast and successful trade, and its sky was reddened by night with the glare of its furnaces, rising like the hot breath of some prostrate Titan, conquered and bowed down by the pitiless cunning of men." The single blot on this industrial idyll is a dangerous labor organization going by the name of the Brotherhood of Bread-Winners, a "roll-call of shirks" whose leadership consists of a loose band of "wandering apostles of plunder." Despite its prosperity, the fine city of Buffland proves remarkably vulnerable to their brand of agitation. By the second day of the strike, "a few tonguey vagrants and convicts from the city and from neighboring towns, who had come to the surface from nobody knew where, were beginning to exercise a wholly unexpected authority. They were going from place to place, haranguing the workmen, preaching what they called socialism, but what was merely riot and plunder."

The Bread-Winners is not a virulently nativist tract. Indeed, a thickly accented German immigrant named Bolty proves to be one of Farnham's most reliable allies. But the foreignness of the mob is marked clearly enough, even if the mob itself is not depicted in the fully venomous language or images of vintage 1880s American nativism. The villainous ringleader of the Brotherhood, Andy Offitt, writes for the *Irish Harp*, for example, and in conversation he decries the American class structure in a distinctive brogue, comparing American laborers to "Roosian scurfs." More than once, Farnham's neighbor tells of the time her late husband calmed a mob of strikers on the Wabash by making "a little speech, complimenting Ireland and the American flag." The Irish mayor, too, expresses his "profound sympathy" for the workers in "this struggle with capital," and he downplays the need for heightened vigilance as the strike approaches. "The workers of Buffland are not thieves and robbers," he avers. And then, with a telling brogue, "I expect their conduct to be that of perr-fect gentlemen."

Hay's polemic point in the novel, ultimately, is to prod "the better classes" to become more involved in the nation's marvelously open political process. After the general strike, the moral of the story goes, the "rich and intelligent" people merely "kept on making money, building fine houses, and bringing up children to hate politics as they did, and in fine to fatten themselves as sheep which should be mutton whenever the butcher was ready." Meanwhile, ominously, "there was not an Irish laborer in the city but knew his way to his ward club as well as to mass." (Apropos of his concern with overseas markets, the future author of the "Open Door Notes" ended this drama of class antagonism with a boosterist plug for the opportunities of the Orient: Arthur Farnham leaves for Japan, asking his love, Alice Belding, "Shall I not bring you the loot of a temple or two? They say the priests have become very corruptible since our missionaries got there—the false religion tumbling before the new.")

The political equation of radicalism with foreign birth was not confined in American discourse to the sharp denunciations of E. L. Godkin and the vague suspicions of John Hay. A string of court decisions and legislative acts between the 1880s and 1900s reveal the depth of the common estimation of political "un-Americanism." The earliest of these, *Chae Chan-ping* v. *United States* (1889) and *Fong Yue-ting* v. *United States* (1893), developed out of the anti-Chinese agitation and legislation of the Exclusion era. Chae Chan-ping, a laborer who had returned to China in 1887 after twelve years in San Francisco, was denied re-entry under the terms of the Scott Act (passed in his absence), which reaffirmed the Exclusion Act and further banned the return of any Chinese laborer who had gone back to China. Chae pursued his re-entry all the way to the Supreme Court, where he was denied. Similarly, Fong Yue-ting petitioned to overturn an Immigration Bureau order expelling him for failure to have a "certificate of residence." He, too, lost his case.

These cases established an important principle in U.S. immigration law, one that would become particularly important for suspected "radicals" or "anarchists" later on: threats posed by immigration were threats to national sovereignty, and therefore the state held the same rights and duties to curb this foreign menace as it did to protect its citizens in time of war. As the majority opinion in *Chae Chan-ping* asserted, it is the "highest duty of every nation to preserve its independence, and give security against foreign aggression and encroachments . . . no matter in what form such aggression and encroachment come, whether from the foreign nation acting in its national character or from the vast hordes of its people crowding in upon us." The court in *Fong Yue-ting* reaffirmed "the right to exclude or expel all aliens or any class of aliens, absolutely or upon certain conditions, in war or in peace, being an inherent right of every sovereign and independent nation, essential to its safety, its independence and its welfare."

In 1891, following a similar line of thinking but applying it to the poison doctrines of socialism rather than to the Yellow Peril, a district-court judge in Texas refused the naturalization petition of one Richard Saur, a German immigrant, on the basis of the petitioner's political beliefs. Discovering that the petitioner was an avowed socialist, Judge Paschal rushed to defend the United States—as had the judge in *Chae Chan-ping*—against foreign aggression. The principles of socialism are "at war with and antagonistic to the principles of the constitution," he pronounced, "un-American, impracticable, and dangerous in the extreme." He went on to opine that "the safety and perpetuity of our free institutions and of constitutional government . . . demand that those who apply for the privilege, honor, and distinction of becoming American citizens should be free from [subversive] doctrines."

This decision remained the exception rather than the rule in U.S. naturalization cases, but its logic—combined with the concerns for "sovereignty" voiced from the bench in both *Chae Chan-ping* and *Fong Yue-ting*—laid the way for deeply significant antiradical, antialien legislation at the federal level early in the twentieth century. Building on this line of thought, the federal immigration act of 1903 for the first time excluded certain immigrants because of their beliefs and associations: section 2 made "anarchists" ineligible for entry. The proximate inspiration for this legislation was the assassination of William McKinley in 1901 at the hand of one Leon Czolgosz. Czolgosz, it turns out, was not an especially dedicated anarchist; nor, in fact, was he an alien, notwithstanding the patently un-American clusters of consonants in his name. But the combination of his foul deed, his strange name, and his vague association with the anarchist movement reignited the antiradical nativism that had smoldered in American political thought since the Haymarket bombing. As ascendant President Theodore Roosevelt had asserted in his annual message only months after the assassination, the opening salvo of the U.S. "war" on anarchism should be the exclusion of "all persons who are known to be believers in anarchistic principles." The United States should put some mechanism in place to discover reliably in every prospective immigrant "some intelligent capacity to appreciate American institutions and act sanely as American citizens."

Further, a new naturalization act in 1906 brought this thinking from the realm of immigration and its exclusions to the realm of naturalized citizenship and its admissions. Under the terms of the new law, not only did a

prospective citizen have to swear that "he" [sic] was not "opposed to organized government," but he had to demonstrate that for the five preceding
years "he has behaved as a man of good moral character attached to the principles of the Constitution . . . and well disposed to the good order and happiness of the same." And what constituted *immoral* behavior? As far as the
courts of the Pacific Northwest were concerned, to take an example, membership in the Industrial Workers of the World did. As historian William
Preston, Jr., comments, any immigrant in the IWW could thus be held responsible for—and denied citizenship on account of—the strident rhetoric
and the revolutionary tactics of the organization as a whole or any of its
members.

Significantly, from the antianarchist immigration bill's passage in 1903
until 1921, the United States excluded only thirty-eight would-be immigrants for their purported anarchism, and deported only fourteen resident
aliens as undesirable anarchists from 1911 until the red scare of 1919. As a
measure for the public safety, in other words, the 1903 act was of negligible
consequence. But as a barometer of official opinion on questions of proper
"Americanism," questions of immigration and its attendant import of ideas,
and questions of who America's "dangerous classes" really were and where
they had come from, the 1903 bar to "anarchists" sums up a vital complex of
ideas that had been taking shape since the labor violence along the B&O line
in 1877. Together with the state's expanded powers of deportation, these antiradical immigration and naturalization laws amount to a decision at the
federal level, not only to disavow homegrown radicalism with a language of
Americanism and un-Americanism, but to export discontent through a machinery of repressive speech codes, unforgiving alien laws, and ever-vigilant
government bureaucracies under the auspices of the Immigration Bureau,
the Bureau of Investigation, and the Attorney General's office. Such measures
to define and enforce legitimate American thinking represent the dark side
of the kind of "Americanization" programs that became so numerous and urgent in the war years and after.

The new immigrants, of course, were far too diverse a group necessarily
to represent any one thing in particular—whether conservatism, radicalism,

striking, strikebreaking, or bomb-throwing. But throughout this period, as the American economic landscape and the nation's demographics both underwent a profound transformation, massive immigration itself provided the general context within which the disposition of American labor was understood on all sides. Those who found labor dangerously militant regarded this as a result of the endless influx of foreigners; those who saw labor as all too tractable attributed this tractability to precisely the same thing. Thus some could worry over the steady stream of "incendiaries" and "agitators" freely entering the body politic from across the seas, while others, like E. A. Ross, lamented the very docility of a foreign workforce whose presence eroded the rights of native labor. "Ivan produces much more than he did at home," Ross commented, "consumes more, and, above all, makes more profit for his employer than the American he displaces. . . . To the employer of unskilled labor this flow of aliens, many of them used to dirt floors, a vegetable diet, and child labor, and ignorant of underclothing, newspapers, and trade unions, is like a rain of manna."

One thing both observers could agree upon, however, was that the growing presence of foreigners somehow threatened an American way of life that was above them. In their profound foreignness in popular American views, immigrant workers shared a niche with the overseas "natives" and "savages" whose lives were to be transformed by the modern wares issuing from American factories. This period of tremendous productivity had brought Americans into unprecedented levels of engagement with diverse peoples both at home and abroad on terms that, from the American perspective, were bound to cast the foreigner as an inferior—as a barbarian whose customs screamed out for revision to an approximation of the American norm; as a relic of some earlier epoch, inexplicably evading the natural laws of "progress"; as a human draft animal whose brawn could be enlisted to carry out the designs of the Anglo-Saxon intellect; as a visitor from the premodern, whose accustomed deprivations threatened to bid down American standards of living; or as an Old World incendiary, reared amid the inequities of a semifeudal regime and now importing dangerous doctrines that had no proper place in a self-governing republic.

The confrontation with such peoples both at home and abroad left powerful traces on the texture of American nationalism, providing new narratives of national grandeur and new idioms of national superiority—and new depths of xenophobic antagonism. In both nativist and imperialist discourses, mere ethnocentrism shaded toward rage, in part because of the peculiar dependence of the "superiors" on their "inferiors" in this instance: precisely by their staggering economic successes, Americans had become bound to the foreign market and the foreign worker, and yet the peoples of the world did not proceed faithfully along the script provided them by American wishes in either case. When an orator like Josiah Strong railed against the incoming hordes or promised an Anglo-Saxon conquest of the world, his very confidence in Anglo-Saxon superiority gave voice to a fear for the well-being of the republic. As historian John Higham has written, "Not all jingoes were nativists or all nativists jingoes, but both the aggressive psychology of the one and the defensive reaction of the other provided instinctive rallying points for a society dubious of its capacity to compose its conflicts."

The historic American encounter with foreign peoples thus took place in intricate relation to the ambivalent American *idea* of foreign peoples: images and stereotypes of the foreigner—by turns menacing, cowed, aggressive, vanquished, needy, or defiant—framed the social and political relations between the United States and its economic participants from around the globe; and these relations, in their turn, had the power to generate a new round of images or to put a new spin on old ones. The confrontation between American merchants with the peoples of Asia, Africa, and Latin America, then, like the confrontation between American factory owners and their immigrant hires, cannot be understood fully apart from the acres of verbiage and imagery produced by the nation's flourishing print culture and its emergent information industries. Gilded Age and Progressive Era magazines, newspapers, novels, travel books, reformist tracts, and academic treatises established the ideological conditions for these encounters by standardizing various preconceptions of the foreigner, and by representing the encounters themselves as unshakable demonstrations of this or that ethnological truth about the character of this nation and the nature of the world's diverse populations.

part two

Images

Demographic apocalypse in the 1890s: "Unrestricted Immigration and Its Results—
A Possible Curiosity of the Twentieth Century,
the Last Yankee." *Frank Leslie's*
Illustrated, 1896

In his 1897 travelogue *Following the Equator*, Mark Twain paused for a moment to pass rather harsh judgment on the state of the Australian aborigines. "They were lazy—always lazy," he wrote. "Surely they could have invented and built a competent house, but they didn't. And they could have invented and developed the agricultural arts, but they didn't. They went naked and houseless, and lived on fish and grubs and worms and wild fruits, and were just plain savages, for all their smartness." Thus did the genre of the travelogue quietly merge with ongoing economic debate over the prospects for tutoring the savage in the arts and habits of civilization. Twain replicated a central concern of current economic discourse, and he ratified and popularized its terms for future consideration of the Australians' outlook.

Like the importance of "civilization" and "savagery" to the American understanding of export markets, Twain's borrowing on the language of development suggests an ideological universe where the logic, the chief idioms, the imagery, and the power of argument in one site of discussion could cross rather easily into usage in a second, quite separate arena—from the missionary's report, to the economist's treatise, to the presidential address, to the travelogue, and back again. American encounters with immigrants at home and with various "natives" abroad were not only structured by the prior experience of actual, face-to-face economic or social exchanges, but mediated by the broad and potent notions of peoplehood, civilization, progress, national destiny, capability, blood, "difference," and hierarchy that saturated the culture in the form of travel writing, soap advertisements, poems, popular journalism, jungle romances, ghetto sketches, novels, reform treatises, anthropological studies, eugenic tracts, and intelligence-testing data.

Part II explores several branches of the culture and knowledge industries in the United States, outlining a broad consensus across the disciplines in these years that, if most of the world's peoples were in dire need of American guidance, so were they utterly undeserving of American munificence. Chapter 3, "Parables of Progress," reconstructs the imaginative cultural geography of places and peoples that circulated in popular consciousness in the travel literature, explorers' accounts, and romantic novels whose narrative gaze scanned the globe, and in the ghetto fictions, social sketches, and reformist tracts that depicted the rising "foreign" districts within the United States. Where the foreigner was permitted to speak at all in such writing, it was rarely to express his or her own subjectivity but, rather, to reflect some truth about modernization, social evolution, the current state of the union, or the nation's patent and manifest destiny. These genres were crucial for the information they conveyed about "America" as a social and political idea.

Though travel writing and like narratives provided the sense of peoplehood that infused American culture, they rested in their turn upon more self-conscious and formal regimes of "knowledge" developed within the academic disciplines. Chapter 4, "Theories of Development," examines the theoretical fretwork of the American conception of the world's peoples as supplied by highly influential and newly professionalized disciplines like anthropology, eugenics, and psychiatry. There may indeed be such a thing as an ideologically disinvested, coolly empirical "fact"; but there is no such thing as an entirely disinvested scientific question. The late nineteenth and early twentieth centuries produced volumes of scientific data and argumentation on questions of evolution, cultural development, genetic makeup, and intelligence, but the questions themselves arose only in the context of economically driven and politically charged encounters of missionaries, exporters, and diplomats with "savages," or of factory foremen, trade unionists, and urban reformers with "greenhorns" and "John Chinamen."

These scholarly data and popular firsthand accounts, taken as neutral ethnological "truths," fed directly back into the loop of political discussions whose highest stakes included the formation of state policies for managing foreign populations—appropriating their lands, extracting their resources or their labor, governing them—either within or without U.S. borders. If Americans came into contact with the diverse peoples of the world primarily through the contingencies of the export and labor markets, the encounters themselves were decisively shaped by the powerful images reeling off the presses of a prolific and ever-accelerating print culture.

Parables of Progress: Travelogues, Ghetto Sketches, and Fictions of the Foreigner

> In all the scorched and exotic places of the earth, Caucasians meet when the day's work is done to preserve the fulness of their heritage by the aspersion of alien things.
>
> —O. *Henry,* Cabbages and Kings *(1904)*

I N EDGAR RICE Burroughs's *Tarzan of the Apes* (1914), the apeman makes first contact with another human being, a lone African hunter, having glimpsed human society only secondhand in some European books he had discovered in his deceased parents' jungle cabin. Rendered through the lens of Tarzan's own naïveté, the narrative captures him now following the hunter, "a sleek and hideous thing of ebony" named Kulonga, through the forest toward Kulonga's village. Tarzan "expected to come to a city of strange houses on wheels, puffing clouds of black smoke from a huge tree stuck in the roof of one of them—or to a sea covered with mighty floating buildings which he had learned were called, variously, ships and boats and steamers and craft." But African society held no such technological wonders. He was "sorely disappointed with the poor little village of the blacks, hidden away in his own jungle, and with not a single house as large as his own cabin upon the distant beach." Worse, he discovered that these people were "more wicked than his own apes, and as savage and as cruel as Sabor [the lioness] herself. Tarzan began to hold his own kind in but low esteem."

Like so many of his compatriots, Burroughs resolved this question of "esteem" by resorting to a logic of race. Tarzan's goal, articulated several pages later, is to find "other white men like himself"; whiteness quickly supplants humanness in Burroughs's conception of what constitutes the apeman's "own kind." Successive volumes will depict Tarzan/Lord Greystoke admirably traversing the landscape of both the "civilized" and the "savage"—from West Africa to Baltimore to Europe and back again—with an ease directly attributable to his roots in both worlds: he outstrips his civilized counterparts by his jungle-bred virility, and he reigns as king in the jungle by virtue of his keen intelligence, his civilized temperament, and, not least, his blue English blood.

But Tarzan's initial "disappointment" with African society in some sense lies at the very heart of the Tarzan myth. His yearning to be fully human, his inchoate longing for *industry* in the form of "strange houses on wheels, puffing clouds of black smoke," and his unflinching judgment that "the poor little village of the blacks" fell decidedly short of the ideal—these elements determine the temper of the narrative, even in its apparent yen for a romantic return to the primal or savage life. If it is true that the Tarzan series reflects a pervasive antimodern impulse in early-twentieth-century American culture—a collective wish for the intense coursing of the blood imagined to characterize life without modern conveniences—it is nonetheless also true that the series casts its lot unambiguously on the side of the industrialized West when it comes to ranking the world's peoples or sifting the notions of relativism and progress.

Millions of Americans learned what little they knew of Africa from *Tarzan of the Apes* and its twenty-two sequels, which is why Burroughs's writing deserves some attention in the first place. But it is also worth noting how little *Tarzan* departed from far more serious writing in this period in many of its essentials. Whether it was Edgar Rice Burroughs imagining the triumphal return of Anglo-Saxondom to the realm of the primeval, Henry Morton Stanley, May French-Sheldon, or Teddy Roosevelt reporting on the Stone Age social conditions in present-day Africa, or Jacob Riis exposing the squalor of the foreign colonies on American soil, narratives of the foreigner provided critical commentary on the theme of social evolution and, by implication, American greatness. When *National Geographic* ran a photograph of a donkey above the caption "An Automobile of the Orient," this, too, expressed a value judgment that was more affirming of American progress than dispassionately descriptive of the lifeways in a North African village.

Drawing away from the "squalor and cheap magnificence" of the Orient at the close of *In the Levant* (1877), Charles Dudley Warner remarked, "I turn again to [the East] with a longing which I cannot explain; it is still the land of the imagination." Land of the imagination indeed. It is the topography of this Western imagination itself, not the exotic land and peoples who are the travel writer's conscious subject, that so often claims the modern reader's attention. The images this roving imagination generated offer a running commentary on precisely the historical processes that, as we have seen, were drawing Americans across the globe in search of markets and millions of foreign laborers to the United States in search of work. If the wheels of industrial "progress" produced ever-sharper contrasts among the lifeways of the world's peoples, travel writers now investigated these contrasts themselves, delivering up the mythic, preindustrial figure of the foreigner as a living symbol of the world left behind. Travelogues now provided myriad fables on the backwardness of distant lands, on the field of opportunity they presented, and on their peculiar inhabitants, whose evolutionary shortfalls and whose lives ostensibly outside of history seemed to recommend either extinction, removal, or reformation under the stewardship of the West.

These genres largely constitute a literature of denigration and debasement, but, as *Tarzan* and Warner's paean to the "land of imagination" themselves suggest, they could also occasionally express a vague yearning. Most common were either accounts of the striking absence of a modern, energized, enlightened spirit in the "dark" corners of the world, or enthusiastic reports of the modest stirrings of progress, as when Warner noted that "Egypt is waking out of its sleep." But accounts of foreign climes, even in their most "backward" aspect, were not always free of a certain wistfulness. Comparing the "sluggish ongoing of life" of Astrakhan with the "furious progress" of the West in 1887, one writer in *The Atlantic Monthly* was forced to concede the charm of that "simple naturalism of places not yet won for enterprise nor exploited by greed with the maniac activity of our machine age. . . . [W]hen I look back at those strange people," he sighed, "not yet cultured enough to be untruthful, nor selfish enough to be dishonest, and think again of their homely faces . . . , of their quiet manners, as graceful as untutored; their simple dignity, without affectation; and their uncalculating hospitality, as eager to entertain a beggar as a king, I pray fervently that civilization may be long in reaching Astrakhan." Shadowing the aggressive literature of social evolution and world supremacy was a quiet antimodern envy, a muted suspicion that the benighted regions of the globe might actually embody a few lessons worth learning.

Interest in accounts of exotic places did not originate in this period, certainly. Richard Burton, David Livingstone, and John Hanning Speke had captivated audiences with their tales of Africa in the preceding decades, and they in turn merely followed the precedents of traveler-raconteurs like Mungo Park in the eighteenth century and, indeed, Marco Polo in the thirteenth. But the decades following Henry M. Stanley's journey in search of Livingstone in 1871 witnessed a relative explosion of productivity in the genre. It is of no trifling significance that James Gordon Bennett, king of the penny presses and publisher of the *New York Herald*, underwrote Stanley's travels, or that Bennett's paper covered Stanley's subsequent adventures beneath banner headlines like "Desperate Encounters with Swarms of Cannibals." The rise of penny journalism, the public's enhanced appetite for novelty and "news," and innovations in print, halftone, and photographic technology—themselves part of the climate of "progress" upon which the travelogue offered oblique commentary—invited reams of popular writing on "the dark continent" and other exotic regions. Writers like Charles Dudley Warner, Mark Twain, May French-Sheldon, Edith Wharton, Richard Harding Davis, and Teddy Roosevelt, carrying on earlier narrative traditions, now were joined by hundreds of less-known writers for *The Atlantic Monthly*, *Harper's Weekly*, the *North American Review*, and (after 1888) *National Geographic*, writing on "The Land of the Incas," "Barbadoes," "Madagascar," or "A Summer Cruise Among the Atlantic Islands."

As we have seen, America's quest for markets abroad, like its reception of foreign immigrants at home, took place at a time when a passion for "progress" defined both the national character as it was popularly conceived and the nature of the world's peoples as they appeared through the ethnocen-

tric lens of an "Anglo-Saxon" cultural mission. In this milieu, popular accounts of the world's peoples—whether fantastic tales like Burroughs's
Tarzan series, or firsthand, nonfiction accounts of the villages along the Nile,
the bazaars of the Orient, or the chattering marketplaces of New York's
Lower East Side—at once fed and *fed upon* existing assumptions regarding
the evolutionary scale of human progress and achievement. In these parables
of progress, the figure of the foreigner served chiefly as a measure of the distance between American "civilization" and some notion of wretched "barbarism" or "savagery"—a bygone era for the "advanced races" of Europe and
North America, a static, prehistoric present for the peoples of Africa and
Latin America or the decaying civilizations of Asia.

In this respect, the common coin of racial or national stereotypes circulating in works like Charles Dudley Warner's *Mummies and Moslems* (1876),
Jacob Riis's *How the Other Half Lives* (1890), O. Henry's *Cabbages and Kings*
(1904), or Edgar Rice Burroughs's *Jungle Tales of Tarzan* (1917) contributed
significantly to the intellectual and ideological climate within which Americans sought and secured foreign markets and in which they greeted foreign
laborers and put them to work. The foreigners of these diverse narratives
served sometimes to condemn the harsh modernity of American "progress";
more often they served to demonstrate and so to trumpet the nation's material and spiritual achievement. In either case, American discourse annexed
this cast of thousands in imperial fashion to a self-absorbed comment on the
United States itself—its accomplishments, its aspirations, its duties, and its
destiny.

"The World's Waste Spaces"

"During the past three centuries," wrote Theodore Roosevelt, "the spread of
the English-speaking peoples over the world's waste spaces has been not only
the most striking feature in the world's history, but also the event of all others most far-reaching in its effects and its importance." The underlying idea
here, of course, is almost too simple to require further comment. "The world
was made for man," wrote Mark Twain caustically, "—the white man." But
between the massive negation entailed by the definition of entire continents

as "waste spaces" on the one hand, and the self-aggrandizement presumed by this "most far-reaching" event in world history on the other, some complex ideas were at work in Roosevelt's outlook. Notions—like Roosevelt's—of Euro-American enlightenment juxtaposed against the world's engulfing regions of barbarism and chaos became increasingly important to the general vocabulary of American nationalism during the four decades from the 1870s to World War I. It is in this respect that travel writing—including Roosevelt's and, for that matter, Mark Twain's—is so significant.

David Spurr, an analyst of Western imperialism, has usefully catalogued a range of logical and stylistic elements that have characterized Euro-American writing on "exotic" places. Certain recurring linguistic patterns and choices, in Spurr's judgment, represent elements in a fairly consistent "rhetoric of empire," whether surfacing in travelogues, novels, journalistic pieces, or the administrative writing of colonial bureaucrats themselves. The various social and political practices associated with a policy of imperialism could never be carried out unless aided and abetted by the culture at large— its dominant assumptions and values, its patterns of respect and contempt, its accepted definitions of things like "merit," "progress," "industry" (in the sense of "effort"), "accomplishment," and "worth." At once reflecting, circulating, and reinforcing such habits of seeing, writing of all sorts may be said to participate in a crucial manner in the political project of empire-building.

Literary and journalistic writing in this period buttressed the logic of empire in a number of ways, according to Spurr. Whether in the factual account of a traveler or the fancied tale of a novelist, the narrator's gaze often lingered over exotic territories as if to possess them, and over "primitive" bodies as if to reduce them to the status of objects. Exotic lands became lovely commodities to be desired and possessed; by rendering indigenous peoples as mere fixtures of that landscape, the very language and logic of a travelogue effaced the "natives" as sentient agents in their own right, and denied the import of their own languages, laws, customs, mores, intellects, histories, and world-views.

If the writer's manner of description communicated the grandiose claims to dominion and the desires aroused within Western travelers by exotic lands (this is itself an imperialistic turn of phrase: there can be no such thing as "exotic"—that is, "imported"—land, except where an imperialistic imagination is placing itself immovably at the very center of things), other literary conventions laid more active claim to the territory under description. By massive efforts of literary negation, entire continents were defined by their presumed emptiness, cultures by their lacks and absences, and peoples by their exemption from the flow of history. *Differently* clothed peoples became "naked savages"; inhabited forests became blank "wilderness"; Africa became "the dark continent." In the span of a few pages on the appearance of "China to the Roving Eye" in *The Changing Chinese* (1914), E. A. Ross noted that there was no common supply of water, no public lighting, no proper chimneys, no window glass, no open lawns or gardens, a pronounced absence of good roads and draft animals, and a scarcity of fuel. Indeed, the landscape and the culture were both defined by what, to Ross, was so notably missing.

Euro-American writers also demonstrated a related tendency to define "natives" as a kind of "wilderness in human form"—so "natural" as to be less than human. It was this view of "natives" that prompted the founders of the American Museum of Natural History, established in 1877, to include cases devoted to Asian, African, and North American peoples among the museum's reptiles, fishes, and stuffed lions. Such assessments of the "natural" made the ultimate appropriation or conquest of these continents as much a certainty as had been the appropriation of North America, a land, in Owen Wister's words, "where Indians and wild animals live unchained."

It was but a quick step from this understanding of "natives" as somehow more animal than their "civilized" counterparts, to out and out *debasement*. "Natives" were openly reviled for their presumed filth, their ignorance, or their treachery. "The Barbadian negro," announced *Harper's* in an 1877 travelogue, "is *sui generis*; there is nothing like him on earth, above it, or under it. He will lie, cheat, and steal beyond all comprehension. He is impudent to a degree hardly to be understood by an American." On the Muslim ritual of bathing, Charles Dudley Warner remarked, "It does seem a hopeless task for men of the color of these to scrub themselves." If the view of foreign peoples as ultranatural implied that they had no concerns or rights that warranted consideration in the West, such outright debasement suggested that, further, they deserved whatever they got.

These rhetorical maneuvers of negative depiction of the "natives" and their "empty" lands were often complemented in travel literature by an inclination among Western writers to match up savagery's lacks and absences with civilization's capabilities; primitive needs with modern duties; the "natives'" negative attributes with America's/Europe's/the West's positive potentialities. The very logic and language of a piece of writing often proposed a course of action toward the pitiful, denigrated savages—a duty to "uplift" them, a "civilizing mission" to carry out among them. Euro-American writing often rendered exotic lands according to their potential as redeemed territories either colonized by or annexed to "civilization." Detached, seemingly neutral descriptions of the landscape could be suddenly disrupted by a daydream about Western settlement, the development of hitherto "unimproved" lands, the tutelage of "backward" races, the restoration of order amid the social chaos of the primitive tribe. "There is no more interesting question of the present day," wrote Richard Harding Davis in *Three Gringos in Venezuela and Central America* (1896), "than that of what is to be done with the world's land which is lying unimproved, whether it shall go to the great power that is willing to turn it to account, or remain with its original owner, who fails to understand its value. The Central Americans are like a gang of semibarbarians in a beautifully furnished house, of which they can understand neither its possibilities of comfort nor its use."

A final element in this overall rhetoric of empire was its erotic charge, its depiction of libidinous primitives in opposition to restrained and properly modest—Christian—moderns, though it was the moderns who traveled halfway around the globe to capture the primitives with a steady pornographic stare. Exploration and travel thus became in many narratives a sexual encounter between a masculine West and feminized natives or primitives. In 1909, Cassell and Company published a book of *Women of All Nations*, promising in one ad that "the fashions range from the laces and frills of the Parisienne down to the skanty skirt of the Fijian belle." This was particularly important for portrayals of those parts of the globe earmarked as colonies or potential colonies—like Fiji. By casting the encounter with various peoples as a story of sexual desire and conquest—by making an individual woman, the "savage beauty," *stand for* an entire people and their land—such accounts

borrowed on the authority of pre-existing sexual relations in order to render
the political themes of hierarchy and possession as thoroughly natural. If the
"geographical" importance of the material excused the otherwise forbidden
interest in women's bodies, so did the tacit romance of the native-as-nude explain away the less agreeable aspects of imperial power and its use. It was but
"natural" for Samoa, for instance, to want to be possessed.

This array of literary elements underlay Roosevelt's deceptively simple
idea of "waste spaces"—regions void of meaningful human activity, and also
wasted in that there were others at the ready to put them to good use. These
rhetorical elements of empire represent not merely habits of description, but
habits of *mind*: only a blurry and imperfect line separates their power to organize speech from their power fully to determine perception. As Charles
Dudley Warner wrote in 1876, on traveling twenty-four days from Cairo and
with the Nubian hills looming into view, "We appear to be getting into real
Africa." "Africa," he rhapsodized,

> *which still keeps its barbarous secret, and dribbles down this commercial*
> *highway the Nile, as it has for thousands of years, its gums and spices and*
> *drugs, its tusks and skins of wild animals, its rude weapons and its cunning*
> *work in silver, its slave-boys and slave-girls. These native boats that we*
> *meet, piled with strange and fragrant merchandise, rowed by antic crews of*
> *Nubians whose ebony bodies shine in the sun as they walk backward and*
> *forward at the long sweeps, chanting a weird, barbarous refrain—what*
> *tropical freights are these for the imagination!*

It is here, in the subtle shifting between "real Africa" and "the imagination,"
that the travel narrative accomplishes its crucial political work.

Among the hallmarks of the Western travelogue, and the quality that
above all else marks the genre as a form of consumption, is the rendering of
the foreign bazaar, the village street scene, or the "savage" encampment as a
prelinguistic human spectacle. The subjects of such scenes do not speak (although sometimes they yell or jabber); they have no independent human
will. Rather, they merely appear, so many fixtures of the natural landscape,
for the benefit of the traveler-narrator, who alone has the capacity to describe,

explain, define, and judge their queer doings for the reader. "Moroccan crowds are a feast to the eye," wrote Edith Wharton in 1919. "The instinct of skilful drapery, the sense of color . . . make the humblest assemblage of donkey-men and water-carriers an ever-renewed delight." Years earlier (1888), she had similarly been taken by "the picturesque populace filling the untidy streets" of Algiers, "the Bedouins . . . and negroes and Jews and half-clothed children, and all the other fantastic figures which go to make up the pageantry of an Eastern street scene." In Brazil, Teddy Roosevelt was enthralled by the "strange and interesting sight" of "utterly wild, friendly savages, circling in [a] slow dance, and chanting their immemorial melodies, in the brilliant tropical moonlight." Throughout the Near East and Africa, Charles Dudley Warner was ever taken with the "swarthy bodies shining in the white sunlight," the "shifting kaleidoscope of races, colors, and graceful attitudes." "The first sight of the colored, pictured, lounging, waiting Orient is enough to drive an impressionable person wild," he wrote; "so much that is novel and picturesque is crowded into a few minutes; so many colors and flying robes; such a display of bare legs and swarthy figures." So unabashed was this propensity of Westerners to stare at such foreign scenes that one Egyptian scholar remarked in 1886, "One of the beliefs of the Europeans is that the gaze has no effect."

But the gaze does have an effect. As with other kinds of consumption, this innocent feasting of the eyes is not divorced from the power relations that frame the encounter of (in this case) East and West. The "pageant," however breathtaking, ever returns to some reminder that "progress" has been made on the Euro-American side of the great human divide, that, although the Orient and Africa might be nice places to visit, there are many reasons one would not want to live there. The term "sumptuousness" may be ill-chosen, explains Wharton of this visual feast of the "Orient": "The nomadic nature of African life persists in spite of palaces and chamberlains and all the elaborate ritual of the Makhzen, and the most pompous rites are likely to end in a dusty gallop of wild tribesmen, and the most princely processions to tail off in a string of half-naked urchins riding bareback donkeys." The grandeur is thin; and the traveler's gaze will always detect the limits of the sham. Indeed, often the traveler's very presence *as* traveler becomes one mark of the immense superiority that the West enjoys over the lands in question. "Many visitors came to inspect our wonderful belongings," wrote Verney Lovett Cameron of his trek across Africa:

> —*watches, guns, pistols, compasses, &c.—and one old man . . . after staring for a long time in mute admiration said, "Oh these white men! They make all these wonderful things, and know how to use them. Surely men who know so much ought never to die." . . . I believe the old gentleman had some idea that we were a few thousand years old and had evolved guns, watches, and all out of our inner consciousness.*

Among the staples of travel reportage was the notion that certain peoples somehow passed their days outside the stream of historic time. One version of this conceit was that the sameness of life was so pronounced and persistent from one generation to the next that a given society was actually suspended in timelessness. The "mongrel subjects of the Khedive" in Egypt, "inheritors of all civilizations and appropriators of none," according to Charles Dudley Warner, "kennel amid these historic ash-heaps, caring for neither the past or the future." The initial ethnographic gesture, as literary scholar Mary Louise Pratt has described it, was to homogenize the people in question "into a collective *they*, which distills down even further into an iconic *he*." The movements of this abstracted specimen are then cast in a timeless present tense. Such descriptions "characterize anything 'he' does not as a particular event in time, but as an instance of a pregiven custom or trait." Euro-Americans perform deeds in historic time (they travel to Africa, discover waterfalls, and name lakes after themselves, for example); "natives," on the other hand, simply *are*.

More common still, particularly in reference to Africa, was the conceit that spatial distance represented temporal distance as well, that other cultures represented fossilized vestiges of "civilized" humanity's dim past. "Do you think our voyage is merely a thousand miles on the Nile?" asked Warner as he led his readers deeper into "mysterious Africa." "We have committed ourselves to a stream that will lead us thousands of years backwards in the ages, into the depths of history."

How vast were the changes that swept the world—East and West—between Henry Morton Stanley's *Herald* dispatches in the 1870s and the African musings of Teddy Roosevelt and Edgar Rice Burroughs in the 1910s. And yet how unchanging the logics and languages by which these writers and others rendered "the dark continent" for a Western readership. In order to perceive the "worth" of the Wangwana, the blacks of Zanzibar, according to Stanley, the European traveler "should not forget the origin of his own race, the condition of the Briton before St. Augustine visited his country, but should rather recall to mind the first state of the 'wild Caledonian,' and the original circumstances and surroundings of Primitive Man." Indeed, one must adopt a view that is evolutionary in the sweep of its understanding, taking into account the vast progress of one's own race in recent millennia and the static timelessness of the African native. "I find that they are a people just emerged into the Iron Epoch, and now thrust forcibly under the notice of nations who have left them behind by the improvements of over 4000 years. They possess beyond doubt all the vices of a people still fixed deeply in barbarism."

This conceit was worked remarkably hard in writings of all sorts. As big game hunter Teddy Roosevelt described the railroad through British East Africa, the rails represented "the eager, masterful, materialistic civilization of today," introduced in a region that does not "differ materially from what it was in Europe in the late Pleistocene"; the life of the tribes there reproduces "conditions of life in Europe as it was led by our ancestors ages before the dawn of anything that could be called civilization." The Andorobo, according to *National Geographic*, "reproduce in a most striking manner the life which we may suppose to have been led by our faraway ancestors or predecessors in the earliest Stone Age," "the life of primitive man not long after he had attained the status of humanity." And Edgar Rice Burroughs would write of a Waziri rite in *The Return of Tarzan*, "The whole sight was as terribly primeval and savage as though it were being staged in the dim dawn of humanity, countless ages in the past."

Of all the world's distant places, Africa may ultimately have been of least concern to most Americans when it came to real and concrete questions of economy and invested interest. But the continent held a place of dispropor-

tionate interest in the geographical imagination. "Africa to-day is the realm
of romance," declared the *North American Review* in 1877. "It is the central
fascination of the scholar, the explorer, the philanthropist, the man of business. It is the one spot of the earth that draws all eyes and hearts to its ma-
jestic mysteries." Explorers' reports had found "a public growing more and
more hungry with every *bonne bouche* these travellers can toss it." Indeed, once
an eager public had lapped up David Livingstone's *Missionary Travels* (1857),
Henry Morton Stanley's *How I Found Livingstone* (1872) and *In Darkest Africa*
(1890), Verney Lovett Cameron's *Across Africa* (1877), Joseph Thomson's *To
the Central African Lakes and Back* (1881), and Mary Kingsley's *Travels in West
Africa* (1897), the continent became a vast, living metaphor: the "dark continent" symbolized all the non-European and non-American portions of the
globe whose savages and cannibals at once resisted and defined the West's
vaunted "civilization." The continent drew its significance, that is, from the
tacit commentary it offered on Western progress.

The difference between savage Africa and the backward civilizations of
behind" by the rapid advances of Western civilization, though along with
the aborigines of Australia they were frequently cited as the most extreme
examples. The decaying civilizations of Asia and the Middle East and the
semibarbarous societies of Latin America, too, represented peoples frozen in
time, bugs in amber displaying the virtues and the vices of an earlier moment in human evolution. As a didactic guide to an Orientalist exhibition in
Paris put it in 1878, Egypt "has no industry at all, properly speaking." After
British colonization had begun in 1882, according to one school textbook,
Egyptian customs persisted "because they have not been sufficiently combat-
ted" and "relegated to the archives of human error."

The difference between savage Africa and the backward civilizations of
the Orient, then, was not a fundamental one. Thus, amid his observations on
village life in China, missionary Arthur Smith could devote an entire chapter
to "The Monotony and Vacuity of Village Life." "A Chinese village is physically and intellectually a fixture," he wrote—if not fully primitive, still im-
mobile and weirdly resistant to normal progress. E. A. Ross felt that China
represented "the European Middle Ages made visible." In 1899, the *North
American Review* announced, "Now, after the sleep of centuries, we look upon

the awakening of China." Among the signs of such an awakening were "the desire for Western learning" and "the spread and success of missionary work." The process of "educating the Chinese mind in the facts and principles of modern life is now going on upon a wide scale." Lafcadio Hearn, writing on Japan in *The Atlantic Monthly*, noted, "The influences of the nineteenth century have little affected the real spirit of Shinto, if they can be said to have done so at all."

On the clash of barbarism and civilization in Central America, meanwhile, O. Henry wrote with some condescension, "The little *opera-bouffe* nations play at government and intrigue until some day a big, silent gunboat glides into the offing and warns them not to break their toys." Along with the conquering gunboat comes a small adventurer "with empty pockets to fill, light of heart, busy-brained—the modern fairy prince, bearing an alarm clock with which, more surely than by the sentimental kiss, to awaken the beautiful tropics from their centuries' sleep." "Centuries' sleep" described precisely the terms in which most writers on the subject understood the torpor of these hopelessly backward regions and peoples.

The presumption of the barbarians' timelessness was most significant in the organic basis it presented for a hierarchic scale of human development. It is one thing to say that two cultures are vastly different, quite another to say that one is grossly behind the other. It is in their "backwardness," their technological and intellectual "behindness," that various peoples earned the Western travel writers' most virulent judgments. For Charles Dudley Warner, the Jews of Jerusalem were but "debased, misbegotten . . . remnants of sin, squalor, and bad living," and Africa, "as we had been taught, lies in heathen darkness." For Teddy Roosevelt, many Africans were "ape-like naked savages, who dwell in the woods and prey on creatures not much wilder or lower than themselves," and much of the continent lay "engulfed in the black oblivion of a lower barbarism." Although May French-Sheldon found some evidence of Africans' capacity in the "appropriation of useful ideas," still, "their brains have the same receptiveness one looks for in children." Even Mary Kingsley, who had a far more sympathetic and keen eye for African cultures than most of her European counterparts (she was alive to the vast differences among tribal cultures, for instance, and she had but harsh

words for the typical European approaches to the task of "civilization"),
could remark unproblematically that "Sierra Leone, charming as it is, has a
sort of Christy Minstrel air about it." And the *North American Review*, for its
part, could declare with no lack of confidence that the majority of the inhabitants of the British West Indies "are incapable of independent progress.
They can advance only under the pressure of the vigorous influences of
northern civilization; without this contract they degenerate and regress."

As this last remark makes clear, debasement carried with it clear policy implications: debasement was the keystone in an ideological arch that
stretched from a bemused condescension toward the quaint ways of queer
peoples on the one hand to a frank argument for the rightful appropriation of
their lands or stewardship over their polity and resources on the other. It is
no surprise that many of the parables of progress that informed American
writing on other regions of the globe carried a frankly imperialistic political
significance. Africa was "not only the land of romance," explained the *North
American Review.* "It is a land of wonderful abundance, animal, mineral, and
vegetable. . . . To it the eyes of commerce, no less than of science, are turned.
'You see you are to lose America as a market,' says an American to an Englishman at the Philadelphia Exposition; 'whither will you go?' 'To Africa,'
was the quick reply."

Teddy Roosevelt is perhaps the best exemplar of these blended literary
and political traditions. In the midst of recounting his travels in the Brazilian wilds, for instance, he paused to predict that "the country when opened
will be a healthy abode for white settlers." Similarly, recounting his safari in
African Game Trails, he reflected that, since islands of "self-produced civilization" in any region of "widespread savagery" are necessarily small and fragile,
"progress is often immensely accelerated by outside invasion and control."
Thus, in many "out-of-the-way regions" of Africa, "the English flag stands
for all that makes life worth living." Indeed, for Roosevelt literal vision and
political vision were deeply enmeshed. "I firmly believe in the future of East
Africa for settlement as a white man's country," he remarked, scanning the
African countryside; "it is an ideal playground" for Euro-American sports-
men and hunters. (And what a playground! On his safari in 1908, Roosevelt
and his son Kermit bagged some 512 animals, including seventeen lions,

eleven elephants, twenty rhinos, eight hippos, nine giraffes, nineteen zebras, forty-seven gazelles of various sorts, four crocodiles, three storks, and a pelican.)

National Geographic, too, found Africa a place "where the white man can live and thrive as well as in Australia, New Zealand, or Canada," and the journal routinely passed judgment on the "natives' " capacities for "improvement" in areas like Samoa, Guam, and the Caribbean. Indeed, *National Geographic* peppered its ostensibly detached reportage on the world's peoples with overt discussions of the colonial project. In 1899, a piece on "Colonial Systems of the World" announced that the 125 colonies, protectorates, dependencies, and "spheres of influence" around the world embraced over five hundred million "natives" and generated $1.5 billion in revenues on imports, roughly 40 percent going to the "mother country" in any given case. Great Britain had "added to her market by bringing the 350 million people of her colonies into colonial relationship," this scientific journal noted with some envy, before going on to consider what the acquisition of Puerto Rico, Cuba, the Philippines, and Hawaii might mean to the United States.

Numbers of the journal over the ensuing months carried features on "The Economic Conditions of the Philippines," "Porto Rico," "Nicaragua and the Isthmian Routes," "The Proposed American Interoceanic Canal in Its Commercial Aspects," and "The Commercial Importance of Samoa." "The day I left [Hong Kong] to return to America," reported one *Geographic* writer in 1900, "I counted over sixty merchant vessels loading and unloading in her harbor. We stand now looking upon the great empire of China, which affords America the most tempting field of trade expansion yet undeveloped in the world." This writer expounded on the theme at length under the frank subhead "Material Value of the Philippines." A piece on "Colonial Government in Borneo" in the fall of 1900 likewise held up one administrator's "splendid . . . success in ruling a savage race" as a suitable model for the United States, which "is about to undertake to rule people of a similar race and characteristics to those in Borneo."

Throughout much of this period, the imperialist project was supported by the greatest parable of all, the comparison of contemporary Africans to their black American counterparts, whose ancestors had been forcibly removed (saved) from the dark continent by slave-traders in centuries past. "To an American, who must necessarily think much of the race problem at home," wrote Teddy Roosevelt, "it is pleasant to be made to realize in vivid fashion the progress the American negro has made, by comparing him with the negro who dwells in Africa untouched, or but lightly touched, by white influence." "No one could fail to be impressed," he wrote of a number of African American and Jamaican blacks he had encountered in Africa, "with the immense advance these men represented as compared with the native negro." Such comparisons not only justified any imperialist designs on Africa as being unquestionably for the Africans' own benefit, but also redeemed blots on the United States' humanitarian record like the slave trade, Jim Crow, and even lynching.

The marked superiority of African Americans to black Africans was also among the lessons written into the structure of the world's fairs from the 1890s to the 1910s. For many white American observers, the state of contemporary African peoples ratified the correctness of an otherwise painful dimension of the American past, and excused present manifestations of the nation's "race problem." The comparison was invoked in praise of American civilization and its state of relative advance, and in the bargain it offered up the African continent as a vast field of opportunity whose fruits simply awaited easy harvest. As the most extreme example of the world's many "waste spaces," Africa actually symbolized the totality of the "uncivilized" world. Though Americans' actual economic and political investments in Africa were slight, American writing on Africa—whether Roosevelt's musings on the continent's promise as a Euro-American "playground," the *North American Review*'s rhapsodizing on this "land of wonderful abundance," or Edith Wharton's cutting remarks on how the region's "most pompous rites" might end in "a dusty gallop of wild tribesmen"—reveals the peculiar lights and shades of American dominance and dependency in the era of rapidly internationalizing markets.

America's "Other Half"

Popular images of the newly arrived immigrant in New York, Chicago, or San Francisco tended to mirror these images of the "native" abroad. Ironically, if American blacks furnished proof of American progress and the nation's capacity to civilize the savage, immigrants, who largely enjoyed more rights and a higher civic status, were often invoked as symbols of unredeemed savagery. Interest in the rising foreign population within American borders was reflected in a range of venues and genres in the burgeoning print culture—domestic travelogues in *Harper's Weekly*, *The Atlantic Monthly*, the *North American Review*, and *National Geographic*; "human-interest" pieces in major metropolitan dailies; reformist tracts by urban progressives like Jacob Riis and Lillian Wald in New York, Emily Greene Balch in Philadelphia, Jane Addams in Chicago, and Robert Woods in Boston; and ghetto sketches by novelists like Stephen Crane and Upton Sinclair.

Given the enormous influx of immigrants in the latter half of the nineteenth century, it is no surprise that writers with a taste for the exotic soon discovered that parts of the United States itself had become a foreign territory. At the east end of Fifty-eighth Street in Manhattan, *Harper's Weekly* noted in 1907, the scene "is almost that of a foreign land. The men you meet are swarthy, black-haired creatures, the buxom dark-eyed women waistless; the children playing upon the pavement call out to each other 'Olga,' and a dozen other names our Pilgrim fathers knew not." Jacob Riis, perhaps the best-known of these urban travel guides, had written in 1890 that in lower Manhattan "one may find for the asking an Italian, a German, a French, African, Spanish, Bohemian, Russian, Scandinavian, Jewish, and Chinese colony. . . . The one thing you shall vainly ask for in the chief city of America is a distinctively American community." Never mind that Riis himself was an immigrant (he had arrived from Denmark at age twenty-one in 1870). More salient to Riis the reformer than his own foreign birth was the overwhelming scale of the immigrant mass, the totality with which the foreigner had laid claim to American soil. In place of New York's older inhabitants had come a "queer conglomerate mass of heterogeneous elements, ever striving and working like whiskey and water in one glass, and with the like result: final union and a prevailing taint of whiskey."

Nor is it surprising that, in rendering the nation's new foreign quarters and colonies, writers like Riis would fall back on the familiar idioms of the travelogue. These narratives typically wend along a Mott Street or a Hester Street as though it were the Nile. A *Harper's* piece on "The Foreign Element

in New York" identified the "Bend" on Mulberry Street as "the most picturesque, squalid, dilapidated, thoroughly interesting and lively New York
colony." One might easily imagine the "prosperous householders" who had
once resided in the area, but now the area had been conquered by "the
swarming, unlucky, unwashed foreigners, each one adding something more
to the general air of dilapidation and to the crust of grime which gives a
dusky tone to all Mulberry things." An adjective like "swarming," of course,
says a great deal about the author's view of the humanity described here:
like the throngs at an Oriental bazaar or the natives along the Congo, the
denizens of Mulberry Bend are thoroughly unindividuated and present a
nearly incomprehensible aspect. Still, like those foreigners across the seas,
these people possess "an inborn feeling for the picturesque. . . . There is a
richness of life and motion and human interest on the street that is certainly
enjoyable." The "Bend," that is, presents another human spectacle, although
here the proper conclusion is not the rightful colonization of the "natives'"
lands but, rather, the vast superiority of the American setting to these newest
American arrivals.

Writers like Jacob Riis and Lillian Wald were largely sympathetic, to be
sure; the chief villain of Riis's *How the Other Half Lives*, for instance, is the
tenement itself, the rank soil from which springs so much regrettable ignorance, immorality, and viciousness. The book ends with a plea for housing reform and for a thoroughgoing revision in American concepts of the common
weal: "Think ye that building shall endure / Which shelters the noble and
crushes the poor?" But Riis's exposé also lingers on the "foreign" with a
rhetoric and a gaze that undermine his nobler intention of a reformist in-
dictment of the emergent industrial-capitalist order.

Indeed, portraits of the immigrant districts from the period's middle-
class or patrician presses often come across as a peculiar hybrid of Stanley's
Africa and Dante's Hell. "Down below Chatham Square," wrote Riis, "in the
old Fourth Ward, where the cradle of the tenement stood, we shall find New
York's Other Half at home, receiving such as care to call and are not afraid."
This spirit of adventure in the journey through the slum is matched by narrative figures of darkness and moral descent that heighten the foreboding of
the overall scene and recall the tone and imagery of the typical account of far

more distant journeys. "We passed through courts and alleys where swarthy Neopolitans were carting bales of rags," reported *Harper's* in the early 1880s; up "dark stairs" to homes consisting of "low, dark rooms, neglected and squalid," where women and children sorted the rags. "Dogs and children were tumbling together on the thresholds just as they do in the cool corridors of Italian towns." (Some of the homes were well cared for, this writer had to concede, but these were "picturesque"—that most gentle of the era's codes for "alien.") The very setting spoke volumes about the inhabitants. Lillian Wald similarly escorted her readers "over broken railways, . . . over dirty mattresses and heaps of refuse, . . . between tall, reeking houses whose fire escapes . . . bulged with household goods of every description. The rain added to the dismal appearance of the streets . . . intensifying the odors which assailed me from every side . . . past odorous fishstands, for the streets were a marketplace, unregulated, unsupervised, unclean; past evil-smelling uncovered garbage cans . . . up into a rear tenement by slimy steps." "That morning's experience," she heaved, "was a baptism by fire."

Most striking in this descriptive genre of hellish exotica is Riis's depiction of an unlicensed drinking establishment in a Lower East Side tenement building. With a voyeur's thrill and a palpable shudder, Riis shows his reader into a room

> *perhaps a dozen feet square, with walls and ceiling that might once have been clean . . . but were now covered with a brown crust that, touched with the end of a club, came off in shuddering showers of crawling bugs, revealing the blacker filth beneath. Grouped about a beer-keg that was propped on the wreck of a broken chair, a foul and ragged host of men and women, on boxes, benches, and stools. Tomato-cans filled at the keg were passed from hand to hand. In the center of the group a sallow, wrinkled hag, evidently the ruler of the feast, dealt out the hideous stuff. A pile of copper coins rattled in her apron.*

Like travelogues, these writings offered, through their treatment of foreign peoples, indirect commentary on the theme of American "progress." First, as in travel accounts of Africa and the Orient, foreign populations in the American city were rendered in a language of blended exoticism and savagery that tacitly posed its own hierarchic or evolutionary scale. Describing the inhabitants of the future twentieth-century American ghetto in his apocalyptic novel *Caesar's Column*, Ignatius Donnelly wrote, "There is no virtue among them. . . . They had almost gotten down to the condition of Australian savages, who, if not prevented by the police, would consummate their animal-like nuptials in the public streets." Such judgments of the immigrant underclass were only slightly more extreme than some of the period's more "realistic" portraits. Jacob Riis, for instance, routinely wrote of the immigrants in the taxonomic narrative tone of the naturalist or travel writer, reducing entire cultures to the generic, singular, and knowable "he." Riis's "Chinaman" "is by nature as clean as the cat, which he resembles in his traits of cruel cunning, and savage fury when aroused." "The Italian," on the other hand, "is gay, lighthearted and, if his fur is not stroked the wrong way, inoffensive as a child."

Such cool ethnological—one wants to say zoological—assessments were reinforced by the dehumanizing effacement of the immigrants' individuality and of any glimmer at all of their distinct personalities. Like the marketplaces of Warner's Egypt or the villages along Stanley's Congo, immigrant ghettos were populated not by individuals, who might speak for themselves and whose recognizable humanity might make a claim on our sympathies, but by crowds, throngs, masses of unindividuated and unspeakably odd folk whose very numbers overwhelmed the capacity for empathy. According to *Harper's*, "The pure type of the Hebrew swarms" on the Lower East Side; "the variety of street life is perfectly bewildering," encompassing "a confusion of pushcarts filled with all manner of merchandise, swarms of little children surrounding the ice cream vendors, the babel of strange tongues, a confusion of ancient and fish-like smells, squalling babies, bawling hucksters, gossiping mothers, and strange business signs in Hebrew characters; venerable Shylocks with long beards and greasy curls." Tours of America's "other half" delivered up the ghetto's inhabitants as a sight to behold—"crowds of half-naked children," "passageways . . . swarming with unwholesome crowds"; the women's "vivid and picturesque costumes [lent] a tinge of color to the otherwise dull monotony of the slums." Amid such scenes, no one seems to be leading a life of sufficient dignity to suggest equality with the imagined community of readers.

It is not just that these peoples are exotic, though indeed the rhetorical distance the narrative places between the observer and the observed actively augments the sense of exoticism at every turn. Bayard Street is "picketed from end to end with the outposts of Israel. Hebrew faces, Hebrew signs, and incessant chatter in the queer lingo that passes for Hebrew on the East Side attend the curious wanderer" all along the way. In Riis's "Jewtown" "the jargon of the street, the signs of the sidewalk, the manner and dress of the people, their unmistakable physiognomy, betray their race at every step. Men with queer skull-caps, venerable beards, and the outlandish long-skirted kaftan of the Russian Jew, elbow the ugliest and the handsomest women in the land. The contrast is startling: The old women are hags; the young, houris."

But more than this, immigrant peoples are not merely exotic; they are fully savage or heathen. Newsboys and other children of the street, significantly called "street arabs," seem "a set of hardened little scoundrels, quite beyond the reach of missionary effort." The inhabitant of Chinatown likewise seemed well beyond the moral reach of Christian civilization: "All attempts to make an effective Christian of John Chinaman will remain abortive in this generation; of the next I have, if anything, less hope. Ages of senseless idolatry, a mere grub-worship, have left him without the essential qualities for appreciating the gentle teachings of a faith whose motives and unselfish spirit are alike beyond his grasp." And as for the Jews of the Lower East Side, they stand "where the new day that dawned on Calvary left them standing, stubbornly refusing to see the light. A visit to a Jewish house of mourning is like bridging the gap of two thousand years. The inexpressibly sad and sorrowful wail for the dead, as it swells and rises in the hush of all sounds of life, comes back from the ages like a mournful echo of the voice of Rachel 'weeping for her children.' "

As in the narrated encounters with North American Indians in the seventeenth and eighteenth centuries, the gender arrangements of these foreign cultures were taken as a sign of their "backwardness," though a broad commitment to women's rights hardly characterized such accounts in other respects. "Down the street comes a file of women carrying enormous bundles of fire-wood on their heads," wrote Riis of Mulberry Bend; "loads of decaying vegetables from the market wagons in their aprons, and each a baby at the breast supported by a sort of sling that prevents it from tumbling down. The women do all the carrying, all the work one sees going on in 'the Bend.' The men sit or stand in the streets, on trucks, or in the open doors of the saloons smoking black clay pipes, talking and gesticulating as if forever on the point of coming to blows." In the Italian section of lower New York, likewise, "women sit in rows, young and old alike with the odd head-covering, pad or turban, that is their badge of servitude—hers to bear the burden as long as she lives—haggling over baskets of frowsy weeds."

This story of the ghetto, of course, has a moral. In economic terms, such scenes of squalor might have been taken to depict the limits or the human costs of "progress." But the lingering attention to the denizens' foreignness rather than to their economic circumstances and their levels of exploitation tacitly suggest a contrary conclusion: these pockets of poverty in the modern industrial city are explained, not by the ravages of capitalism, but by the innate racial character of their inhabitants. If domestic travel literature began with the bemused discovery of an imported population, it ended—by its exoticizing rhetoric and gaze—in the effective export of human misery and want. Wretchedness, evidently, was never homegrown, but only came ashore with the immigrants themselves. For instance, Italians and Jews, noted Riis, "carry their slums with them wherever they go, if allowed to do it"; the Italian immigrant "reproduces conditions of destitution and disorder which, set in the frame-work of Mediterranean exuberance, are the delight of the artist, but in a matter-of-fact American community become its danger and reproach."

Barbarian Virtues

If such writings on the foreigner did most often offer at least oblique commentary on the theme of American progress, the comparison did not in every single instance redound to the savages' discredit. "On Indian persons, real and constructed, have been played out both the first impulses and the second thoughts of American culture," writes historian Curtis Hinsley. In first impulse the Indian is but a savage whose very presence is an obstacle to great developments and whose demise is foreordained; on second thought the savage becomes far nobler, the barbarous existence more enticing. This dynamic ambivalence—the paradoxical intertwining of the impulse to dominate and a sentimental idealization—characterized American visions not only of Indians, but also of those "savages" encountered elsewhere around the globe and in the foreign districts of New York or Chicago. Alongside the unblinking pronouncements of American (or Western, or simply "white") superiority lurked the sneaking suspicion that the world's many barbarians somehow had it better.

"There are many humorous things in the world," wrote Mark Twain in *Following the Equator*; "among them is the white man's notion that he is less savage than the other savages." This even-handed regard for the world's "other savages" could coexist with an unflappable self-conception of supremacy (recall Twain's own assessment of the "lazy—always lazy" Australians). But this egalitarian or relativist strain had a long intellectual pedigree; it dated at the least to the sixteenth century, when French essayist Michel de Montaigne, in his famous piece on cannibalism, frankly preferred Brazilian barbarism to the European variety. "I consider it more barbarous to eat a man alive than to eat him dead," he averred in a passage on Europe's punitive customs of rack and torture. "We are justified . . . in calling these people barbarians by reference to the laws of reason, but not in comparison with ourselves, who surpass them in every kind of barbarity." Elements of this Western intellectual tradition include paradoxical self-criticisms, such as Montaigne's essay, and romantic idealizations, notably the "noble savage" of the late eighteenth and early nineteenth centuries. This exaltation of savagery encompassed a complex of ideas that were not always logically aligned: the typical savage, in such formulations, could be sweet and gentle or admirably rough and fearsome; civilization could be lamentably effete or, as in Montaigne's formulation, more savage than we like to admit.

Perhaps the most complete American expression of the sentiment until late in the century was Herman Melville's bucolic portrait of barbarous existence in *Typee: A Peep at Polynesian Life* (1846). The so-called civilized societies of Europe and North America had not cornered the market on the human virtues, he wrote. On the contrary, such virtues

> *flourish in greater abundance and attain greater strength among many barbarous people. The hospitality of the wild Arab, the courage of the North American Indian, and the faithful friendships of some of the Polynesian nations, far surpass any thing of a similar kind among the polished communities of Europe. If truth and justice, and the better principles of our nature, cannot exist unless enforced by the statute-book, how are we to account for the social condition of the Typees? So pure and upright were they in all the relations of life, that . . . I was soon led to exclaim in amazement, "Are these the ferocious savages, the blood-thirsty cannibals of whom I have heard such frightful tales? They deal more kindly with each other, and are more humane, than many who study essays on virtue and benevolence, and who repeat every night that beautiful prayer breathed first by the lips of the divine and gentle Jesus."*

Indeed, when all is said and done, civilization, "for every advantage she imparts, holds a hundred evils in reserve"; and "the white civilized man" is in fact "the most ferocious animal on the face of the earth."

This notion, long lingering in Euro-American thought, received an invigorated round of expression toward the century's end, when the "polish" of Europe and America's "polished communities" took on an almost unbearably high gloss—when work was increasingly rationalized by bureaucracy, when nature's rhythms were lost and the day's tempo was dictated exclusively by the tick of the clock, when the aesthetic pleasures of natural greenery choked behind a veil of industrial smoke or perished beneath harsh slabs of urban pavement, and when fashions, comforts, and conveniences of a thousand kinds seemed to interfere with civilized humanity's hold on "authentic" life. Now, atop long-standing pleas in behalf of the superiority of barbarous life, came zealous appeals for the strenuous life in politics, for naturalism in literature, and for primitivism in the arts. Each represented a version of a particularly modern strain of antimodernism; and each derived some moral for the West from a stylized parable of the primitive.

Even Tarzan owed his popularity to precisely this guarded preference for the primitive and for a version of "manliness" that was imagined in primitivistic terms. "*Mon Dieu!*" cries the thinly civilized apeman, having sampled the modern pleasures of Parisian culture in *The Return of Tarzan* (1913), "but they are all alike. Cheating, murdering, lying, fighting, and all for things that the beasts of the jungle would not deign to possess—money to purchase the effeminate pleasures of weaklings. And yet withal bound down by silly customs that make them slaves to their unhappy lot while firm in the belief that they be the lords of creation enjoying the only real pleasures of existence." Although Tarzan is here including African culture, too, among the human vanities, the logic of the series certainly exempted Africans from the charge of "overcivilization." Later, when Tarzan was named king of the Waziri, "The last remnant of his civilization was forgotten—he was a primitive man to the fullest now; reveling in the freedom of the fierce, wild life he loved, gloating in his kingship among these wild blacks." Likewise, when he had encountered the tribe of Kadour ben Saden in Algeria, "Here were people after his own heart! Their wild, rough lives, filled with danger and hardship, appealed to this half-savage man as nothing had appealed to him in the midst of the effeminate civilization of the great cities he had visited."

In an extended piece "On Being Civilized Too Much" (1897), *The Atlantic Monthly* reflected upon humanity's constitution as "a compound of feeling and intellect."

> *In the savage, feeling predominates, and the intellect plays a very subordinate part. But now take your savage in hand, cut his hair, put trousers on his legs, give him a common school education, an air-tight stove, and a daily newspaper, and presently his intellect will develop, and will exercise more and more control over his feelings. Pursue the process a little further, and soon you will have a creature who is what we call over-sophisticated and effete—a being in whom the springs of action are . . . paralyzed or perverted by the undue predominance of the intellect.*

To remain "close to nature," on the other hand, is to "preserve certain primeval impulses," chiefly "the instinct of pugnacity, the instinct of pity, and the instinct of pride. Nature herself has decided against the man who has lost these primeval impulses. He does not survive, he does not conquer and overspread the earth: and this appears most plainly when the instinct of pugnacity is considered."

This wistful view of the savage was common enough, its logic elastic enough, that it could color political discussion on both sides of the imperialism debate at the turn of the century. "Civilized man," wrote Teddy Roosevelt with palpable misgiving, "now usually passes his life under conditions which eliminate the intensity of terror felt by his ancestors when death by violence was their normal end." His rousing call to the nation to live "The Strenuous Life" amounted to a political program based precisely on recovering this "intensity." Roosevelt decried "the doctrine of ignoble ease," the "slothful ease" that was the prerogative of "the over-civilized man, who has lost the great fighting, masterful virtues," and he pursued this logic to endorse a policy of mastery—violent if need be—in the Philippines, Cuba, Puerto Rico, and Hawaii. It was in this vein, indeed, that, in a letter to G. Stanley Hall, Roosevelt proposed restoring civilization by recovering the "barbarian virtues."

Through the lens of Mark Twain's nascent relativism, on the other hand, European and American treatment of "natives" became the condemnatory acid test of "civilization" and its shortcomings. "The Whites always mean well when they take human fish out of the ocean and try to make them dry and warm and happy and comfortable in a chicken coop," he wrote of British policy in the South Pacific;

> *but the kindest hearted white man can always be depended on to prove himself inadequate when he deals with savages. He cannot turn the situation around and imagine how he would like it to have a well-meaning savage transfer him from his house and his church and his clothes and his books and his choice food to a hideous wilderness of sand and rocks and snow. . . . This would be hell to him; and if he had any wisdom he would know that his own civilization is a hell to the savage.*

Much writing on immigrants in the United States also bore traces of this tradition; there is a striking affinity between the noble savage of the travelogue and the immigrant greenhorn of turn-of-the-century fiction and ghetto sketches. *Harper's*, for instance, having depicted the "swarming, unlucky, unwashed foreigners" of Mulberry Bend, nonetheless concluded that they were a "simple, honest, light-hearted people," displaying a notable "gentleness." The language here and elsewhere echoes travelers' accounts of the Samoans' "open and amiable" natural disposition, the "innocence" of the tribes around Lake Victoria, the "extremely hospitable" and "charming" peoples of Uganda, or the "leading virtue" of hospitality among the Hawaiian natives.

Like the attraction to African or Pacific natives, the attraction to "simple, honest, light-hearted" immigrants within the American literary imagination was often animated by some form of antimodernism. "We live in an age in which the impact of materialized forces is well-nigh irresistible," wrote Theodore Dreiser in *Jennie Gerhardt* (1911);

> *the spiritual nature is overwhelmed by shock. The tremendous and complicated development of our material civilization, the multiplicity, and variety, of our social forms, the depth, subtlety, and sophistry of our imaginative impressions, gathered, remultiplied, and disseminated by such agencies as the railroad, the express and the post office, the telephone, the telegraph, the newspaper, and, in short, the whole machinery of social intercourse—these elements of existence combine to produce what may be termed a kaleidoscopic glitter, a dazzling and confusing phantasmagoria of life that wearies and stultifies the mental and moral nature.*

Amid these wearying and stultifying elements of modern life walks Jennie Gerhardt, a German American woman whose simplicity and goodness evoke the primitive virtues of Melville's "pure and upright" Typees, notwithstanding Jennie's European parentage. She was a product of "the innate affection of the untutored"; she had a "simple unaffected recognition of the primal facts of life"; she was "better than some who do the so-called superior thinking"; she was "natural, sympathetic, emotional, with no schooling in the ways of polite society, but with a feeling for the beauty of life and the lovely things in human relationship"; she was, as far as suitor Lester Kane was concerned, "the most perfect thing under the sun, even if she was a little out of my world"; and, it turns out in the end, she was something of a mystic, subject to clairvoyant visions.

Jennie's simplicity and untutored purity win her the affections, first of Senator Brander, and then of Lester Kane, both inhabitants of that stultifying world ruled by railroads, telegraphs, telephones, and newspapers. The latter takes her in and tutors her "into an understanding of the usages and customs of comfortable existence"—he civilizes her, that is, even if he is not willing to marry her. The class and gender dimensions of Jennie's noble savagery should not be missed: the novel clearly draws upon a tradition of *noblesse oblige* that had long characterized discussion of patriarchy and class relations. So, too, does the innocent's confrontation with a harsher, jaded social world represent a variation on the long-standing literary theme of country and city. But it is also worth noting the significance of Jennie's *foreignness*—her status as an import—to Dreiser's overall critique of American modernity and its dehumanizing social conventions. As with Melville's Typee, Jennie Gerhardt's innate goodness derives less from her social location in this world than from her origins in another world, far removed.

Perhaps the most pronounced treatment of the immigrant in this vein is Jurgis Rudkus, the ruddy Lithuanian greenhorn in Upton Sinclair's *The Jungle* (1906). At the very core of this treatment, obviously, is Sinclair's assertion that the modern American city—Chicago, in this instance—is a "jungle": "Here in this huge city, with its stores of heaped-up wealth, human creatures might be hunted down and destroyed by the wild-beast powers of nature, just as truly as ever they were in the days of the caveman!" Ultimately, Jurgis comes to see "the world of civilization" as "a world in which nothing counted but brutal might, an order devised by those who possessed it for the subjugation of those who did not." As in most literature employing the icon of the noble savage, the surprising savagery of civilization is a necessary precondition or a foil for the surprising gentility of the savage.

Within this setting of a generally savage civilization, the putative "savages" occupy a moral plane quite removed from their civilized counterparts, "who surpass them in every kind of barbarity," as Montaigne had put it. Sinclair touches on the theme of the immigrants' inborn simplicity and the simple naturalism of their customs at once. *The Jungle* opens with a classic ethnographic account of a Lithuanian wedding on the preindustrial pattern, though set in the midst of the industrial squalor of Chicago's back of the yards. That the immigrants spend so much on the fleeting pleasures of *veselija*, a traditional wedding fête, "is very imprudent, it is tragic," remarks Sinclair,

> *but, ah, it is so beautiful. Bit by bit these poor people have given up every-thing else, but to this they cling with all the power of their souls—they can-not give up the* veselija*! To do that would not mean merely being defeated, but to acknowledge defeat. . . . The* veselija *has come down to them from a far-off time, a time when money was made for man and not man for money—when the fruits of the earth belonged to the person who tilled it, and when plenty and to spare was the reward of honest toil.*

Like Dreiser's *Jennie Gerhardt*, *The Jungle* relies upon the figure of the premodern immigrant as a moral counterpoint in its critique of the industrial-capitalist order. The foreignness of the Lithuanian immigrants is critical to Sinclair's condemnation; the embattled oasis of the premodern Lithuanian ghetto is among the chief symbols of the perils posed by the en-croachment of the modern. Already "modern" values have invaded the en-clave—young immigrant "vipers" attend the wedding, having absorbed the wanton selfishness of industrial Chicago itself. They "no longer cared about the laws of the *veselija*" but, rather, "came in crowds and filled themselves with a fine dinner and sneaked off."

The plot of *The Jungle* turns, its social critique depends, not only upon what happens *to* Jurgis Rudkus in turn-of-the-century Chicago—the grind-ing labor, the poverty, and the string of injustices he endures—but what happens *within* him. At the outset, simplicity and guilelessness are his chief traits; this innocent who had formerly "dressed hogs himself in the forest of Lithuania" is now dashed and buffeted by the bewildering currents of Pack-ingtown, "the greatest aggregation of capital and labour ever gathered in one place." His exploitation registers as a kind of immediate and visceral dis-comfort, never as anything so cerebral as discontent. But he eventually learns "to take all the miracles and terrors for granted." He grows accustomed to modernity, and as he does, like the partially Americanized "vipers" at the opening wedding fête, Jurgis changes for the worse. His nobility begins to fade; the noble savage becomes merely savage—"savage . . . with those who would wreck [his drink-induced happiness], and with the world, and with his life."

As Jurgis hits bottom—like the savages in the Tarzan series or in the writings of Teddy Roosevelt and others—the line between savage and animal begins to blur. When Jurgis hunts down and assaults his wife's seducer, "in a flash he had bent down and sunk his teeth into the man's cheek; and when they tore him away he was dripping with blood, and little ribbons of skin were hanging in his mouth. . . . He fought like a tiger." Once in jail "he was like a wild beast that had glutted itself; he was in a dull stupor of satisfaction." "They had put him behind bars, as if he had been a wild beast"; and indeed, he paced up and down his cell "like a wild beast."

Throughout the narrative, it is never Jurgis's savagery that earns reproach, only the social order that robbed him of his simple nobility. The essential antimodernism of the piece is reinforced at the end, in the terms by which Sinclair presents the panacea of socialism: the first sight of the socialist speaker who sends Jurgis down the road of political radicalization "was like coming suddenly upon some wild sight of Nature—a mountain forest lashed by a tempest, a ship tossed about on a stormy sea." He is not merely some craggy-featured soapbox orator; rather, his program represents a retreat from the modern, a return to a more "natural," bucolic order—not, one guesses, altogether unlike the one from which Jurgis Rudkus had originally come, "a far-off time . . . when the fruits of the earth belonged to the person who tilled it, and when plenty and to spare was the reward of honest toil."

To note the similarities between representations of immigrant primitives like Jurgis Rudkus or Jennie Gerhardt and the savage inhabitants of Roosevelt's "waste spaces" is not to equate the social position of white (albeit premodern) Europeans with nonwhite peoples within the dominant American political imagination. Nor is noting the strain of positive commentary on savages, their nobility, or their blessedly uncomplicated lifeways to lose sight of how overwhelmingly negative most depictions of them actually were. There was certainly a wistful streak in turn-of-the-century American culture, as the enormity and the costs of modern "progress" became clear, but the overall weight of the culture never fell close to anything like envy or misgiving.

Still, this cultural use of the primitive—whether the grass-skirted native of the Pacific isles or the "picturesque," "brown-skinned" residents of lower Manhattan's Mulberry Bend—constituted an important element in the running parable of American progress. Even in 1917, as American nativism mounted, *National Geographic* could depict "Our Foreign-Born Citizens" as an assemblage whose outstanding characteristic was its nearly terminal *quaintness.* A series of ethnographic photos shot by reformer Frederic Howe at Ellis Island supported the observation that the immigrants (Dutch, in this instance) displayed a "contentment with simple pleasures that cannot be excelled." As in the journal's treatment of overseas peoples, the ethnographic gaze lingered over subjects' sartorial difference as a marker of difference much more profound—"the typical headdress of the Italian women," "Montenegrins in their native costumes," "Norwegian children in peasant costume" all symbolized an earlier era, before "simple pleasures" had indeed been lost. "In matters of costume," offered the writer, perhaps referring obliquely to much more than mere matters of costume, "Americanization often proceeds all but too rapidly."

In *Jungle Tales of Tarzan* (1916), the apeman kidnaps an African boy named Tibo and sets about raising him himself, hoping to pass on all the advantages of his own dual background as both blue-blooded Anglo-Saxon and virile jungle savage. One day, after they have spent a fair amount of time together, Tarzan notes that Tibo is finally attempting to mimic him, to learn from the apeman's example: "For the first time there entered his dull, Negroid mind a vague desire to emulate his savage foster parent." But, ultimately, the black child lacked "the divine spark" that permitted white people to benefit from experience and training. "In imagination he was wanting," remarks Edgar Rice Burroughs, "and imagination is but another name for super-intelligence. Imagination it is which builds bridges, and cities, and empires. The beasts know it not, the blacks only a little, while to one in a hundred thousand of the earth's dominant race it is given as a gift from heaven that man may not perish from the earth." Tarzan's experiment in environmentalism and uplift runs aground on a stubborn hereditarian shoal.

Burroughs's comments on the imaginative "super-intelligence" of whites over blacks suggest a close relationship between the common parlance of novels, magazines, and other popular forms on the one hand and the rarefied discourses of ethnology and biology on the other. Burroughs's own explanation of human difference was at once psychological, Darwinian, and, one might say, theological. Other writers drew upon vocabularies of the biological sciences or genetics. Scientific notions of evolution, heredity, and "survival of the fittest," if often misapplied, were nonetheless popularized far beyond the limits of an academically engaged audience in myriad fictions, poems, and adventurers' accounts. For every anthropologist who wondered whether contemporary savages might stand as "living representatives of the early Stone Age," there was a novelist describing Africa as a "prehistoric planet."

Popular imagery of the foreigner thus partook, directly and indirectly, of the myriad theoretical pronouncements that were issuing from the sciences and other academic disciplines throughout these years. Writers in these genres drew from various intellectual traditions with differing degrees of conscious intentionality and with differing degrees of real expertise. Some seemed to rely upon taxonomic traditions dating back to French naturalist Comte de Buffon and the eighteenth-century sciences. Their writing resembles nothing so much as those naturalists' accounts, like Buffon's *Natural History*, that translate specific, onetime observations into grand and immutable general laws: a single behavior observed in a single instance becomes a generic taxonomic principle. Though a traveler's knowledge was naturally restricted by the temporal bounds and the social circumstances of his or her visit, the conventions of travel writing, like the conventions of taxonomy in natural science, did away with all interpretive modesty: the badger is indolent and the ape is intractable, pronounced the naturalist; the Barbadian is thievish, the Wagogo a coward and a poltroon, declared the travel writer.

Others drew upon a vague, often unrefined Darwinism. But if "evolution" promised to mitigate the unforgiving notion of hierarchy by setting all of humanity on a common trajectory of development, so, ultimately, did it break that promise by suggesting a developmental distance that was so great as to be unbridgeable. (Even if ascending the evolutionary scale toward our own condition of civilization, in other words, the Wagogo was *still* a poltroon.) In general, it did not matter whether the social distances among peoples and cultures reflected differences in innate ability or merely in the degree of evolutionary progress, so great did such differences seem.

Throughout these years, the fields of anthropology, biology, and the sciences of the mind most heavily influenced popular conceptions of the world's peoples, their relative merits and capacities, their dominant traits, and their prospects for economic advancement, assimilation, or colonial rule. While diverse works like *Tarzan of the Apes*, *How the Other Half Lives*, *The Jungle*, *African Game Trails*, and *National Geographic* all suggested a human hierarchy extending upward from lowliest savagery to the vaunted civilizations of Europe and the United States, scholarly works like *Ancient Society*, *Heredity in Relation to Eugenics*, and *Feeble-Mindedness* elaborated that hierarchy and explained why its internal order was unlikely ever to change. While fantasists and observers like Burroughs, Riis, Wharton, and Roosevelt furnished the most popular images of the world's peoples for a celebration of national progress and entitlement, anthropologists like Lewis Henry Morgan, biologists like Charles Davenport, and psychologists like Henry Herbert Goddard and Lewis Terman furnished the necessary theories.

Theories of Development: Scholarly Disciplines and the Hierarchy of Peoples

> The adult who retains the more numerous fetal, infantile or simian traits, is unquestionably inferior to him whose development has progressed beyond them. . . . Measured by these criteria, the European or white race stands at the head of the list, the African or negro at its foot. . . . All parts of the body have been minutely scanned, measured and weighed, in order to erect a science of the comparative anatomy of the races.
>
> —*D. G. Brinton,* Races and Peoples *(1890)*

AMONG THE STUDY questions in John Fiske's 1907 primer, *A History of the United States for Schools*, was the instruction "Mention some country whose civilization is of a low grade, and tell why it is low." Another asked, "Are the Indians that [James Fenimore] Cooper tells us about in his *Leather Stocking* tales . . . true and real ones, or rather better?" By the turn of the century, arrangements of hierarchy were integral to scholarly conceptions of the world's peoples (including, evidently, schoolchildren's conceptions); indeed, *ranking* peoples had become a reflexive pursuit in a number of academic disciplines, including anthropology, biology, genetics, psychology, historiography, and even linguistics. ("Barbaric languages" lack durability, wrote Fiske in an explication of superior and inferior linguistic cultures; "numerals and personal pronouns which the Aryan has preserved for fifty centuries get lost every few years in Polynesia.")

The mainspring of such investigation was evolutionism, a model whose central tenets in one form or another had by the late nineteenth century swept across biology, anthropology, some schools of historiography, and the rising sciences of the mind and human intelligence. In the realm of social thought, bastardized notions of "the survival of the fittest" became indispensable for expressing a certain meanness of spirit. But when it came to theorizing the relationships among the world's peoples, of far greater portent was the revolution in the conception of human *temporality* wrought by Darwinian thinking and its emphasis on linear development. Classical ethnology had focused upon the question of human unity within a theoretical framework of biological stasis and a temporal frame limited by the master narrative of Genesis. By the 1870s and after, social evolutionism had become focused upon the problem of development, within a theoretical framework of biological dynamism and a temporal frame vastly expanded by the discoveries and theories of modern archaeology. By 1875, one anthropologist could assert that "it would be pure moonshine, in the present state of knowledge, to study Anthropology on any other basis than the basis of development." Two years later, in *Ancient Society*, Lewis Henry Morgan would flatly declare, "It can now be asserted upon convincing evidence that savagery preceded barbarism in all the tribes of mankind as barbarism is known to have preceded civilization. The history of the human race is one in source, one in experience, and in progress."

This evolutionary bent in the scholarship set contemporary savagery squarely at the center of inquiry, although savagery held little significance in its own right. Rather, savage society was primarily understood to offer an important window on civilized society's distant past. In their ruthless development, white savages had left black savages far behind; black savages now represented a missing link in the evolutionary chain extending backward in time. As historian George Stocking, Jr., has characterized the scholarship of the period, during the reign of evolutionism in the 1870s and after, the dark-skinned peoples of the world promised to shed new light on how "the ape had developed into the British gentleman."

The ascendant Euro-American fetish of evolutionary development had tremendous consequences for the U.S. encounter with foreign peoples: it provided a narrative for otherwise disparate and disjointed images of the world's nations and tribes, and it tacitly endorsed a very particular set of political and social relationships. By its very popularity, including its misapplications, evolutionism became a secular counterpart to an earlier religious discourse of the Christian civilizing mission among the "heathen." White Europeans and Americans in both cases supposedly enjoyed exclusive knowledge of the one proper way. In this instance, the proper way was marked not by God's favor but by nature's: the range of human existence represented a naturally unfolding, linear progression of developmental stages along which white peoples had quite obviously traveled the farthest. This doctrine would have a great deal to suggest both in the realm of trade, where the cultivation of markets so nicely comported with the elevation of the species, and in the realm of politics, where the industrialized West could assume stewardship over the "lower orders" of Africa, Asia, the Americas, and the Pacific without troubling with sticky questions of rights and representation.

The relationship among academic disciplines like anthropology or psychiatry and the narrative genres examined earlier, such as the travelogue, was complex and often paradoxical. On the one hand, nineteenth-century scholars relied heavily upon travelers, missionaries, colonial officials, explorers, and naturalists for their data. Formal ethnographic fieldwork had not yet become a commonplace; in the era of "armchair anthropology," the grand theories of human development encompassed a terrain of human geography far broader than had yet been examined firsthand by the ethnologist. The volume of travel writing and firsthand description of far-flung peoples and places was an irresistible source for those who would theorize the developmental relationship of savagery to civilization. Science thus remained largely at the mercy of travelers' haphazard impressions.

But, on the other hand, the most popular of these theories themselves—like evolutionism—quietly came to inform both the gaze and the voice of travel writing, so that theories that had been derived in part from earlier travelers' accounts of Africa or the Pacific actually structured later travelers' impressions of those same regions, as theoretical and descriptive writing folded into each other. Compelling propositions—that present-day savages represented living fossils of Stone Age mentalities and lifeways, for instance—were repeated in an endless and self-sustaining loop of observation and theory. By the time Teddy Roosevelt wrote of the "railroad through the Pleistocene" in Africa in 1910, the phrase occupied the status of both an un-self-conscious impression of observable fact and a deeply embedded, reflexive commitment to evolutionist thinking. Evolutionism had become naturalized; the proposition drew authority from its own repetition.

In a series of observations gathered as "Primitive Man—Emotional" and "Primitive Man—Intellectual" (1876), Herbert Spencer encapsulated the scientific assessment of the savage as a creature of retarded development: the savage had "the mind of a child and the passions of a man." The sketch in outline included "impulsiveness" as the savage's calling card—a pronounced "improvidence" whose tendency was ever toward the immediate gratification of desire. As for intellectual qualities, savages may demonstrate "acute senses and quick perceptions," but in proportion as "mental energies go out in restless perception, they cannot go out in deliberate thought." Purely imitative, they demonstrate but a small departure "from the brute type of mind."

Whether a given theorist imagined the social distances between peoples temporally (as did many evolutionists, who regarded contemporary savagery as a fossil of an earlier period) or developmentally (as did many psychologists, who saw savagery as a kind of retardation in the process of the individual life cycle recapitulating the life cycle of the species), most did picture the diversity of humankind as ranging along a hierarchic scale, from the brute or childish savage, barely removed from the beasts of the field, to the refined white European. Nor were such explanatory models reserved for the specialized discourse of the scientific community. Looking over the Midway Plaisance at the World's Columbian Exposition in 1893, a writer for the *Chicago Tribune* exclaimed, "What an opportunity was here afforded to the scientific mind to descend the spiral of evolution, tracing humanity in its highest phases down almost to its animalistic origins." Eleven years later, the Louisiana Purchase Exposition in St. Louis included an ambitious anthropology exhibit in which, according to a reporter for *Harper's*, "primitive folk will occupy habitations erected by themselves out of materials brought for the purpose, and will live and work in their accustomed ways." The excitement of the exhibit derived from the fact that the exposition grounds would thus present "every stage in industrial progress with the developments in the arts, languages, social customs, and beliefs characteristic of each stage of human advancement." Thus the fairs and the reportage of the fairs, like various works in literary naturalism and other more popular venues, disseminated not only the substance of evolutionary thinking but its moral: movement along the evolutionary path was not merely onward, it was most decidedly—and portentously—upward.

Cultures

Debates had raged in the natural sciences and ethnology throughout the mid-nineteenth century between monogenists, who believed in a single origin of humanity in accordance with Genesis, and polygenists, who believed that the varieties of humanity and the profound differences among peoples could only be explained by a model of multiple origins. The brand of social evolutionism that dominated discussion in the wake of Darwin's discoveries seemed at first to solve the problem in favor of the monogenists: humanity had originated at a single site of creation, and then fanned out across the globe in myriad migrations whose disparate destinations had then worked a kind of environmental alchemy over the course of thousands of years. Differences in color, stature, physiognomy, and custom could all be explained by the diverse evolutionary paths followed by various peoples in their wanderings from the original site of creation.

But if earlier monogenism had tended to soften the edges of scientific racism by positing an essential unity among all humans, the new evolutionist argument, though proceeding from the assumption of a single site of origin, still left room for some of the most radically racist ideas of the polygenists. Indeed, as George Stocking, Jr., has written, social evolutionism is best seen as a *synthesis* of monogenism and polygenism. Whereas polygenists had argued that differences between Africans and Europeans, for instance, were so vast as to discount a shared ancestry, social evolutionists now argued that despite their shared ancestry these two peoples had developed along such wildly divergent trajectories that whatever commonalities they had shared in dim antiquity were now moot. Their differences, if merely differences of relatively recent development, were nonetheless unbridgeable. As Darwin himself had written of a group of Indians at Tierra del Fuego in 1839, they were "stunted in their growth, their hideous faces daubed with white paint, their skins filthy and greasy, their voices discordant, their gestures violent and without dignity." Outward signs invited musing on inner character. Darwin doubted their capacity for domestic affection and wondered whether they were capable of experiencing any pleasure in life. "How little can the higher powers of the mind be brought into play? What is there for imagination to picture, for reason to compare, for judgment to decide upon?" "For my own part," he concluded in *The Descent of Man* (1871),

I would as soon be descended from that heroic little monkey, who braved his dreaded enemy in order to save the life of his keeper; or from that old baboon, who, descending from the mountains, carried away in triumph his young comrade from a crowd of astonished dogs—as from a savage who delights to torture his enemies, offers up bloody sacrifices, practises infanticide without remorse, treats his wives like slaves, knows no decency, and is haunted by the grossest superstitions.

Among the polygenist survivals in evolutionist thinking were an emphasis on biological classification; a posited linkage between physical type and cultural standing; and the maintenance of the polygenists' rigid racial hierarchy, now cast within a temporal sequence of progressive stages. Though humanity had indeed been a single "homogenous race" at the dawn of time, remarked early evolutionist Alfred Wallace, present differences ran so deep that one could "fairly assert that there were many originally distinct races of men." Human unity, in other words, was a theoretical truth whose practical value was inconsequential. Like the polygenists whose intellectual edifice they were engaged in dismantling, most evolutionists measured an enormous distance between diverse human groups; and, also like the polygenists, they assigned unmistakable, hierarchic value to those differences.

If humanity was united by a single creation, then what was the basis of the evolutionists' hierarchy? The hallmarks of classical evolutionism included three types of assumptions.

The first was a cluster of ideas regarding the mechanisms of human development: natural growth is from simplicity to complexity; humanity shares a single psychic nature; development of social and cultural forms depends upon the interaction between human nature and the conditions of the environment; variations among human groups reflect the cumulative results of such interactions in differing environments across time. The entire spectrum of such social and cultural developments was presumed to be governed by laws that were not only discoverable by science, but that operated uniformly in past times as well as present. Thus the continuity between past and present was discernible to the trained eye, as were certain relics of the past that had survived into the present. It was in this vein, for instance, that James Frazer, a British theorist of comparative religions and customs, looked to the "popular superstitions and the customs of the peasantry" in modern Europe for clues to the "primitive religion of the Aryans."

The second class of assumptions had to do with the measure of social and cultural differences, and with the interpretation of such measurements. It is here that the evolutionists' value judgments begin to emerge: human control over nature is the primary criterion for measuring development; scientific and technological progress tend to be accompanied by many other social and cultural developments; thus human groups can be objectively ordered based upon measures of technology and their states of knowledge; "lower" societies, by this measure, represent "earlier" stages of human development.

And the third parcel of assumptions dealt with the significance of these discoveries for the understanding of contemporary humanity: "savage" and "barbaric" societies can be used to reconstruct the historical sweep of human time; vestigial survivals from lower forms now embedded in civilized societies testify to the mechanisms of development. Objective science thus pointed the way to frank assessments of relative human worth. "On the whole the civilized man is not only wider and more capable than the savage," wrote British anthropologist Edward Tylor in 1871, "but also better and happier."

Typical studies in early evolutionist thinking fixed upon cultural forms such as religion, language, mythology, sexual practices, kinship systems, and law as clues to the proper mapping of human progress, and so the field was crowded with titles like *Primal Law*, *Primitive Marriage*, *Primitive Paternity*, *The Origin and Development of Moral Ideas*, *Kinship and Marriage in Early Ara-*

bia, The Material Culture of the Simpler Peoples, or *A Treatise on Certain Early Forms of Superstition and Society.* Others hinted more directly at the stakes of such inquiry: "From Spell to Prayer," "On the Limits of Savage Religion," or "On the Tasmanians as Representatives of Palaeolithic Man."

In 1877, Lewis Henry Morgan published *Ancient Society,* the most complete single-volume consolidation of evolutionist thinking to appear in the United States. The book's subtitle conveys much about the author's outlook: *Researches in the Lines of Human Progress from Savagery Through Barbarism to Civilization.* Morgan's opening discussion of "Ethnical Periods" could not be more straightforward: "Mankind commenced their career at the bottom of the scale," he asserted, "and worked their way up from savagery to civilization through the slow accumulation of experimental knowledge. As it is undeniable that portions of the human family have existed in a state of savagery, other portions in a state of barbarism, and still other portions in a state of civilization, it seems equally so that these three distinct conditions are connected with each other in a natural as well as necessary sequence of progress."

"The experience of mankind has run in nearly uniform channels," asserted Morgan, though in his view it has clearly carried some peoples much further than others. *Ancient Society* represents a highly methodical attempt to map those channels, and thus to chart the history of human progress. Morgan launched an ambitious inquiry into the "ideas, passions, and aspirations" of developing humanity, as these were reflected in the interrelated realms of invention, discovery, and technological innovation on the one hand, and primary institutions on the other. His areas of focus included subsistence, government, language, the family, religion, house life and architecture, and property relations.

On this basis, Morgan ventured to classify the entire spectrum of human experience into seven subdivisions, from Africa's "ethnical chaos of savagery and barbarism" to the rapidly industrializing United States:

1. *Lower Savagery:* from the "infancy of the human race" to the acquisition of a fish subsistence and a knowledge of the use of fire.
2. *Middle Savagery:* from the use of fire to the invention of the bow

and arrow. (Contemporary exemplars included Australians and most Polynesians.)

3. *Upper Savagery:* from the bow and arrow to the art of pottery. (Contemporary exemplars included Athapascan tribes of Hudson Bay Territory, Columbia Valley tribes, and certain coastal tribes of North and South America.)

4. *Lower Barbarism:* from pottery—which presupposes village life and considerable advancement in the simple arts—to the domestication of animals in the Eastern Hemisphere, or the cultivation of maize and plants by irrigation in the Western. (Contemporary exemplars included Indian tribes of the United States east of the Missouri.)

5. *Middle Barbarism:* from the domestication of animals or irrigation to the smelting of iron ore. (Contemporary exemplars included Village Indians of New Mexico, Mexico, Central America, and Peru.)

6. *Upper Barbarism:* from iron to the creation of a phonetic alphabet. (Morgan noted no contemporary exemplars, but pointed to the Grecian tribes of the Homeric age and Germanic tribes in Caesar's time.)

7. *Civilization:* commences with the phonetic alphabet and the production of literary records (subdivided into ancient and modern).

If the evolutionist's view was founded upon notions of social fluidity and biological dynamism, still the hierarchy established by the evolutionary model was unforgiving and fixed. It is significant that many of Morgan's "ancient societies" were in fact contemporary, like Australians and the Iroquois. In a telling discussion of the *gens,* a unit of social organization antedating the tribe or clan in his model, Morgan began "with the gens as it now exists among the American aborigines, where it is found in its archaic form." This peculiar certainty that something that "now exists" in another culture is also "archaic" represents the intellectual mainspring of the evolutionist project. Morgan similarly identified a particular type of social organization found among Australians as "the most primitive form of society hitherto discovered," and of special import because of "the contingent probability that the remote progenitors of our own Aryan family were once similarly organized." Such cultural fossils in contemporary savagery pointed directly to the hierarchic scale implicit in the evolutionist paradigm: "The Australians rank below the polynesians, and far below the American aborigines. They stand below the African Negro and near the bottom of the scale. Their social institutions, therefore, must approach the primitive type as nearly as those of any existing people."

The so-called savages of Australia, Africa, and the Americas drew the greatest attention in such scientific discussions, from Darwin, Morgan, and Tylor on down, but they were by no means the only peoples whose state was thought to be particularly revealing of the grand mosaic of human development. Among the most thorough treatments of European peoples within this tradition was William Z. Ripley's *Races of Europe* (1899), a sprawling study that originated as a series of lectures at the Lowell Institute in Massachusetts in 1896. "All students would agree with Spencer that 'feeble unorganized societies are at the mercy of their surroundings,'" wrote Ripley; but civilized society raised some vexing questions about heredity and environment, about the relationship between humanity and nature. Did civilization mark humankind's passage from a "natural" state to an "artificial" one? Or did it merely reflect a perfected adaptation to nature (rather than a freedom from it)? Ripley's comments on the force of environment and civilization's struggle to adapt recalled not only Darwin's fatal struggle for survival, but also the contemporary crisis of "overproduction" that was so much on the minds of those now educated in the wants of civilized life. "The varieties of [nature's] resources," he offered, quoting Lord Bryce, "differing in different regions, prescribed the kind of industry for which each spot is fitted; and the competition of nations, growing always keener, forces each to maintain itself in the struggle by using to the utmost every facility for the production or transportation of products."

Ripley's investigation of such struggle led him through a dense thicket (six hundred pages dense) on the three races of Europe—the Teutonic, the Alpine, and the Mediterranean—their geographical and political circumstances, their cephalic indexes (head size and shape), their physical statures,

STAKING A NEW CLAIM.

Uncle Sam scrambles toward the fabled
China market. *New York Herald*, 1898

ALL SIZES AND GOOD FITS FOR ALL THE FAMILY.

The United States outfits
the Philippines (and
"family"—Cuba, Puerto
Rico, and Hawaii) for self-
government. Here the
metaphor of the fitting
room dovetails neatly with
actual U.S. aspirations for
international trade and the
capture of foreign markets,
which revolved with such
regularity around the concerns of textile manufac-
ture and export. *New York
Herald*, 1898

The dress and the authoritative bearing of Tagalog census enumerators under U.S. guidance (facing page) contrast sharply with the traditional garb and lifeways of the Philippines. *National Geographic*, 1905

COURTESY OF THE NATIONAL GEOGRAPHIC SOCIETY

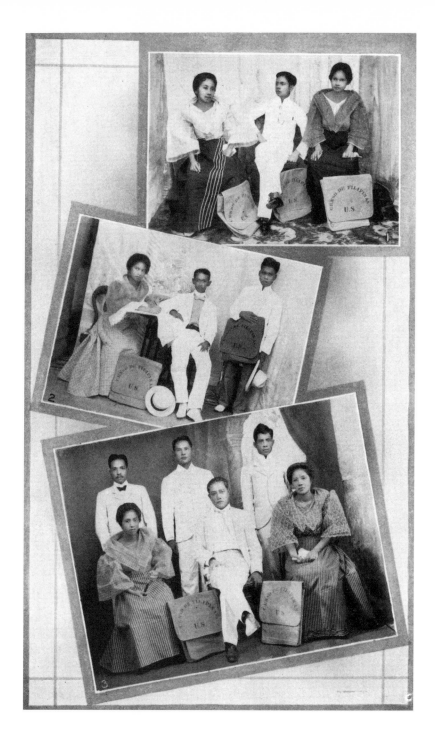

The Chinaman at bat. Anxiety over labor competition merges with a more generalized anxiety over the fate of true "Americanism." *Harper's Weekly*, 1880s

COURTESY OF THE BEINECKE RARE BOOK AND MANUSCRIPT LIBRARY, YALE UNIVERSITY

Native Americans driven out of the East; Chinese immigrants driven out of the West; American blacks (background) await their orders. *Harper's Weekly*, 1880s

COURTESY OF THE BEINECKE RARE BOOK AND MANUSCRIPT LIBRARY, YALE UNIVERSITY

A GORILLA ON THE LOOSE.

"A Gorilla on the Loose"—*Harper's Weekly*'s depiction of the brute force of labor in the wake of the 1877 B&O strike. The "gorilla" in this instance exhibits some visual echoes of the standard depiction of Irishness in popular iconography

COURTESY OF THE BEINECKE RARE BOOK AND MANUSCRIPT LIBRARY, YALE UNIVERSITY

The wages of universal male suffrage according to Thomas Nast: German socialism and intemperance. *Harper's Weekly*, 1880s

COURTESY OF THE
BEINECKE RARE BOOK
AND MANUSCRIPT LIBRARY,
YALE UNIVERSITY

Taking up the needle trades: Jewish sweatshop workers on New York's
Lower East Side, 1890. Jacob Riis, *How the Other Half Lives*

COURTESY OF THE MUSEUM OF THE CITY OF NEW YORK

"Bringing the World to Columbus": an advertisement for an exposition in
Columbus, Ohio, dramatizes the confrontation of U.S. civilization with various
stages of barbarism and savagery. Postcard, 1919

COURTESY OF LOUISE NEWMAN

Tarzan and his adopted son, an African native named Tibo. A visual recapitulation of the text's equation of African blackness with African bestiality. Edgar Rice Burroughs, *Jungle Tales of Tarzan*, 1916–17

The arrival of the white man and the encounter with African savagery: Henry Stanley in Africa. *Harper's Weekly*, 1878

COURTESY OF THE BEINECKE RARE BOOK AND MANUSCRIPT LIBRARY, YALE UNIVERSITY

A REFUTATION OF DARWINISM.

Dennis (*at the Zoo.*). "Tim, there's thim that sez we was all iv us the loike iv that onct; sure I don't belave it."

Darwinism refuted by the apelike Irishman. *Harper's Weekly*, 1883

COURTESY OF THE BEINECKE RARE BOOK AND MANUSCRIPT LIBRARY, YALE UNIVERSITY

WHAT SHALL THE HARVEST BE?

Uncle Sam tending the garden of exotic transplants: "What shall the harvest be?" Though the cartoon seems at first glance a testimony to the powers of environmentalism ("Great Opportunities," "Public School," "Free Press"), the racial assumptions of the depiction rather argue the power of heredity

COURTESY OF THE LIBRARY AND ARCHIVE OF ELLIS ISLAND

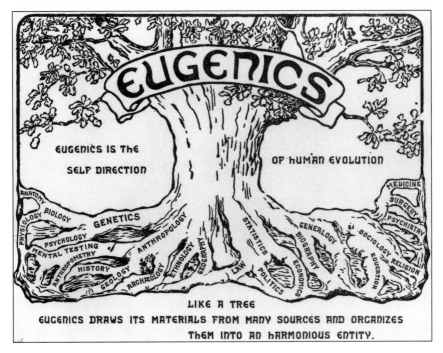

The science of eugenics, thoroughly rooted in the learning of twenty-five disciplines. Second International Congress of Eugenics, held at the American Museum of Natural History in New York, 1921. *Pamphlet of the Race Betterment Foundation*, 1921

Cradle as war zone: "troubles" in the form of eugenically unsound babies. Postcard, c. 1910s

COURTESY OF LOUISE NEWMAN

"The Minnesota Baby," winner of a "Race Betterment" contest as the ideal type at the First National Conference on Race Betterment, Battle Creek, Michigan, 1914. *Pamphlet of the Race Betterment Foundation, 1914*

"Uncle Sam's Thanksgiving Dinner," Thomas Nast's idealized vision of the United States'
congeries of peoples under the benign sway of self-government and universal suffrage

COURTESY OF THE BEINECKE RARE BOOK AND MANUSCRIPT LIBRARY, YALE UNIVERSITY

"The Ignorant Vote—Honors Are
Easy." The Southern Negro and
the Northern (Irish) immigrant
are suspended in equipoise on the
scales of civic virtue, showing
Thomas Nast's misgivings about
self-government and universal
suffrage. *Harper's Weekly*, 1876

COURTESY OF THE BEINECKE RARE
BOOK AND MANUSCRIPT LIBRARY,
YALE UNIVERSITY

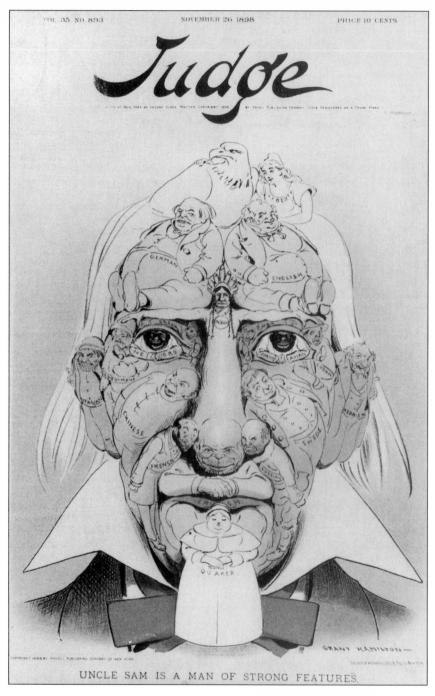

An ambivalent vision of the assimilability of peoples. The composite
portrait of a recognizable Uncle Sam may suggest assimilation; but the
distinctive and unchanging character of each of the parts (the "strong features")
indicates some doubt as to national homogenization. *Judge*, 1898

Uncle Sam's "polyglot boardinghouse," as Theodore Roosevelt was to call it. Here it is the Irish lodger who causes the most headaches

COURTESY OF THE CORBIS-BETTMANN ARCHIVES

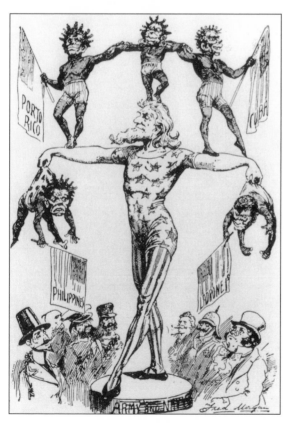

Parvenu Uncle Sam "supporting" his new imperial charges, much to the surprise of the onlooking European powers. *Philadelphia Inquirer*, 1898

"Madonnas of Many Lands": "Bedouin Mother and Child." "The father of this little nomad may be a warlike bandit with a cloudy notion of property rights and other details of the civilized code . . ." The visual lexicon of the exotic and the text's unabashed acceptance of human hierarchy at once reflect and reinforce popular American assumptions regarding the barbarism and the virtue of the world's peoples. *National Geographic*, 1917

COURTESY OF THE NATIONAL GEOGRAPHIC SOCIETY

"Madonnas of Many Lands": the industrial arts of the South Seas. "This device is at a disadvantage when compared to an American cradle . . ." *National Geographic*, 1917

COURTESY OF THE NATIONAL GEOGRAPHIC SOCIETY

"Madonnas of Many Lands": "Motherhood in the Philippines." "After his mother, Uncle Sam is his best friend . . ." Aside from the frank imperialism of its caption, this illustration also indicates the ways in which the imperialistic and the pornographic gazes could converge, given the strictures of Victorian culture regarding feminine modesty. *National Geographic*, 1917

COURTESY OF THE NATIONAL GEOGRAPHIC SOCIETY

and their modes of government. Significantly, though the bulk of the volume is given over to the relative strengths and weaknesses of the European races and their subdivisions (Slav, Celt, Gaul, and the like), the bottom line, for Ripley, turns out to be the racial prospect—given the environmental and hereditarian laws of human adaptability—for the European colonization of non-European climes. "Teutonic peoples are exceedingly unelastic in power of adaptation in tropical climates," he noted; therefore, "great problems for science remain to be solved before the statesmen can safely proceed to people those tropical regions of the earth so lately apportioned among European states."

By the late nineteenth century, a counter-evolutionary intellectual tradition was in formation. As early as 1887, in an essay on comparative phonetics, anthropologist Franz Boas wondered whether European observers were misinterpreting various sounds in primitive languages based on faulty preconceptions derived from the phonetics of their own European languages. The query pointed Boas to a much larger problem: perhaps, as in phonetics, savage cultural practices that evolutionists treated as imperfect approximations of the presumed European pinnacle were in fact unrelated developments, independent of and separate from those practices that set the Eurocentric evolutionary standard. Boas formalized his critique in "Human Faculty as Determined by Race" (1894) and "The Limitations of the Comparative Method of Anthropology" (1896). Though "civilized man" had "conquered the forces of nature and compelled them to serve him," and might justly be "proud of his wonderful achievements," there still remained no proof that civilization caused an increase of faculty among its members, or that currently "civilized" peoples alone possessed the capacity for civilization. The evolutionists' scale of races was a shaky construct.

Moreover, the evolutionist argument rested squarely on the unproven assumption that ethnological phenomena develop everywhere in the same manner—that the path toward "civilization" is inexorable and unilinear, that there is one way and one way only for a people, a trait, a custom to develop. "The fact that many fundamental features of culture are universal, or at least occur in many isolated places, interpreted by the assumption that the same features must always have developed from the same causes, leads to the conclusion that there is one grand system according to which mankind has developed everywhere." But, on the contrary, argued Boas, "the same phenomena may develop in a multitude of ways." The divergent internal logic of two cultures itself may explain differing paths of development; but it is easier still to identify intermarriage, war, slavery, and trade as a few of the external forces that have intervened in various peoples' development, disrupting the evolutionists' tidy scheme of universal stages by introducing foreign elements, as it were, out of sequence.

In *The Mind of Primitive Man* (1911), Boas laid out a comprehensive critique of classical evolutionism, laying bare and investigating the ethnocentric assumptions undergirding evolutionary thinking. The evolutionists' hierarchy was suspect on its face, he argued, noting that "a race is commonly described as the lower, the more fundamentally it differs from our own." Here Boas brought two common assumptions in particular under scrutiny: that the achievement of civilizations was due above all to aptitude, and that the European races ("or, taking the notion in its extreme form, the Northwest European type") represented the "highest" development of humankind. European civilization had arisen not by aptitude but by blind chance: through processes of diffusion and physical assimilation, savage European tribes were particularly quick to adopt the ways of civilized European tribes. Besides, from Boas's standpoint, given recent archaeological revisions in the time frame for human development, the evolutionists' notions of "higher" and "lower" types lost all force. If modern humanity was about one hundred thousand years old, what difference if various cultures were a paltry few thousand years apart developmentally? In his contribution to the Dillingham Immigration Commission report in successive years, Boas added to this overall critique a radically environmentalist argument regarding "Changes in Bodily Form of Descendants of Immigrants" (1912), noting the power of environment fundamentally to destabilize and alter racial types.

The Boasian view was in ascendance in the United States early in the century, and this critique of evolutionism gained ground in this country far more quickly than it did in Europe. But even as late as World War I, evolutionism, not cultural relativism, still carried the day in popular discussion. Boas himself, it is worth noting, had absorbed a good dose of the evolutionists' hereditarian reasoning. In the article that was the forerunner to *The Mind of Primitive Man*, Boas's most far-reaching critique of evolutionism, the relativist conceded, "We find that on the average the size of the brain of the negroid races is less than the size of the brain of the other races; and the difference in favor of the mongoloid and white races is so great, that we are justified in assuming a certain correlation between their mental ability and the increased size of their brain." Boas's most bitter adversaries could have comfortably applauded this assessment.

But the triumph of a harder, more thoroughly racist hereditarianism was more complete in the court of public opinion and among policy-makers. The Panama-Pacific International Exposition in San Francisco (1915), for instance, was one great paean to evolution and hierarchy. In 1912, Herbert Hoover, then an international mining engineer, had proposed to the fair's directors that they stage a great pageant to portray the racial drama of westward expansion. The pageant would begin with "the innumerable conflicts of the Northern and Southern branches of the Aryan race" in the reaches of European antiquity, and end in "the last great conflict of [northern Aryans and Latins] for the actual possession of the land" in California. "There the meekly religious Southerner vanished like a mist before the more virile Northerner."

The fair itself was neither less dramatic nor less racially invested than Hoover's vision of Darwinian struggle. The Fountain of the Psychology of Life, for instance, featured groupings of sculptures titled *The Dawn of Life*, *Natural Selection*, and *Survival of the Fittest*, which encapsulated the saga of "primitive man." "Onward these primitive people pass through life," a guidebook to the fair explained. "You can see them if you look up on the Tower. On they march, in that upward climb of civilization." San Diego's Panama-California Exposition that same year, though significantly smaller, went the Panama-Pacific one better by setting "the science of man" at the thematic center of its exhibits. Four years after Boas's critique of racial formalism in *The Mind of Primitive Man*, the Smithsonian's Aleš Hrdlička and other physical anthropologists mounted an ambitious educational display on "the Physical Evolution of Man" and "the Evolution of Culture" as though such processes were nowhere in dispute.

Between the ascendance of evolutionism in the 1870s and the expositions of the 1910s, then, the harshest edges of the evolutionist paradigm had come to the fore. It was no longer so much the dynamism of the processes as the stasis of the hierarchy that claimed attention in public discussion. This dimension of evolutionist thought, of course, was not altogether new. As John Fiske had written in "The Progress from Brute to Man" way back in 1873, "The capability of progress . . . is by no means shared alike by all races of men." After granting "the Aryan and Semitic" races special status as exhibiting such capability in marked degree, then begrudgingly mentioning "the Chinese and Japanese, the Copts of Egypt, and a few of the highest American races" as distant runners-up, Fiske asserted, "The small-brained races—the Australians and Papuans, the Hottentots, and the majority of tribes constituting the wide-spread Malay and American families—appear almost wholly incapable of progress, even under the guidance of higher races. The most that can be said for them is, that they are somewhat more imitative and somewhat more teachable than any brute animals." By the 1910s, this dimension of evolutionism—this adherence to the *innateness* of capability—had begun to overshadow all else.

Genes

The position of biology and "race" throughout these debates was ambiguous. On the one hand, when scholars like Edward B. Tylor, the leading evolutionist in British anthropology, spoke of "race," most often the term was meant to include a cultural dimension that was not strictly biological—and, indeed, depending on the context, the cultural, nonbiological, nonheritable dimension might overshadow the connotations of biology and "blood" inhering in the term in more recent times. In this such scholars differed from their predecessors, for whom "race" itself lay at the very heart of the question of single or multiple creation. But on the other hand, when Tylor himself arranged a series of "races" into a hierarchy based on "culture," best to worst, he rather conspicuously arranged them in accordance with the customary racial ordering from light to dark: Italian, Chinese, Aztec, Tahitian, Australian. Given the Lamarckian assumption of the inheritance of acquired characteristics, such "cultures" might have an unshakably "racial" character.

James Frazer, too, amid a debate over "primitive" religious practices, could posit as a given that "civilisation varies on the whole . . . directly with complexion, increasing or diminishing with the blanching or darkening of the skin." As George Stocking, Jr., explains, for many anthropologists in this period categories of "habitual behavior became instinctive, and cultural inheritance became part of biological heredity."

By the early twentieth century, however, a second intellectual current had emerged in which the primacy of race was anything but ambiguous. As one speaker told the Race Betterment Congress at the Panama-California Exposition, people "will not prosper without proper selection any more than vegetables would if indiscriminately planted." He went on to define "two distinct lines in the improvement of the race": "One is by favorable environment; and the other, ten thousand times more important, is by selection of the best individuals through a series of generations." The intellectual principles of eugenics may have overlapped a great deal with evolutionism and with the leading strands of anthropological thought on questions of culture and environment, in other words; but among the biologically minded proponents of eugenics, culture was but a sideshow: practically speaking, heredity was all.

Indeed, the relationship between eugenics and the classical Darwinian paradigm was peculiar: eugenics was at once rigidly predicated upon the principle of selection, and yet it also represented a complete loss of faith that *natural* selection could operate within the conditions of advanced civilization. Though certainly no eugenicist, Darwin himself had written in *The Descent of Man:*

> *With savages, the weak in body or mind are soon eliminated. . . . We civilized men, on the other hand, do our utmost to check the process of elimination; we build asylums for the imbecile, the maimed, and the sick; we institute poor-laws; and our medical men exert their utmost skill to save the life of everyone to the last moment. . . . Thus, the weak members of civilized societies propagate their kind. No one who has attended to the breeding of domestic animals will doubt that this must be highly injurious to the race of man.*

The eugenics movement on both sides of the Atlantic represented this concern writ large; and in the context of the times, questions of "breeding" quickly boiled down to the matter of "superior" and "inferior" races.

The widely recognized founder of eugenics was Francis Galton, a British naturalist and statistician and a cousin of Charles Darwin. Galton's interest in heredity, race, and character dated to the 1860s, when he began a "purely ethnological inquiry into the mental peculiarities of different races." In 1865, he published "Hereditary Talent and Character," a treatise purporting to demonstrate that "human mental qualities" could be manipulated or cultivated in precisely the way that breeders controlled the qualities of domesticated animals through selection. "What an extraordinary effect might be produced on our race," he exclaimed, were scientific principles employed to "unite in marriage those who possessed the finest and most suitable natures, mental, moral, and physical!"

Galton followed this up with *Hereditary Genius* in 1869 and then *Natural Inheritance* in 1889, a vast study of statistical correlations among various traits and their descent through generations. ("Whenever you can," he had once advised, "count.") Insofar as this work was devoted to questions of race, it focused on differences between "civilized" whites and "savage" nonwhites. Indeed, Galton had explored southern Africa firsthand in the 1850s, and had published an account of his adventures under the title *The Art of Travel.* The requirements of civilization, he now ventured, had bred into advanced Europeans "the instinct of continuous steady labour" and had bred out the "wild, untameable restlessness" that was "innate with savages." Like most British scientists, however, Galton remained most interested in questions of class— the heritable qualities of civilized society's "better element," in the parlance of the day, and the ways in which, using newly gained knowledge in genetics, humanity might actually manipulate evolutionary processes in order to breed out the unwanted qualities that characterized the rougher element.

It was in the United States that genetics and eugenics became most closely aligned with race thinking. Like biologists working independently in several countries toward the century's end, Galton had discovered the long-overlooked work of Gregor Mendel, an Austrian monk who had experimented broadly with the hybridization of sweet peas in the 1850s and '60s.

After breeding some thirty thousand plants, Mendel was able to announce to the scientific world that certain characteristics were definitely determined by hereditarily transmitted "elements." His findings, the basis of Mendelian genetics, had received relatively little notice among a generation whose overriding concern was with evolutionism, adaptation, and change. Mendelian genetics, after all, described a sort of biological *stability*. But in the political and social climate of the late nineteenth and early twentieth centuries, Mendel's findings took on new significance. For a generation concerned with industrialization, the proliferation of slums, the massive migrations from countryside to city, and the attending social ills of crime, prostitution, intemperance, and disease, any scientific system of portraiture of the population and its prospects was bound to spark interest. By 1910, most American biologists accepted some form of Mendelian principles; and in the American setting, such genetic portraiture was bound to take on racial connotations.

Eugenics as an intellectual project thus holds a dual place in the history of the United States at this historical moment of expanding imperial horizons and massive labor migrations. On the one hand, like anthropology, eugenics was a genre of representation, which served up the world's peoples and made them "known" according to an established body of scientific principles—the Serb is savage, the Gypsy is lawless, the Italian is excitable, the Bulgarian is stolid, the Slav is careless and given to fits of cruelty. (And all of these peoples, it turns out, tend to be disturbingly prolific in comparison to the Anglo-Saxon.)

On the other hand, the eugenics movement in the United States was itself largely a creature of the bedeviling immigration question; indeed, it is impossible to disentangle eugenic views of race and races from the political occasion of their articulation. If eugenicists were committed to the principle of white supremacy, the immigration debates that drove much of the research ensured that the differences *within* the white race would actually receive more attention. As Ruth Benedict remarked from the vantage point of the 1940s, the racist literature of the United States in this period dealt surprisingly little with "the Negro." The case was so thoroughly closed on the nonwhite races, in other words, that they scarcely warranted discussion when it came to questions of "breeding" and the biological engineering of society.

Rather, the racists' "constant injunction is that Old America should limit immigration on a 'racial' basis and should keep its blood free from mixture with that of the inferior non-Nordics we have carelessly admitted." Scientific racism in the United States became largely "a spectacle of immigrants of one decade condemning to everlasting inferiority the immigrants of a later decade." What imperialism was to anthropology, in short, immigration was to American eugenics. The so-called new immigrants from places like Greece, Russia, Poland, and Italy captivated scholarly attention as scientists now set out to survey, quantify, and assess what one eugenicist referred to as "the great strains of human protoplasm . . . coursing through the country."

If the story of the initial eugenic idea begins with Galton, the history of eugenics as a budding intellectual movement in the United States properly begins in the political movement to restrict immigration. The Immigration Restriction League, founded in 1894 by Anglo-Saxon patricians Prescott Hall, Robert DeCourcy Ward, and Charles Warren, espoused a frank Anglo-Saxon supremacism whose early rhetoric, if lacking the specialized language of eugenics, did have distinctly biological implications. By early in the new century, the league was indeed employing a language of racial hygiene. "We should see to it that the breeding of the human race in this country receives the attention which it so surely deserves," the league submitted to a congressional committee charged with investigating the issue of immigration. "A considerable proportion of the immigrants now coming are from races and countries . . . which have not progressed, but have been backward, downtrodden, and relatively useless for centuries." Prescott Hall added that the league did not oppose all immigration, only that which "lowers the mental, moral, and physical average of our people." In this connection he noted ominously that, of recent immigration, "three-fifths were of the Slavic and Iberic races of southern and eastern Europe."

Francis Amasa Walker, president of MIT and superintendent of the U.S. Census in 1870 and 1880, also stepped forward to make the statistical case that the nation's immigrants were breeding at a far higher rate than native-born Americans. In an *Atlantic Monthly* piece in 1896, Walker wondered why "every foul and stagnant pool of population in Europe, in which no breath of intellectual or industrial life has stirred for ages," should gain such easy entry to the United States. "These people have no history behind them which is of a nature to give encouragement," he wrote of the new immigrants.

> *They have none of the inherited instincts and tendencies which made it comparatively easy to deal with the immigration of the olden time. They are beaten men from beaten races; representing the worst failures in the struggle for existence. . . . They have none of the ideas and aptitudes which fit men to take up readily and easily the problem of self-care and self-government, such as belong to those who are descended from the tribes that met under the oaktrees of old Germany to make laws and choose chieftains.*

It was in the political climate generated by such concerns that Mendel's work on sweet peas was rediscovered and embraced; that Galton's writings gained favor; that a rising generation of experimental scientists rallied to the challenges posed by genetic and eugenic doctrine; and that an institutional framework for genetic research was erected in the United States. The American Breeders' Association (ABA) was founded in 1903 by a group of agricultural breeders and academic biologists in direct response to the rediscovery of Mendel's work. In 1906, at the urging of Charles Davenport, a pioneer in biometry at the University of Chicago and an avid admirer of Francis Galton, the ABA established a Eugenics Section "to investigate and report on heredity in the human race" and to "emphasize the value of superior blood and the menace to society of inferior blood."

Davenport had established his reputation as a biologist with his work on the Mendelian inheritance of certain traits among chickens, and later of hair and skin color among humans. He now turned his attention to eugenics. His overarching convictions were, first, that humans ought to be judged upon their merits as biological breeding stock; and, second, that from infancy each person carried biological "unit characters" in the blood, to which could be traced a wide variety of stable "traits," from intelligence to artistic ability to hysteria. Indeed, the full catalogue of traits attributable to "unit characters"—including physical traits, mental traits, and pathological traits—was what made the theory so comprehensive and thus so socially and politically significant. Here, indeed, was the key to all human potentiality.

Impassioned by the explanatory power of genetics in all fields of human activity, Davenport devoted himself to the problem of building a network of institutions to carry out eugenic research and to set policy. Davenport was able to attract a significant grant from the Carnegie Institution to found a station for genetic research at Cold Spring Harbor, Long Island, in 1904. The primary object of the station was to recast classical selection experiments along Mendelian lines, and to pursue "the analytic and experimental study of the causes of specific differentiation—of race change." And in 1910, Davenport established the Eugenics Record Office (ERO), whose small army of field-workers fanned out across the countryside to collect data on hereditary conditions such as "dementia," "shiftlessness," and "criminalism" and to gather information on the relatives of "defectives." Soon the installation at Cold Spring Harbor had become a clearinghouse for data and information generated by similar, though less spectacularly endowed organizations like the American Eugenics Society, the Eugenics Research Association, the Galton Society, the Institute of Family Relations, and the Race Betterment Foundation. The ERO's publication, *Eugenical News*, first appeared in 1916 under the editorship of Davenport and ERO Director Harry Laughlin.

Under Davenport's leadership, the Eugenics Section of the American Breeders' Association established ten research committees, devoted to areas such as Feeble-Mindedness, the Heredity of Criminality, Sterilization and Other Means of Eliminating Defective Germ Plasm, and the Heredity of Insanity. Of course there was a research committee on Immigration, too; and Davenport chose none other than Prescott Hall and Robert DeCourcy Ward of the Immigration Restriction League to head it. Given the figures on immigration during this period (8.7 million came ashore between 1901 and 1910), the immigration question was precisely the site where the eugenic stakes in innate character were the highest. "The idea of a 'melting-pot' belongs to a pre-Mendelian age," wrote Davenport. "Now we recognize that characters are inherited as units and do not readily break up."

In *Heredity in Relation to Eugenics* (1911), Davenport assessed the "unit characters" of recent immigrant groups and ventured his best estimations of what the enormous influx of South and East Europeans might mean for the genetic makeup of the country. The earliest European settlers, of course, represented the ideal: a host of royalist refugees had sought asylum in America after the execution of Charles I (1649), for instance, and "by this means was enriched a germ plasm which easily developed such traits as good manners, high culture, and the ability to lead in all social affairs." Although the new immigration represented quite a departure overall, not all the news was bad. Germans and Scandinavians, for instance, were free of genetic flaws. German unit characters included thrift, intelligence, and honesty; and Scandinavians inherited a "love of independence in thought, action, chastity, self-control of other sorts, and a love of agricultural pursuits."

The Irish, on the other hand, were in Davenport's estimation genetically given to "alcoholism, considerable mental defectiveness, and a tendency to tuberculosis." Even the Irish penchant for machine politics and "graft" was traceable to their blood inheritance. Italians, meanwhile, inherited a "tendency for crimes of personal violence"; and Jews' defective blood, seen most readily in a vicious, race-specific brand of individualism and materialism, set them directly on "the opposite extreme from the early English and more recent Scandinavian immigration with their ideals of community life in the open country, advancement by the sweat of their brow, and the uprearing of their families in the fear of God and the love of country." In the long run, Davenport fretted, not only would the infusion of new blood make the population "darker in pigmentation, [and] smaller in stature," but—and here was the real crux of the eugenicists' interest in germ plasm and characterology—the future American would be "more given to crimes of larceny, kidnapping, assault, murder, rape, and sex-immorality." Under then current rates of immigration, "the ratio of insanity in the population will rapidly increase."

On its "biologic side," therefore, the question became "How can we keep out defective germ plasm while we admit that which is strong?" What was needed, in Davenport's view, was a way "to classify immigrants for admission or rejection on the basis of the probable performance of their germ plasm." Here Davenport recommended that screening at Ellis Island approximate the methods of what was then becoming the chief mode of operation of the Eugenics Records Office, the eugenic "survey" of a person's background carried out by a field-worker trained not only in the administration of a detailed biological questionnaire, but in the minute observation and detection of hu-

man defects. This method, Davenport predicted with confidence, would allow "200,000 Europeans [per year] to our citizenship with equanimity"—as
against, say, the one million who had arrived in 1910.

"Eugenics has to do with racial development," wrote Davenport in the
preamble to his "Eugenics Credo" (1916). "It accepts the fact of differences
in people—physical differences, mental differences, differences in emotional
control. It is based on the principle that nothing can take the place of innate
qualities. While it recognizes the value of culture it insists that culture [i.e.,
cultivation] of a trait is futile, where the germs of the trait are absent." The
notion of "Americanization" in these eugenic terms was sentimental and un-
scientific. So-called assimilation could provide only a pitifully thin veneer
over the inborn unit characters that in all likelihood inadequately outfitted
rude Slavic or Italian peasants for the political and social requirements of life
in an industrial democracy. No race per se was dangerous, cautioned Davenport, "only those individuals whose somatic traits or germinal determiners
are . . . bad." But even so, race did offer useful clues as to the likely clusters
of such defective individuals.

Among the most important and popular expressions of the rising eugenic view of immigration was *The Passing of the Great Race* (1916) by Madison Grant, a New York eugenicist and officer of the American Museum of
Natural History. For Grant, too, "Moral, intellectual, and spiritual attributes
are as persistent as physical characters and are transmitted substantially un-
changed from generation to generation." *The Passing of the Great Race* is an
extended diatribe against Americans' democratic faith in environmentalism,
the "pathetic" belief, in Grant's view, that American institutions are hardy
enough to take in and transform the world's diverse populations. Grant did
not have the scientific training or competence of a Davenport or a Galton—
he had run no biological studies of hair color or correlation coefficients on
hereditary traits, that is—but he certainly fancied himself a legitimate scientific authority, and his work was indeed received that way in many quarters.

Grant, like William Z. Ripley, divided the peoples of Europe into three
races—Nordic, Alpine, and Mediterranean—whose physical, mental, and
emotional differences were as deeply seated as they were plainly observed.
The old-stock, Nordic American's liberal immigration policies, in his view,

were tantamount to "suicidal ethics which are exterminating his own race." Grant took issue with Franz Boas and others who emphasized the influence of environment and the potential for changes—even changes in physical characteristics—among newly arrived immigrant populations. What the melting pot (a biological—not a cultural—contrivance) really accomplishes, Grant argued, is best exemplified by "the racial mixture which we call Mexican, and which is now engaged in demonstrating its incapacity for self-government." Here, then, is the underlying peril of the "melting-pot" ideal: the mixture of two races, in the long run, yields a race reverting to the "lower type." "The cross between a white man and an Indian is an Indian; the cross between a white man and a negro is a negro; the cross between a white man and a Hindu is a Hindu; and the cross between any of the three European races and a Jew is a Jew."

This combination of immutable racial traits and an ineluctable tendency toward decline among any multiracial crosses spelled danger indeed for the republic. Like Davenport, Grant considered the new immigration to consist largely of "the weak, the broken, and the mentally crippled of all races drawn from the lowest stratum of the Mediterranean basin and the Balkans, together with hordes of the wretched, submerged populations of the Polish Ghettos." In cities like New York, "old stock" Americans were being "literally driven off the streets" by "swarms" of immigrants—primarily Polish Jews—who "adopt the language of the native American; they wear his clothes; they steal his name; and they are beginning to take his women, but they seldom adopt his religion or understand his ideals."

Predictably, Grant reserved harsh judgment for American blacks, too, who had become "a serious drag on civilization" from the moment "they were given the rights of citizenship and were incorporated in the body politic." But the inferior races of Europe posed the greater threat. Alpines and Mediterraneans were in fact "western extensions of an Asiatic subspecies and neither of them can be considered as exclusively European." But because of their nominal whiteness, unlike African Americans in the age of Jim Crow, these inferior race types had their run of the country's important social and economic arenas. Too proud to compete with such flotsam, Nordics were abandoning the field altogether: declining birthrates among old-stock

Americans were directly attributable to the new immigration; and the combination of the Nordics' decline and the Alpines' and Mediterraneans' frightening fecundity meant that the new, inferior immigrant was not only *dis*placing, but literally *re*placing the rightful heirs of the great republic. (The Nordic myth, it is worth noting, underwent significant revision during World War I. Grant's good friend Henry Fairfield Osborn now traced the blood of the Kaiser back to the "Wild Tartars," exposing the Germans as round-headed Tartar impostors to Nordic greatness.)

Specious as such scientific doctrines may sound today, eugenics was scarcely the province of an intellectual fringe or a cabal of crackpots. In various of its elements, eugenic thought was popular thought in the early decades of the twentieth century, disseminated—not least—by the vigorous debate over immigration restriction itself. But beyond its currency in political discourse, by the 1910s eugenics was the stuff of world's-fair exhibits like the Race Betterment booth at the Panama-California Exposition in San Diego, and eugenics had entered the curriculum of many major universities through the disciplines of biology, sociology, genetics, and psychology. Even Tarzan of the Apes (significantly, in a chapter titled "Heredity") demonstrated a gallantry and a subtle social grace toward Jane that represented "the hall-mark of his aristocratic birth, the natural outcropping of many generations of fine breeding, an hereditary instinct of graciousness which a lifetime of uncouth and savage training and environment could not eradicate." La, the high priestess of Opar in *The Return of Tarzan*, likewise explained the purity of her "strain" in eugenic terms: "For countless ages my foremothers were high priestesses—the sacred office descends from mother to daughter. Our husbands are chosen for us from the noblest in the land. The most perfect man, mentally and physically, is selected to be the husband of the high priestess."

By the 1920s, eugenic arguments had become standard fare in magazines like *Good Housekeeping* and *The Saturday Evening Post*, beneath headlines like "Danger That World Scum Will Demoralize America." As this headline suggests, the significance of the gene in the American imagination resided perhaps less in its power to explain the processes of human development than in its power to suggest how the various peoples of the world *ranked*, and to give name to the irretrievable biological chaos that they threatened for the republic.

Minds

Sciences of mind and mental capability predated eugenics by several decades. As early as the 1830s, pioneer craniometrist Samuel Morton occupied himself by measuring the amount of birdshot that could be poured into the specimen skulls representing "Caucasians," "Mongolians," "Malays," "Americans," and "Ethiopians." In 1839, his *Crania Americana* had rather predictably ranked the world's races (Teutonic family of the Caucasian group on top) according to their cranial capacities and hence their presumed capacities for mental effort. Even Herbert Spencer, whose brand of evolutionism drew upon Lamarck's notion of acquired physical characteristics, could remark with portent that, because of their disparate developmental paths and the cumulative effects of their disparate life experiences (read: racial experiences), Europeans might have "from ten to thirty cubic inches more brain than the Papuan." Recapitulation theory, too, by which the individual was presumed to pass through precisely the developmental stages of the species as a whole, lent Spencer and psychologists like G. Stanley Hall a suggestive lexicon for comparing mentalities. "The intellectual traits of the uncivilized," wrote Spencer, ". . . are traits recurring in the children of the civilized." That savages were "like children" was no longer merely a metaphorical flight, but was rigorously grounded in the hypothesis that "inferior" peoples were stranded in an ancestral stage of "superior" types, and that "civilized" children, unlike their primitive counterparts, literally *outgrew* their own "savagery."

Scientific measures of intelligence had become more feverish still by the turn of the century. From a purely economic standpoint, laypersons may have been most interested in scholarly conclusions regarding evolution and relative degrees or rates of development. It was the foreordained path of evolution, after all, that suggested that "waste spaces" might be made over into markets, that civilized peoples owed savages some guidance. But from a political standpoint, what mattered most was mind: as the engines of industry sent Americans out across the globe to forge new relationships with the world's peoples, as industry drew more and more foreign peoples ashore at Angel Island, Castle Garden, and Ellis Island, other questions arose. What were these peoples capable of, and how might they behave as participants in the nation's—or the empire's—governance?

The policy implications of scientific work on intelligence were plain enough. As race theorist Benjamin Kidd wrote in *The Control of the Tropics* (1898), the peoples of tropical Africa "represent the same stage in the history of the development of the race that the child does in the history of the development of the individual. The tropics will not, therefore, be developed by the natives themselves." In debates over imperialism as in debates over immigration, the key for Americans resided in the question of "fitness for self-government." In response to those who wondered whether God would have created a race of people actually incapable of self-government, Josiah Strong argued that modern science had shown "that races develop in the course of centuries as individuals do in years, and that an undeveloped race, which is incapable of self-government, is no more a reflection on the Almighty than is an undeveloped child who is incapable of self-government. The opinions of men who in this enlightened day believe that the Filipinos are capable of self-government because everybody is, are not worth considering." Intelligence, then, measured and coolly represented according to the doctrines of modern science, became inextricably linked to questions of imperialist economic development and the imperatives of colonial administration.

By the turn of the century, of course, there was already a fairly long history by which the question of intelligence had become entwined with questions of nativity and race. In his *Observations on an Ethnic Classification of Idiots* (1866), to cite just the most glaring instance, John Langdon Haydon Down—famed for his identification of "Down's syndrome"—found that "a very large number of congenital idiots are typical Mongols." Of one European specimen he wrote, "the boy's aspect is such that it is difficult to realize that he is the child of Europeans." Thus did "Mongoloidism" enter the lexicon of American psychology and contiguous fields—a medical metaphor for a package of presumed "Mongolian" racial traits. Similarly, Edward Drinker Cope, in *The Origin of the Fittest* (1887), had identified four groups of "lower" human forms by comparing them with the children of white males: non-white races, all women, South Europeans, and lower classes within the superior races. South Europeans were trapped in a more childlike, primitive state as adults than their Northern counterparts, according to Cope, because the South European climate imposed an earlier cessation of maturation.

The growing cottage industry in intelligence measurement at the turn of the century shared many things in common with the eugenics movement—personnel, for one thing, as eugenicists frequently turned their attention to problems of mental capacity, and as many psychologists and intelligence experts gravitated to the hereditarian models provided by genetics. Like eugenics, too, scholarship on intelligence had a direct bearing on the immigration question. (Cope's work on South Europeans, for instance, led him to agitate for a restrictive immigration policy on scientific grounds.) Indeed, the legal history of immigration and naturalization betrays a close affinity between restrictionism and various fields dedicated to the mind: classes excluded from immigration by law included lunatics and idiots (1882), epileptics and insane persons (1903), imbeciles and feeble-minded persons (1907), and "persons of constitutional psychopathic inferiority" (1917).

The first decade of the twentieth century, when Frenchman Alfred Binet abandoned the medical approach of craniometry in favor of a psychological approach to the measure of intelligence, represents a watershed in the study of human intellect. Binet developed an empirical test of the ability to reason that might render intellectual capacity as an easily calculated and comparable "mental age." (In 1912, a German psychologist developed the formula for IQ: the division of mental age by chronological age, times one hundred.) Binet himself saw the test's value not in its ability to rank pupils according to mental worth, but primarily in the gross distinctions it would enable between "normal" and "retarded" subjects. In the United States, however, a feverish round of intelligence testing began with the quick disposal of three of Binet's cardinal precepts: he had warned that (1) the test scores did not measure anything innate or permanent about a subject's "intelligence"; (2) the test was not a device for ranking normal children; and (3) low scores should not be used to mark anyone as innately incapable. In the general pro-eugenics climate, however, Americans rushed not only to sweep aside these caveats, but to wed the quest for a reliable measure of intelligence with a hereditarian notion of capability and its basis. Americans insisted upon the permanence and the innateness of intelligence as revealed by the Binet tests, and further insisted that the tests could be used to rank races and classes.

The key figure in this development of a hereditarian conception of intelligence was Henry Herbert Goddard, the expert on "feeble-mindedness" whose keen observations added the scientific category of "morons" to the earlier, two-tiered scheme of "idiots" and "imbeciles." (Morons, according to Goddard, were "high-grade defectives" who might actually be taught a thing or two.) It was Goddard who translated Binet into English and popularized the Binet scale in the United States. Like many other enthusiasts of Mendelian genetics, Goddard approached intelligence in a manner that had immediate consequences in the realm of social outlook and even social policy. "The people who are doing the drudgery," he wrote with certainty, "are, as a rule, in their proper places." As for policy, in *Feeble-Mindedness: Its Causes and Consequences* (1914), Goddard advanced the eugenic argument that "it is perfectly clear that no feeble-minded person should ever be allowed to marry or to become a parent." The moron's chief threat to society resided precisely in his or her *partial* abilities to function: unlike the "idiot," for example, the moron might take a job, meet a mate, and raise children (whose IQ of course could be no more promising). This prospect, multiplied by the masses, augured poorly indeed for the republic.

Here again, the immigration question was crucial. In 1912, Goddard was invited by the United States Public Health Service to administer the Binet tests to incoming immigrants at Ellis Island. His findings were eye-opening. As Goddard later reported in the *Journal of Delinquency*, "One can hardly escape the conviction that the intelligence of the average 'third class' [steerage] immigrant is low, perhaps of moron grade." Indeed, based on small samples ranging in number from sixteen to thirty-nine, he concluded that 83 percent of Jews disembarking at Ellis Island were feeble-minded; 80 percent of Hungarians; 79 percent of Italians; and 87 percent of Russians. In *Feeble-Mindedness*, although Goddard did not discuss the immigration question in any concentrated fashion, the mental condition of the foreign element constituted a running motif. Nationality was dutifully noted for each of the 327 cases of feeble-mindedness discussed in the volume; and out of 164 cases that Goddard attributed to hereditary causes, forty-nine were in people of foreign parentage and another seven were immigrants themselves. Of an additional thirty-five cases whose causes Goddard labeled as "probably hereditary," six were people of foreign parentage and three were immigrants.

Goddard's suspicion that the inspection and screening procedures at Ellis Island were flawed likewise peppered this discussion. The problem of immigration officials mistakenly passing "morons" or "imbeciles" is prevalent enough to warrant an index entry ("Immigration inspectors passed"); and several of the cases present cautionary tales on precisely this theme. One Italian "moron of the slow phlegmatic type" entered the country at age three, and "probably seemed normal at that time but the mother's defect also passed." A "cheerful imbecile of low grade" from Russia had been rightly detained at Castle Garden, but was later allowed entry when that immigration station burned down and there was no place to keep him. And another Russian defective, named Hattie, was permitted entry at age three; "whether her condition should have been detected at that time it is very difficult to say; [but] she is so very low grade now that it would seem as though she must have shown it even at that age."

The problem posed by immigration was twofold. First, since Goddard's debt to Davenport and the eugenicists was great (*Feeble-Mindedness* includes chapters on "Mendel's Law of Inheritance" and "Eugenics"), he assumed without question that the new immigrant races disproportionately carried undesirable unit characters like feeble-mindedness. Second, even for those whose mental capacities were normal, migration to a more complex society could pose some real challenges. In this respect, intelligence, though fixed, was still situational. As Goddard admitted, quoting Binet, "A French peasant may be normal in a rural community but feeble-minded in Paris." Similarly, an unskilled laborer from the Calabrian countryside or a peddler from the Russian shtetl, however "normal" in the Old World setting, might present the character of a moron in the vastly more complex social setting of a modern urban industrial center like New York or Chicago.

Though H. H. Goddard brought the Binet test to the United States, Lewis Terman popularized it. Terman, too, dispensed almost entirely with the idea that environmental influences might have some sway on intelligence. Children of "superior social classes," he argued, for example, scored higher on the tests "due, for the most part, to a superiority in original endowment." It was Terman who, in *The Measurement of Intelligence* (1916), gave the science of intelligence testing its most unabashedly racial spin. As he wrote of a group whose IQ he measured at 70 to 80, this level of intelligence

> *is very, very common among Spanish-Indian and Mexican families of the Southwest and also among negroes. Their dullness seems to be racial, or at least inherent in the family stocks from which they come. The fact that one meets this type with such extraordinary frequency among Indians, Mexicans, and negroes suggests quite forcibly that the whole question of racial differences in mental traits will have to be taken up anew and by experimental methods. The writer predicts that when this is done there will be discovered enormously significant racial differences in general intelligence, differences which cannot be wiped out by any scheme of mental culture. . . . There is no possibility at present of convincing society that they should not be allowed to reproduce, although from a eugenic point of view they constitute a grave problem because of their unusually prolific breeding.*

In defining the category "dull normals," Terman likewise used West European races as the standard: such defectives were "far enough below the actual average intelligence among races of western European descent that they cannot make normal school progress."

The racialist assumptions that were merely latent in much of the early writing on intelligence testing became more and more pronounced as the field developed. During World War I, Robert Yerkes, president of the American Psychological Association and chair of the Eugenics Research Association's Committee on Inheritance of Mental Traits, embarked on an ambitious project to measure the intelligence of the nation's two million draftees. Although his assumptions may have been little different from those of Goddard or Terman, Yerkes's results were cast in far more frankly racialist language and form. His 1921 report included a chapter on "Relation of Intelligence Ratings to Nativity," for instance; and he reported unequivocally that the groups at the bottom of the pyramid—Poles, Italians, Russians, Greeks, and Turks—produced many times the proportion of D scores that their English or Dutch counterparts did, and only a slim fraction of the A and B scores. Measured by a compilation either of their best scores or of their worst, Yerkes's testees of foreign birth scored about half as well (or failed about twice as often) as the white draft overall.

As a coda to this entire chapter in American psychometry, Carl Brigham, an assistant professor of psychology at Princeton, reanalyzed Yerkes's data and formulated an even stronger racialist statement on the new immigrants in *A Study of American Intelligence* (1923). According to Brigham, Yerkes's army tests presented "an opportunity for a national inventory of our own mental capacity, and the mental capacity of those we have invited to live with us." Nor was the picture pleasing: 46 percent of the Poles, over 42 percent of the Italians, and 39 percent of the Russians who took Yerkes's test, Brigham now announced, had scored at or below the Negro average. Although Brigham also found that, the longer an immigrant had lived in the United States, the higher he or she was likely to score—a finding that might easily have been marshaled toward an environmentalist argument—he chose, rather, to attribute the change to "a gradual deterioration of the class of immigrants . . . who came to this country in each succeeding five-year period since 1902." As the proportion of "Nordic" blood had decreased with each successive year of immigration, in other words, so had the aggregate IQ of the immigrants.

"There can be no doubt," Brigham pronounced, "that recent history has shown a movement of inferior peoples or inferior representatives of peoples to this country." Since 1901, about ten million "Alpine and Mediterranean types" had entered the country. Given their average performance on the tests, and allowing for a return rate of roughly one-third to three-eighths back to the Old World, the United States had willingly embraced "over 2,000,000 immigrants below the average negro." Beyond this problem of the sheer numerical onslaught of undesirable types, moreover, was the mounting evidence of racial "admixture" among Nordic, Alpine, and Mediterranean types, for mixture could only dull the intellectual peaks of the higher types. The 1920 census showed over seven million native-born whites of mixed parentage, according to Brigham, "a fact which indicates clearly the number of crosses between the native born stock and the European importations." Striking a familiar eugenic chord, Brigham asserted that there was "no reason why legal steps should not be taken which would ensure a continuously progressive upward evolution." The following year, Congress took precisely such a step by passing the Johnson-Reed Immigration Act, which was calculated to curtail vastly the influx of undesirable racial types from Eastern and Southern Europe and Asia.

Significantly, the same exposition that became a popular forum for the Race Betterment Foundation and the program of eugenics in 1915 also served as an early forum for the popularization of intelligence testing. Significantly, too, the exposition itself was a celebration of the opening of the Panama Canal and all that would portend for the expanding American commercial empire and for the mingling of peoples through the dynamics of world communication, travel, and trade. It was at San Diego's Panama-California Exposition, before the Education Congress, that Lewis Terman unveiled "The Stanford Revision and Extension of the Binet Scale." His forthcoming book would demonstrate, he announced, that a correlation between race and intelligence could indeed be proved.

Until Yerkes and Brigham came along in the late 1910s and early '20s, race and nationality actually took up but a small corner of the writing on intelligence and inheritance. The immigration question occupied only a few pages of Davenport's *Heredity in Relation to Eugenics*, a single paragraph in Terman's *Measurement of Intelligence*, and scattered snatches in Goddard's *Feeble-Mindedness.* But racial assumptions did lie at the very core of the investigation of intelligence, however scarcely they were articulated; and, more important, these studies themselves did become central to the popular generic conception of "the immigrant." If the inferior European races took up no more than an occasional page in these studies of hereditary merit, that is, these scholars' findings on hereditary merit fully dominated American discussion of who exactly were the people who daily thronged the gangplanks at Ellis Island.

As Edward Said has remarked, "There is never interpretation, understanding, and then knowledge where there is no *interest.*" Not only were these branches of the mounting knowledge industry entwined with one another and with discourses of immigration and nativism, but so were they entwined with the imperial project of exploration and acquisition. Researchers in anthropology, for instance, rode into the "dark" regions of the globe on the machinery of empire, just as empires themselves made use of anthropological or ethnographic "knowledge." James Frazer self-consciously provided his compatriots with a tour of the peoples "of rudimentary culture" whose fate had fallen "in the hands" of "our imperial race." Franz Boas, perhaps more responsibly, advocated the establishment of an Oriental school at Columbia University because "our commerce and political intercourse with Eastern Asia are rapidly expanding." New circumstances required "a better knowledge of the people and of the countries with which we are dealing." "Most important of all in the present juncture [1903]," Boas added, "would seem to be that opportunity be given for acquiring knowledge in matters pertaining to the Philippine Islands."

Political implications suffused the scholarly pursuit. "A savage brought up in a cultivated society," commented one writer in *Popular Science Monthly* in 1903, "will not only retain his dark skin, but is likely also to have the incoherent mind of his race." The very questions of cultural diversity and relative intelligence were driven by the possibilities for contact—either the importation of a "savage" into "cultivated society," or the export of cultivated social conditions and the trappings of the modern to the savage climes of Africa or Oceania. The incoherence of mind—whether the "savage" Malay's or the dull Irishman's—suddenly mattered so much precisely because peoples were now finding one another and coming together at such an accelerated pace. Presenting cases of "borderline efficiency" (commensurate with Goddard's "morons"), Lewis Terman noted that among the laboring classes "there are thousands like them. They are the world's 'hewers of wood and drawers of water.' . . . These boys are uneducable beyond the merest rudiments of training. No amount of school instruction will ever make them intelligent voters or capable citizens in the true sense of the word." A sobering thought for a nation whose polity had so recently come to include over twenty million newly arrived hewers of wood from the most "backward" regions of Europe, Asia, and the Americas.

In *Human Efficiency and Levels of Intelligence* (1920), Henry Herbert Goddard devoted an entire chapter to "Democracy and Mental Levels." Summing up the high civic stakes of recent findings on human achievement, Goddard asked, "Can we hope to have a successful democracy when the average mentality [of the populace] is thirteen?" The prospects turned out to be not so bad, in Goddard's estimation, as long as there was some careful political and social engineering from above. "In a democracy every man is supposed to do his part," he wrote. "What that part is can only be determined by knowing his mental capacity." Intelligence testing, that is, would show the way. Democracy is indeed possible even among low-grade defectives as long as "there is a sufficiently large group of people of high intelligence to control the situation."

Unlike his earlier work at Ellis Island, *Human Efficiency* made the case without reference to race. But clearly, given the trends across the disciplines—including anthropology, historiography, sociology, psychology, and genetic biology—such thinking about mentality and democracy was going to have potent implications for the view of foreign peoples, whether they resided on American soil or on distant shores. The study of comparative cultures at once derived from and fed into American discussions of global economic relationships—the material conditions of savage societies, their needs, their prospects for "advancement," and the inherent right by which Euro-Americans might step in to make better use of the unimproved "waste spaces" that the savage occupied but in no way possessed. Contemporary studies of genetic makeup and native intelligence, on the other hand, derived from and fed into discussions of politics. What were the inherent capacities of the world's peoples? To what extent could they be assimilated to complex forms of social and political organization? And what were the prospects for their governance, either as immigrants at home or as colonized subjects abroad?

part three

Politics

The machinery of empire: "Primary Pupils in a Municipal School, Manila." The school itself and the visual conventions of its depiction were both important to the justification and maintenance of U.S. hegemony in the Philippines. *National Geographic*, 1905

COURTESY OF THE NATIONAL GEOGRAPHIC SOCIETY

· · · · · · · · ·

In 1917, *National Geographic* ran a series of plates devoted to "mother love" around the world. Beneath a "Bedouin Mother and Child" the caption read, "The father of this little nomad may be a warlike bandit with a cloudy notion of property rights and other details of the civilized code; his mother a simple daughter of the desert with a childish curiosity and fondness for gaudy trinkets, but her babe has the divine heritage of mother love as truly as the most fortunate child of our own land." Beneath a woman in New Guinea carrying a baby in a sling: "This device is at a disadvantage when compared with an American cradle, but it is a touching evidence of maternal inventiveness and industry at work for baby's safety even in the South Seas." And beneath a plate depicting "Motherhood in the Philippines," this baby "doesn't know that, after his mother, Uncle Sam is his best friend. Had he belonged to an earlier generation his childhood would have been spent at work in the fields until he was old enough to join father in head-hunting."

Although the benign tone seems to say that underneath it all the diverse members of the human family are really quite alike, the commentary moves inexorably from the absence of a "civilized code," to the comparative "disadvantage" of the primitive's industrial arts, to one savage baby's supreme good fortune in having been rescued by a beneficent foreign state from the lifeways of his parents. In much of the writing on foreign climes—both popular and academic—there may be a gently nagging wistfulness about the simple naturalism of the premodern world, but finally there is a dead certainty in the verity and value of Western progress. The world, it turns out, is mostly populated by bandits and head-hunters whose retarded development is self-evident; the necessity of Western stewardship over the rest of the world is the only conclusion to be drawn. As refracted through the prism of Gilded Age and Progressive Era information industries, various foreign peoples' "cloudy notions of property rights" or the "disadvantageous" devices of their material culture inevitably pointed toward a set of propositions in the realm of politics and governance.

It is not merely coincidental that, as William McKinley embarked upon a policy of imperialism in the Philippines, he employed a vocabulary that linked this exercise in "uplift" across the Pacific to the acculturation of immigrants within U.S. borders. His phrase "benevolent assimilation" is wonderfully suggestive not only of the power of paternalism to mask violent social and political realities, but also of the affinities in American discourse between subject peoples abroad and immigrants at home—problem populations whose "difference" stood in the way of successful republican citizenship. Racial discourse in both cases rendered "assimilation" as urgent as it was doubtful. The question became, how would the United States maintain its economic relations with these peoples as consumers abroad and workers at home without being degraded by their "savage" presence? How would Americans benevolently assimilate these diverse peoples without becoming tainted by their patent inferiority in the process?

Part III examines the twin discourses of naturalization and empire. Republican ideology provided the terms by which foreigners were understood, and yet republicanism itself was constituted by boundaries of public virtue marked off by these same foreign peoples. Chapter 5, "Accents of Menace," examines heated American discussion of immigration, not as a supply of cheap labor for the nation's industry, but as a supply of future citizens. In the figure of the radical-as-un-American, of course, the two questions were joined. But antiradicalism occupied only one corner of a broader debate over "the foreign element" in America. Throughout this debate, immigrants were measured against idealized republican virtues of wisdom, self-possession, and forbearance. By their shortfall—as theorized ethnologically, and as evidenced in the conduct of their urban political machines—they highlighted the prevalence of these virtues among Americans of the "older stock," and so helped to constitute the very notion of proper Americanism.

Chapter 6, "Children of Barbarism," traces parallel ideas of citizenship and virtue as expressed on questions of intervention, empire, or annexation in regions like Samoa, Hawaii, the Philippines, Cuba, and Puerto Rico. If racial notions of a superior Anglo-Saxon peoplehood justified policies of imperial conquest abroad, so did they generate considerable anxiety about the fate of a free republic that had taken on too many "undesirable" elements. Like immigrants, the "natives" in America's far-flung empire tested the bounds of ideal citizenship and taxed the concept of fitness for self-government. Ultimately, like American Indians in the conquered West and African Americans in the post-Reconstruction South, they were disqualified from the constitutional principle of the consent of the governed.

As long as the immigrants—whether Celtic, Slavic, Hebrew, or Mongolian—were thought to fall well short of Anglo-Saxon genius, their presence aroused fears about the smooth functioning of the republic. As long as savages were thought to embody "the minds of children and the passions of adults," in Spencer's formulation, they were no candidates for republican self-rule—nor, in fact, did they have any rights that the United States was bound to respect. If the economics of the era brought these diverse millions under the sway of U.S. power or direct governance both within and without U.S. borders, the information industries' dominant ethnological images suggested how perilous this expansion of the polity might be. Among the mainsprings of the period's politics, then, was a tension between the imperatives of the market, which swallowed more and more peoples no matter who, and the imperatives of republican government, which set a high premium indeed upon the exclusionary notions of civic virtue and "fitness for self-government."

Accents of Menace: Immigrants in the Republic

> Vast additions have been made to our population . . . to whom American political and social ideals appeal but faintly, if at all, and who carry in their very blood traditions which give universal suffrage an air of menace to many of the things which civilized men hold most dear.
>
> —The Nation, *1877*

THE FAVORED METAPHORS for American diversity—melting pot, mosaic, potato salad, stew—all tend to present the relationship among the nation's peoples as neutral and even-handed. Pleasing though they may be, such celebratory conceits evade the power differentials, the coercion, the tensions, and the conflict that have characterized the American social order since the era of European settlement. What room does a clever metaphor like "melting pot" or "mosaic" leave to reckon seriously with the animosities marshaled under the banner of racialism or nativism? With legal issues such as eligibility versus ineligibility for citizenship? With historical facts of racial hierarchy, conquest, or slavery? With the differential political trajectories charted by citizenship through the coerced processes of slavery and emancipation, say, versus citizenship through voluntary migration and naturalization? Madison Grant captured the contests for power inherent in American diversity from one side of the social divide; figures like Horace Kallen, Mary Antin, and W.E.B. Du Bois caught it from the other. Americanization ought not to be a crushing imperative to conform, wrote Kallen; the whole point of democracy was not to conceal or suppress "difference" but, rather, to grant diverse peoples the freedom to cultivate their particular "ancestral endowments." Thus questions of assimilation and pluralism (or, for Grant, invasion and unassimilability) could never be fully divorced from questions of power and its disposition.

The peoples of the United States did not come together in a simple process of politically neutral adding-and-stirring. Some entered the polity willfully through migration, others through enslavement and eventual liberation, and still others through conquest, dispossession, and absorption. As different peoples have entered the polity along widely differing lines, so have they enjoyed or suffered widely divergent statuses. Questions about who is in fact "fit for self-government" have been crucial to the history of American diversity in the making from the American Revolution onward.

This query had gender at its very root; among the core contradictions of citizenship in the United States is that while *in*dependence was seen initially as a prerequisite for fit citizenship, *dependence*—upon either husband or father—continued to be among the hallmarks of proper womanhood, and none seemed so destabilizing to the social order as the independent woman. Womanly virtue thus disqualified civic virtue, and vice versa. The question of fitness for self-government most often turned out to be a racial query as well: the Revolution may have altered the lines of authority radically from the Crown to "the people," but it left untouched various Enlightenment assumptions about who "the people" properly ought to be. This experiment in republican government demanded an extraordinary moral character in the people—it called for a polity that was disciplined, virtuous, self-sacrificing, productive, far-seeing, wise—traits that were all racially inscribed in eighteenth-century Euro-American thought. (The definition of the word "Negro" in an encyclopedia published in Philadelphia in 1790, for instance, included "idleness, treachery, revenge, debauchery, nastiness, and intemperance.") If the external authority of monarchy was to be loosened, members of the polity themselves were going to have to exhibit truly fabulous powers of self-control, self-possession, and often self-denial. And, according to Euro-American thinking at the time, "race" was one key to the distribution of these virtues and so to the question of fitness for self-government. Thus even free blacks were most often denied the full rights of citizenship; and thus the nation's first naturalization law limited the prospect of naturalized citizenship to "free white persons."

Nor had the racial imperatives of self-government faded by the late nineteenth and early twentieth centuries. Thomas Bailey Aldrich, the New England poet and former editor of *The Atlantic Monthly*, looked over the bedraggled immigrants disembarking at the docks of East Boston in 1892 and, economically combining the languages of criminality, disease, and race, pronounced upon their undesirability. These "jailbirds, professional murderers, amateur lepers ('moon-eyed' or otherwise) and human gorillas," he wrote a friend, "should be closely questioned at our gates." That same year, he composed a fretful poem on "The Unguarded Gates," a nativist repudiation of the open-armed magnanimity voiced in Emma Lazarus's "New Colossus." "Wide open and unguarded stand our gates," Aldrich warned,

> And through them passes a wild motley throng—
> Men from the Volga and the Tartar steppes,
> Featureless figures from the Hoang-Ho,
> Malayan, Scythian, Teuton, Kelt, and Slav,
> Flying the Old World's poverty and scorn;
> These bringing with them unknown gods and rites,
> Those, tiger passions, here to stretch their claws.
> In street and alley what strange tongues are these,
> Accents of menace alien to our air,
> Voices that once the Tower of Babel knew!

By the 1910s, as we have seen, such dimly articulated racial fears of "wild motley throngs" and "human gorillas" had become a highly codified science. San Francisco's Panama-Pacific International Exposition in 1915 not only popularized current anthropological, psychometric, and eugenic thinking on questions of race and the relative merits of the world's peoples, but brought these directly to bear on the issue of American diversity and the prospects for smooth governance. In addition to the Race Betterment booth, whose aim was to "present the evidence of race deterioration, [and] to show the possibility of race improvement," the U.S. Department of Labor exhibit in the Palace of Mines and Metallurgy overtly addressed the issue of immigration and the changing (read: deteriorating) face of the American polity. An electrical diagram depicted the waves of immigration between 1820 and 1914, and the exhibit supplied "statistical facts for 1914 as to races of alien arrivals; occupations of those admitted; routes of entry followed by admitted aliens; distribution of persons admitted; causes of exclusion; and arrests and deportations by classes." A motion picture about Ellis Island underscored the general sense of the exhibit that, from the point of view of biology, the population of the country was changing, and it was changing decidedly for the worse. The scientific discourses of anthropology, psychometry, biology, and the like—the work of scholars like H. H. Goddard, Charles Davenport, and Lewis Terman—thus bore directly on questions of fit citizenship and the nation's political prospects in the face of the new immigration.

Cogs in the Machine

The first large-scale electoral confrontation between natives and immigrants in the United States occurred in the mid-nineteenth century and after, when a number of forces converged to produce a new political creature on the American scene, the boss and his machine. In *The American Commonwealth* (1893) James Bryce described the "droves of squalid men" who, accompanied by a ward agent, marched before the magistrate to register to vote, though they looked as though they were but fresh from steerage. The immigrants "obtain votes after three or four years' residence at most (often less)," Bryce worried, "but they are not fit for the suffrage. . . . Neither from Central Europe nor from Ireland do they bring much knowledge of the methods of free government, and from Ireland they bring a suspicion of all government."

Machine politics had burst upon the national consciousness in the 1860s and '70s, amid revelations of the rapacious spirit and the fiscal irresponsibility of William Marcy Tweed's Democratic ring in New York. (Tweed allowed the city's municipal debt to increase from $30 million to $90 million in just four years in the late 1860s—a sure way to attract attention—while party regulars enjoyed enormous kickbacks on various city contracts.) But in fact the basic patterns of the rising style of boss politics predated the Civil War.

In cities like New York, it was at mid-century that the machine model began to take shape, as the expanded franchise, rapid industrialization and urban growth, massive immigration, revised city charters, and greatly expanded governmental functions all converged to alter the rules of municipal politics.

Machine politics has long been associated with the Irish, though the timing of Irish immigration, rather than Irishness itself, may provide a more useful key to the genesis of the new urban politics. The relatively high percentage of English-speakers among the Irish immigrants did give this group a distinct edge over other arrivals in gaining access to the New World political arena, as did the Irish premigration experience—however bitter—with Anglo-Saxon political traditions and institutions. Catholic Emancipation in Ireland in 1829, on what also turned out to be the eve of a period of massive Irish exodus, had granted some Irish immigrants firsthand experience not only in the general business of political participation but in the more specific and terribly important business of using the ballot as a weapon of the weak. Since the poor must always outnumber the wealthy under capitalism, the Irish peasantry and tenancy discovered, the inequities of the social order themselves generated certain natural advantages in the electoral order: once they had the right to vote and hold office, the Catholic working class and poor relied on their sheer numbers to wage a campaign to wrest a modicum of political power from their wealthier neighbors.

Premigration experience may have helped, then; but timing was still everything. In the 1840s and after, as the Irish pulled ashore in America in phenomenal numbers, they settled in cities whose mechanisms of governance were newly ripe for capture by a proletarian bloc. The franchise had just been expanded to include the propertyless, first of all; and so, as the Irish enjoyed the legal status of "free white persons" under reigning naturalization law, they were well placed to take advantage of universal white male suffrage. But more than this, they were arriving in cities whose sharpening class and ethnic segregation, geographic schemes of electoral representation, structures of government, and expanding municipal functions all conspired to repay precisely the brands of political reciprocity and allegiance that in retrospect appear so critical to the functioning of the classic machine. Crowded into precincts and wards whose class (and often ethnic) homogeneity easily translated into a harmony of political interests, immigrant voters were able to elect their compatriots to numerous posts in city government. In the days before civil-service reform, those posts, in their turn, could be used to generate further appointments for friends and relatives in the expanding public-employment sector that characterized the industrializing city—street cleaning and ditch-digging; policing and schoolteaching; the construction of streets, municipal buildings, parks, and trolley lines. Dispensing such concrete favors in exchange for votes, the machine could generate astonishing rates of loyalty: public coffers in effect bought votes for the next election. "Is it any wonder that [the Irishman] has a tender spot in his heart for old New York," asked party functionary George Washington Plunkitt, "when he is on its salary list the mornin' after he lands?"

The machine functioned, then, by a peculiar combination of iron discipline and a flexible, glad-handed approach to patronage jobs and municipal monies. Accurate and steady communication and unbending obedience flowed up the chain of command from block captains to precinct captains to district or ward captains to the boss himself. Nowhere in American politics has there been such a tight, efficient web of disciplined face-to-face relationships, reaching from the alderman's or mayor's office down to every single block of an urban working-class ward. A good boss knew the vote of virtually every voter in his bailiwick, and loyalties were both repaid and reinforced with a job laying rail for the city trolley, a goose at Christmastime, or an influential visit to the city jail to help get a brother or a cousin out of trouble. "The great mass of people are interested in only three things—" said Boston boss Martin Lomasney philosophically, "food, clothing, and shelter. A politician in a district like mine sees to it that his people get these things. If he does, then he doesn't have to worry about their loyalty and support." One German ward boss in Detroit summed up his party's platform, "Bread, meat und coal, vat in h——l else do ve vant?"

Recalling a campaign to unseat a deeply entrenched ward boss in Chicago, reformer Jane Addams had to admit that she and her idealistic allies had failed for some time to comprehend the realities of a neighborhood where "politics deal so directly with getting a job and earning a living." "We soon discovered," she wrote, "that approximately one out of every five voters in the nineteenth ward at that time held a job dependent upon the good will of the alderman." The other four out of every five voters, one might surmise, were either friends or relatives of the one machine-beholden patronage worker. In an 1898 article for *The Outlook*, Addams had enumerated some of the other services performed by the machine on behalf of its newest citizens: "The Alderman . . . bails out his constituents when they are arrested, or says a good word to the police justice when they appear before him for trial; uses his 'pull' with the magistrate when they are likely to be fined for a civil misdemeanor, or sees what he can do to 'fix matters up' with the State's attorney when the charge is really a serious one." She noted, "Primitive people, such as the south Italian peasants who live in the Nineteenth Ward, deep down in their hearts admire nothing so much as the good man." These ward bosses, from the immigrant perspective, patently represented "good men." Under these circumstances, an exceedingly close relationship developed between immigrants and political bosses, one consequence of which was the increasing centrality of immigrant institutions like the neighborhood saloon to the daily business of municipal governance. As muckraking journalist Lincoln Steffens caustically remarked in *The Shame of the Cities* (1904), a practical joker nearly emptied the House of Delegates in St. Louis by paying a boy to rush into the assembly room shouting, "Mister, your saloon is on fire!"

The pattern varied from one city to the next, but between the 1860s and the New Deal some version of this machine model reigned in cities across the country—Boston, New York, Pittsburgh, Philadelphia, Chicago, Detroit, Jersey City, St. Louis, Kansas City, San Francisco, San Antonio. Its chief ingredients everywhere were universal male suffrage; an ethnically and class-segregated urban geography whose representative scheme assured that Irish working-class neighborhoods, for example, could send Irish candidates to city assembly; an expanding municipal treasury and store of patronage jobs, with which to repay the loyalties of the faithful in a strict and unambiguous favors-for-votes arrangement; and a tight chain of communication and command, by which the needs of the city's residents could be administered.

And immigrants. Indeed, chief among the ingredients for boss politics was the steady stream of potential voters from Europe. "Ward politics is built up out of racial, religious, industrial affiliations," wrote Boston reformer Robert Woods; "out of blood kinship; out of childhood associations, youthful camaraderie, general neighborhood sociability." The Tweed scandal itself had convinced many that the mass of immigrants now threatened the republic—"Irish Catholic despotism rules the City of New York, the Metropolis of free America," shuddered the *Times.* The reformist Citizens' Association announced that New York had become but a "common sewer" for the "dregs" of Europe.

This impression would intensify in the latter decades of the century. The overwhelming number of immigrants, whose needs were many in these days before the welfare state and whose ethnic allegiances were easily tapped— this army of foreign-born voters proved both the reason for being and the mode of operation of the big-city machine. According to the 1890 census, immigrants and their children constituted as much as 70 or 80 percent of the population in Milwaukee, New York, Chicago, Detroit, and Buffalo; and they accounted for well over 60 percent in San Francisco, St. Paul, Cleveland, Jersey City, St. Louis, Cincinnati, Brooklyn, Pittsburgh, Boston, Rochester, Newark, and Providence. It was the foreign-born population, with its critical amalgam of economic need, social cohesion, and numerical supremacy, that kept the machine running, in some cities well into the twentieth century. Everywhere the machine's pantheon of heroes included names that could only conjure up images of the Ellis Island throngs: Hugh O'Brien, Patrick Collins, John "Honey Fitz" Fitzgerald, and James Michael Curley (Boston); "Honest John" Kelly, "Slippery Dick" Connolly, Richard Croker, and Charles Murphy (New York); "Hinky Dink" Kenna, "King" Michael McDonald, and "Bath House John" Coughlin (Chicago); Henry Kelly (San Antonio); "Uncle Henry" Ziegenhein (St. Louis); "Big Jim" Pendergast, Tom Pendergast, and Joe Shannon (Kansas City); Chris Magee and William Flinn (Pittsburgh); Abraham Ruef and Eugene Schmitz (San Francisco).

Lincoln Steffens cautioned that the American fixation on boss politics as an immigrant or alien problem actually got in the way of realistic solutions. When he had set out to review the political scene in urban America, he wrote in 1904, one New Yorker had predicted that he would "find that the

Irish, the Catholic Irish, were at the bottom of it everywhere." But Steffens found corruption in the German city of St. Louis and the Scandinavian city of Minneapolis as well. " 'Ah, but they are all foreign populations,' " was the reply. He then found similar corruption in Philadelphia, the "purest American community of all"; New York and Chicago, "both mongrel-bred" cities, at that time represented veritable triumphs of reform and good government. "The 'foreign element' excuse is one of the hypocritical lies that save us from the clear sight of ourselves," Steffens warned.

Few among the native upper and middle classes, however, shared Steffens's view. Reformer William Allen White described Tammany boss Richard Croker as a "prosimian bulk of bone and sinew—a sort of human megatherium who has come crashing up from the swamps splashed with the slime of pre-Adamite wickedness!" It was this view—dovetailing as it did with the general view of immigrants as decidedly unrepublican simian brutes—that more often characterized native discussion of the machine and its followers. Beginning with Thomas Nast's *New York Times* cartoons of the Tweed Ring and its apelike Irish pawns in the early 1870s, political activity and discussion in opposition to the machine carried a sharp anti-immigrant edge. If the specter of machine corruption never did register as fiercely in the nativist imagination as issues of job competition and foreign radicalism, still it was in the context of the immigrants' increasing electoral power and its perceived abuses that Michigan voters, for example, voted to disenfranchise aliens by a constitutional amendment in 1894.

As municipal electoral battles took shape in one city after another across the country, as machines squared off against reform coalitions for city-council seats and the like, the geographical lines that described the contest (central neighborhoods versus the suburban periphery) most often coincided with class lines and ethnocultural lines as well (working class versus upper and middle classes; immigrants versus natives; Catholics versus Protestants; wets versus drys). Municipal reform in this period, then, assumed a distinct pattern that urban historian Howard Chudacoff has called "disciplining the center," whereby not only the political practices but also many of the social customs and cultural values of the immigrant working classes in the city's inner industrial wards became fair game for native reformers' zealous attentions. As political conflict between periphery and center took shape in Cincinnati in the 1880s, for instance, one member of an old, pre–Civil War family denounced the German and Irish residents at the city's core as "illiterates, full of superstition and semi-barbarism," who regarded "progressive civilization" as an "encroachment upon their superior rights, independence, and personal liberty." Cultural questions such as temperance or Sabbatarianism, which often lay at the heart of a given locale's political divisions, became part of the general question of the requisites of sound municipal governance.

Thus, even if Progressive reformers relied on a universalist language of governmental "efficiency" and the quest for the "public good," some elements of their program smacked of a class and ethnic particularism no less striking than that of the boss and his compatriot/clients. The apocalyptic tones that often accompanied Progressive discussion of the urban center hint at the almost missionary righteousness that reformers brought to their struggle to wrest control of the city out of the hands of unreliable foreigners. As Judge William Howard Taft predicted (incorrectly, it turned out) at what seemed to him the dawn of a new reformist day in Cincinnati, "The clouds are beginning to break over this Sodom of ours and the sun of decency is beginning to dispel the moral miasma that has rested on us now for so many years." It was in this context that even a sympathetic reformer like Jane Addams might comment upon the disposition of the "primitive peoples" at the urban core and their blissful dependence upon the corrupt boss and his henchmen.

A number of Progressive reforms ultimately did chip away at the power of the bosses, though many machines were able to adapt and to survive well beyond the Progressive Era. (Indeed, with some credibility, the Cook County machine in Chicago could brag of delivering Illinois—and so the U.S. presidency—to the Democrats as late as 1960.) The most significant and common antiboss measures included civil-service reform, whose abstracted mechanisms for discovering "merit" made it far more difficult for politicians to dole out patronage jobs on the basis of party loyalty alone; the institution of the Australian (secret) ballot, which limited machines' ability to track and enforce voter loyalty in the polling place; various redistricting schemes, including "at large," citywide electoral districts, which diluted the concentrated power of ethnic voting blocs; and frankly antidemocratic registration requirements, whose red tape and paper slowed the march of the machine's army of immigrant voters (living as well as dead). Historical forces, too, such as immigration restriction in the 1920s and the commandeering of welfare functions by the federal government in the 1930s, dealt blows to the machine in its twilight.

In the era of its reign, however, far from toppling the republic, as many reformers feared, the machine performed many crucial functions in integrating the mass of immigrants into the American polity. Machine politics assimilated the newcomers to practices of civic participation that were often well out of their ken in the Old World—even despite the corruption involved, the invitation to join a political party and to become an active voter was no small thing to generations for whom "politics" had generally referred to a sealed arena reserved for distant nobles. Machines gave a human face to the abstract relationship between citizen and state as well. Though no one would call the process fair—machines most often favored one ethnic group over the others, and sometimes brutally so—bosses did funnel important goods and services to the populations who most needed them before the birth of the modern welfare state; and they ushered unskilled workers into suitable positions in the public sector in the era before public-works programs. Though men participated in machine politics more directly and benefited more clearly than women, ward politicians understood the *household* as the basic unit of immigrant social organization, and they tended to approach their voter/clients with their familial responsibilities, ties, and needs firmly in mind. As the South End boss of Boston Martin Lomasney once told Lincoln Steffens, "There's got to be in every ward somebody that any bloke can come to—no matter what he's done—and get help. Help, you understand, none of your law and justice, but help."

Thus, as a nascent social-welfare agency at a moment when the urban working classes and poor were exceptionally vulnerable, the machine may well have *preserved* the institutions of the republic by dampening the wrath of the so-called dangerous classes against the rapacious and unrepentant capitalism of the turn-of-the-century elite. Remarking on the "nationalizing

influence" of party politics in the 1890s, a most optimistic observer identified the machine as the very "secret" of "the powerful solvent influence which
American civilization exerts upon the enormous deposits of alien population
thrown upon this country by the torrent of emigration." It was the truly democratic openness of the machine above all else that might transform the
immigrant masses into reliable republican citizens, in this view. But for
most, the unsavory workings of the urban machine merely provided concrete
evidence of the period's broader ethnological certainty: that some peoples
and races were simply unfit for self-government.

An Ethnological Animal Show

"If universal suffrage has worked ill in our cities, as it certainly has," wrote
James Russell Lowell in "Democracy" (1884), "this has been mainly because
the hands that wielded it were untrained to its use. There the election of a
majority of the trustees of the public money is controlled by the most ignorant and vicious of a population which has come to us from abroad, wholly
unpracticed in self-government and incapable of assimilation by American
habits and methods."

The phrase "incapable of assimilation" carries with it an air of the irre-
versible and innate, but others were even more straightforward about the
hereditarian, racial dimension of this unfitness for self-government. In the
early 1880s, one Midwestern congressman warned that democratic governance required a homogenous population; republican institutions surely
would not flourish in the midst of an "ethnological animal show." For others,
the language and logic of ethnology became indispensable for assessing the
merits of the various immigrant groups themselves. Nativism in this period
increasingly relied upon the language and logic of biology, from the racialized republicanism that characterized the anti-Chinese campaign in the
1870s, to that cult of Anglo-Saxonism called the Immigration Restriction
League in the 1890s, to the frank eugenic program of the American Breeders' Association and the Galton Society in the early decades of the twentieth
century. The convergence of racialism and republicanism governing the immigration debate was expressed most starkly in an exchange on the floor of

Congress in the early 1920s, as that body debated a racialist immigration-restriction bill that was soon to become law. "Is it the gentleman's idea," one congressman asked another, "that the primary object of this bill is to discriminate against certain people?"

> MR. O'CONNOR of New York: I believe that the committee and the proponents of this bill believe that, in order to preserve the ideals of this country, it is necessary to discriminate against certain races.
>
> MR. MACLAFFERTY: That is fairly put. Would you discriminate against Asiatic races?
>
> MR. O'CONNOR of New York: I believe it is a well-founded tradition of America.
>
> MR. MACLAFFERTY: Is it discrimination?
>
> MR. O'CONNOR of New York: It is.
>
> MR. MACLAFFERTY: Is it necessary?
>
> MR. O'CONNOR of New York: It may be.
>
> MR. MACLAFFERTY: Is necessary discrimination ever justified?
>
> MR. O'CONNOR of New York: Sometimes.
>
> MR. MACLAFFERTY: Very good.

The idea of American citizenship, of course, was racialized at its core and at its inception. The significance and the ramifications of the "free white persons" clause of the 1790 naturalization act cannot be overestimated. Overtly racial objections to incoming immigrants were advanced as early as mid-century, when a consensus gradually formed as to the undesirability of the Irish—the first non-Anglo-Saxon group whose frightful numbers suggested a full-fledged political crisis for the receiving country. Couched in a racial language of "Irishism" or "Celtism," the argument was put forward by patrician natives that the immigrants were "constitutionally incapable of intelligent participation in the governance of the nation." The Massachusetts State Board of Charities, for example, identified the immigrants' "inherited organic imperfection, vitiated constitution, or *poor stock*" as the chief cause of their pauperism and public dependency. In the wake of the Emancipation Proclamation, one writer in *The Atlantic Monthly* argued, "it is impossible to name any standard of requisites for the full rights of citizenship which will give the vote to the Celt and exclude the negro." And in response to the Fenian raid on Canada in 1866, a fanciful Irish nationalist plot to free Ireland by drawing the United States into a war with Great Britain, *The Atlantic Monthly* again commented that "all the qualities which go to make a republican, in the true sense of the term, are wanting in the Irish nature"; "to the Celtic mind, when anything comes in the guise of a law, there is an accompanying seizure of moral paralysis." As that journal concluded thirty years later, "A Celt . . . lacks the solidity, the balance, the judgment, the moral staying power of the Anglo-Saxon"—solidity, balance, judgment, and moral staying power, of course, representing the keystones of a self-governing republic.

As the exchange among congressmen with names like MacLafferty and O'Connor might begin to suggest, by the twentieth century—in no small measure because of the political power they had come to wield through their urban machines—the Irish had become, for many, honorary Anglo-Saxons or Nordics. Germans, too, sometimes assumed the status as honorary "old-stock" Americans, though upon their arrival in the mid-nineteenth century they had not exactly been greeted as blood relatives of the Revolutionary generation. The slippages here were significant; consistency has rarely been among the hallmarks of American race thinking. By the end of the century, no less an arbiter of Anglo-Saxon propriety than Henry Cabot Lodge could write of a kinship between English-speaking natives and Celtic immigrants; and sociologist E. A. Ross could soften the edges of anti-Irish invective, arguing that the Celt's drunk-tank criminality was largely a matter not of "cupidity nor brutality nor lust," but merely of "conviviality and weak control of impulses."

But whether individual speakers pegged the Irish and Germans as "undesirable" or not, clearly an impressive consensus was forming on the mass of so-called new immigrants from Southern and Eastern Europe—the Greeks, Poles, Italians, Slovenes, Ruthenians, Armenians, Russian and Polish Jews, Sicilians, Hungarians, and Bohemians, whose numbers reliably registered between a quarter- and a half-million per year in the 1890s and topped the one-million mark four times between 1901 and 1910. They were roundly denounced as unfit citizens for this self-governing polity; and the denunciations themselves increasingly relied upon the earthy agricultural—which is to say, Mendelian—vocabulary of superior and inferior "stocks." Whereas at one time it had been only the Irish who lacked "the qualities which go to make a republican," by the 1890s Francis Amasa Walker, former superintendent of the U.S. Census, could paint *all* new immigrants as "beaten men from beaten races," lacking the "ideas and aptitudes which fit men to take up . . . the problem of self-care and self-government." By the end of the century, even some within the growing women's-suffrage movement paradoxically embraced this construction of "fit" and "unfit" citizenship, parsed along racial lines. Anglo-Saxon women's votes, according to this argument, would serve as an electoral bulwark against the pernicious influences of the degraded foreign and Negro vote.

Though applied to the Irish as early as the 1850s, the racialism of American nativism had stepped up considerably in the 1870s in response to Chinese immigration. "If there be any truth whatever in Darwin's scientific theory of Natural Selection," wrote John Swinton in 1870, "it must be admitted that a nation like ours would run a fearful risk from the degradation of its race existence." He went on to assert that "liberty is a conception of the White race, not of the Yellow or Red or Black," and to worry over the "*tainted hordes*, vast and dense," that currently inhabited American cities. This equation of race with a capacity for liberty was nowhere more plainly articulated than in a report of the Joint Special Congressional Committee to Investigate Chinese Immigration in 1877:

> *The safety of republican institutions requires that the exercise of the franchise shall be only by those who have a love and appreciation for our institutions, and this rule excludes the great mass of the Chinese from the ballot as a necessary measure for public safety. . . . An indigestible mass in the community,*

distinct in language, pagan in religion, inferior in mental and moral qual-
ities, and all peculiarities, is an undesirable element in a republic, but be-
comes especially so if political power is placed in its hands.
The safety of the State demands that such power shall not be so placed.

The report went on to worry over the "vast hive from which the Chinese may swarm," and to reiterate that "the Mongolian race seems to have no desire for progress and to have no conception of representative and free institutions." The committee had gathered much valuable testimony on the differences between "the Asiatic and Caucasian races" that might be "particularly interesting to the ethnologist." Among other things, decades before H. H. Goddard had begun his inquiries, this congressional committee had discovered that "there is not sufficient brain capacity in the Chinese to furnish motive power for self-government." Upon the point of morals, too, "there is no Aryan or European race which is not far superior to the Chinese as a class."

Given the dynamics of the party system in the 1870s, and particularly the process by which anti-Chinese agitation came to the national agenda via the legislative halls of California, the labor-competition issue tended to dominate discussion of the Chinese question right up until the passage of the Chinese Exclusion Act. But this racial strain of argumentation—the innate Chinese incapacity for self-rule and the corresponding racial propensity for despotism—constituted a consistent leitmotif throughout the public debates. The Chinese were so vulnerable to exclusion in the first place, recall, because as "aliens ineligible to citizenship" they had neither voice nor political might to counter the assault against them; and they were ineligible to citizenship precisely on racial grounds—they were not the "free white persons" (or, after 1870, the "persons of African nativity or descent") required by American naturalization law.

The law itself became one of the chief sites of Asian American resistance—and the courts became the chief site for the articulation of a distinctly racial understanding of republican citizenship—as various petitioners stepped forward to challenge the legal and ethnological reasoning of the free-white-persons clause. In the first such case, one Ah Yup petitioned for citizenship in California in 1878 on the grounds that, since the Chinese were neither clearly "white" nor clearly "of African descent"—the only two designations spelled out in naturalization law at the time—their status had yet to be ruled upon in a court of law. The judge chose to frame the question, "Is a person of the Mongolian race a 'white person'?" and easily arrived at a negative reply. No current usages either in the vernacular or among ethnologists would number Mongolians among "whites" or "Caucasians," the court ruled, and so the Chinese could not gain entry under the legal aegis of the "white persons" clause. Moreover, since Congress had revised the law by adding Africans to "white persons" without taking up the case of any others, "whatever latitudinarian construction might otherwise have been given to the term 'white person,' it is entirely clear that congress intended by this legislation to exclude Mongolians from the right of naturalization." The white-persons clause admitted of no *in*clusionary reading.

The Chinese Exclusion Act opened a new chapter in the legal history of Chinese immigration. Would-be immigrants swamped the courts with over seven thousand cases in the first decade after Exclusion, and since the law proved to be far more difficult to administer and enforce than it had been to rally support for and to pass, a number of these cases were decided in favor of the Chinese entrants. Soon, too, a cat-and-mouse game took shape between Chinese "paper sons" (immigrants whose forged documentation depicted them as the sons of Chinese merchants or of Chinese born in the United States and therefore as eligible entrants) and U.S. immigration inspectors, who attempted to expose their ruse through a grueling procedure of harsh and remarkably minute questioning.

But because the Chinese Exclusion Act itself had failed to name any other Asian groups, Asian immigration from other sources continued in the wake of Exclusion (over a hundred thousand Japanese immigrants came ashore between 1890 and 1910, for instance, and several thousand Indians, Turks, Armenians, Filipinos, and Pacific Islanders). Thus the legal question of naturalization first broached by *Ah Yup* remained live. These years saw a cavalcade of East and South Asian petitioners following *Ah Yup* in challenging the white-persons clause of naturalization law in the courts. A number of these were decided on precisely the ethnological basis that *Ah Yup* had been in 1878: Hawaiians were not "white persons," for example (*Kanaka Nian*, 1889), nor were Burmese (*Po*, 1894), nor were Japanese (*Saito*, 1894; *Yamashita*, 1902; *Buntaro Kumagai*, 1908; *Bessho*, 1910; and *Ozawa*, 1922), nor were Filipinos (*Mallari*, 1916; *Rallos* 1917). Petitioners from South Asia and the Middle East, on the other hand, fared somewhat better: Syrians were sometimes turned away (*Shahid*, 1913), but often they were found to be legal "white persons" (*Najour*, 1909; *Mudarri*, 1910; *Ellis*, 1910; and, on appeal, *Dow* v. *United States*, 1915). Likewise, East Indians could fall on either side of the color line—perhaps "white" (*Thind*, 1920) and then, on appeal, not (*United States* v. *Thind*, 1923).

Throughout these legal contests, however, only the ethnological boundaries of whiteness were in dispute. The cases uniformly pivoted upon the definition of "white persons," leaving wholly untouched the core presumption that only certain races represented "fit" citizens in the self-governing republic. As a South Carolina judge remarked in the case of a Syrian petitioner in 1914, in relying upon the phrase "white persons" to frame naturalization law, the first Congress "neither expected nor desired immigrants from any other quarter" than Western Europe—"certainly not from Syria." "The average citizen of the United States," he went on with a candor that now seems appalling, "was at that time firmly convinced of the superiority of his own white European race over the rest of the world. . . . He had enslaved many of the American Indians on that ground. He would have enslaved a Moor, a Bedouin, a Syrian, a Turk, or an East Indian of sufficiently dark complexion with equal readiness on the same plea if he could have caught him."

For some, it was neither an illogical nor a terribly long leap from the necessary exclusion of the inferior Chinese to the necessary exclusion of the inferior European races. As the U.S. consul at Budapest remarked in the early 1890s, "These Slovacks are not a good acquisition for us to make, since they appear to have so many items in common with the Chinese." Restrictionists like Senator Henry Cabot Lodge readily concurred: the new immigration, comprising "races most alien to the body of the American people," now threatened the prized homogeneity that was presumed to ensure the smooth governance of the republic; and not only were they different, but their difference in and of itself hardly recommended them as fellow citizens. The new immigrants in general, wrote Lodge, "do not promise well for the standard of civilization of the United States." Citing a State Department report on the "almost revolting" character of many of the new immigrants, Lodge elsewhere declared that not only was "our immigration changing in point of race," but that it was in fact "deteriorating."

Intellectual debate on the relative merits of European immigration in the 1880s thus gave way to fierce and unbridled restrictionist agitation in the 1890s. Out of an array of New England civic and ancestral organizations such as the Massachusetts Society for Promoting Good Citizenship and the Sons of the American Revolution sprang a new, frankly restrictionist organization in 1894. Founded by Charles Warren, Robert DeCourcy Ward, and Prescott Farnsworth Hall in Boston, the Immigration Restriction League combined the civic ideals of New England patricians like Henry Cabot Lodge with the racialist ideologies then current in the Harvard curriculum. The impact of immigration was best calculated not by the material prosperity immigrants generated or the troubling labor competition they represented, by these lights, but by the purely civic question of America's traditional Anglo-Saxon political grandeur and its disruption by these swarthy streams of obvious inferiors. What would be the civic impact of "these degraded races that seek our shores"? Vida Scudder asked in her novel of the settlement house, *A Listener in Babel* (1903). Would these aliens supplant "the governing race" in the United States?

Although perhaps never terribly impressive in sheer numbers, the Immigration Restriction League's membership rolls did read like a *Who's Who* of American education and civic leadership, and so the league wielded significant influence in public discussion and, ultimately, in the halls of power. The league's first president was historian John Fiske. Over the years, its officers and members included college presidents like A. Lawrence Lowell (Harvard), William DeWitt Hyde (Bowdoin), and David Starr Jordan (Stanford); social scientists like John R. Commons, Edward A. Ross, William Z. Ripley, and Richmond Mayo Smith; social workers like Robert Woods; and philanthropists like Joseph Lee, Henry Lee Higginson, and Samuel Capen. Within a year of its establishment in Boston, the New England organization greeted affiliate chapters in Albany, Brooklyn, Chicago, Milwaukee, New

York, and Philadelphia, and nominally statewide chapters in Alabama and Montana.

Befitting the marked presence of prominent educators within its ranks, the league identified public education among its chief tasks. "Public opinion," the *Immigration Restriction League Constitution* announced, must be helped to recognize "the necessity of a further exclusion of elements undesirable for citizenship or injurious to our national character." The league energetically educated "public opinion" by sending speakers to address local civic groups and voluntary associations, by distributing literature and leaflets, and by engaging in direct lobbying in Washington. Within a year of its founding, the organization would boast that over five hundred daily newspapers were receiving league literature, and a good many of these were reprinting it in their columns or on their editorial pages. After the turn of the century, the league also had modest success in reaching organized labor.

Although some members, like Robert DeC. Ward, might insist that no immigrants should be excluded from the country on the grounds of race alone, the creeping racialism of the league was fairly plain. The *Constitution's* reference to "elements undesirable or injurious to our national character" itself hinted at the racial underpinnings of the organization's restrictionist logic. Prescott Hall could write unambiguously of "the objectionable races" now entering the country; or, in an early letter to the editor of the *Boston Journal*, he could describe the new immigrants' relationship to the "native American stock" and worry over the possibility that they might "pollute the Yankee blood." Likewise, Albert Shaw, editor of the *American Review of Reviews*, could warn against immigration as a willful and inexplicable consent, on the part of old-stock Americans, "to spoil their breed of pedigree stock by allowing the introduction of the refuse of the murder-breed of Southern Europe." James H. Patten could warn of the "brownish" races of Southern Europe and the threat they posed to white America; Robert Woods could remark with some envy on the national composition of England, embracing "the vigorous Anglo-Saxon race, without contaminating mixture."

Nor is it coincidental that Henry Cabot Lodge's Ph.D. dissertation at Harvard, a treatise on Anglo-Saxon land law, had exalted the Teutonic virtues of the English—virtues that had survived intact in no small part because of the Anglo-Saxons' "purity of race," "free from the injurious influences of the Roman and Celtic peoples." Now, in the early 1890s, in a piece on "The Distribution of Ability in the United States" (1892) that "classified by race and occupation all persons of foreign birth who have gained distinction in this country," Lodge demonstrated that Great Britain had supplied "three-fourths of the *ability* furnished from outside sources." The non-Anglo-Saxon millions were furnishing something altogether different.

Most league members drank deeply of the racially romantic, Anglo-Saxonist or Teutonist myths of liberty and the nation's political origins in the primeval forests of Germany; their brand of nativism carried a pronounced strain of hereditarianism from the outset. Americans must drop the notion that "a man is a man," wrote Harvard Professor Nathaniel Southgate Shaler in the nativist magazine *America.* "The truth is that a man is what his ancestral experience has made him." This hereditarian thinking would become more and more pronounced in the league's restrictionist reasoning, ultimately merging entirely with the eugenic arguments of Charles Davenport, Harry Laughlin, and the Eugenics Research Association. In a recommendation to the Dillingham Immigration Commission under the aegis of the league in 1911, Prescott Hall argued:

> *Recent investigations in biology show that heredity is a far more important factor in the progress of any species than environment. . . . The same arguments which induce us to segregate criminals and feeble-minded and thus prevent their breeding apply to excluding from our borders individuals whose multiplying here is likely to lower the average of our people. We should exercise at least as much care in admitting human beings as we exercise in relation to animals or insect pests or disease germs. Yet it is true that we are to-day actually taking more care in the selection . . . of a Hereford bull or a Southdown ewe, imported for the improvement of our cattle and sheep, than we are taking in the selection of alien men and women who are coming here to be the fathers and mothers of future American children.*

A considerable number of current immigrants, Hall went on, were from races and countries that had been "relatively useless for centuries."

If race was the preferred idiom of the Immigration Restriction League on the question of "fit" and "unfit" citizens, literacy was its preferred legislative tool for many years. Lodge originally sponsored a bill in 1897 that would limit immigration to those who could read and write in their own languages, convinced that the device would effectively curtail the influx of undesirable races from Southern and Eastern Europe. The bill passed that year, only to be vetoed by President Cleveland. Objecting to the cant of "undesirability," the president commented that "within recent memory . . . the same thing was said of immigrants who, with their descendants . . . now number among our best citizens." Similar literacy bills or literacy provisions went down to defeat or veto in 1902, 1903, 1904, 1907, 1909, 1913, and 1915. Although veto messages (Cleveland, Taft, and Wilson) typically invoked American tradition and the vaunted principles of asylum and opportunity, clearly the failure of the literacy bills owed in greater part to a powerful coalition of business interests whose reliance on immigrant labor ultimately outweighed the racial distaste for non-Anglo-Saxon citizenship.

But throughout these years, the starker racial argument was in ascendance. Indeed, a literacy bill was finally passed over Wilson's veto in 1917; by then, however, the racialist, eugenic strain of American nativism was often frankly posed, without the concealing cloak of the more environmentalist—and hence more optimistic and humanitarian—concern for literacy. As Jeremiah Jenks wrote in 1909, "Up to the present time we have attempted to sift the immigrants as they come in through Ellis Island, on an individualistic basis." But it was now worth asking, "What are the racial characteristics, if any, by which we might venture to exclude or give preference to certain classes of immigrants?" Given the wealth of information being made available through Davenport's eugenic-research station at Cold Spring Harbor and through the vast and growing network of eugenics societies, perhaps it was now possible "to discover some test to show whether some may be better fitted for American citizenship than others." Race proved to be precisely that test, as suggested by the Immigration Commission's *Dictionary of Races or Peoples* (1911), which hinted darkly at the changing "source" and "character" of current immigration and worried over the wildly prolific birthrates of groups like Italians in every country they came to inhabit. The 1917 immigration act's provision of an Asiatic Barred Zone—effectively extending the Chinese Exclusion Act to the rest of Asia—on strict white-supremacist grounds was a dramatic sign of just how powerfully and overtly race thinking was shaping the public debate.

It was precisely at this juncture that scholarly treatises on race, genetics, and intelligence like Charles Davenport's *Heredity in Relation to Eugenics*, Madison Grant's *Passing of the Great Race*, Henry Herbert Goddard's *Feeble-Mindedness*, and Robert Yerkes's army intelligence tests attained such a purchase on American political discussion. Indeed, figures like Grant and Harry Laughlin, the director of the Eugenics Records Office at Cold Spring Harbor, became prime witnesses in congressional hearings on the question of immigration. In the latter 1910s and early 1920s, race itself became written into the formulas that would soon govern the legal rates of immigration of the world's peoples. As one congressman put it during a debate on what would finally become the National Origins Act of 1924, "We have admitted the dregs of Europe until America has been orientalized, Europeanized, Africanized, and mongrelized to that insidious degree that our genius, stability, greatness, and promise of advancement and achievement are actually menaced. . . . I should like to exclude all foreigners for years to come, at least until we can ascertain whether or not the foreign and discordant element now in what many are pleased to term 'our great melting-pot' will melt into real American citizens."

The formula finally agreed upon—quotas based on a percentage of any given group's U.S. population in the 1890 census—did not "exclude all foreigners for years to come"; but it did *nearly* exclude those who, according to the racial doctrines of the time, were most problematic in terms of their fitness for self-government and their promise for the general level of civilization in the republic. As the immigration commissioner noted with satisfaction after the National Origins Act had become law, the immigrants daily disembarking at Ellis Island now all "looked exactly like Americans."

Immigrant Voices: Descent and Dissent

The average immigrant of today, wrote Mary Antin in 1914, "like the immigrant of 1620, comes to build . . . a civilized home under a civilized government, which diminishes the amount of barbarity in the world." It is hard to know how, in the course of their everyday lives, ordinary immigrants experienced their status as despised and inferior "stock" in their adopted country, or to what extent they concerned themselves with or were even aware of the discourse on "fitness" and "unfitness" for self-government. It is clear, however, that those articulate immigrant writers and leaders who have left an imprint on the historical record did respond to the racialist argument; and, like Mary Antin, a Jewish refugee from the Russian town of Polotsk, they responded to it as a slander.

The peculiar tension in American political culture between the ideal of universal inclusion and the fact of very real and often harsh exclusion has historically posed a common dilemma for those who would cross into the polity from anywhere without: do we stake our claim to American participation on sameness (we are no different from those who already enjoy the rights and privileges of citizenship), or on difference (we have special gifts that will benefit the republic)? The question has generated a range of responses, yet the general patterns are strikingly similar from one group to the next. The question echoes throughout the debates between Booker T. Washington and W.E.B. Du Bois regarding African American inclusion, for instance, and between Carrie Chapman Catt and Alice Paul regarding the political status of American women. Among immigrant commentators, the differences separating assimilationists, pluralists, and various ethnic nationalists were wide indeed. But each in his or her way did advance some version of the argument that the new immigrants were indeed fit for self-government and worthy of American democracy.

One answer to the charge of unfitness for self-government was the straightforward political claim that, far from representing unassimilable foreigners, the immigrants—often by virtue of their very foreignness—represented *pre-eminent* "Americans." As Michael Kruszka, a Polish leader in Milwaukee, declared, "I am an ardent Pole and at the same time an American. I do not see where one contradicts the other." Indeed, Poles were uniquely fitted to appreciate and enjoy American liberty, because, living under the despotic rule of Russians, Prussians, and Austrians in their own conquered and divided land, they required a free country in which to be themselves. Given the bars to Polish cultural and political aspiration during the period of partition, being Polish was in fact for Kruszka the very point of being *in* America: "In the New World we have the best opportunity to exist as Poles," he wrote in 1885. And for this very reason, Poles, though ever loyal to the homeland, could understand the blessings of liberty and carry its responsibilities with a greater enthusiasm and depth of understanding than could ordinary "Americans." Similar arguments were advanced regarding Jews and the Irish.

Perhaps the most thoroughgoing example of this dual sensibility was the Italian activity around the commemoration of Christopher Columbus's voyage. Carlo Barsotti, founder of the immigrant journal *Il Progresso Italo-Americano*, spearheaded the effort in 1892 to mark the four hundredth anniversary of Columbus's landing, and over the next several years the commemoration generated mass rallies and ostentatious parades in Italian colonies across the country. In 1909, when the New York legislature approved a bill making Columbus Day an official holiday, some thirty thousand Italian immigrants marched to Columbus Circle, at once demonstrating an unshakable Italianness and laying claim to an unassailable Americanism. Revolutionary War hero Tadeusz Kościuszko held a similar value for immigrant Poles; for the Irish—at least before the Anglo-American rapprochement of the 1890s—it was their historic hatred for England and the wonderful compatibility of Irish national aspirations and America's pedigree as a colony in revolt. As immigrant poet and political leader John Boyle O'Reilly wrote in "The Exile of the Gael," "The hearts we bring for Freedom are washed in the surge of tears; / And we claim our right by a people's fight outliving a thousand years." Not their willingness to turn away from former allegiances, therefore, but their very commitment to Old World struggle and their hearts cleansed with the sorrows of national oppression constituted the chief Irish claim to America. In *The Americanization of Edward Bok* (1920), the Dutch author probed the national specificity of true "Americanism": "There are thousands of American-born," he concluded philosophically, "who need Americanization just as much as do the foreign-born."

Others, leaving true Americanism to the Americans, nonetheless argued forcefully on behalf of their own and their fellow immigrants' civic reliability. Norwegian leader Knute Nelson, a U.S. senator from Minnesota, tried to warn his Senate colleagues away from a blind bigotry with this telling analogy in 1896: "As the good wife, though loving her mother, still gives her husband the uppermost place in her affections, so do the foreign-born sons and daughters of Minnesota, though loving the lands of their birth, still place [America] uppermost and foremost in their love and affection." Cleverly invoking the dual yet quite "natural" allegiances of kinship and law (birth and marriage), Nelson thus sought to naturalize the notion of dual national loyalties.

Loyalty was one thing, and immigrant commentators had a wealth of symbols at their disposal to prove their special affinity to the adopted country, whether they were Irish, Polish, Czech, Norwegian, German, or Russian Jews. But racial character was quite another: loyalty aside, were the immigrants fit for the republic? This was a tougher matter. The three dominant political idioms through which immigrant commentators argued their "fitness" were assimilationism, pluralism, and nationalism. Each in its way sought to articulate the merits of the newly arrived immigrants and to stake a particular claim upon American democracy.

Of course the period's most famous statement on assimilation is Israel Zangwill's 1908 play, *The Melting Pot*, in which, now safely in America, the Jewish immigrant David Quixano falls in love with the daughter of an anti-Semitic baron from the very city where Quixano's parents had been murdered in a pogrom. The play's central romance thus gives a whole new dimension to the concept of fresh beginnings and escape from the past, while its finer touches (like the maid Kathleen O'Reilly's occasional exclamation, "*Oy vey!*") convey both the large and small ways that cultures collide and reshape one another in the New World. Here all races and peoples come together, cries Quixano at the drama's crescendo; "what a stirring and a seething! Celt and Latin, Slav and Teuton, Greek and Syrian—black and yellow . . . how the great Alchemist melts and fuses them with his purging flame! Here shall they all unite to build the Republic of Man and the Kingdom of God." In this last line, Zangwill identifies both the secular and the religious dimensions of the tremendous human drama of migration and mutual accommodation; and, affirming a national messianism that had by then had many incarnations in American political culture, he provided the innovative twist that—the fears of natives like Josiah Strong or Henry Cabot Lodge to the contrary—the massive influx of alien races *was* the nation's destined greatness. Only by the absorption of these millions could the nation fulfill its divine promise.

We tend to think of assimilation as an erosion of cultural tradition rather than as a deliberate political program per se; and certainly cultural patterns can change with time—languages fade, new tastes arise, romances spark across ethnic lines—without any mindful political intent. Where assimilation does seem to be political at all, moreover, it most often appears an accommodation or a surrender. But at a moment when notions of "unassimilability" were so central to the host society's hostility to the newcomers, assimilationism could in fact carry a concealed blade of protest. Zangwill's assertion that American diversity could be symphonic rather than discordant, that is, was not without political poignance for a generation steeped in the teachings of Darwin, Mendel, and Galton.

The best exemplar of this submerged political tendency in assimilationism was Mary Antin, who, by her assiduous study and her accomplishment in American letters, was to become a darling among American literary gatekeepers like Ellery Sedgwick, Thomas Bailey Aldrich's successor at *The Atlantic Monthly*. Her widely hailed autobiography, *The Promised Land* (1912), was not a testament to the powers of the republic to absorb the wretched refuse from across the seas so much as it was a testament to the extraordinary powers of the immigrants to transform themselves. "I was born, I have lived, and I have been made over," the book begins. "I am absolutely other than the person whose story I have to tell." This "making over" not only becomes the central focus of the heroine's individual life, but, quite pointedly, it provides the baseline for a critique of then current assertions that this or that people—Aldrich's "human gorillas"—could never be successfully incorporated into the body politic.

Throughout *The Promised Land*, Antin's tale of transformation unfolds primarily in the realm of culture; it is a tale of discarded and adopted social customs and habits of mind. From the moment of arrival, Antin's father, who had preceded the family by some years, instructed the rest of the family in the ways of the New World. "We did not want to be 'greenhorns,' and gave the strictest attention to my father's instructions." The initial education included lessons in the use of unaccustomed objects (such as "a curious piece of furniture on runners, which he called 'rocking-chair'") and an introduction to "a dazzlingly beautiful palace called a 'department store,'" where the family exchanged "our hateful homemade European costumes" for "real American machine-made garments." "With our despised immigrant clothing we shed also our impossible Hebrew names," she recalls. Thus did Maryashe become Mary. "We had to . . . be dressed from head to foot in American clothing; we had to learn the mysteries of the iron stove, the washboard, and the speaking-tube; we had to learn to trade with the fruit peddler through the window, and not to be afraid of the policeman; and, above all, we had to learn English." "In after years," she later remarks,

> *when I passed as an American among Americans, if I was suddenly made aware of the past that lay forgotten,—if a letter from Russia, or a paragraph in the newspaper, or a conversation overheard in the street-car, suddenly reminded me of what I might have been,—I thought it miracle enough that I, Mashke, the granddaughter of Raphael the Russian, born to a humble destiny, should be at home in an American metropolis, be free to fashion my own life, and should dream my dreams in English phrases.*

The self-loathing implicit in this description of the greenhorn's metamorphosis is so palpable as to preclude, on first glance, any interpretation of cultural or political resistance on Antin's part. But the resistance lies paradoxically in the totality of her transformation. That Antin can assimilate, and can assimilate so utterly, becomes the core principle in a quiet politics of antinativism throughout the autobiography. The foreign-born Jewess can, in fact, pass as "an American among Americans." Though her style is far more staid, one nonetheless thinks of James Joyce, whose "vengeful virtuosity" in the English language, as one critic has put it, stood as a monument of rebuttal to the unending English claims of Irish inferiority. Antin's flamboyant Americanization should silence the likes of Henry Cabot Lodge once and for all. And her own seemingly extraordinary "thoughts and conduct," by her account, were not unusual, but "typical of the attitude of the intelligent immigrant child toward American institutions."

Your immigrant inspectors will tell you what poverty the foreigner brings in his baggage, what want in his pockets. Let the overgrown boy of twelve, reverently drawing his letters in the baby class, testify to the noble dreams and high ideals that may be hidden beneath the greasy caftan of the immigrant. Speaking for the Jews, at least, I know I am safe in inviting such an investigation.

Elsewhere, she challenges her reader (pointedly referred to as "my American friend"), "Think, every time you pass the greasy alien on the street, that he was born thousands of years before the oldest native American; and he may have something to communicate to you, when you two shall have learned a common language. Remember that his very physiognomy is a cipher the key to which it behooves you to search for most diligently."

In a paean to the assimilative workings of the public-school system (a chapter entitled "My Country"), Antin goes on to describe her childish thrill at the story of the American Revolution and her own attempt at a suitable poem for the occasion of a Washington celebration, demonstrating all along a capacity for an almost rhapsodic American patriotism that could only have taken the wind out of the naysayers of the Immigration Restriction League or the Eugenics Research Association. The U.S. Constitution, according to this Russian Jewish schoolgirl's Washington Day poem, was a "blessed guide to man . . . which says, 'One and all of mankind are alike, excepting none.'" *The Promised Land* ends with a claim on America that, again, against the backdrop of the policy debates of the 1910s, carried a sharp, if muted, political charge: "America is the youngest of the nations, and inherits all that went before in history. And I am the youngest of America's children, and into my hands is given all her priceless heritage."

The political edge of Antin's assimilationism came most starkly to the fore in *They Who Knock at Our Gates* (1914), an inquiry into the practices and policies by which the United States greeted its newest inhabitants. "The restrictionists could afford to hold their peace while the Government tries out a logical method of dealing with the immigrant," Antin had written to Mary Austen in 1912. "It is hardly fair to call immigration a burden before a consistent National effort has been made to turn it into a resource." *They Who Knock* at once challenges the common critique of the current immigration, and advocates and outlines precisely such a "National effort," consisting chiefly of public expenditures for classes in civics and English to help digest the masses of new immigrants into the body politic.

They Who Knock is framed by three questions of civic import: Do we have the moral right to regulate immigration? What is the nature of the present immigration? Is immigration good for us? (Her use of "we" and "us" was itself a point of some contention. Some old-stock Americans, like Antin's fellow Bostonian Barrett Wendell, objected to her self-inclusion in the body of "Americans" as "an irritating habit.") Of course, Antin answered all three questions in a manner favorable to the immigrants. Among her opening gambits was an appeal to the tenets of true Americanism and to the wishes of the founding fathers. America rested upon "the doctrines of liberty and equality," she argued. "A faithful American is one who understands these doctrines and applies them in his life." "Strip the alien down to his anatomy, you still find a *man*, a creature made in the image of God; and concerning such a one we have definite instructions from the founders of the Republic."

But Americans in the age of eugenics were now turning away from these creatures of God, the oppressed who hungered for freedom and aid. *Why?* "What have the experts and statisticians done so to pervert our minds? They have filled volumes with facts and figures, comparing the immigrants to-day with the immigrants of other days, classifying them as to race, nationality, and culture, tabulating their occupations, analyzing their savings, probing their motives, prophesying their ultimate destiny." Science had been improperly brought to bear on the moral question of America's disposition toward the immigrants, Antin protested. "By all means register the cephalic index of the alien . . . but do not let it determine his right to life, liberty, and the pursuit of happiness."

Antin ultimately concluded that the animus toward the new immigrants not only violated hallowed American principle, but overlooked mountains of evidence as to the newcomers' overall contribution to the nation. "Our brains, our wealth, our ambitions flow in channels dug by immigrants," she asserted. "Not the immigrant is ruining our country"—and here her political passions reached their very heights—"but the venal politicians who try to make the immigrant the scapegoat for all the sins of untrammeled capitalism." Here, indeed, in *The Promised Land* and *They Who Knock*, is an assimilationism every bit as militant in its pride and strident in its politics as it is accommodating to an imagined Anglo-Saxon mainstream.

The boundary between Antin's brand of vindictive assimilationism and the softer shades of cultural pluralism could be blurry indeed. (Where exactly to locate, for example, Knute Nelson's image of the immigrant as both devoted wife to the New World and dutiful daughter to the Old?) But many, of course, were far more skeptical, or even downright hostile to assimilationism. Abraham Cahan's 1894 novella *Yekl* is an elegant argument not only that assimilation is undesirable (Yekl's mean-spirited social impulses all derive from the greenhorn's desire to prove himself a real "Yankee feller"), but that, at bottom, it is impossible as well. However fiercely Yekl insists upon his Americanism, he is forever betrayed by his "Semitic eyes" or his "Semitic smile." For Cahan, as for his contemporaries among the Jewish intelligentsia like Abraham Liessen, Leon Kobrin, and Morris Winchevsky, Jewishness was a racial identity, permanently etched in the flesh and bone of the natural order, never to be completely shed like some unwanted or outgrown piece of clothing. Decades later, in *The Rise of David Levinsky* (1917), though Cahan himself had become partially assimilated into the English-language literary mainstream (his Yiddish-speaking colleagues wryly referred to him as "Yekl"), he wrote in the voice of his successful and "assimilated" protagonist, "I cannot escape from my old self. My past and present do not comport well."

For thinkers along this line, Mary Antin's assimilationist argument for inclusion on the basis of sameness clearly would not do. The boldest, most thoroughgoing theorist of the pluralist alternative—inclusion on the basis of difference—was Horace Kallen, a Silesian Jewish immigrant who studied philosophy at Harvard under William James. Kallen was the son of a Latvian rabbi who was expelled from Bismarck's Germany as an "alien Jew." His family immigrated to the United States in 1887, when Horace was five. His youth amid the pulls of secular Americanism and traditional Judaism seems to have given Kallen a keen sense of cultural multiplicity; his graduate work with James gave him a language for honing and expressing this sense. He wrote his dissertation on the nature of truth; much of Kallen's later commentary can be seen as an effort to translate James's thinking into the social sphere of an increasingly diverse United States.

Kallen's cleanest statement of his emergent social philosophy of pluralism was a 1915 essay, "Democracy Versus the Melting-Pot." As expressed here, pluralism consisted of five major interlocking propositions.

First, he argued, what was commonly meant by the term "assimilation" was not an even-handed exchange or a melding of cultures at all but, rather, the predominance of one culture over the others. Assimilation most often implied coerced conformity to an Anglo-Saxon norm, "a transmutation . . . of Jews, Slavs, Poles, Frenchmen, Germans, Hindus, Scandinavians and so on into beings similar in background, tradition, outlook and spirit to the descendants of the British colonists, the Anglo-Saxon stock."

Hence, second, for Kallen assimilationism was inherently hierarchical and antidemocratic. "In 1776 all men were as good as their betters," he wrote, with a characteristic—if misplaced—zeal for the democratic golden age of the Revolutionary era; "today men are permanently worse than their betters." "The first immigrants in the land simply through the accident of being first have become its aristocracy, its chief protagonists of the pride of blood." Kallen's rhetoric of aristocracy and his hint at a kind of cultural primogeniture carried a tacit accusation that those who laid most urgent and forceful claim to proper Americanism were, in fact, deeply *un*-American in their commitment to hierarchy and in their hostility to true democracy. And their brand of assimilationism was not only antidemocratic, he added, but coercive: Mary Antin to the contrary, the Anglo-supremacist public-school system crushed the spirit of prospective Americans, fitting them as mere cogs in an industrial machine whose workings favored the American upper classes—that is, the "firstborn." The enforced assimilationism of American education amounted to nothing less than a "Pecksniffian efficiency-press" that ground the spontaneity and spark out of the immigrants' children.

Assimilation may be a kind of defeat or surrender from the standpoint of ethnic and racial minorities; fortunately, however, Kallen posited in his third proposition, the assimilationist ideal would never be fully attained: the melting pot simply would not, in the long run, melt people down. In explaining his position, Kallen laid out a series of developmental stages that the immigrant was presumed to pass through in his or her cultural odyssey in the New World. First was a period of "economic eagerness" and voluntary conformism, during which the immigrant embraced assimilation as an economic strategy. Inasmuch as "difference" itself was a handicap in the marketplace, the immigrant sought consciously to eradicate it. But once the newcomer had attained a certain level of achievement and independence, assimilation slowed down markedly and even came to a stop. Finally, at the next stage a process of "dissimilation" began: the arts, life, and ideals of nationality became central and paramount; and "difference" shifted in status from disadvantage to distinction. "All the while the immigrant has been uttering his life in the English language and behaving like an American in matters economic and political, and continues to do so." But, ironically, "the institutions of the republic" have liberated ethnic consciousness and social autonomy. True Americanization "does not repress ethnic or national identity, but liberates it and gratifies it."

For Kallen, ethnic identity, ancestry, heritage, and ethnic culture all represented primordial, immutable bonds—categories of experience that could never be shed. "People may change their clothes, their politics, their spouses, their religions, their philosophies . . . but they cannot change their grandfathers. Jews or Poles or Anglo-Saxons, in order to cease being Jews or Poles or Anglo-Saxons, would have to cease to be." Something that looks like "assimilation" may occasionally take place, but only most superficially; apparent assimilation always turns out to be but a transitory stage on the way toward a new, more profound understanding of one's primordial bonds and affinities.

Kallen's fourth contention, then, was that cultural retention—the embrace of one's true identity and cultural heritage, the insistence upon holding one's ground—was ennobling. Ethnic and racial identity, the primordial connection to one's particular group, represented the very seat of human meaning. Kallen used the term "self-realization" to describe the prospect of attaining the pinnacle of one's potentialities, a height to be reached only by embracing national or ethnic particularity. After passing through the temporary stage of assimilation, "the wop changes into a proud Italian; the hunky into a proud nationalist Slav. They recall the spiritual heritage of their nationality, and their cultural abjectness gives way to cultural pride." In the particularism of ethnic identity, in other words, lies human dignity itself. Contrariwise, assimilation in the American setting could only mean absorption into a wholly undignified modernist mass:

> *In these days of ready-made garments, factory-made furniture, refrigerating plants, boiler-plate movies and radio, it is almost impossible that the mass of the inhabitants of the United States should wear other than uniform clothes, use other than uniform furniture . . . or eat anything but the same sorts of food, read anything but the same syndicated hokum, see anything but the same standardized romances and hear anything but the same broadcasted barbarisms.*

In addition to resisting the antidemocratic impulses of assimilationism, pluralism in Kallen's view ennobled the spirit and provided an oasis in the cultural desert of modern, mechanized, mass-produced, and mass-consumed living.

For all of these reasons—and this was Kallen's fifth and crowning contention—pluralism represented what was best not only for the individual, but for democracy and for American governance. Here again he appealed to the hallowed rhetoric of an early-American political tradition, the language of inalienable rights. "The selfhood which is inalienable in people," he declared, "and for the realization of which they require inalienable liberty, is ancestrally determined, and the happiness which they pursue has its form implied in ancestral endowment. This is what democracy in operation assumes. There are human capacities which it is the function of the state to liberate and protect. . . . Government under the democratic conception is merely an instrument, not an end." Though he may have agreed with the likes of Madison Grant or Charles Davenport on the *fact* of "ancestral endowment," Kallen saw such endowments as sacred, and he thought the proper function of government not to defend itself against such diverse and distinct endowments but, on the contrary, to liberate them and to benefit by them. Ethnic particularism, because it is the very seat of human meaning, is also the very point of political liberty. Would the dominant classes in the United States choose wisely in dealing with diversity, Kallen asked; or would "vanity blind them and fear constrain them, turning the promise of liberty into the fact of tyranny?"

Kallen's argument certainly had its weakness. He was mistaken, for instance, in his insistence upon a democratic golden age in 1776; and his notion of the stability of ethnic "essences" was discredited in subsequent decades. But "Democracy Versus the Melting-Pot" was nonetheless a sharp answer to those who, like the eugenicists and the 100-percent Americans, sought to defend the United States *from* diversity. Not only did immigrants' "difference" not imperil the republic, Kallen argued; such difference was the republic's very reason for being. "Democracy involves not the elimination of differences," but their "perfection and conservation."

Given his concern for primordial attachments and the sanctity of group identities, it is not surprising that, in addition to his carefully theorized pluralism, Kallen was also sympathetic to that brand of Jewish group feeling represented by Zionism. Which brings up a third major immigrant response to Anglo-Saxon hostility: liberationist nationalism on behalf of the homeland. Across the country, immigrant nationalist organizations like the Clan na Gael, the Knights of Zion, the Polish National Alliance, the Indian nationalist Ghadr Party, and the Society to Revive China; myriad protomilitarist gymnastics and drill clubs; politicized literary works like Mariano Azuela's *Los de abajo* [*The Underdogs*] (1915); and political rallies like the Irish Race Conventions of the 1910s all testified to the power of nationalist sentiment among these communities in exile. In 1911, when Francisco Madero's revolutionary forces won a temporary victory at Juárez, ten thousand Mexicans and Mexican Americans marched across the border from El Paso, accompanied by a brass band, to salute the Maderistas. During World War I, some two hundred thousand Poles donned American military uniforms, many on the promise that an allied victory would guarantee an independent Poland after over a century of partition and foreign rule.

Like Antin's assimilationism and Kallen's pluralism, immigrant efforts expended on behalf of Old World liberation frequently expressed a pragmatic hope for New World political redemption. As Irish nationalist Michael Davitt implored a Cooper Union audience in 1880, "Aid us in Ireland to remove the stain of degradation from your birth and the Irish race here in America will get the respect you deserve." If the nativist argument about "unfitness for self-government" held so much power in American discussion, many nationalists implied, surely it was in part because so many of the immigrants hailed from lands where self-government was unknown.

This is not to say that immigrant nationalisms arose solely in response to New World slanders. On the contrary, emigration and nationalism often represented two divergent responses to the same sets of economic and political circumstances in a given region; immigrants from many countries felt a natural affinity with the nationalists' sensibility, and they formed a natural, ready-made audience for nationalist polemics. American aspirations, that is, often had little to do with their nationalist leanings. Disproportionately touched by the woes of the Old World—whether famine, pogroms, or the dislocations caused by intrusive foreign powers—immigrants were disproportionately drawn to nationalist solutions to the problems of land distribution, ethnic violence, or foreign domination, even if they had addressed these issues for themselves by fleeing. The period of greatest outmigration from a given region coincided by definition with a period of widespread distress; Old World nationalism typically spoke to precisely this feature of a group's collective history.

The very experience of migration, too, could promote nationalism. As Polish émigré Agaton Giller theorized in 1879, emigrants were particularly ripe for enlistment in nationalist causes, because their experience abroad sharpened for them—in many cases for the very first time—the sense of distinct ethnic or national peoplehood. The Polish migrant "feels foreign and misunderstood here," he explained, "and so he looks for people who would be able to understand him, and he finds Poles who have arrived from other provinces." The commonality of language and ideas that the migrant found among fellow migrants in the midst of a foreign culture broke down the intense localisms and village allegiances that had reigned in the old country, and awakened a sense of national distinctiveness. The migrant began to feel "but a particle" of a larger mass. After his ethnic consciousness has begun to stir, "if he is found by one who is able to . . . make him recognize the obligations which go along with this character—then this simple man, hitherto passive and dim to the national cause, changes into an individual consciously and actively serving [nationalist] ideas."

But if they were generated by the process of migration and derived in part from an unflagging, "homeward" orientation toward the Old World, immigrant nationalisms were nonetheless inflected and influenced by the political hostilities of the New. If Irish America was to be "the avenging wolfhound of Irish nationalism," as Michael Davitt put it, for instance, some Irish Americans saw the prospect of a free, self-determining, and internationally respected Ireland as the avenging wolfhound of the downtrodden and despised Celtic exiles in the United States. "I cannot feel that America is my country," wrote the fiery Irish nationalist Jeremiah O'Donovan Rossa in 1898; "I am made to see that the English power, and the English influence and the English hate, and the English boycott against the Irishman is to-day as active in America as it is in Ireland." If Old World nationalism remained primary for Rossa and others, it was still thoroughly entwined with New World politics and struggle.

One particularly stark example of the distinctly American aims of an Old World nationalist movement was the flourishing of Chinese nationalism after the failed boycott movement of 1905. Sun Yat-sen, the charismatic leader from Hsiang-shan, had organized his first revolutionary group, the Society to Revive China, in Hawaii in 1894. Trips to the mainland United States in 1896 and 1904 yielded little in the way of political support. Sun's view that the issue of U.S. immigration policy was an unfortunate diversion from the more important aim of revolution in China hurt him among a population whose vulnerable political and legal status owed directly to the reigning naturalization law and to Exclusion.

But in the wake of the boycott, which the Chinese government had helped to crush, Sun's anti-Manchu program gained interest among Chinese immigrants. It became increasingly accepted, in the years after 1905, that the fate of the overseas Chinese was inextricably intertwined with the fate of the Chinese nation itself. "One should know," an anonymous poet wrote on the wall of a detention barrack at the Angel Island Immigration Station, "that when the country is weak, the people's spirit dies. / Why else do we come to this place to be imprisoned?" By 1909, Sun had become enormously popular among the immigrants, and branches of his Chinese Nationalist League were established across the mainland United States and in Hawaii. By 1911, Sun was drawing hundreds to his rallies, and the Chinese in the

United States were collecting formidable sums of money to support Chinese revolution. The immigrants enjoyed a moment of restored hope when the revolution triumphed in 1912; but soon, when Sun's party was expelled from the new government, dissident activity continued among the Chinese Nationalist League, now in support of Sun's Revolutionary Party, Kuomintang.

Except in those instances when it fit nicely with U.S. policies and needs—as when the Poles flocked to American recruiting stations during World War I—immigrant nationalism rarely deflected Anglo-Saxon hostility in quite the way its adherents might have liked. Chinese nationalism became more evidence for the "unassimilability" of the Chinese and of their stubborn lack of interest in proper "American" concerns. Irish zeal for the homeland simply convinced nativists that these rebels lived, as *The Atlantic Monthly* put it, "in a world of unrealities almost inconceivable to a cool Saxon brain."

But Old World nationalisms did represent an important brand of the political pride by which immigrants continually challenged the Anglo-Saxonist slanders of the late nineteenth and early twentieth centuries. Like Michael Kruszka's assertion that to be unbendingly Polish was to be pre-eminently American; like Mary Antin's efforts to demonstrate the astonishing powers of the "unassimilable" masses to assimilate with a vengeance; and like Horace Kallen's carefully crafted theory that not only could democracy withstand racial and cultural differences, but indeed it *depended* upon and found its meaning in such differences, the nationalism of the Irish, Polish, Indian, Chinese, Mexican, or Jewish enclaves throughout the United States powerfully argued that these peoples were indeed "fit for self-government" on *either* side of the U.S. border. If many Americans were certain of the barbarism that characterized those "wild motley throngs" clamoring at the nation's gates, immigrants themselves were apt to understand American injustices and the failures of American democracy in precisely the same terms. A park ranger in the 1970s, visiting the long-abandoned Angel Island detention barrack in San Francisco Bay (where unwanted Chinese immigrants had been held while they awaited their turn to be grilled by immigration inspectors), found these words carved into the walls:

If there comes a day when I will have attained my ambition and become
successful,
I will certainly behead the barbarians and spare not a single blade of grass.

As Horace Kallen recognized, in U.S. political culture the presumably open, even-handed nature of democracy itself has often been responsible for—or at least its defense has been the occasion for—the nation's most *anti-democratic* impulses. Given the racial valences of Enlightenment thinking on self-possession and virtue, from the inception of the new nation the utopian depth of the experiment in self-governance itself foreclosed on the full and equal participation of those deemed to be outside the proper realm of "the people." Democracy, flatly, was too delicate to be entrusted to just any old assemblage of chance comers.

This same "liberty-loving" yet exclusionary logic came forcefully into play in the latter half of the nineteenth century, as the Irish, the Germans, and the new immigrants from Southern and Eastern Europe pressed the boundaries of what had traditionally been considered to be the coextensive territories of whiteness and fit citizenship. Asian immigrants resided entirely outside the pale of civic virtue; and beyond the question of naturalization, the very presence of Chinese newcomers—and later Asians in general—could be excluded outright by law (as indeed they were in 1882, 1917, and 1924). But immigrants from places like Greece, Russia, Italy, or Finland posed a special problem: they were "white" enough to enter the polity as "free white persons," and yet they seemed not to possess the very properties of whiteness—its virtue, its wisdom, its capacity for self-sacrifice—that had suggested the racial qualification for citizenship in the first place. If the ethnological facts were not plain enough, the rise of corrupt urban machines clinched the case: their cogs meshed precisely where the immigrants' overwhelming numbers, their considerable desperation, and their evident disregard for the sanctity of civic responsibility came together.

The U.S. response to these millions of immigrants in the late nineteenth and early twentieth centuries represented a massive revision of "race" itself—a reflexive ideological effort to align the reigning racial conceptions of fit citizenship with the dawning social reality of a polyglot citizenry encompassing ever-larger proportions of patently *unfit* "white persons." It was in this context that Francis Amasa Walker would speak of the "beaten men of beaten races," or that Representative Alden McClure of Ohio would worry for the safety of republican institutions amid the "ethnological animal show" that was the United States in the era of mass immigration.

The nativists' agenda ultimately triumphed in the restrictive legislative acts of 1917, 1921, and 1924 not simply because their racial interpretations had gained the upper hand in American political discourse. On the contrary, restrictive legislation in those years would probably have gone down to defeat, as it had in previous years, had the needs of American employers continued to require the unhindered influx of cheap labor. Shifting needs in manufacturing and the contingencies of coalition politics, that is, not racial ideology pure and simple, explain the shifts in U.S. immigration policy in the early decades of the twentieth century. The advent of an African American proletariat in the industrial cities of the North, the rising tide of anti-radicalism after the war, the mild depression of 1920, and the general maturation of industrial capitalism, which now set a higher premium on trained workers and a relatively lower premium on an abundance of unskilled labor, all converged to tip American business's long-standing support of immigration.

But even so, it is worth noting that the language of restriction did shift significantly between the mid-nineteenth century and the early twentieth. The racial lexicon of "fit" and "unfit" citizenship did eclipse the economic arguments of labor competition within national discussion of immigration policy. From the essentially psychiatric exclusionary categories that were written into immigration law beginning in the late nineteenth century (banning "lunatics," "idiots," and "persons likely to become a public charge," for instance), to the frankly racial categories that framed the quota system, it was the civic concern for a reliable citizenry that uniformly drove the restrictionist legislative agenda after about the 1880s. Over this same period, immigration became more a matter of sovereignty than of commerce, as far as the legislature was concerned. The Alien Contract Labor Law of 1885 marks one of the last pieces of major restrictive legislation whose terms and logic were economic rather than civic.

Throughout this period, the needs of the economy and the needs of the republic were at odds. This tension between capitalism's imperative for cheap and abundant labor on the one hand and republicanism's imperative for a reliable citizenry on the other proved critical to the dynamics of U.S. nationalism. Until the restrictionist temper of the World War I years, profound economic dependence upon foreign labor mingled with a keen civic anxiety regarding the virtue of foreign citizens. This domestic dimension of American nationalism mirrored the U.S. reach across the waters: here, too, economic forces brought more and more foreigners under the purview of the United States—either as consumers or as potential colonial subjects—in a manner that raised questions about the racial outlook for the once-Anglo-Saxon republic. American nationalism, as it was played out both inside and outside of U.S. borders, thus became a peculiar compound of arrogance and anxiety, global reach and parochial vision.

Children of Barbarism: Republican Imperatives and Imperial Wards

> It would be better to abandon this com-
> bined garden and Gibraltar of the Pacific
> [i.e., the Philippines] . . . than to apply
> any academic arrangement of self-
> government to these children. They are
> not capable of self-government. How
> could they be? They are not a self-
> governing race. . . . What alchemy will
> change the oriental quality of their blood
> and set the self-governing currents of the
> American pouring through their Malay
> veins? How shall they, in the twinkling of
> an eye, be exalted to the heights of self-
> governing people which required a thou-
> sand years for us to reach, Anglo-Saxons
> though we are?
>
> —*Albert Beveridge to the*
> *U.S. Senate, January 1900*

AMID HEATED DEBATE over the disposition of the Philippines in 1899, Whitelaw Reid, owner of the *New York Tribune*, candidly declared, "It is time to begin teaching the American people the absurdity of that clause in the Declaration of Independence which derives all just powers of government from the consent of the governed." No such constitutional niceties were required, the expansionist argument now went, among peoples who were innately unfit for the tasks and rigors inherent in self-government. New circumstances in Spain's former colonies gave free rein to a set of racially inflected ideas about self-possession and governance—the proposition, for example, that consent itself was beyond the intellectual and moral reach of certain backward races.

American expansionism had its economic engines, to be sure: the outward thrust for new markets and its ancillary requisites of coaling stations and naval bases had brought the United States into close encounters with the peoples of Hawaii, Samoa, the Philippines, Puerto Rico, Guam, and Cuba in the first place. As Henry Cabot Lodge remarked to President McKinley in May 1898, the nation's domestic market "is not enough for our teeming industries." Were the United States to acquire the Philippine archipelago, for example, and protect it with a high tariff wall, "its ten million inhabitants, as they advance in civilization, would have to buy our goods, and we should have so much additional market for our home manufactures." "Our largest trade must henceforth be with Asia," seconded Indiana Senator Albert Beveridge. "Where shall we turn for consumers of our surplus? . . . The Philippines gives us a base at the door of all the East."

But once that encounter had taken place, pressing questions arose in the political realm. Just as immigration taxed the workings of American democracy, so the nation's expansive mission abroad—the migration of the state, as it were—brought under American influence more and more peoples whose racial character spelled trouble to Anglo-Saxon supremacists. What would be the political relationship between Americans and the peoples of the potential colonies? Was citizenship thinkable? If not, could a free republic hold an array of lands in despotic dependency and still remain a free republic? Could it be, asked Mark Twain in his anti-imperialist tract, "To the Person Sitting in Darkness" (1901), "that there are two kinds of Civilization—one for home consumption and one for the heathen market?" Untroubled by the contradiction, for his part Senator Beveridge railed against the very idea that the peoples of the Pacific could ever be "self-governing" in quite the way of the masterful Anglo-Saxons. "How dare any man prostitute this expression ["self-governing race"] . . . to a race of Malay children of barbarism?" he stormed.

The complexities and possible contradictions were evident at once. As Theodore Roosevelt pronounced in his popular appeal for a renewed racial and "manly" vigor, "The Strenuous Life" (1899), "Many of [the Philippine] people are utterly unfit for self-government, and show no signs of becoming fit. Others may in time become fit, but at present can only take part in self-government under a wise supervision, at once firm and beneficent. We have driven Spanish tyranny from the islands. If we now let it be replaced by savage anarchy, our work has been for harm and not for good."

Trouble, then, potentially lay in either direction. To let peoples like the Filipinos have their hard-won independence would be to refuse a sacred national duty and to invite calamity upon these hapless natives in the form of an inevitable reversion to savagery. And yet American stewardship of these inferior peoples raised problems of its own: How did Americans propose to rule a group that they had defined as innately unruly? What precisely would it mean to let them "take part" in self-governance only under "supervision"? Could such supervision indeed remain "beneficent" if it were rejected—even violently so—by those who were allegedly in need of it? And what was the imagined duration of U.S. involvement lurking in the assertion that these peoples might "in time" achieve the requisite civic habits of independence and self-governance?

American discussion of expansionism and national policy was tensely strung between the poles of duty and distrust, of missionary zeal and the missionary's skepticism toward the prospect of the heathen's redemption. Like Francis Amasa Walker's "beaten men from beaten races" or Lord Bryce's "droves of squalid men" who now took up their place in the urban, working-class wards of the American polity, the "savage" Caribbean and Pacific natives who came under the sway of U.S. power at the turn of the century sorely tested American ideals of liberty, governance, and consent. As Teddy Roosevelt wrote to Brooks Adams, "In the long run civilized man finds he can keep the peace only by subduing his barbarian neighbor." This was a version of "keeping the peace" that, beginning with the wars of 1898–1902, would characterize American foreign policy throughout much of the twentieth century, and would indeed become a central tenet in the canons of American nationalism.

Imperialism and Anti-Imperialism

Expansionism did not spring upon the United States from nowhere in the summer of 1898. No nation whose history had been so expansive—including trans-Atlantic migration, settlement, and conquest; trans-Appalachian migration; the Louisiana Purchase and Indian Removal; Manifest Destiny; the Mexican War, and the annexations of Texas, California, the Southwestern territories, and Alaska—could plausibly feign surprise when, at the end of the very decade in which the superintendent of the census had declared the frontier "closed," a new frontier opened up farther west, across the Pacific. "We had not pondered [the 1890 census] a single decade," remarked Woodrow Wilson, "before we made new frontiers for ourselves beyond the seas." But many felt at the time that trans-Pacific expansion represented something altogether new; and this has become a comforting conceit for later generations. Disavowing the continuity in the nation's expansionist history allows for phrases like "the imperialist moment of 1899," or the "imperialist experiment in the Philippines," as though this fleeting episode were utterly detached from the balance of U.S. history—as though it *were* fleeting.

In fact, the entire period from 1876 to 1917 is best understood as an imperialist epoch. These years witnessed Indian wars in the West, the last phase in the subjugation of the continent in the 1870s; trans-Pacific involvement in Samoa, Hawaii, Wake, Guam, and the Philippines, and Caribbean interventions in Cuba and Puerto Rico at the century's close; and a number of Latin American interventions in the 1900s and 1910s, including the taking of Panama. Expansionism likewise held a conspicuous place in cultural ritual, celebration, and representation throughout the period—in popular fiction, in Wild West shows, in the novel cultural form of motion pictures (whose earliest narrative endeavors included re-enactments of the U.S. war in the Philippines, staged in the jungles of New Jersey), and in the string of lavish world's fairs from Philadelphia (1876) to Chicago (1893) to St. Louis (1904) to San Francisco (1915), each profoundly structured by the aspersions, the aspirations, and the national self-ascriptions associated with empire.

Despite such a diffuse currency, however, the issue of empire did come into exceptionally sharp focus in 1898, when the war with Spain raised urgent questions regarding military necessity (would the United States "need" Hawaii as a way station to the Asian theater?) and the spoils of war (how should vanquished Spain's colonies be disposed?). Now Americans were called upon to debate directly and to pronounce upon the fate of a variety of peoples who inhabited what might conceivably become "isthmian approaches" and trans-Pacific coaling stations and bases for a far-flung American empire. The United States had established its first governing presence overseas, in Samoa (along with Germany and Great Britain), in 1890. Now, eight years later, as Spain retreated from its colonies and U.S. naval and ground forces spread from the Caribbean to the Far East, policy-makers pondered questions of territorial status and governance in Hawaii, whose white elites had been seeking annexation ever since their coup against Queen Liliuokalani in 1893; and in Cuba, Puerto Rico, and the Philippines, whose liberation from Spain left many questions open regarding their future, their potential peril at the hands of yet other European predators, and their proper political relationship to their American "allies."

Here one sees with unremitting clarity the tension between, on the one hand, aggrandizing national designs, and, on the other, civic fears of those strange peoples whom national aggrandizement had rather suddenly brought into the compass of U.S. concern. Both economic aspiration and long-standing tradition of racial *noblesse oblige* seemed to dictate that these "island treasures" simply be taken by the United States, these savage populations gradually "uplifted" and "civilized" under the tutelage of their racial betters. And yet, as commentators from across the political spectrum noted, precisely the racial inferiority that suggested U.S. stewardship over these peoples in the first place also raised vexing questions about their presence within the bounds of the self-governing republic. As New York Senator Carl Schurz wrote in 1899, the consequences following "the admission of the Spanish creoles and the negroes of the West India islands and of the Malays and Tagals of the Philippines to participation in the conduct of our government is so alarming that you instinctively pause before taking the step." Americans did pause, therefore, before taking the step. And though they did ultimately take the step of assuming "the white man's burden" in the Caribbean and the Pacific, the various political arrangements under which these islands entered the U.S. sphere—ingeniously excluding their "participation in the conduct of our government"—reflected the very alarm of which Schurz had spoken.

Certainly one of the dominant strains in the discussion of U.S. policy toward the peoples of the Caribbean and the Pacific was good old spread-eagled, racialist, masculinist bluster and venom. Albert Beveridge's impassioned Senate speech in January 1900 offered the clearest distillation of the nationalist imperatives now commonly evoked by proponents of expansionism—economic, racial, religious, and political concerns all atangle. "The Philippines are ours forever," Beveridge announced.

> *And just beyond the Philippines are China's illimitable markets. We will not retreat from either. We will not repudiate our duty in the Orient. We will not renounce our part in the mission of our race, trustees under God, of the civilization of the world. And we will move forward to our work, not howling out regrets like slaves whipped to their burdens, but with gratitude for a task worthy of our strength, and thanksgiving to Almighty God that He has marked us as His chosen people, henceforth to lead in the regeneration of the world.*

But the presumed Anglo-Saxon superiority that justified American expansion over distant reaches of the globe also called into question the proper relationship between the United States and its new, inferior stewards. As Teddy Roosevelt wrote to Rudyard Kipling, in dealing with the Philippines he had first to deal with "the jack-fools who seriously think that any group of pirates and head-hunters needs nothing but independence in order that it may be turned forthwith into a dark-hued New England town meeting." "Only the exceptional people have ever succeeded in the experiment of self-government," he remarked elsewhere, "because its needs, its interest, and its successful working imply the existence within the heart of the average citizen of certain very high qualities. There must be control. There must be mastery, somewhere, and if there is no self-control and self-mastery, the control and the mastery will ultimately be imposed from without." Having liberated these peoples so lacking in republican virtue, the United States could now only succeed Spain as the power who, by force if necessary, would impose "control and mastery" upon them from without.

Even Beveridge had to concede the perils of governance in a case so shaky as that of the Filipinos. "It will be hard for Americans who have not studied them to understand the people," he said, ". . . My own belief is that there are not 100 men among them who comprehend what Anglo-Saxon self-government even means, and there are over 5,000,000 people to be governed." But for Beveridge and others, the contradictions were easily resolved. The Declaration of Independence, first of all, was never meant to apply to peoples like the Filipinos. And though that particular piece of American political tradition did not apply in the case of the Philippines, there was nevertheless one that did: Manifest Destiny. "God has not been preparing the English-speaking and Teutonic peoples for a thousand years for nothing but vain self-contemplation and self-admiration," insisted Beveridge, echoing the mid-century expansionist orators on Mexico and the West. "No! He has made us the master organizers of the world to establish system where chaos reigns. He has given us the spirit of progress to overwhelm the forces of reaction throughout the earth. He has made us adept in government that we may administer government among savage and senile peoples. Were it not for such a force as this the world would relapse into barbarism and night."

William Howard Taft, who was to become the Philippine commissioner in 1900, also calculated that 90 percent of the Philippine population was "in a hopeless condition of ignorance, and utterly unable intelligently to wield political control." "Our little brown brothers," in his formulation, would need "fifty or one hundred years" of close supervision "to develop anything resembling Anglo-Saxon political principles and skills." Likewise, the popular Philippine exhibit at the St. Louis World's Fair in 1904 was a living monument to the idea of the Filipino's unfitness for self-government. As one journalist remarked, this authentic re-creation of the Filipinos' savage lifeways amid an imported assemblage of genuine Philippine thatched huts "disabused [Americans] of any impression that the natives could take care of themselves." The task, as it was articulated in policy circles and in street-level discussion, then, would be not only to take these islands but to "take care of" their people—to draw them under U.S. control without granting any of the rights or privileges that, in the hands of such "savages," might expose the nation's porous political culture to inferior influences or taint.

As Albert Beveridge's unceremonious scrapping of the Declaration of Independence might suggest, expansionist thought did generate its own heated opposition. On June 2, 1898, a month after Admiral Dewey's victory over the Spanish in Manila Bay had lent the imperialism question its unexpected urgency, Boston reformer Gamaliel Bradford called a meeting at Faneuil Hall to protest the "insane and wicked ambition which is driving the nation to ruin." His call brought forward hundreds of prominent reformers and aging abolitionists. Over the course of the summer and autumn, the protest broadened, and in November the movement crystallized in the New England Anti-Imperialist League. Sensing its growing strength, the league made an ambitious promise to President McKinley to deliver an anti-imperialist petition bearing no fewer than ten million signatures. But within the next several months, although the league had gone national and claimed over seventy thousand members, the petition drive died out at a miserable five thousand signatures; and the United States, meanwhile, strengthened its hold on Samoa, annexed Hawaii outright, and extended its influence in various forms over Cuba, Puerto Rico, the Philippines, Wake, and Guam.

The momentum of these events should not conceal the breadth of anti-imperialist sentiment. In the Senate vote on the Treaty of Paris (by which Spain ceded the Philippines to the United States), one staunch and unambiguous anti-imperialist resolution was defeated by the single tie-breaking vote of Vice President Garret Hobart; a watered-down resolution actually passed by a vote of twenty-six to twenty-two. Even so enthusiastic an imperialist as Henry Cabot Lodge had to admit that the battle over ratification had been "the closest, hardest fight I have ever known."

Nor should the league be mistaken for the anti-imperialist movement itself. Led by ex-abolitionist George Boutwell and a prestigious body of forty-one officers—a veritable *Who's Who*, including Andrew Carnegie, Carl Schurz, Benjamin Harrison, Jane Addams, Grover Cleveland, Moorfield Storey, and E. L. Godkin—the league ultimately failed to gather disparate anti-imperialists at the grassroots level. By its strategy of bringing political pressure to bear primarily through the nation's "better elements," the league neglected many of its natural allies—African Americans, immigrants, and labor most notably. Moreover, by its genteel reformist style, its old republicanist stance, its Anglo-Saxon biases, and its didactic social bearing, the league fully alienated many others.

The arguments against imperialism in 1899 were so varied as to preclude any viable political coalition; it was this, rather than any *absence* of opposition, that expansionists like Roosevelt and Lodge exploited in their effort to make imperialist designs into national policies. We must stand "shoulder to shoulder," exhorted anti-imperialist leader Erving Winslow, "Republican, Democrat, Socialist, Populist, Gold-man, Silver-man, and Mugwump, for the one momentous, vital, paramount issue, Anti-Imperialism and the preservation of the Republic." Winslow knew something about such motley coalition-building: he and fellow "Mugwump" reformers had broken with their beloved Republican Party on principle in 1884, and their alliance with the Democrats had helped to put Grover Cleveland in the White House.

Still, "standing shoulder to shoulder" with diverse anti-imperialists at century's end was easier said than done. Indeed, deep differences among their visions of "the Republic" and its virtues within this assembly made a unified statement on this "paramount issue" impossible. Anti-imperialist Mark Twain could acidly denounce "the Blessings-of-Civilization Trust" and its mistreatment of the so-called savages; anti-imperialist Samuel Gompers frankly worried over "an inundation of Mongolians" swarming to the U.S. mainland to overwhelm white labor. Andrew Carnegie could object that a colonial adventure in the tropics would provoke Europe, alienate Latin America, and so jeopardize important foreign markets for American goods; his anti-imperialist "ally" Eugene Debs, meanwhile, rather bristled at the prospect of "making a market by the force of arms and at the expense of . . . a people whose only offense has been their love of freedom and self-control." John Mitchell, the African American editor of the *Richmond Planet*, could object that the United States should not export its race prejudice across the Pacific; and white supremacist "Pitchfork" Ben Tillman of South Carolina shuddered at the notion of *importing* "any more colored men into the body politic." The anti-imperialist movement thus inherited long-standing feuds of Anglophiles with immigrants, capital with labor, radicals with conservatives, goldbugs with silverites, and African Americans with white Southern aristocrats.

E. L. Godkin had rather impressively conveyed the ideological tensions within anti-imperialist thought when he amassed the objections to Hawaiian annexation in a piece for *The Nation* as early as January 1898. Among the reasons to oppose imperialism, according to Godkin, were:

The sudden departure from our traditions; the absence from our system of any machinery for governing dependencies; the admission of alien, inferior, and mongrel races to our nationality; the opening of fresh fields to carpet-baggers, speculators, and corruptionists; the un-Americanism of governing a large body of people against their will, and by persons not responsible to them; the entrance on a policy of conquest and annexation while our own continent is still unreclaimed, our population unassimilated, and many of our most serious political problems still unsolved; and finally the danger of the endorsement of a gross fraud for the first time by a Christian nation.

Godkin here spins out a veritable color wheel of high principle and low invective. High-sounding appeals to the best principles of the Constitution—what Lincoln might have meant by the "better angels of our nature"—shade into frank denunciations of "mongrel races" and insinuating allusions to the "unassimilated" peoples and unsolved problems within this "Christian" nation. In a single breath, Godkin endorses the aspirations of a people spurning government "against their will" by an outside power, *and* he fears for the future of that outside power itself, should this "inferior" people gain admission to nationality. The ease with which Godkin makes these moves illuminates what a peculiar beast American anti-imperialism could be.

In the present context, the most significant ideological strands were those that linked many anti-imperialists—like Godkin—with their presumed enemies in the expansionist camp. It is true that some articulated a radical and uncompromising anti-imperialism. Just a few weeks after fighting had broken out in Manila in 1899, for instance, Harvard philosopher William James denounced the "brutal piracy" of U.S. policy, calling for freedom for the Filipinos, whether " 'fit' or 'unfit,' "—"home rule . . . and whatever anarchy may go with it until the Filipinos learn from each other, not from us, how to govern themselves." Mark Twain, too, declared in a letter to Albert Sonnichsen, whose *Ten Months a Captive Among Filipinos* offered a rare, sympathetic portrait of the independence movement, "The hearts of men are about alike, all over the world, no matter what their skin-complexions may be." Wherever one finds a nation "whose hearts are not debauched," he went on, "the civilization that obtains in that nation is high, and its possessors may be trusted to be able to govern themselves about as well as we, the subjects of Mr. Croker, could do it for them."

But two decidedly racialist (paradoxically, *imperialist*) strains of anti-imperialist comment did unite many dissenters with their avowed political adversaries. One we might call the constitutionalist argument: Godkin's concern, for instance, over the proposed "departure from our traditions," the nation's lack of suitable legal "machinery for governing dependencies," the "opening of fresh fields to carpet-baggers, speculators, and corruptionists"—in a word, the "un-Americanism" of the project. Though perhaps advancing the cause of Philippine independence, such argument was inherently imperialist in that it identified not Filipinos but Americans, and their hallowed traditions, as the real victims of expansion and violent dispossession.

Like their counterparts in the expansionist camp, that is, these combatants in the debate took but little account of Filipino lives. "Much as we abhor the war of 'criminal aggression' in the Philippines," ran the Anti-Imperialist League's platform, "greatly as we regret that the blood of the Filipinos is on American hands, *we more deeply resent the betrayal of American institutions at home. The real firing line is not in the suburbs of Manila. The foe is of our own household. The attempt in 1861 was to divide the country. That of 1899 is to destroy its fundamental principles and noblest ideals." The duration of the protracted slaughter in the Philippines "is but an incident in a contest that must go on until the Declaration of Independence and the Constitution of the United States are rescued from the hands of their betrayers." The league did recoil at the "needless horror" of the slaughter in the Philippines but, finally, saw this as merely incidental to the weightier matter of democracy's peril at home.

In some cases such reasoning may have been but a rhetorical ploy, an effort to win over an American audience by enumerating the costs of empire in strictly American terms. But the constitutionalist argument is suspect in that it was so often combined, as in Godkin's formulation, with a second, fundamentally imperialist strain of thinking, an overtly racialist disdain for the "alien, inferior, and mongrel races" of the Philippines. And Godkin was scarcely the worst in this regard. Even the German '48er and onetime aboli-

tionist Carl Schurz worried that, should any of the Caribbean or Pacific islands be admitted to the union on equal footing with the other states, "they
will not only be permitted to govern themselves as to their home concerns,
but will take part in governing the whole republic, in governing us, by sending senators and representatives into our Congress to help make our laws,
and by voting for president and vice-president to give our national government its executive." It was here that Schurz opined how "alarming" was the
prospect of granting the peoples of the former Spanish colonies the right to
participate "in the conduct of our government."

Many whites from Southern and border states were less restrained on the
racial question, if this can be called restraint. Sharpening the polemic edge
on Schurz's basic premise, Representative Champ Clark of Missouri snapped,
"No matter whether they are fit to govern themselves or not, they are not fit
to govern us [applause]." But, questions of innate fitness aside, if Southern
history taught nothing else it at least taught that racial diversity was not to
be taken lightly in a self-governing republic, and that racial homogeneity
represented a virtue in and of itself. As "Pitchfork" Ben Tillman explained,
Southerners "understand and realize what it is to have two races side by side
that can not mix or mingle without deterioration and injury to both and the
ultimate destruction of the civilization of the higher." As a senator from
South Carolina, "with 750,000 colored population and only 500,000 whites,
I realize what you [expansionists] are doing, while you don't; and I would
save this country from the injection into it of another race question which
can only breed bloodshed and a costly war and the loss of the lives of our
brave soldiers."

Tillman's colleague in the Senate, John Daniel of Virginia, raised this
racial specter in sexual terms, moving quickly from annexation as a kind of
figurative miscegenation to the certainty of literally mingled blood: "Today
we are the United States of America," he warned. "Tomorrow . . . we will be
the United States of America and Asia. It is a marriage of nations. This twain
will become one flesh. They become bone of our bone and flesh of our flesh.
Henceforth and forever, according to the terminology of this treaty, the Filipinos and Americans are one."

Given the stresses that expansion into the world's "waste spaces" was perceived to put on the functioning of republican government and on the very notion of competent citizenship, it is not surprising that the ranks of the anti-imperialist movement would be populated by many who were even more virulent in their racism than imperialists like Albert Beveridge. Racialism thus constituted the very ground upon which the imperialism question was largely debated among white Americans: some espoused expansionism because of their pronounced racial disdain for the peoples of the Pacific and elsewhere; some opposed expansion based on precisely the same set of presuppositions and patterns of disdain. As one senator put it during the debate over Hawaiian annexation in 1898, "How can we endure our shame when a Chinese senator from Hawaii, with his pigtail hanging down his back, with his pagan joss [idol] in his hand, shall rise from his [honored seat in the Senate] . . . and in pidgin English proceed to chop logic with George Frisbee Hoar or Henry Cabot Lodge?" Or, as Major General John Dickman wrote with perhaps more candor still when Cubans accused the United States of harboring plans for annexation, "You ought to see them squirm when I tell them that your Uncle Samuel has too many niggers already."

This impulse, too, had a rather long pedigree in American political thinking: during Senate debate over Mexican annexation fifty years earlier, one Southern senator had expressed anxiety over the nation's receiving "not merely the white citizens of California and New Mexico, but the peons, negroes, and Indians of all sorts, the wild tribe of Comanches, the bug-and-lizard-eating 'Diggers,' and other half-monkey savages in those countries, *as equal citizens of the United States.*" However attractive might be the riches held out by expansionism, in other words, from a civic standpoint racial isolation had much to recommend it.

From the debate on Hawaii in the summer of 1898, then, to the conclusion of the war against Philippine independence in 1902 (and, indeed, up through the Wilson administration, which passed new Organic Acts for both Puerto Rico and the Philippines), white Americans articulated a double-edged disdain for the "children of barbarism" who populated the islands of the Caribbean and the Pacific. One argument ran that such backward peoples were fit for nothing but domination by a progressive power like the United States—indeed, that the United States was divinely "intended" for just such a task; the other, that their savagery itself presented a compelling reason to let these peoples alone. "Tis not more than two months since ye larned whether they were islands or canned goods," quipped Finley Peter Dunne's organic wit, Mr. Dooley. But the unresolved fate of these hitherto obscure islands were "makin' puzzles f'r our poor tired heads" just the same. "Ivry night, whin I'm countin' up the cash," Dooley moaned, "I'm askin' meself will I annex Cubia or lave it to the Cubians? Will I take Porther Ricky or put it by? An' what shud I do with the Ph'lippeens? Oh, what shud I do with thim?" Should such places be taken? And how could they be smoothly governed?

The Disposition of "Our New Island Treasures"

Anti-imperialists may have lost every battle over U.S. policy between the Hawaiian annexation debate in 1898 and the passage of the various acts determining U.S. governance in the Caribbean and the Philippines early in the new century. But the mechanisms of governance developed in these areas did reflect the broad, undergirding consensus on race that united many anti-imperialists with their triumphant expansionist counterparts. Each region found itself gripped in U.S. possession only at arm's length: the United States held them, to be sure, but at a safe distance from anything approximating full citizenship, equality, or participation in the sacred workings of self-government.

Hawaii was a peculiar case among the territories seized in this period in that it had a sizable population of European and American settlers who, after the revolution staged against Queen Liliuokalani in 1893, held political control of the islands and actively sought admission to the United States. According to a census in 1896, native Hawaiians constituted 28 percent of the population; Japanese, 22 percent; Americans and Europeans, 22 percent; Chinese, 20 percent; and racially mixed peoples, 8 percent. But the terms of the 1894 Constitution drawn up by whites made it very difficult for the multiethnic nonwhite plurality to participate in the governance of the islands (after the revolution, the franchise was narrowed from fourteen thousand to only twenty-eight hundred, many of whom were employees of Dole

Pineapple). Among other things, the qualifications for suffrage included a pledge to support the new Hawaiian Constitution, which in its turn provided for eventual annexation to the United States. The very aspiration of Hawaiian independence, that is, was grounds for disenfranchisement. Thus, although three-quarters of the population were, in racialist estimations of the day, only questionably capable of self-government, the islands did have a "natural" white aristocracy who not only held jealously the reins of power but did so avowedly toward the end of ultimate annexation to the United States. Once annexation had been accomplished, would the terms of statehood allow the exclusive rule of this white minority to continue?

President Cleveland had rebuffed the annexationists' hopes in 1893; an annexation treaty put forward by McKinley in 1897 failed to win the necessary two-thirds vote. Throughout these years, antiannexationist sentiment drew upon a cluster of principles that were at bottom racial and that, by now, are quite familiar: the population of the islands was too dissimilar from the existing American population to be safely admitted; the well-established principle of Chinese Exclusion precluded any arrangement that would allow for the admission of a population like Hawaii's; Asian and Pacific ("tropical") peoples were as unsuited to the rigors of American political culture as Anglo-Saxons were to tropical climates; and the United States had never had a happy result from its experiments with "inferior" races. Asked one senator from Indiana, in what was to become a standard refrain throughout the debate, "Shall great public issues affecting the vital interests of all our people be submitted for determination to the Senators and Representatives from Hawaii?"

The war with Spain was a turning-point in the debate. Now the pressing issue of military necessity, not the abstract principles of governance, decided the question. The islands were hailed as an indispensable way station for the U.S. fleet in the Pacific, notwithstanding the reasonable objection of Representative Champ Clark that, if Dewey's "great victory proves anything at all about these islands, it is that we have no earthly use for them, for he could not have done better if we owned all the islands in all the seas." Congressional opposition to annexation creaked and collapsed in July 1898, in part under the weight of the emboldened wartime rhetoric of national destiny, in part under the weight of the compelling (if specious) argument of "military necessity." In late summer, the Hawaiian flag came down for the last time and the U.S. flag was raised amid the mournful weeping of the relatively few native Hawaiians who showed up for the ceremony.

Their sorrow was well founded. The government that Congress established for the Territory of Hawaii extended Chinese Exclusion to the islands, and it limited U.S. citizenship to "all white persons, including Portuguese, and persons of African descent, and all persons descended from the Hawaiian race . . . who were citizens of the Republic of Hawaii immediately prior to transfer [of sovereignty]." Property qualifications to hold office in either the Senate or the House of Representatives of Hawaii ensured that governance remained in the hands of the white elite; and a combination of property and literacy qualifications (in addition to a rigorous set of procedural rules) significantly narrowed the franchise. Further, every applicant for suffrage would be examined by a board of registration that held broad discretion to pronounce upon his qualifications, including the power to summon its own witnesses. Leaving nothing at all to chance, Congress also provided that private citizens, too, had the right to challenge and to cross-examine any person whose claims to eligibility for the vote they deemed questionable. This rather impressive array of obstacles to political participation led one Southern legislator, William Kitchin of North Carolina, to remark that the laws were "very like ours"—that is, very like the laws that disenfranchised blacks across the "redeemed" South in the wake of Reconstruction.

Hawaiian petitions for statehood were rejected in 1903, 1911, 1913, and 1915. Thus the United States took the Hawaiian Islands without, as it were, taking the Hawaiians. The practical effect of this political limbo was perhaps best summed up by the secretary of the Hawaiian Sugar Planters' Association, testifying before Congress in 1910: "The Asiatic has had only an economic value in the social equation," he asserted. "So far as the institutions, laws, customs, and language of the permanent population go, his presence is no more felt than is that of the cattle on the ranges." This presumption would be contested in myriad ways for many years to come, just as Asians had contested similar presumptions in the courts and in the culture of the American West. As a statement of political *intent*, however, the secretary had voiced an impeccable truth regarding the civic standing of the "Asiatic" in American—and now Hawaiian—political culture.

Cuba represented yet another variation on this pattern of the United States' assuming control of a territory without opening itself up to the hazards of democratic participation. Given the outpourings of American sympathy for Cubans who suffered the yoke and the lash of Spanish General Valeriano "Butcher" Weyler in the years leading up to the Spanish-Cuban-American War, one might have expected some enthusiasm for the idea of Cuban independence in the years after the Spanish were vanquished. But if Cuba was personified as a white damsel in distress in the melodramas of American political discourse through mid-1898, the island symbolically became a guileless plantation "darky" once discussion had turned to the political fate of the newly freed island—an unruly, decidedly black male whose claims to political independence were made ridiculous by his disqualifying racial traits. Indeed, political cartoons of the era demonstrate precisely this transformation in the Cubans' image among North Americans.

As historian Louis Perez, Jr., has found, the Cubans' unfitness for self-government was the central theme of U.S. debate once Spain had been removed from the picture, particularly among those military and political figures engaged in the day-to-day business of administering the island's affairs in the interim. "Why[,] those people are no more fit for self-government than gunpowder is for hell," declared General William Schafter. Others, if less colorful in their pronouncements, concurred with Schafter's assessment. General Samuel Young: the "insurgents are a lot of degenerates, absolutely devoid of honor and gratitude. They are no more capable of self-government than the savages of Africa." Major George Barbour, the U.S. sanitary commissioner in Santiago de Cuba: the Cubans "are stupid, given to lying and doing all things in the wrong way. . . . Under our supervision . . . the people of Cuba may become a useful race and a credit to the world; but to attempt to set them afloat as a nation, during this generation, would be a great mistake." And Governor General Leonard Wood: "We are dealing with a race that has steadily been going down for a hundred years and into which we have to infuse new life, new principles and new methods of doing things." When the United States declared war on Spain, Wood asserted, it had become "responsible for the welfare of the people, politically, mentally and morally."

The chief task of American stewardship in the wake of Spain's departure was to establish stable and reliable mechanisms for Cuban government. Ironically, what Cuba had most to be protected *from*, in American eyes, was the overzealous program of Cuban *independentistas*. As a start, the United States enacted Cuban franchise legislation whose restrictions reduced the electorate to roughly 5 percent of the island's population. The restrictions were designed to keep power out of the hands of Cuba's "mass of ignorant and incompetent" inhabitants, in Secretary of War Elihu Root's phrase, and so to weaken the independence movement, whose most radical force was among the lower classes. Or so Americans thought. Despite the narrow franchise, the *independentistas* prevailed in municipal and assembly elections in 1900; Americans would have to find another way of achieving "stable" government on the island.

The eventual instrument of U.S. aims in Cuba was a parcel of provisions designed by Root in 1901 and incorporated into a treaty with Cuba as the Platt Amendment in 1903. Deftly navigating within the difficult parameters of U.S. concern on the matter—a congressional amendment to the U.S. Declaration of War with Spain had proscribed the annexation of Cuba, and yet the idea of true independence for the island was rejected as absurd—Root's proposal, like the provisions for government in the Territory of Hawaii, assumed U.S. control over Cuba without quite assuming any Cubans. The Platt Amendment forbade Cubans to enter into treaties with foreign powers on their own behalf; it limited the Cuban government's power to assume or contract public debt; it provided for the cession of necessary lands to the United States for coaling and naval stations; and, most significantly, it granted the United States "the right to intervene for the preservation of Cuban independence, the maintenance of a government adequate for the protection of life, property, and individual liberty."

At the heart of this arrangement was the U.S. certainty that Cubans were not fit to manage their own affairs. Though Cuba might be protected from the predatory powers of Europe, warned Albert Beveridge, "the welfare of the Cuban people was still open to attack from another enemy and at their weakest point. That point was within and that enemy was themselves." If it was Americans' business to see that the Cubans were not destroyed by any foreign power, was it not also their duty to see that Cubans were not destroyed by their own incapacities? For his part, Elihu Root asserted that the character of the Cubans themselves would "require the restraining influence of the [the United States] for many years to come," and he flatly declared that this proposal represented the "extreme limit" of U.S. "indulgence" in the matter of Cuban independence. Thus did one Caribbean dream of independence sink in the American waters of race and self-governance. As revolutionist José Martí had wondered back on the eve of U.S. intervention in the war with Spain, "Once the United States is in Cuba who will get her out?"

Governmental affairs in Puerto Rico assumed yet a third configuration, though to precisely the same effect. Spanish military rule in Puerto Rico officially came to an end on October 18, 1898, when U.S. Major General John Brooke became the island's military governor. (Spain retained nominal sovereignty until the treaty of peace was ratified.) Most significant for the inhabitants of Puerto Rico, as for those of the Philippines, was a provision in the Treaty of Paris stipulating that "the civil rights and political status of the native inhabitants of the territories hereby ceded to the United States shall be determined by Congress." For the time, the military governor maintained his rule on the island just as he had before the treaty was signed; he prepared the island—or so he thought—for the governmental status of a "territory" whose eventual political fate would be statehood. President McKinley, too, acted at first as though Puerto Rico could expect to go the way of Alaska and other U.S. territories, with the single foreboding exception that in his scheme the president and the Senate of the United States would undertake certain decisions and appointments for the islands that in other territories devolved upon the people themselves. "I have not thought it wise to commit the entire government of the island to officers selected by the people," he explained, "because I doubt whether in habits, training, and experience they are such as to fit them to exercise at once so large a degree of self-government."

Though many continued to assume that Puerto Rico would enjoy normal territorial status, the doubts voiced by McKinley and others were in ascendance in the critical legislative months of early 1900. An initial bill introduced by Senator Foraker of Ohio (chairman of the Committee on the Pacific Islands and Puerto Rico) specified that inhabitants of the island would be deemed "citizens of the United States," and that all legal proceedings conducted by this body politic "shall run in the name of 'The United States of America, island of Puerto Rico.' " But a massive revision of that bill in ensuing months resulted in a novel governmental status for Puerto Rico, the creation of a legal entity virtually unknown elsewhere in American history. Inhabitants were no longer "citizens of the United States," for example, but, rather, "citizens of Porto Rico, and as such entitled to the protection of the United States." The revised version also did away with all references to the U.S. Constitution as providing the legal framework for the islands; and it revoked one of the major rights of other American territorial governments, the right to elect one delegate to serve as a nonvoting member of the United States House of Representatives. A Senate report justifying the changes stated baldly that, since Puerto Ricans represented an "illiterate" population of a "wholly different character," they were "unacquainted" with traditions of self-government and were "incapable of exercising the rights and privileges guaranteed by the Constitution." "If we should acquire territory populated by an intelligent, capable and law-abiding people," the report ran, "to whom the right of self-government could be safely conceded, we might at once, with propriety and certainly within the scope of our constitutional power, incorporate that territory and people into the Union as an integral part of our territory, and, by making them a State as a constituent part of the United States, and extend to them at once the Constitution of the United States." Were the territory inhabited by the politically unfit, on the other hand, as was the case in Puerto Rico, it behooved Congress to "hold the territory as a mere possession" and to "govern the people thereof as their situation and the necessities of their case might seem to require."

Throughout continued debates over statehood and citizenship for Puerto Ricans in the 1900s and 1910s, the racialist argument regarding "fit" republicanism held tremendous sway. In 1912, William Atkinson Jones, chair of the Committee on Insular Affairs, submitted a second Organic Act for

Puerto Rico, which would pass only after five more years of bitter debate and periodic shelving. The major article of the bill granted U.S. citizenship to Puerto Ricans, a point that would be debated with some rancor until the Jones Act passed in 1917. The war with Spain had bequeathed to the United States "an incongruous, inharmonious, and entirely unassimilable people," declared one Texas congressman in a rather backhanded plea for Puerto Rican independence early on in this drawn-out discussion. In both the Philippines and the West Indies, "we got a people who can make no contribution to our political institutions, no contribution to our civilization in any way, that we would regard as valuable." "Political mixing with alien people is as dangerous and unprofitable to the State as physical mixing is sinful and hurtful to us as a people," he warned. Echoed a Mississippi senator in 1917, as the question still loomed, "I think we have enough of that element in the body politic already to menace the nation with mongrelization." As far as he was concerned, "It is a misfortune to take that class of people into the body politic. They will never, no, not in a thousand years, understand the genius of our government or share our ideals of government."

The final terms of the Jones Act did grant Puerto Ricans U.S. citizenship, but also imposed literacy and property requirements for suffrage that privileged Puerto Rican whites and effectively disenfranchised 70 percent of the adult male population of the island. Thus, as one historian has put it, did the United States impose "a system of government less democratic than the government previously allowed by autocratic Spain."

The Philippines represented at once the most complex and the simplest of these imperialist forays: complex because the battle was so hard-fought on the part of Filipinos set on independence, simple because here, at the barrel of a gun and under the "tutelage" of a bureaucratic colonial administration, Filipinos succumbed to U.S. imperial power in its most naked form. Tensions arose soon after Admiral Dewey's victory over the Spanish fleet in Manila Bay in May 1898. Like their Cuban counterparts, Filipinos had to wonder about the role of the United States in their country once the Spanish tyrants had been vanquished. Nationalist leader Emilio Aguinaldo entered into a military partnership with the United States with the understanding, as he put it in his diary, that "the United States would at least recognize the independence of the Philippines under the protection of the U.S. Navy." On this point Aguinaldo settled for the oral assurances of E. Spencer Pratt, the U.S. consul at Singapore, who purported to speak for Admiral Dewey. Aguinaldo also took solace in American political tradition itself: "I have studied attentively the Constitution of the United States," he told U.S. General T. M. Anderson, "and I find in it no authority for colonies, and I have no fear."

Although the Englishman who served as interpreter for the Aguinaldo-Pratt discussions swore that Aguinaldo's version was correct, Washington (and Dewey himself) disavowed any such promise of Philippine independence. Dewey did deem the Filipinos "far superior in intelligence and more capable of self-government than the natives of Cuba," but still he kept his distance, avoiding what he called "any entangling alliance" with the Filipino insurgents. Thus, as the Spanish regime in Manila toppled, U.S. and Philippine forces were already jockeying for potential control of the city. But as the War Department cabled the U.S. general in the field, "There must be no joint occupation with the insurgents. . . . The insurgents and all others must recognize the military occupation and authority of the United States."

What ensued, after several tense months during which Aguinaldo vainly continued to pursue recognition for the independence movement, was the United States' first land war in Asia. Filipinos had lodged a list of grievances against the U.S. occupying force, among them its failure to include the Filipino army in the Spanish capitulation at Manila, its aggressive expansion beyond the boundaries of Manila proper, its seizure of several small Philippine craft, and its insulting prohibition against the flying of the Philippine flag. U.S. troops, for their part, were "just itching to get at the 'niggers,'" according to one contemporary report. Hostilities broke out between Aguinaldo's troops and the U.S. Army on the outskirts of Manila on February 4, 1899, and organized warfare continued in one form or another until the last of the insurgents surrendered in May 1902. Sporadic violence punctuated later years as well.

This was a brutal war. Approximately three thousand Filipino soldiers died on the very first day of fighting alone. Nor was this the quick, token, face-saving skirmish that General Elwell Otis had predicted of the Filipinos.

Rather, after that first, extraordinarily grim day of battle, the war rolled on for some eleven hundred additional days—a conventional war of set-piece battles from February to May of 1899, followed, upon Aguinaldo's orders to disperse, by a protracted guerrilla war that dragged well into the spring of 1902. Estimates vary wildly, but most modern historians set the death toll at around 220,000 for the Filipinos (attributed to the war and to the indirect ravages of war—pestilence, disease, and famine) and forty-two hundred for the Americans. Some set the Filipino toll as high as a million, once all war-derived health perils have been duly considered.

Most Americans were stunned by the tenacity of what they thought a hopelessly outmatched enemy. As one editorial in *The Call* summarized early on, General Otis's " 'crushing blows' do not crush. We have probably killed thousands. . . . Our troops have pushed the unavailing butchery of war with uncomplaining endurance and dash. Yet the barefooted enemy, remembering his hut burned and his paddy field destroyed, lurks in the jungle and fights."

On the U.S. side, the savagery of the war certainly derived from the racial preconceptions of this "barefooted," "savage" enemy. As a correspondent for the *Philadelphia Ledger* explained, "It is not civilized warfare, but we are not dealing with a civilized people. The only thing they know and fear is force, violence, and brutality, and we give it to them." Such views were axiomatic among American military leaders in the Philippines, many of whom, including Generals Wesley Merritt, Adna Chaffee, and Jacob ("Hell Roarin' Jake") Smith, had cut their military teeth in the Indian Wars of the American West. But racial thinking permeated the ranks from boots to brass. As one Kingston, New York, volunteer wrote home in May 1899, in a letter that was widely circulated in the press as far away as San Francisco, "Last night one of our boys was found shot and his stomach cut open. Immediately orders were received from General Wheaton to burn the town and kill every native in sight; which was done to a finish. About 1,000 men, women and children were reported killed. I am probably growing hard-hearted, for I am in my glory when I can sight my gun on some dark skin and pull the trigger."

Thus among American soldiers the distinction between Filipino combatants and Filipino civilians blurred and often vanished altogether over the years of warfare—one private reported that his company had been ordered to open fire on a native wedding party. More and more reports of U.S. atrocities filtered back home. American techniques for obtaining intelligence commonly included the "water cure"—a torture in which enormous volumes of water were forced down the throat of the victim while interrogators knelt or jumped on his distended abdomen. Historically constant casualty-to-kill ratios were dramatically reversed in the Philippines, with the Filipino dead outnumbering the wounded by fifteen to one. A Washington volunteer could identify "this shooting of human beings" as a " 'hot game' [that] beats rabbit hunting all to pieces." By 1902, General Smith had ordered the summary death, not of actual Filipino combatants, but of "all persons . . . *who are capable of bearing arms* in actual hostilities against the United States." When asked by a marine commander where the line should be drawn between mere children and potential combatants, Smith replied, "ten years of age." In reporting Smith's new orders for the conduct of the war, American newspapers in April 1902 blared the headline "Samar to Be Made 'A Howling Wilderness.' " Echoing generations of pioneers who had waged war against "savages" across North America, one veteran of the Philippine war later explained, "The only good Filipino is a dead one. Take no prisoners; lead is cheaper than rice."

The killing wore on, even after Aguinaldo himself was captured in the spring of 1901. The problem of governance, meanwhile, remained. McKinley had appointed a civilian commission consisting of Jacob Gould Schurman (the president of Cornell University), Charles Denby (former minister to China), and Dean Worcester (an ornithologist whose researches had acquainted him with the peoples of the Philippines). The commission pledged to the Filipinos "the most ample liberty of self-government" possible, consistent with "a wise, just, stable, effective, and economical administration of public affairs." Given long-standing American assumptions regarding race and "fitness for self-government," Filipinos were rightly skeptical as to how much "liberty of self-government" this would actually turn out to be. Apolinario Mabini, president of the Philippine Cabinet, responded sharply to the commission's pledge, declaring that, even if the United States granted Filipinos all the rights of the U.S. Constitution (which itself was unlikely), American racism would still undermine the Filipinos' standing.

Once the war had broken out, moreover, the very fact of this violent bid for independence paradoxically became grist for the American contention that such independence was beyond the Filipinos' capabilities. "The war on the part of the Filipinos has been conducted with the barbarous cruelty common among uncivilized races," declared Secretary of War Elihu Root, as if to prove that the Filipinos' aim of political independence was plainly illegitimate. Even a popular gift-book published in Chicago as the war still raged, *Exciting Experiences in Our Wars with Spain and the Filipinos* (1899), was inclined to draw lessons on Filipino mental capacity from the fact of their belligerence: the natives "are not capable of deep cognition or continued logical thought," according to this account; "such a thing as acting upon settled conclusions from logical deductions is not possible with them. No better example of this could be given than that of their foolish attack on the Americans. . . . They were not able to grasp the situation nor to restrain themselves." Frederick Funston, a general in the field, put the matter more plainly still:

> *I am afraid some people at home will lie awake nights worrying about the ethics of this war, thinking that our enemy is fighting for the right of self-government. The word independent, which these people roll over their tongues so glibly, is to them a word, and not much more. It means with them simply a license to raise hell, and if they get control they would raise a fine crop of it. They are, as a rule, an illiterate, semi-savage people, who are waging war, not against tyranny, but against Anglo-Saxon order and decency.*

In an attempt to win the trust of the Filipinos, McKinley in 1900 appointed a second Philippine commission to establish civil administration on the islands, this one headed by William Howard Taft. The very language of the second commission's charge was telling: in an effort to "secure the confidence and the affection of the Filipinos," ran the report that authorized the new commission, the United States would have "(so far as the public safety permits) to let them in all local affairs govern themselves in their own way." This parenthetic concern for the public safety in the face of Filipino self-rule was more than a running leitmotif in American discussion: it was—as in Hawaii, Cuba, and Puerto Rico—a bedrock, structuring principle. At one extreme, General Arthur MacArthur's brash but widely shared opinion, according to Dean Worcester, was that "what the Filipinos needed was 'military government pinned to their backs for ten years with bayonets.'" Softer words were spoken by Commissioner Taft, who identified the U.S. task in the Philippines as preparing "a whole people for self-government, and that problem includes not only the teaching of that people how to read, write and figure in arithmetic, but also to teach them how to labor." But whether one saw the task as brute control (like MacArthur) or mere tutelage (like Taft), the bottom line was much the same: as Taft himself put it, "We must have a self-governing people before we turn this government over to them." Real independence would have to wait.

"Ye-es," said Secretary Root, candidly summing up the legal situation of the archipelago, "as near as I can make out the Constitution follows the flag—but doesn't quite catch up with it." The United States continued to hold the Philippines in this problematic status—pursuing what McKinley had called "benevolent assimilation"—until the Philippine Autonomy Act became law under Woodrow Wilson in 1916. In the language of the new law's preamble, "It was never the intention of the people of the United States in the incipiency of the War with Spain to make it a war of conquest or for territorial aggrandizement"; indeed, "it has always been the purpose of the people of the United States to . . . recognize [Philippine] independence as soon as a stable government can be established." By 1916, it had become "desirable to place in the hands of the people of the Philippines as large a control of their domestic affairs as can be given them" without impairing the exercise of the rights of sovereignty by the United States, thus setting the Philippines on a road toward "all the privileges of complete independence." The Philippine Autonomy Act replaced the former commission and Philippine Assembly with a Senate and House of Representatives to be elected by the Filipinos themselves. The governor general, appointed by the president of the United States, possessed a veto that could be overridden, but any item passed over his veto was subject to approval or rejection by the president.

In each of these cases, then, where it was tempered at all, the impetus to acquire new territories and their peoples was tempered primarily by a pervasive fear among American whites that the people themselves, by their very degeneracy or savagery, held the power to bring the self-governing republic down in ruin. For enthusiastic expansionists like Albert Beveridge, Theodore Roosevelt, or Henry Cabot Lodge, this was simply a matter of unapologetically seizing the islands in the name of progress and assuming the responsibility of both tutoring and governing the natives as their patent racial superiors. For anti-imperialists like Champ Clark, Ben Tillman, and Carl Schurz, better to leave the islands alone completely. If most expansionists doubted that these people would ever participate smoothly in America's democratic culture (approximating, in Roosevelt's phrase, some kind of "dark-hued New England town meeting"), many anti-imperialists worried about the fate of the United States' democratic culture itself upon the infusion of such "dark hues." Combatants on either side of the question could fiercely disagree on the economic merits of an expansionist policy. So could they dispute the proper interpretation of political "consent," and whether or not Hawaiians, Cubans, Puerto Ricans, or Filipinos were competent to enter into such a social compact and to cast votes on their own behalf. But upon one point there was broad agreement: these peoples were not competent to cast votes that would in any way influence the lives of white Americans.

The fact of American stewardship over these peoples and the ingenious mechanisms of that stewardship—the political arrangements by which Americans seized control of the islands without ceding any of the reciprocal powers inherent in democratic governance—embody the deep racial ambivalence within American thinking on questions of empire: such inferior peoples ought to be brought under American influence, but, emphatically, they ought not to be brought close enough to influence America. We want the Philippines, much of the popular press clamored, but we do not want the Filipinos. From the standpoint of political voice, at any rate, in the Pacific and the Caribbean between 1898 and 1903 the United States found four different ways of attaining exactly this.

Anglo-Saxon Empire and America's Non-Anglo-Saxons

Race, it was plain, lay at the heart of these cases for combatants on every side of the discussion. As Filipino leader Apolinario Mabini put it, even if Americans were to grant the Filipinos "all, absolutely all, the rights and liberties of American citizens"—itself too sanguine a hope for most to entertain—race hatred would still undermine this status. Thus within the American polity it was the nation's racialized minorities—African Americans and immigrants—who tended to articulate the sharpest, most egalitarian, and most democratically animated critiques of empire. While the American trade-union movement worried over the impact of so-called coolie labor in the case of annexation; while many socialists dismissed native resistance in the Pacific and the Caribbean as irrelevant in the face of the mechanistic forces of maturing capitalism; while Mugwump reformers and Southern Democrats fretted over the havoc that imperialism might wreak, not on the far-flung islands, but on America's republican institutions themselves; and while others lodged their protests in a frank language of national "mongrelization" or racial degeneration, many among the United States' maligned, non-Anglo-Saxon minorities forged a critique of imperialist designs and conduct from the vantage point of the conquered, and insisted on the broad principle of the right to self-determination. "It is a sorry, though true, fact," wrote one African American observer, "that wherever this government controls, injustice to the dark race prevails. The people of Cuba, Porto Rico, Hawaii and Manila know it as well as do the wronged Indian and outraged black man in the United States." Or, as Irish nationalist Bourke Cochran asked on the floor of the Senate, "Is it part of the principles of our free, independent government to proceed to civilize a weaker people by first shooting and then robbing them?"

Of course, even among these dissenters there was no unanimity on the *terms* of dissent. For African Americans in particular the issues were many. The entire expansionist enterprise had begun amid the hopeful talk of "liberating" the Spanish colonies and of the fruits to be won for blacks on the proving-ground of national belonging, the battlefield. Powerful sentiments regarding the "duties" of citizenship died hard and only unevenly once the cause of liberation had given way to the quest for domination. For some, most disconcerting was the evident reconciliation of the white North and the white South as they faced the external enemies of Spain and—especially—the Filipinos. As the editor of the *Norfolk Recorder* worried in the summer of 1898, "The closer the North and South get together by this war, the harder [the Negro] will have to fight to maintain a footing." The *Indianapolis Free-man* likewise hoped that "in the great act of complete conciliation between north and south . . . the Negroes will not be ground to dust between the upper and nether millstone of national cohesion." Imperialism constituted a rather foreboding coda to the War Between the States. Nor did it ease the tensions within African American political discussion that the Republicans, the long-beloved party of Lincoln, now championed a new racial oppression in the form of American empire, while the hated Democrats represented the legitimate opposition.

There was also significant disagreement over what, precisely, American empire would mean for the annexed territories. Some saw the islands of the Caribbean and the Pacific as an attractive refuge for persecuted blacks from the American South, and backed various programs of U.S. annexation and black resettlement; others were certain that it was only a matter of time before American patterns of racial hatred and violence tainted the onetime racial calm of these tropical paradises. Still others, like journalist Ida B. Wells, felt that, whatever the outcomes in places like Cuba and the Philippines, the United States had no business assuming burdens of any kind abroad until it could protect blacks from lynch mobs here at home. And some, particularly after U.S. control of the islands was a *fait accompli*, voiced a dim hope that in further diversifying its population the United States might overcome once and for all the harsh white-over-black dynamics of its civic and social life.

But whatever the particulars of their stance on imperialism, most African Americans did have to reckon in some fashion with the scissor grip of their own racial identity and civic aspirations on the one hand, and the ever-sharpening affinity between American nationalism and white supremacism on the other. As the election of 1900 approached, Howard University sociologist Kelly Miller asked, "Will the Negro stultify himself" by endorsing the self-aggrandizing designs of American nationalism, "and become part of the movement which must end in his own humiliation?" It was this inevitable racial lens, and the tremendously high stakes of the imperialism debate for American blacks, that lent such power and urgency to much African American anti-imperialism.

Among the most common concerns expressed by black dissenters was that, in this period of Jim Crow legislation, massive disenfranchisement, and rampant antiblack violence and lynching at home, the United States was simply going to export a bitter cargo of Mississippi- or Louisiana-style racial practices abroad. This became a running theme in African American commentary, beginning with the annexation of Hawaii, which *Richmond Planet* editor John Mitchell characterized immediately as "The Rape of the Islands." The "black natives of the Hawaiian islands," as one black writer in Colorado called them, would soon enough "wish the infernal regions to open and receive them rather than bear the torments, persecutions and abuses" that U.S. hegemony surely held in store for them. The same argument quickly applied to the former Spanish colonies as well. "The color line is being fastly drawn here," one black missionary wrote from Cuba in the summer of 1898, "and the Cubans [are] abused as Negroes." In the Philippines, meanwhile, white American soldiers' treatment of Filipinos *and* black American soldiers (all of whom they routinely lumped together as "niggers") prompted one black soldier to comment that it was "enough to make a colored man hate the flag of the United States." In addition to the widespread and widely reported savagery in the U.S. conduct of the war against this "dark-hued" foe, blacks objected to the daily slights presented by the establishment of "white-only" accommodations for the American military, or popular soldiers' ballads like "I Don't Like a Nigger Nohow."

Comment on the nation's racially freighted policy in the Philippines was constant and quite sharp among black journalists and clergy. "We would rather be called traitors," declared the *Chicago Broad Ax*, flatly, "than permit ourselves to shoulder a musket for the purpose of deliberately murdering Filipinos who are fighting for liberty and independence." To black missionary H.C.C. Astwood, U.S. imperialism was a "diabolical outrage": "American manliness and the spirit of the fathers are trampled under the feet of the imperialists," he wrote. Early on in the war against the Philippines, Edward Cooper, editor of the *Colored American*, had noted that a comparison between the "enlightened civilization" of the United States and the "customs of barbarians" in the Philippines would "not appear to our advantage." John Mitchell of the *Planet* also sighed with notable irony, "With the government acquiescing in the oppression and butchery of a dark race in this country and the enslaving and slaughtering of a dark race in the Philippines, we think it time to call all missionaries home and have them work on our own people."

As the election of 1900 neared, a group of black Democrats issued a public anti-imperialist statement under the aegis of the Negro National Democratic League. "We insist that the subjugation of any people is 'criminal aggression,'" the league announced. "Whether the people who will be affected by such a policy be or consider themselves Negroes is of but little moment. They are by nature entitled to liberty and freedom. We being an oppressed people . . . should be the 'loudest in our protestations against the oppression of others.'"

Nor were such bitter critiques limited to those who observed far-off events from the vantage point of the U.S. mainland: African American soldiers in the field were perhaps even more appalled by the racist sentiments and deeds they witnessed among their white fellow soldiers, and they often denounced quite sharply the policy of expansion whose battle lines they were defending. By mid-1900, there were over two thousand black regulars serving in the Philippines, including two Negro volunteer regiments, the Forty-eighth and Forty-ninth Infantry, who had been recruited specifically for service there. "The whites have begun to establish their diabolical race hatred in all its home rancor," reported one black infantryman, noting that white Americans had even endeavored "to propagate the [race] phobia among the Spaniards and Filipinos so as to be sure of the foundation of their supremacy when the civil rule . . . is established."

In a letter reprinted in the *Cleveland Gazette*, another complained, "The poor whites don't believe that anyone has a right to live but the white American, or to enjoy any rights or privileges that the white man enjoys." "I have mingled freely with the natives," wrote another,

and I must confess they have a just grievance. All this never would have occurred if the army of occupation would have treated them as people. The Spaniards, even if their laws were hard, were polite and treated them with some consideration; but the Americans, as soon as they saw that the native troops were desirous of sharing in the glories as well as the hardships of the hard-won battles with the Americans, began to apply home treatment for colored peoples: cursed them as damned niggers.

As for the approaching election in the United States, "Party be damned!" he wrote of the so-called Party of Lincoln. "We don't want these islands, not in the way we are to get them, and for Heaven's sake, put the party in power that pledged itself against this highway robbery. Expansion is too clean a name for it." In the *Savannah Tribune,* even one soldier who persisted in seeing the Philippines as offering "the best opportunities of the century" for "our people" had to concede that "color prejudice has kept close in the wake of the flag."

Instances of black desertion to join the Filipino insurgents numbered only about a dozen, yet these received considerable attention among white officials and in the press. White deserters, reported *New York Herald* journalist Stephen Bonsal, were most often merely "lazy and idle," whereas black deserters were far more likely to leave U.S. ranks for ideological reasons, or even to jump sides. The most notorious of these cases was David Fagen of the Twenty-fourth Infantry, who deserted in November 1899, evidently after coming across a placard from Aguinaldo addressed "To the Colored American Soldier." "It is without honor that you are spilling your costly blood," such broadsides proclaimed. "You must consider your situation and your history, and take charge that the blood . . . of Sam Hose proclaims vengeance." (Sam Hose had been the victim of a particularly gruesome and infamous lynching in Coweta County, Georgia, earlier that year.)

Fagen took a commission in the insurgent army and appealed to other black soldiers to do the same. When Fagen's (Filipino) outfit surrendered in 1901, the American escaped, becoming the subject of wild rumor and speculation on both sides of the Pacific. General Funston put a $600 bounty on him, and took great pleasure in Fagen's capture and beheading at the hands of a Filipino scout in late 1901. "Fagen was a traitor and died a traitor's death," opined one black editor in Indianapolis; "but," he went on, reflecting African Americans' inherent ambivalence during this war for Anglo-Saxon glory, "he was a man no doubt prompted by honest motives to help a weaker side, and one with which he felt allied by ties that bind."

The issues confronting recently arrived immigrants from Europe during this period may not have been so highly charged or, ultimately, so fraught with peril as for American blacks, whose rights and personal safety at home were under siege just as the United States embarked on this imperialist adventure among the "savages" overseas. But as non-Anglo-Saxons in the midst of this national crusade for Anglo-Saxon supremacy, immigrants did share some fundamental concerns with African Americans, and much immigrant commentary echoed precisely the concerns and the sensibilities voiced in the black press and in letters from black soldiers. Like African Americans, many immigrants had been drawn to the initial humanitarian and liberatory rhetoric of McKinley's war against Spain, and they, too, were stunned to find themselves on the aggressing end of a war for "Anglo-Saxon" conquest. One Polish American journal summed up its view of Cuban "liberation" in a front-page cartoon in 1900: a Cuban is seated on a bench reading a newspaper; a poster behind him proclaims that the U.S. Army will remain in Cuba only until law and order reign, while the blaring headlines of his newspaper announce various lynchings across the United States. Remarks the Cuban, "When I read of these atrocities, I come to the conclusion that my old, bloody friend Weyler is now the chief commander of the United States."

Like many African Americans, immigrants from Europe's underdog nations expressed a profound sympathy with the oppressed inhabitants of the Pacific and Caribbean islands, no matter that it was suddenly their adopted country that was now doing the oppressing. "Those miserable foreigners in Manila, Cuba, Porto Rico or wherever you please," wrote Irish nationalist James Jeffrey Roche, "if they are not ready to accept and adopt every 'Yankee notion' offered them, are manifestly unfit for self-government, and our equally manifest duty and destiny is to pitchfork our institutions down their throats, or, failing that, to govern them ourselves in the good old, time-honored 'Anglo-Saxon' way." Thus were the natural interests of Filipinos, Cubans, Puerto Ricans, and the Irish on both sides of the Atlantic at once comprehended and articulated as being in wonderful alignment.

Roche also gave the lie to the American pretentions toward "civilizing" the savages in a fetching little piece of doggerel, which he cast as an exchange between Uncle Sam, who is "green" when it comes to the business of empire, and John Bull, his mentor:

Said Samuel Green, a 'prentice hand,
"I don't exactly understand.
Suppose this heathen locks his store,

And don't give us an open door."
But Burglar Bull he winked his eye:
"Open a winder then, says I.
And if he kicks when we surprise him,
Let's take our clubs and civilize him!"

Chief among the political accents in immigrant discussion of American policy was Old World nationalism—a sense that the injuries and woes of an Ireland or a Poland could shed an unerring light on the plight of a Cuba or a Philippine archipelago. When Father McKinnon, the chaplain of the First California Volunteer Regiment, lectured in favor of American expansionism on the grounds that Filipinos were incapable of "understanding what freedom means," he was heckled for making "the English argument." "Why shouldn't they be free?" one member of his largely Irish New York audience shouted before being escorted from the hall. Patrick Ford, the fiery editor of the *Irish World*, continually condemned U.S. policy in the unmistakable strains of a liberatory philosophy developed under the Saxon's heel in Ireland. "Today the Filipinos are treated in their own country by their would-be foreign masters the same way the Irish were treated by the English in 1798," wrote Ford. "Like the Irish, they see their religion insulted and their most sacred rights infringed on by insolent foreigners, who are trying to steal their country from them. They would be deserving of contempt if they did not resist to the last the 'benevolent assimilation' William McKinley would force upon them." It also seems to have been a feeling of affinity with the Filipinos, based in part upon an admiration for their dauntless spirit of rebellion, that led Irish American soldiers in the Philippines to nickname the insurgents, almost affectionately, "the smoked Irish" and "the O'Hoolies."

Poles, too, invoked the plight of their homeland (then partitioned among Prussia, Russia, and Austria) in denouncing American policy toward the former Spanish colonies. *Dziennik Chicagoski* decried the self-proclaimed U.S. role as "culture-bearers" (*kulturtraegerzy*) in the Philippines, employing a word whose German root implicitly likened McKinley's policies to Bismarck's anti-Catholic and Slavophobic *Kulturkampf* policies in Prussian Poland. The journal further questioned the logic by which the United States seemed willing to kill off half of the Filipino population in order to "lift" the other half out of "barbarism." In Manila, as in Poland, violence and victimization seemed to be among the chief blessings of "civilization" and "culture-bearing." In *Zgoda*, the Chicago-based organ of the Polish National Alliance, Stefan Barszczewski likewise argued that "the Filipinos are defending their independence, and our government should not be treating them as it is." "It could very well be that the Filipinos are completely incapable of self-government," he conceded; "but that does not exclude their right of fighting for the liberty of their native land." Like Ford, Roche, and other nationalists from Ireland, Barszczewski set his compass on the imperialism question according to the lights of an Old World struggle whose own racial logic—in this case Teuton versus Slav—had proscribed the cultural practices and defined the rights of an oppressed majority.

Unlike African Americans, however, Europeans could find an alternative location for themselves on the racially keyed map of New World political identity: if their status as non-Anglo-Saxons in some instances gave rise to a fierce dissent against the brute Anglo-Saxonist arrogance of U.S. conduct, their status as "whites" also offered a way comfortably to embrace their adopted country's aggrandizing mission as their own. The limits of political affinity among European immigrants and the Filipinos were indicated most suggestively in an editorial in Milwaukee's *Kuryer Polski* soon after fighting had broken out in Manila in 1899. "For us Poles, this war is not necessarily pleasant," wrote Michael Kruszka. "Traditionally we always stand on the side of the oppressed; since we have repeatedly taken up arms in defense of our independence, we naturally sympathize with all other peoples struggling for independence—even if they be half-savage Malays." Kruszka's "even if" here points up the possibility of the immigrants' accepting the racialist terms of imperial discourse, although they themselves were the subject of like prejudices on the part of German or English rulers on one side of the Atlantic and American rulers like Henry Cabot Lodge on the other. Kruszka ultimately decided that, since the Filipinos came nowhere near the Poles in terms of "civilization," they could indeed benefit from the stewardship of a country like the United States.

Many immigrant commentators went even further down this road than

Michael Kruszka. Indeed, the discourse of empire, though premised on precisely the same racial principles of republican exclusivity as immigration restriction, worked considerable magic in transforming unwanted immigrants—as "white" Europeans—into the very stuff of good American citizenship. In a piece titled "Why We Don't Want the Philippines," the Irish American editor of the *Catholic Citizen*, Humphrey Desmond, advanced the familiar argument that imperialism would mean "American citizenship is to be diluted by Malay citizenship, and that America's democracy is to stand the trial of working itself out among inferior people." Elsewhere he had insisted that "our acquisitions should be civilized Caucasian communities, such as can adapt to our democratic system." The Lower East Side's *Yiddishes Tageblatt*, too, likened the Filipino insurgents to the Biblical Levites, who, bedazzled by their newfound freedom, had mistaken Moses, their beneficent liberator, for an enemy. Just so, Aguinaldo and his followers were "so savage and confused by their freedom that they do not recognize their liberators and their friends." And even the generally sympathetic *Boston Pilot* could lapse into the white-supremacist logic so common in American anti-imperialism: " 'The Philippine vote' will become an important, possibly a decisive, factor in a national election. Dost like the picture?"

Central to discussion of the United States' "large policies" abroad, the capabilities and rights of the natives of the new island possessions, and, if only by inference, the civic standing of non-Anglo-Saxons within the American polity, then, was the notion of the "White Man's Burden." Rudyard Kipling's noxious poem of that title had exhorted Americans to assume the British imperial mantle of white supremacy and to govern these islands' "newcaught, sullen peoples, half-devil and half-child." Could the republican imperative of reasoned self-government be squared with the nation's taking on several million imperial wards? And what of the "ties that bind," as the *Indianapolis Freeman* had put it, which united non-Anglo-Saxons within the American polity with the new, non-Anglo-Saxon wards of the state in Hawaii, Cuba, Puerto Rico, and the Philippines? What did McKinley's notion of "benevolent assimilation" abroad portend for the inclusion of the so-called inferior races—whether Negro, Celt, Slav, or Hebrew—*within* U.S. borders? Just what sort of transformation was American citizenship undergoing?

In response to Kipling, H. T. Johnson, a black clergyman and editor of the *Christian Recorder*, protested that imperialism constituted a burden not for the white man but for the black:

Pile on the Black Man's Burden.
  'Tis nearest at your door;
Why heed long bleeding Cuba,
  or dark Hawaii's shore?
Hail ye your fearless armies,
  Which menace feeble folks
Who fight with clubs and arrows
  and brook your rifle's smoke.

For his part, James Jeffrey Roche quipped, "The 'White Man's Burden' . . . is never so heavy that he cannot carry it out of the door or window of the house which he has just burglarized." Roche, like so many of his Celtic compatri- ots, and like so many other non-Anglo-Saxons now on the American scene, thought he knew a larceny when he saw one.

A popular book on the territories of expansionist concern appeared at the turn of the century under the title *Our New Island Treasures and Their Peoples.* As historian Oscar Campomanes has remarked, the title tells all: the frankly economic rendering of the islands as "treasures" nicely conveys U.S. aspira- tion in these regions, while the logical bifurcation between possession and rejection—"our" islands and "their" peoples—indicates a major source of American ambivalence, a hangover from the days of "the winning of the West." What happens when "waste spaces" turn out to be populated? Can territories be taken and their peoples disowned? What is the desirable polit- ical status of those who happen to inhabit "our treasures"?

Like the "winning of the West," the extension of American power into the Caribbean and the Pacific required a very particular pattern of certainties regarding the relative merit of diverse cultures and humanity's prospects for self-governance. Summing up the Supreme Court's ruling in the so-called in- sular cases (a series of cases determining the rules under which persons and commodities could move between the new possessions and the United

States), William Howard Taft quipped, four of the judges ruled that the Constitution does follow the flag, four ruled that it does not, and the ninth ruled that it sometimes follows the flag and sometimes does not, and he would determine which is which.

Nor did questions of U.S. expansion and the fate of subjected peoples end with the territories ceded by Spain. In his annual message of 1901, Teddy Roosevelt declared that intervention among "barbarous and semi-barbarous peoples" was "a most regrettable but necessary international police duty which must be performed for the sake of the welfare of mankind." Indeed, his "corollary" to the Monroe Doctrine extended to the entire hemisphere precisely the principle that the United States had developed in Hawaii, Cuba, Puerto Rico, and the Philippines in the preceding years: the right of the United States to control strategic areas in the Caribbean and the Americas without opening itself up to the perceived hazards of annexing any alien or barbarous populations.

As Roosevelt wrote in a letter to the Senate regarding U.S. conduct in Santo Domingo and Haiti, "Our position is explicitly and unreservedly that under no circumstances do we intend to acquire [these territories]. . . . Even if the two republics desired to become a part of the United States, the United States would certainly refuse its assent." But when it came to collecting customs receipts or maintaining the "stability" necessary for American business transactions, the sovereignty of the republics was of relatively little concern. The United States intervened in Santo Domingo in 1904, sent a commission in 1908, and established a military government in 1916. As one American observer wrote in 1920, "The Government of Santo Domingo has been absolutely in the hands of the military forces of the United States" since November 1916. "How absolutely one is not prepared to appreciate until one goes to the country. A Rear Admiral of the United States Navy is the President of the republic, and his cabinet is made up of officers of the United States Marine Corps. There is no semblance of a Dominican legislative body."

Similarly, the United States undertook the occupation of Port-au-Prince, Haiti, in 1915, ostensibly "to help the Haitian people and prevent them from being exploited by irresponsible revolutionists." Invoking Haiti's proud history as a free republic, Booker T. Washington warned that "the white men sent [by the United States] must be able to be white men in a black man's country if their work is to be fundamental." But the United States disregarded Haiti's traditions of governance and its long-standing Constitution, hand-picking instead a puppet regime; and Americans demonstrated little respect for the individual inhabitants of the black republic. As one editorial in *Outlook* put it, the Haitians evidently attempted to receive the Americans as friends, but "the troops apparently treated the Haitians as enemies."

As the prominent black Philadelphian Chris J. Perry had predicted back at the turn of the century, the scourge of the Cubans was going to turn out to be more deadly than scorpions: Americans would block Cuban independence, he warned, "by alleging a desire to teach her people self-government." The "Anglo-Saxon begins with you by an appeal to heaven to witness his innocence and honesty, and ends by 'stealing your spoons.'" By the era of the Great War, the regime of the Platt Amendment, diverse in its formal structures but the same in its effects, had been extended across the nation's "new frontiers" in the Caribbean and the Pacific. While Woodrow Wilson was busy making the world safe for democracy in the wake of the war, the *de jure* president of the Dominican Republic went to the Paris peace conference to present his country's case, fully expecting that amid all the talk about self-determination and the integrity of territories the League of Nations might extend benevolent supervision to the Western Hemisphere. "Mr. Wilson," as *The Nation* reported, "could not find time to see him."

Conclusion: The Temper of U.S. Nationalism—Coming of Age in the Philippines

The isolation of the United States is at an end, not because we chose to go into the politics of the world, but because, by the sheer genius of this people and the growth of our power, we have become a determining factor in the history of mankind.

—*Woodrow Wilson, 1919*

The United States—bounded on the north by the North Pole; on the south by the Antarctic Region; on the east by the first chapter of the Book of Genesis and on the west by the Day of Judgment . . .

—*Arthur Bird,* Looking Forward *(1899)*

IT IS ONE of the strange throughlines in the history of U.S. nationalism that since at least the mid-nineteenth century Americans have fancied their country as the savior of the world's peoples—redeemer nation, civilizer, beacon of liberty, asylum of the oppressed—even as they have expressed profound anxiety that the world's peoples might ultimately prove the ruin of the republic. The period between the Philadelphia Exposition of 1876 and World War I was a critical epoch in the twin development of these contending ideas. Americans erected a magnificent statue in New York Harbor beckoning the "tempest-tost" and "wretched" refugees of the Old World through the "golden door" of new hope, and yet they developed in succeeding decades an elaborate biological explanation of the superiority of "old-stock" Americans and the undesirability of the "backward" or "useless" races who were overrepresented among the newer immigration. The restrictive immigration legislation of 1917 and 1924 announced that—Emma Lazarus's pretty sentiments to the contrary—nothing would threaten the republic quite so much as leaving the golden door ajar. Likewise, if Americans embarked on a mission to "uplift" the savages of Asia, the Pacific, and the Americas, they also devised an ingenious array of legal and political mechanisms by which the uplifted savages themselves might be held at bay. What America had to offer seemed too good *not* to extend to the benighted peoples of the world (by force, if necessary); but what those people threatened to return in the bargain ultimately seemed too bad to risk.

My focus on the years 1876 to 1917 in this book is meant to redress two striking failures of our national memory—one regarding immigration; the other, imperialism.

Recent debates over immigration have revolved around highly idealized images of the "good" European immigrant of a bygone era. In comparison with the "bad" Latino and Asian immigrants of today, the story goes, the nineteenth century's Irish, Italian, Jewish, Polish, Greek, or Lithuanian immigrants came ashore with a healthier respect for American ideals, with a willingness to shed their Old World customs in favor of American ways, and, underneath it all, with a shared cultural foundation in the "Western" traditions that formed the core of the United States' mainstream culture. Sure, these immigrants sometimes seemed like trouble, it is conceded; but they never posed the fundamental threat to the republic that today's less assimilable immigrants do.

It is useful to know, in this connection, that—however safely "assimilated" now—at the moment of their arrival the waves of European immigrants constituted a full-blown political crisis in the United States, and that it was a crisis articulated in exactly the terms used today by the likes of Patrick Buchanan, Pete Wilson, or *Border Watch* in reference to Asian and Latin American immigrants. "Fitness for self-government" has dropped out of the nation's political vocabulary over the course of the twentieth century; but only, one suspects, because, in the age of mass-mediated electoral culture, the bureaucratic administrative state, dwindling voter turnout, and escalating voter cynicism, Americans have largely ceased to think of themselves as "self-governing" at all. Meanwhile, the racial valences survive, even if notions of popular sovereignty do not. The myth of yesterday's "good" European immigrant resides at the heart of this popular misreading of the period, screening the fact that today's "bad" immigration represents *precisely* the threat that the republic has faced and overcome many times before. Evidently the capacity of the republic to withstand its own diversity is greater than the capacity of many citizens to imagine an America that departs significantly from the demographic status quo (and lives to tell about it—in English).

The second piece of public amnesia addressed here concerns turn-of-the-century empire-building, an area even more striking for the totality of its disappearance from popular discussion. Current renditions of U.S. history thoroughly expunge the Philippine-American War and related engagements in Cuba, Puerto Rico, and Guam to the extent that these warrant not even a paragraph in many high-school textbooks, and scarcely that in many college texts. Not only do most Americans know nothing about the conduct of the Philippine-American War; many do not even know that such a war took place.

The stakes are quite high for Americans' national self-conception. In expurgating the period of U.S. expansionism that bridges the nineteenth and twentieth centuries, Americans adopt a broken narrative that casts Manifest Destiny and continental expansionism falsely adrift from "modern" U.S. history, and obscures the extent to which the modern state was built, and modern nationalism generated, in close relation to the imperialist project. The effect is to mystify U.S. involvement in global affairs by hiding the very moment when global power was so lustily seized. If there is no turn-of-the-century expansionism, then Manifest Destiny becomes an irrelevance of dim antiquity, and both the Wilsonian internationalism and the Cold War interventionism of the twentieth century can be imagined as developing upon an entirely different epistemological footing. Without the Philippines, in other words, it becomes easy to suppose a radical historical disjuncture separating the plains wars of the mid-nineteenth century and the Southeast Asian wars of the mid-twentieth: that U.S. soldiers referred to areas within Vietnam as

"Indian Country" becomes a matter of simple metaphor, not of deeper ideology. But our first land war in Asia was fought not in 1950–53 but in 1899–1902, and it was waged largely by American officers who had received their practical training in campaigns against the "savages" of the Western plains in the 1870s.

This erasure has generally allowed a view that the United States has played its part as a power on the world scene only reluctantly. The triumph of American innocence, as Stuart Creighton Miller has called this willful revision, constitutes a pillar of twentieth-century American liberalism. Unabashed discussion of racial conquest has long faded from American political discourse; there is simply no longer a place in national self-conceptions for the rhetoric of "waste spaces" and of "unfitness for self-government," or for the glorious war against "savages" that obtained in Theodore Roosevelt's day. And yet Americans still find themselves in possession of an empire marked by myriad alliances with pliant dictators, by an unbroken history of military interventions, by a twelve-digit defense budget, and by a global network of military bases—and so they have some explaining to do.

One of the most robust explanations is that Americans never asked for the worldwide power and influence that they ultimately wielded. The United States ascended to global power "by the sheer genius of this people," according to Woodrow Wilson, and "not because we chose to go into the politics of the world." As Henry Luce put it in his famous article inaugurating the "American Century" a generation later, the United States had become a world power "blindly, unintentionally, accidentally and really in spite of ourselves." More recently still, in his musings on the modern presidency in a PBS documentary on *TR,* historian David McCullough asserted that Teddy Roosevelt understood that "America, like it or not, would have to play a large part in the world."

Like it or not. This is the real significance of the disappearance of the Philippine-American War from national memory; this is what is at stake in forgetting what was once proudly adopted as a grand imperialist design. When we recall and squarely face U.S. conduct in the Philippines at the dawn of Pacific empire in 1899, we can neither utter the phrase "like it or not" nor pass off the U.S. rise to global predominance as blind, unintentional, or accidental. Despite some opposition, the United States consciously chose imperial power along with the antidemocratic baggage and even the bloodshed that entailed; and many Americans—none more than Teddy Roosevelt—*liked it.*

As Americans await their next intervention abroad and debate the merits of the newest immigrant arrivals at home in terms not wholly unlike those employed by Henry Cabot Lodge in the 1890s, they would do well to reckon in a serious way with the continuities in their own history—from the wars on the plains to the Cold War's boundless "defense perimeter," from the eugenicists' fears for the delicacy of self-governance to the pious concerns a century later for the capacity of the republic to absorb peoples who are "so foreign" to the "mainstream" culture. It is in this crucible of foreign policy and immigration that dominant notions of Americanism and citizenship are largely formed; it is through this perpetually self-renewing narrative of encounter that many Americans receive their historical sense of *place,* their notion of what "America," as a political idea, is meant to be. "Unless we keep the barbarian virtues, gaining the civilized ones will be of little avail," Roosevelt warned at the dawn of the twentieth century. But unless we can shed the civilized *vices,* one might object, any talk of virtue is for naught. And among the chief vices of American "civilization," in our day as in his, has been this nation's failure to match its worldwide economic, political, and military reach with anything better than a desperately parochial understanding of the world's peoples themselves.

INTRODUCTION

3 "waste spaces": Theodore Roosevelt, *The Winning of the West* [1889–96] (Lincoln: University of Nebraska Press, 1995), vol. I, p.1.

3 "these continents should be reserved . . .": ibid., vol. III, p. 44.

4 "rat-eyed young men": Louise Mayo, *The Ambivalent Image: Nineteenth-Century America's Perception of the Jew* (Rutherford, N.J.: Fairleigh Dickinson University Press, 1988), p. 54.

8 "the cause lost . . .": Jacqueline Denise Goldsby, "After Great Pain: The Cultural Logic of Lynching and the Problem of Realist Representation in America, 1882–1922," unpublished Ph.D. dissertation, Yale University, 1998, vol. I, p. 65.

8 "open liberal modernity": Nicholas Thomas, *Colonialism's Culture: Anthropology, Travel, and Government* (Princeton, N.J.: Princeton University Press, 1994), p. 12.

PART I: MARKETS

1. EXPORT MARKETS

15 "We thank thee . . .": J. S. Ingram, *The Centennial Exposition, Described and Illustrated* (Philadelphia: Hubbard Bros., 1876), p. 82.

15 "that giant wonder . . .": ibid., p. 763.

16 "show-cases filled with dresses . . .": ibid., p. 159.

16   "Unquestionably international trade . . .": ibid., pp. 767–68.

16   "an almost unlimited field . . .": Robert Rydell, *All the World's a Fair: Visions of Empire at American International Expositions, 1876–1916* (Chicago: University of Chicago Press, 1984), p. 29.

16   "for the sole purpose . . .": Walter LaFeber, *The American Search for Opportunity, 1865–1913*, vol. II in *The Cambridge History of American Foreign Relations* (Cambridge: Cambridge University Press, 1993), p. xiv.

17   "The mysteries of Africa . . .": Josiah Strong, *Our Country: Its Possible Future and Its Present Crisis* (New York: Baker and Taylor, 1886), pp. 14, 15.

18   "At least one-third . . .": Charles S. Campbell, Jr., *The Transformation of American Foreign Relations, 1865–1900* (New York: Harper & Row, 1976), p. 109.

18   "Our manufactures have outgrown . . .": James Lorence, *Organized Business and the Myth of the China Market: The American Asiatic Association, 1898–1937*, in *Transactions of the American Philosophical Society*, vol. 71, pt. 4 (1981), p. 10.

19   "our surplus will soon roll back . . .": Campbell, *Transformation of American Foreign Relations*, p. 85.

19   "Abundance clutched . . .": James Jeffrey Roche, *The V-A-S-E and Other Bric-a-Brac* (Boston: Richard Badger, 1900), pp. 57–58.

21   "Multiply your ships . . .": Walter LaFeber, *The New Empire: An Interpretation of American Expansion, 1860–1898* (Ithaca, N.Y.: American Historical Association/Cornell University Press, 1963), p. 27.

21   "the drawbridge between . . .": ibid., p. 29.

22   "We must have new markets . . .": LaFeber, *Search for Opportunity*, p. 158.

22   "find markets . . ."; "vast undeveloped fields . . .": Thomas McCormick, *China Market: America's Quest for Informal Empire, 1893–1901* (Chicago: Quadrangle, 1967), pp. 37, 38.

22   "The fostering, the developing . . .": LaFeber, *New Empire*, p. 41.

22   "The diplomacy of the present administration . . .": Thomas Paterson, *Major Problems in American Foreign Policy: Documents and Essays* (Lexington, Mass.: D. C. Heath, 1978), p. 330.

23   "stands face to face . . .": Brooks Adams, *America's Economic Supremacy* (New York: Macmillan, 1900), p. 72.

23   "more dangerous . . .": ibid., p. 89.

23   "On the existence . . ."; "for governments are simply . . .": ibid., p. 133.

23   "If America is destined . . ."; ibid., p. 131.

24   "a resting spot in the midocean . . .": LaFeber, *New Empire*, p. 35.

24   "influenced by the idea . . .": Campbell, *Transformation of American Foreign Relations*, p. 101.

25   "to bring about peace . . .": LaFeber, *New Empire*, pp. 46–47.

26   "extensive field . . ."; "the key to national wealth . . .": Michael Hunt, *The Making of a Special Relationship: The United States and China to 1914* (New York: Columbia University Press, 1983), pp. 12, 90.

26   "our interests in what was once . . .": Lorence, *Organized Business and the Myth*, p. 25.

27   "From the earliest times . . .": Adams, *America's Economic Supremacy, p. 72.*

27   "Our geographical position . . ."; "the great problem of the future": Adams, *America's Economic Supremacy*, p. 194.

27   "the prize . . .": McCormick, *China Market*, p. 129.

27   "You can see at once . . .": Charles S. Campbell, Jr., *Special Business Interests and the Open Door Policy* [1951] (Hamden, Conn.: Archon Books, 1968), p. 20.

31   "[throw] back a considerable . . .": Adams, *America's Economic Supremacy*, p. 105.

31   "In the field of trade . . .": McCormick, *China Market*, p. 130.

32   *"These are precisely the districts . . .":* Paterson, *Major Problems*, p. 303 (emphasis added).

32   "Earnestly desirous . . .": ibid., p. 298.

33   "We have done the Chinks . . .": Richard Drinnon, *Facing West: The Metaphysics of Indian-Hating and Empire Building* (Minneapolis: University of Minnesota Press, 1980), p. 277.

33   "preserve Chinese territorial . . .": Paterson, *Major Problems*, p. 299.

34   "99 percent of China . . .": Paul A. Varg, *The Making of a Myth: The United States and China, 1897–1912* (East Lansing: Michigan State University Press, 1968), p. 38.

35   "in obedience to the call . . .": Lorence, *Organized Business and the Myth*, p. 43.

35   "when a Chinaman of today . . .": *Harper's Weekly*, May 18, 1907, p. 743.

36   "Sales success in the Orient . . .": *Asia*, Jan. 1921, p. 96.

36   "In China there are . . .": Campbell, *Special Business Interests*, p. 12.

36   "hostile to all improvement . . .": Stuart Creighton Miller, *The Unwelcome Immigrant: The American Image of the Chinese, 1785–1882* (Berkeley: University of California Press, 1969), p. 35.

37   "a pocket-comb . . .": Arthur Smith, *Chinese Characteristics* (London: Oliphant, Anderson, and Farrier, 1900), p. 128.

37   "dread of the unknown . . . dropping ancestor worship . . .": Edward A. Ross, *The Changing Chinese* (New York: Century, 1912), p. 69.

40   "is ours by *natural laws*": LaFeber, *Search for Opportunity*, p. 26.

40   "When money can be borrowed . . .": Lloyd Gardner, "A Progressive Foreign Policy, 1900–1921," in William Appleman Williams, ed., *From Colony to Empire: Essays in the History of American Foreign Relations* (New York: John Wiley and Sons, 1972), p. 217.

41   "While the great powers of Europe . . .": LaFeber, *New Empire*, p. 105.

41   "What we want . . .": LaFeber, *Search for Opportunity*, pp. 76–77.

42   "We have good money . . .": José Trías Monge, *Puerto Rico: The Trials of the Oldest Colony in the World* (New Haven: Yale University Press, 1997), p. 27.

43   "Once the United States . . .": Philip Foner, *The Spanish-Cuban-American War and the Birth of American Imperialism* (New York: Monthly Review Press, 1972), p. xxx.

43   "the extreme limit . . .": Louis Perez, Jr., *Cuba: Between Reform and Revolution* (New York: Oxford University Press, 1995), p. 187.

43   ". . . The civil rights and political status . . .": Monge, *Puerto Rico*, p. 27.

44   ". . . foreign to the United States . . .": *Downes* v. *Bidwell* (1901), 182 U.S. 244.

44   "treated as a mere chattel . . ."; "spectacle of terrible . . .": Monge, *Puerto Rico*, pp. 48, 52.

45   "The United States now holds . . ."; "I do not think . . . ": Stephen Randall, *Columbia and the United States: Hegemony and Independence* (Athens: University of Georgia Press, 1992), pp. 83, 85–86.

45   ". . . shall have the right . . .": Paterson, *Major Problems*, pp. 328–29.

46   "land hunger . . .": ibid., pp. 329–30.

46   ". . . the flag of his nation . . .": John M. Hart, *Revolutionary Mexico: The Coming and Process of the Mexican Revolution* (Berkeley: University of California Press, 1987), p. 276.

47   "With the present industrial activity . . .": Gardner, "Progressive Foreign Policy," p. 236.

47   "If the United States as compared . . .": Frederick Pike, *The United States and Latin America: Myths and Stereotypes of Civilization and Nature* (Austin: University of Texas Press, 1992), p. 147.

48   "a nation of half-breeds": ibid., p. 146.

48   "firmness is essential . . .": ibid., p. 211.

48   "the victim of a bad start . . .": Edward A. Ross, *South of Panama* (New York: Century, 1915), preface, n.p.

48   "Chronic wrongdoing . . .": Paterson, *Major Problems*, pp. 329–30.

49   "not only away from Europe . . .": Charles Dudley Warner, *Mummies and Moslems* (Hartford, Conn.: American, 1876), p. 119.

49   "The fierce wild life . . .": Archibald Roosevelt, ed., *Theodore Roosevelt on Race, Riots, Reds, Crime* (West Sayville, N.Y.: Probe, 1968), pp. 78–79.

49   "wanderers on a prehistoric planet": quoted in Michael Adas, *Machines as the Measure of Man: Science, Technology, and Ideologies of Western Dominance* (Ithaca, N.Y.: Cornell University Press, 1989), p. 165.

50   "The Indians are entitled . . .": Reginald Horsman, *Race and Manifest Destiny: The Origins of American Racial Anglo-Saxonism* (Cambridge, Mass.: Harvard University Press, 1982), p. 202.

50   "as a passion over all . . .": Lewis Henry Morgan, *Ancient Society* [1877] (Cleveland: World Publishing, 1963), p. 6.

51   "all modern, successful civilization . . .": Pike, *The United States and Latin America*, p. 176.

51   "the introduction of the Arts . . ."; "when the hunter shall be transformed . . .": Robert Berkhofer, *The White Man's Indian: Images of the American Indian from Columbus to the Present* (New York: Vintage, 1978), pp. 146, 151.

52   "We have . . . the absolute need . . .": ibid., p. 173.

53   ". . . there is no single Chinese custom . . .": Arthur H. Smith, *Village Life in China: A Study in Sociology* (New York: Fleming H. Revell, 1899), p. 346.

53   "Firearms command respect . . .": Adas, *Machines as the Measure*, pp. 160–61.

54   "Men rise in the scale . . .": Strong, *Our Country*, p. 101.

54   "direct relation between the missionary . . .": Lorence, *Organized Business and the Myth*, p. 55.

54   "Missionaries are the pioneers . . .": McCormick, *China Market*, p. 66.

55   "He . . . Lacked the Power . . .": *Asia*, May 1921, pp. 426, 428.

55   "There is no place . . .": O. Henry, *Cabbages and Kings* [1904] (New York: Penguin, 1993), p. 153.

56   "were followed by large crowds . . .": Rydell, *All the World's a Fair*, p. 14.

2. LABOR MARKETS

60   "emigration to America": *National Geographic*, Dec. 1909, p. 1063.

61   "The sources of our national wealth . . .": Alexander Saxton, *The Indispensable Enemy: Labor and the Anti-Chinese Movement in California* (Berkeley: University of California Press, 1971), p. 274.

62   "Where Braddock and his men . . .": Frederick Jackson Turner, "The West and American Ideals" (1914), in Frederick Jackson Turner, *The Frontier in American History* (Tucson: University of Arizona Press, 1986), p. 300.

62   "the terrible little Ellis Island . . .": Henry James, *The American Scene* (New York: Library of America, 1993), pp. 425, 427.

62   "gross aliens to a man . . .": ibid., p. 545.

62   "Jews, Injuns, Chinamen . . .": Frederick Pike, *The United States and Latin America: Myths and Stereotypes of Civilization and Nature* (Austin: University of Texas Press, 1992), p. 179.

63   "The wheels of industry . . .": Peter Roberts, *The New Immigration: A Study of the Industrial and Social Life of Southeast Europeans in America* (New York: Macmillan, 1912), p. viii.

63   "The ebb and flow . . .": John R. Commons, *Industrial Goodwill* (New York: McGraw-Hill, 1919), p. 1.

63   "With comparatively few exceptions . . .": Mark Wyman, *Round Trip to America: The Immigrants Return to Europe, 1880–1930* (Ithaca, N.Y.: Cornell University Press, 1993), p. 34.

64   "The free lands are gone . . .": Frederick Jackson Turner, "The Problem of the West" (1896), in Turner, *Frontier in American History*, p. 219.

65   "The changing character of immigration . . .": John R. Commons, *Races and Immigrants in America* (New York: Macmillan, 1907), pp. 133–34.

65   "the most stupid man . . .": Wyman, *Round Trip to America*, p. 45.

65   "Those who bring anything . . .": E. A. Ross, *The Old World in the New: The Significance of Past and Present Immigration to the American People* (New York: Century, 1913), p. 195.

66   "Switzerland of America . . .": Philip Taylor, *The Distant Magnet: European Emigration to the U.S.A.* (New York: Harper & Row, 1971), pp. 72–73.

66   "To Labouring Men . . .": ibid., p. 74.

66   "the great commercial centre . . .": ibid., p. 71.

66   "a great hunt for emigrants": Ross, *Old World in the New*, p. 196.

67   "as the locusts covered Egypt": Taylor, *Distant Magnet*, p. 81.

67   "For a small sum . . .": Yuji Ichioka, *The Issei: The World of First Generation Japanese Immigrants, 1885–1924* (New York: Free Press, 1988), p. 63.

67   "The real agents . . .": Oscar Handlin, ed., *Immigration as a Factor in American History* (Englewood Cliffs, N.J.: Prentice-Hall, 1959), p. 56.

68   "it would be difficult . . .": Thomas Kessner, *The Golden Door: Italian and Jewish Immigrant Mobility in New York City, 1880–1915* (New York: Oxford University Press, 1977), p. 58.

68   "A laboring population . . .": Wyman, *Round Trip to America*, p. 15.

69   "Last week we employed . . .": James Barrett, "Unity and Fragmentation: Class, Race, and Ethnicity on Chicago's South Side, 1900–1922," in Dirk Hoerder, ed., *"Struggle a Hard Battle": Essays on Working-Class Immigrants* (DeKalb: Northern Illinois University Press, 1986), p. 235.

69   "The only device . . .": Commons, *Races and Immigrants*, p. 150.

70   "the tall, dark-complexioned . . .": Handlin, *Immigration as a Factor*, p. 68.

70   "We must steer clear . . .": ibid., pp. 66–67.

70 "... understands that he is ...": Neil Foley, *The White Scourge: Mexicans, Blacks, and Poor Whites in Texas Cotton Culture* (Berkeley: University of California Press, 1997), pp. 36–37.

70 "These people are good laborers ...": Michael Karni, "Finnish Immigrant Leftists in America: The Golden Years, 1900–1918," in Hoerder, ed., *"Struggle a Hard Battle,"* p. 212.

71 "American industry had a place ...": Roberts, *The New Immigration*, p. 50.

71 "in the matter of picking and packing ...": Sucheng Chan, *This Bittersweet Soil: The Chinese in California Agriculture, 1860–1910* (Berkeley: University of California Press, 1986), p. 334.

71 "the peculiar genius ...": Nancy Green, *Ready-to-Wear and Ready-to-Work: A Century of Industry and Immigrants in Paris and New York* (Durham, N.C.: Duke University Press, 1997), p. 189.

71 "the Jewish people ...": ibid., p. 190.

71 "The Italian, like the Jew ...": ibid., pp. 192–93.

72 "excel as miners ...": 61st Cong., 3rd sess., doc. no. 662, *Reports of the Immigration Commission Dictionary of Races and Peoples* (Washington, D.C.: Government Printing Office, 1911), pp. 23, 47, 112, 129, 72.

72 "You don't want to work there ...": Wyman, *Round Trip to America*, p. 54.

72 "My people are not in America ...": Ardis Cameron, *Radicals of the Worst Sort: Laboring Women in Lawrence, Massachusetts, 1860–1912* (Urbana: University of Illinois Press, 1993), p. 101.

73 "we have bigger outputs ...": Ross, *Old World in the New*, p. 197.

73 "do not know to purchase ...": Gwendolyn Mink, *Old Labor and New Immigrants in American Political Development: Union, Party, and State, 1875–1920* (Ithaca, N.Y.: Cornell University Press, 1986), p. 109.

73 "an immigrant community ...": Green, *Ready-to-Wear*, p. 171.

74 "Commodities are produced to be sold ...": Commons, *Races and Immigrants*, p. 157.

74 "The competition of races ...": ibid., p. 151.

74 "neediest, meekest laborers ...": Ross, *Old World in the New*, p. 198.

74 "the backward parts of Europe . . .": ibid., p. 209.

74 "With the insweep of the unintelligible . . .": ibid., p. 216.

75 "the Mediterranean race . . .": Frederick Jackson Turner, "Social Forces in American History" [1910], in Turner, *Frontier in American History*, pp. 316–17.

75 "degraded Asiatics": Elmer Sandemeyer, *The Anti-Chinese Movement in California* (Urbana: University of Illinois Press, 1973), p. 42.

75 "We want the Chinese *trade* . . .": ibid., p. 42.

76 "unless protective measures . . .": Mink, *Old Labor*, p. 71.

76 "ignorant tools . . .": *New York Times*, July 9, 1870, p. 1.

76 "long-tailed barbarians . . .": Mink, *Old Labor*, pp. 78–79.

77 "the lowest and most degraded . . .": *New York Times*, July 1, 1870, p. 1.

77 "The Chinamen labor for such pitiful wages . . .": *Atlantic Monthly*, Nov. 1871, p. 598.

77 "Reilly can *outdo* Ah San . . .": Edward A. Ross, *The Changing Chinese* (New York: Century, 1912), p. 47.

77 "The Chinese can live cheaper . . .": Mink, *Old Labor*, p. 76.

77 "another kind of tawny slave labor"; "the laborers that had come from Europe": *New York Times*, July 1, 1870, p. 1.

77 "there is not sufficient brain capacity . . .": *Congressional Record*, 44th Cong., 2nd sess., vol. 5, pt. 3, 1877, p. 2005.

78 "The Chinese have reduced wages . . .": ibid., p. 2004.

78 "drive the Chinaman out . . .": *New York Times*, April 3, 1877, p. 4.

78 "We declare that the Chinaman . . .": Mink, *Old Labor*, p. 82.

79 "directly or indirectly . . .": Roger Daniels, *The Politics of Prejudice: The Anti-Japanese Movement in California, and the Struggle for Japanese Exclusion* (New York: Atheneum, 1977), p. 18.

79 "to restrain the great influx . . .": Shih-Shan Henry Tsai, *The Chinese Experience in America* (Bloomington: Indiana University Press, 1986), p. 59.

79 "Every country owes . . .": Saxton, *Indispensable Enemy*, pp. 147–48.

80   ". . . even Chinese and Japanese . . .": Ignatius Donnelly, *Caesar's Column: A Story of the Twentieth Century* [1890] (Cambridge, Mass.: Belknap Press of Harvard University Press, 1960), p. 38.

82   "The foreign shylocks are rushing . . .": Daniels, *Politics of Prejudice*, p. 20.

82   "We keep out pauper-made goods . . .": ibid., p. 22.

82   "We declare our belief . . .": Ichioka, *Issei*, pp. 98–99.

82   "your union will under no circumstances . . .": ibid., p. 99.

83   "Every incoming coolie . . ."; "can not be *unionized* . . .": ibid., p. 100.

83   "Once the war with Russia . . .": Daniels, *Politics of Prejudice*, p. 25.

83   *Chronicle* headlines in this period: ibid., p. 25.

83   "complete orientalization . . .": ibid., p. 26.

83   "We view with alarm . . .": Ichioka, *Issei*, p. 121.

84   "the patronizing or employing . . .": ibid., p. 139.

84   "contribute nothing to the growth . . .": Daniels, *Politics of Prejudice*, p. 27.

84   "Ill fares the land . . .": ibid., p. 46.

84   "We are anxious . . .": Ichioka, *Issei*, p. 36.

85   "In the matter of Chinese . . .": Daniels, *Politics of Prejudice*, p. 55.

85   "torrent of peon poison": Foley, *White Scourge*, p. 47.

85   "slim-legged [Mexican] peons . . .": Mario Garcia, *Desert Immigrants: The Mexicans of El Paso, 1880–1920* (New Haven: Yale University Press, 1981), p. 104.

85   "Cheap labor . . .": ibid., p. 103.

86   "the refuse and sweepings of Europe . . .": *Memorial: The Other Side of the Chinese Question* (Woodward and Co., 1886), pp. 8–9.

86   "The immigrant from across the Atlantic . . .": Esther Baldwin, *Must the Chinese Go?* (New York: Elkins, 1890), pp. 29–30.

86   "been inclined, as a rule . . .": *Atlantic Monthly*, Nov. 1912, p. 694.

86   "The Dago works . . .": Mink, *Old Labor*, p. 229.

86   "Slovenians, Italians . . .": ibid., p. 230.

87   ". . . all legislative measures . . .": ibid., p. 232.

87   "in the position of any other asylum . . .": John Higham, *Strangers in the Land: Patterns of American Nativism, 1865–1925* [1955] (New York: Atheneum, 1978), pp. 71–72.

87   "The subject of the exclusion . . .": Daniels, *Coming to America*, p. 31.

88   " 'Barbarians, savages, illiterate Anarchists . . .' . . .": Philip Foner, ed., *The Autobiographies of the Haymarket Martyrs* (New York: Pathfinder, 1969), pp. 59, 60.

89   "our wonderful fervent girls": Maxine Schwartz Seller, "The Uprising of the Twenty Thousand: Sex, Class, and Ethnicity in the Shirtwaist Makers' Strike of 1909," in Hoerder, ed., *"Struggle a Hard Battle,"* p. 268.

89   "the emigrants' strike": Green, *Ready-to-Wear*, p. 50.

89   "There has appeared in great force . . .": Mink, *Old Labor*, p. 66.

90   "Why Does Overproduction Cause Starvation?": Philip Foner, *The Workingmen's Party of the United States: A History of the First Marxist Party in the Americas* (Minneapolis: MEP Publications, 1984), p. 79.

90   "We now have the communists . . .": ibid., p. 88.

91   "probably an amalgamation . . .": ibid., p. 73.

91   "vast additions . . .": Richard Slotkin, *The Fatal Environment: The Myth of the Frontier in the Age of Industrialization, 1800–1890* (Middletown, Conn.: Wesleyan University Press, 1985), p. 495.

91   "Any hour the mob chooses . . .": Foner, *Workingmen's Party*, p. 72.

91   "Its air was filled . . .": John Hay, *The Bread-Winners: A Social Study* (New York: Harper & Brothers, 1884), p. 7.

92   "roll-call of shirks": ibid., p. 82.

92   "wandering apostles of plunder": ibid., p. 239.

92   "a few tonguey vagrants . . .": ibid., p. 215.

92   "Roosian scurfs": ibid., pp. 89, 78.

92   "a little speech . . .": ibid., p. 225.

92   "profound sympathy . . .": ibid., p. 187.

92   "rich and intelligent . . ."; "there was not an Irish laborer . . .": ibid., pp. 246–47.

93   "Shall I not bring you . . .": ibid., p. 314.

93   "highest duty of every nation . . .": *Chae Chan-ping* v. *United States* (1889), 130 U.S. 606.

93   "the right to exclude . . .": *Fong Yue-ting* v. *United States* (1893), 149 U.S. 698.

94   "at war with and antagonistic to . . .": *Ex Parte Saur* (1891), 81 F. 355.

94   "all persons who are known . . .": William Preston, Jr., *Aliens and Dissenters: Federal Suppression of Radicals, 1903–1933* (New York: Harper & Row, 1963), p. 31.

95   "opposed to organized government . . .": ibid., p. 67.

96   "Ivan produces much more . . .": Ross, *Old World in the New*, pp. 197–98.

97   "Not all jingoes were nativists . . .": Higham, *Strangers in the Land*, p. 76.

PART II: IMAGES

101   "They were lazy—always lazy . . .": Mark Twain, *Following the Equator: A Journey Around the World* [1897] (New York: Dover, 1989), p. 207.

3. PARABLES OF PROGRESS

105   "a sleek and hideous thing of ebony . . .": Edgar Rice Burroughs, *Tarzan of the Apes* [1914] (New York: Signet, 1990), pp. 90, 104.

106   "other white men . . .": ibid., p. 120.

107   "An Automobile of the Orient": *National Geographic*, March 1917, p. 259.

107   "squalor and cheap magnificence . . .": Charles Dudley Warner, *In the Levant* [1877] (Boston: Houghton Mifflin, 1901), p. 547.

107   "Egypt is waking . . .": Charles Dudley Warner, *Mummies and Moslems* pp. 430–31.

107   "sluggish ongoing of life . . .": *Atlantic Monthly*, Dec. 1887, p. 813.

108   "Desperate Encounters . . .": *New York Herald,* Nov. 24, 1877, p. 3.

109   "During the past three centuries . . .": Theodore Roosevelt, *The Winning of the West* [1889–96] (Lincoln: University of Nebraska Press, 1995), vol. I, p. 1.

109   "The world was made for man . . .": Mark Twain, *Following the Equator: A Journey Around the World* [1897] (New York: Dover, 1989), p. 186.

111   "where Indians and wild animals . . .": Owen Wister, *The Virginian* [1902] (New York: Viking Penguin, 1988), p. 69.

111   "The Barbadian negro . . .": *Harper's New Monthly Magazine*, Feb. 1877, p. 387.

111   "It does seem a hopeless task . . .": Warner, *Mummies and Moslems*, p. 83.

112   "There is no more interesting question . . .": David Spurr, *The Rhetoric of Empire: Colonial Discourse in Journalism, Travel Writing, and Imperial Administration* (Durham, N.C.: Duke University Press, 1993), p. 31.

112   "the fashions range from . . .": *National Geographic*, Nov. 1909, advertising pages at back, n.p.

113   "We appear to be getting into real Africa . . .": Warner, *Mummies and Moslems*, p. 234.

114   "Moroccan crowds are a feast to the eye . . .": Edith Wharton, "In Morocco" [1919], in Sarah Bird Wright, ed., *Edith Wharton Abroad: Selected Travel Writings, 1888–1920* (New York: St. Martin's Griffin, 1995), pp. 187, 188.

114   "the picturesque populace . . .": Edith Wharton, "The Cruise of the Vanadis," in ibid., p. 41.

114   "strange and interesting sight . . .": Theodore Roosevelt, *Through the Brazilian Wilderness* (New York: Scribner, 1914), p. 219.

114   "swarthy bodies shining . . .": Warner, *In the Levant*, pp. 16, 439.

114   "The first sight of the colored . . .": Warner, *Mummies and Moslems*, p. 31.

114   "One of the beliefs of the Europeans . . .": Timothy Mitchell, *Colonizing Egypt* (Berkeley: University of California Press, 1988), p. 2.

114   "The nomadic nature of African life . . .": Wharton, "In Morocco," p. 188.

115   "Many visitors came to inspect . . .": Verney Lovett Cameron, *Across Africa* (London: Daldy Isbister, 1877), vol. I, p. 100.

115   "mongrel subjects of the Khedive . . .": Warner, *Mummies and Moslems*, p. 110.

115   "into a collective *they* . . .": Mary Louise Pratt, *Imperial Eyes: Travel Writing and Transculturation* (New York: Routledge, 1992), p. 64.

115   "Do you think our voyage . . .": Warner, *Mummies and Moslems*, p. 119.

116   "should not forget the origin . . ."; "I find that they are . . .": Henry Morton Stanley, *Through the Dark Continent* [1899] (New York: Dover, 1988), vol. I, p. 38.

116   "the eager, masterful, materialistic . . ."; "conditions of life . . .": Theodore Roosevelt, *African Game Trails: An Account of the African Wanderings of an American Hunter-Naturalist* (New York: Scribner, 1910), p. 2.

116   "reproduce in a most striking manner . . .": *National Geographic*, March 1909, p. 217.

116   "The whole sight was . . .": Edgar Rice Burroughs, *The Return of Tarzan* [1913] (New York: Ballantine, 1963), p. 149.

117   "Africa to-day is the realm of romance . . ."; "a public growing . . .": *North American Review*, July 1877, p. 147.

117   "has no industry at all . . .": Mitchell, *Colonizing Egypt*, p. 9.

117   "because they have not been . . .": ibid., p. 99.

117   ". . . A Chinese village . . .": Arthur H. Smith, *Village Life in China: A Study in Sociology* (New York: Fleming H. Revell, 1899), p. 312.

117   "the European Middle Ages . . .": Edward A. Ross, *The Changing Chinese* (New York: Century, 1912), p. 3.

117   "Now, after the sleep . . .": *North American Review*, Feb. 1899, pp. 230, 233, 236, 238.

118   "The influences of the nineteenth century . . .": *Atlantic Monthly*, May 1897, p. 678.

118   "The little *opera-bouffe* . . .": O. Henry, *Cabbages and Kings* [1904] (New York: Penguin, 1993), p. 7.

118   "debased, misbegotten . . .": Warner, *In the Levant*, pp. 63–64.

118   "as we had been taught . . .": Warner, *Mummies and Moslems*, p. 29.

118   "ape-like naked savages . . .": Roosevelt, *African Game Trails*, pp. x, 405.

118   "appropriation of useful ideas . . .": May French-Sheldon, *Sultan to Sultan: Adventures Among the Masai and Their Tribes of East Africa* (Boston: Arena, 1892), p. 342.

119   "Sierra Leone . . .": Mary Kingsley, *West African Studies* [1899] (New York: Barnes and Noble, 1964), p. 53.

119   "are incapable of independent progress . . .": *North American Review*, March 1906, p. 428.

119   "not only the land of romance . . .": ibid., July 1877, p. 149.

119   "the country when opened . . .": Roosevelt, *Through the Brazilian Wilderness*, p. 225.

119 "self-produced civilization . . .": Roosevelt, *African Game Trails*, p. 432.

119 "out-of-the-way regions . . .": H. W. Brands, *T.R.: The Last Romantic* (New York: Basic Books, 1997), p. 649.

119 "I firmly believe . . .": Roosevelt, *African Game Trails*, p. 173.

119 some 512 animals: ibid., pp. 532–33.

120 "where the white man can live . . .": *National Geographic*, March 1900, p. 91.

120 ". . . added to her market . . .": ibid., Jan. 1899, pp. 21, 23, 24–25.

120 Numbers of the journal: *National Geographic*, Feb., March, June–Aug. 1899.

120 "The day I left . . .": ibid., Jan. 1900, pp. 5, 7.

120 "splendid . . . success in ruling . . .": ibid., Sept. 1900, pp. 362–63.

120 "To an American . . ."; "No one could fail . . .": Brands, *T.R.*, p. 650.

122 "is almost that of a foreign land . . .": *Harper's Weekly*, Feb. 9, 1907, p. 193.

122 "one may find for the asking . . .": Jacob A. Riis, *How the Other Half Lives: Studies Among the Tenements of New York* [1890] (New York: Hill and Wang, 1967), p. 15.

122 "queer conglomerate mass . . .": ibid., p. 16.

123 "the most picturesque . . ."; "an inborn feeling . . .": *Harper's Weekly*, June 29, 1895, p. 607.

123 "Think ye that building shall . . .": Riis, *How the Other Half Lives*, p. 226.

123 "Down below Chatham Square . . .": ibid., p. 21.

124 "We passed through courts . . .": "Italian Life in New York" [c. 1880], in *New York: A Collection from Harper's Magazine* (New York: Gallery, 1991), pp. 244–45.

124 "over broken railways . . .": *Atlantic Monthly*, March 1915, p. 290.

124 "perhaps a dozen feet square . . .": Riis, *How the Other Half Lives*, p. 53.

125 "There is no virtue among them . . .": Ignatius Donnelly, *Caesar's Column: A Story of the Twentieth Century* [1890] (Cambridge, Mass.: Belknap Press of Harvard University Press, 1960), p. 41.

125 "is by nature as clean as the cat . . .": Riis, *How the Other Half Lives*, pp. 71–72.

125   "The Italian . . .": ibid., p. 41.

125   "The pure type of the Hebrew . . .": *Harper's Weekly*, Aug. 3, 1895, p. 725.

125   "crowds of half-naked children . . .": Riis, *How the Other Half Lives*, pp. 100, 43, 41.

126   "picketed from end to end . . .": ibid., p. 43.

126   "Jewtown"; "the jargon of the street . . .": ibid., p. 77.

126   "a set of hardened little scoundrels . . .": ibid., p. 148.

126   "All attempts to make . . .": ibid., p. 68.

126   "where the new day . . .": ibid., p. 83.

127   "Down the street comes a file . . .": ibid., p. 45.

127   "women sit in rows . . .": ibid., pp. 43–44.

127   "carry their slums . . ."; "reproduces conditions of destitution . . .": ibid., pp. 20, 37.

127   "On Indian persons . . .": Curtis Hinsley, "Zunis and Brahmins: Cultural Ambivalence in the Gilded Age," in George Stocking, Jr., ed., *Romantic Motives: Essays on Anthropological Sensibility* (Madison: University of Wisconsin Press, 1989), p. 169.

128   "There are many humorous things . . .": Twain, *Following the Equator*, p. 213.

128   "I consider it more barbarous . . .": Michel de Montaigne, "On Cannibals" [1580], in *Essays* (New York: Penguin, 1958), pp. 113–14.

129   "flourish in greater abundance . . .": Herman Melville, *Typee: A Peep at Polynesian Life* [1846] (New York: Signet, 1964), p. 228.

129   "for every advantage . . .": ibid., pp. 144–45.

130   "*Mon Dieu!* . . .": Burroughs, *Return of Tarzan*, p. 17.

130   "The last remnant . . .": ibid., p. 149.

130   "Here were people . . .": ibid., p. 70.

130   ". . . In the savage, feeling predominates . . .": *Atlantic Monthly*, June 1897, pp. 838–39.

130   "close to nature . . .": ibid., p. 839.

131   "Civilized man . . .": Roosevelt, *African Game Trails*, p. 239.

131 "the doctrine of ignoble ease . . .": Theodore Roosevelt, "The Strenuous Life" [1899], in Theodore Roosevelt, *The Strenuous Life* (New York: Review of Reviews, 1910), pp. 3, 9.

131 "The Whites always mean well . . .": Twain, *Following the Equator*, p. 267.

132 "swarming, unlucky . . .": *Harper's Weekly*, June 29, 1895, p. 607.

132 "open and amiable . . .": *National Geographic*, June 1899, p. 217; March 1909, p. 233; June 1899, pp. 207, 211.

132 "We live in an age . . .": Theodore Dreiser, *Jennie Gerhardt* [1911] (New York: Penguin, 1989), p. 132.

132 "the innate affection of the untutored . . .": ibid., pp. 164–65, 229, 337, 381, 419–20.

133 "into an understanding . . .": ibid., p. 199.

133 "Here in this huge city . . .": Upton Sinclair, *The Jungle* [1906] (New York: Penguin, 1985), p. 140.

133 "the world of civilization . . .": ibid., p. 278.

134 "is very imprudent . . .": ibid., p. 18.

134 "no longer cared . . .": ibid., p. 20.

134 "dressed hogs . . ."; "the greatest aggregation . . .": ibid., pp. 47, 51.

134 "to take all the miracles . . .": ibid., p. 249.

135 "savage . . . with those . . .": ibid., p. 166.

135 "in a flash . . .": ibid., p. 183.

135 "he was like a wild beast . . .": ibid., p. 185.

135 "They had put him behind bars . . .": ibid., pp. 191, 193.

135 "was like coming suddenly upon . . .": ibid., p. 358.

135 "a far-off time . . .": ibid., p. 18.

136 "contentment with simple pleasures . . .": *National Geographic*, Feb. 1917, pp. 99, 101, 105, 113, 115.

136 "For the first time . . .": Edgar Rice Burroughs, *Jungle Tales of Tarzan* [1916–17] (New York: Ballantine, 1997), p. 236.

137   "living representatives . . .": George Stocking, Jr., *Victorian Anthropology* (New York: Free Press, 1987), p. 176.

4. THEORIES OF DEVELOPMENT

139   "Mention some country . . .": John Fiske, *A History of the United States for Schools* (Boston: Houghton Mifflin, 1907), p. 345.

139   "Are the Indians . . .": ibid., p. 16.

139   "Barbaric languages . . .": John Fiske, *Myths and Myth Makers: Old Tales and Superstitions Interpreted by Comparative Mythology* (Boston: Osgood, 1873), p. 149.

140   "it would be pure moonshine . . .": George Stocking, Jr., *Victorian Anthropology* (New York: Free Press, 1987), p. 185.

140   "It can now be asserted . . .": Eliot Barkan and Ronald Bush, eds., *Prehistories of the Modern: The Primitivist Culture of Modernism* (Stanford, Calif.: Stanford University Press, 1995), p. 32.

140   "the ape had developed . . .": Stocking, Jr., *Victorian Anthropology*, p. 185.

142   "the mind of a child . . .": ibid., pp. 225–26.

142   "What an opportunity . . .": Robert Rydell, *All the World's a Fair: Visions of Empire at American International Expositions, 1876–1916* (Chicago: University of Chicago Press, 1984), p. 65.

142   "primitive folk will occupy . . .": *Harper's Weekly*, April 30, 1904, p. 684.

144   "stunted in their growth . . .": David Spurr, *The Rhetoric of Empire: Colonial Discourse in Journalism, Travel Writing, and Imperial Administration* (Durham, N.C.: Duke University Press, 1993), pp. 63–64.

144   "For my own part . . .": Charles Darwin, *The Descent of Man and Selection in Relation to Sex* [1871] (Princeton, N.J.: Princeton University Press, 1981), pp. 404–5.

144   "homogenous race . . .": Stocking, Jr., *Victorian Anthropology*, p. 148.

145   "popular superstitions . . .": George Stocking, Jr., *After Tylor: British Social Anthropology, 1888–1951* (Madison: University of Wisconsin Press, 1995), p. 139.

145   "On the whole . . .": Stocking, Jr., *Victorian Anthropology*, p. 162.

146   "Mankind commenced their career . . .": Lewis Henry Morgan, *Ancient Society: Or, Researches in the Lines of Human Progress from Savagery Through Barbarism to Civilization* [1877] (Cleveland: World Publishing, 1963), p. 3.

146   "The experience of mankind . . .": ibid., p. 8.

146   "ethnical chaos of savagery . . .": ibid., p. 16.

147   "with the gens as it now exists . . .": ibid., p. 64.

147   "the most primitive form of society . . .": ibid., p. 49.

148   "All students would agree . . .": William Z. Ripley, *Races of Europe: A Sociological Study* (New York: Appleton, 1899), pp. 10, 11.

148   "The varieties of [nature's] resources . . .": ibid., p. 11.

149   "Teutonic peoples . . .": ibid., pp. 584, 589.

149   "civilized man . . .": George W. Stocking, Jr., ed., *A Franz Boas Reader: The Shaping of American Anthropology, 1883–1911* (New York: Basic Books, 1974), pp. 221–42.

149   "The fact that many fundamental . . .": Franz Boas, "Methods of Cultural Anthropology," in Franz Boas, *Race, Language, and Culture* [1940] (Chicago: University of Chicago Press, 1982), pp. 275, 273.

150   "a race is commonly described . . .": Franz Boas, *The Mind of Primitive Man* (New York: Macmillan, 1911), p. 20.

150   "or, taking the notion . . .": ibid., p. 21.

151   "We find that on the average . . .": Elazar Barkan, *The Retreat of Scientific Racism: Changing Conceptions of Race in Britain and the United States Between the World Wars* (Cambridge: Cambridge University Press, 1992), p. 86.

151   "the innumerable conflicts . . .": Rydell, *All the World's a Fair*, p. 211.

151   "Onward these primitive people . . .": ibid.

152   "The capability of progress . . .": John Fiske, "The Progress from Brute to Man," *North American Review*, Oct. 1873, p. 255.

153   "civilisation varies on the whole . . .": Adam Kuper, *The Invention of Primitive Society: Transformation of an Illusion* (New York: Routledge, 1988), p. 105.

153   "habitual behavior became instinctive . . .": Stocking, Jr., *Victorian Anthropology*, p. 235.

153   "will not prosper . . .": Rydell, *All the World's a Fair*, p. 224.

153   "With savages, the weak . . .": Darwin, *The Descent of Man*, p. 168.

154   "purely ethnological inquiry . . ."; "human mental qualities": Stocking, Jr., *Victorian Anthropology*, p. 94.

154 "What an extraordinary effect . . .": Francis Galton, "Hereditary Talent and Character" [1865], in Russell Jacoby and Naomi Glauberman, eds., *The Bell Curve Debate: History, Documents, Opinions* (New York: Times Books, 1995), p. 393.

154 "Whenever you can . . .": Daniel Kevles, *In the Name of Eugenics: Genetics and the Uses of Human Heredity* (Berkeley: University of California Press, 1985), p. 7.

154 "the instinct of continuous steady labour . . .": Stocking, Jr., *Victorian Anthropology*, pp. 94–95.

156 "constant injunction is that . . .": Ruth Benedict, *Race: Science and Politics* [1940] (Westport, Conn.: Greenwood Press, 1982), pp. 126–27.

156 "the great strains of human protoplasm . . .": Kevles, *In the Name of Eugenics*, p. 54.

156 "We should see to it . . .": *Reports of the Immigration Commission: Statements and Recommendations Submitted by Societies and Organizations Interested in the Subject of Immigration* (Washington, D.C.: Government Printing Office, 1910), pp. 107, 111.

156 "every foul and stagnant pool . . .": Allan Chase, *The Legacy of Malthus: The Social Cost of the New Scientific Racism* [1975] (Urbana: University of Illinois Press, 1980), p. 110.

157 "to investigate and report on . . .": ibid., p. 114.

158 "the analytic and experimental study . . .": Garland Allen, "Eugenics Comes to America," in Jacoby and Glauberman, eds., *Bell Curve Debate*, p. 447.

158 "The idea of a 'melting-pot' belongs . . .": Kevles, *In the Name of Eugenics*, p. 47.

159 "by this means was enriched . . .": Charles B. Davenport, *Heredity in Relation to Eugenics* (New York: H. Holt, 1911), p. 207.

159 "love of independence . . .": ibid., p. 214.

159 "alcoholism, considerable mental defectiveness . . ." . . . ". . . love of country": ibid., pp. 212–20.

159 "darker in pigmentation . . .": ibid., p. 219.

159 "How can we keep out defective . . .": ibid., p. 221.

159 "to classify immigrants . . .": ibid., p. 222.

160 "Eugenics has to do . . .": Chase, *Legacy of Malthus*, pp. 161–62.

160 "only those individuals . . .": Davenport, *Heredity in Relation*, p. 222.

160 "Moral, intellectual, and spiritual . . .": Chase, *Legacy of Malthus*, p. 170.

161 "suicidal ethics . . .": Madison Grant, *The Passing of the Great Race; or, The Racial Basis of European History* (New York: Scribner, 1916), p. 80.

161 "the racial mixture . . ."; "The cross between . . .": ibid., pp. 15–16.

161 "the weak, the broken . . ." . . . ". . . or understand his ideals": ibid., p. 81.

161 "a serious drag on civilization . . .": ibid., p. 73.

161 "western extensions of an Asiatic subspecies . . .": Chase, *Legacy of Malthus*, p. 170.

162 "Wild Tartars": ibid., p. 185.

162 "the hall-mark of his aristocratic birth . . .": Edgar Rice Burroughs, *Tarzan of the Apes* [1914] (New York: Signet, 1990), p. 202.

162 "For countless ages . . .": Edgar Rice Burroughs, *The Return of Tarzan* [1913] (New York: Ballantine, 1963), pp. 173–74.

162 "Danger That World Scum . . .": Chase, *Legacy of Malthus*, p. 173.

163 "from ten to thirty cubic inches . . .": Stocking, Jr., *Victorian Anthropology*, p. 141.

163 "The intellectual traits of the uncivilized . . .": Stephen Jay Gould, *The Mismeasure of Man* (New York: Norton, 1981), p. 117.

164 "represent the same stage . . .": ibid., p. 118.

164 "that races develop . . .": ibid., pp. 118–19.

164 "a very large number of congenital idiots . . .": ibid., pp. 134–35.

166 "high-grade defectives": ibid., p. 158.

166 "The people who are doing the drudgery . . .": ibid., p. 161.

166 "it is perfectly clear . . .": Henry Herbert Goddard, *Feeble-Mindedness: Its Causes and Consequences* [1914] (New York: Macmillan, 1926), p. 561.

166 "One can hardly escape the conviction . . .": Henry Herbert Goddard, "Mental Tests and the Immigrant," *Journal of Delinquency*, Sept. 1917, p. 1.

167 "moron of the slow phlegmatic type . . .": Goddard, *Feeble-Mindedness*, pp. 121–22.

167 "cheerful imbecile of low grade": ibid., p. 234.

167 "whether her condition . . .": ibid., p. 432.

167 "A French peasant may be normal . . .": ibid., p. 573.

168 "superior social classes . . .": Lewis M. Terman, *The Measurement of Intelligence: An Explanation of and a Complete Guide for the Use of the Stanford Revision and Extension of the Binet-Simon Intelligence Scale* (Boston: Houghton Mifflin, 1916), p. 72.

168 "is very, very common . . .": ibid., pp. 91–92.

168 "far enough below the actual average . . .": ibid., p. 92.

169 "an opportunity for a national inventory . . .": Carl Brigham, *A Study of American Intelligence* (1923), in Jacoby and Glauberman, eds., *Bell Curve Debate*, p. 572.

169 "a gradual deterioration . . .": Leon Kamin, "The Pioneers of IQ Testing," in ibid., p. 494.

169 "There can be no doubt . . .": Brigham, *Study of American Intelligence*, p. 577.

169 "over 2,000,000 immigrants . . .": ibid., p. 577.

170 "a fact which indicates clearly . . .": ibid., p. 580.

170 "no reason why legal steps . . .": ibid., p. 581.

170 "There is never interpretation . . .": Edward Said, *Covering Islam: How the Media and the Experts Determine How We See the Rest of the World* (New York: Pantheon, 1981), p. 157.

171 "of rudimentary culture . . .": Stocking, Jr., *After Tylor*, p. 147.

171 "our commerce and political intercourse . . .": Boas to Morris K. Jessup [1903], in Stocking, Jr., ed., *Franz Boas Reader*, pp. 295, 296.

171 "A savage brought up . . .": George W. Stocking, Jr., *Race, Culture, and Evolution: Essays in the History of Anthropology* (Chicago: University of Chicago Press, 1968), p. 132.

171 "borderline efficiency . . .": Terman, *Measurement of Intelligence*, p. 91.

172 "Can we hope to have . . .": Henry Herbert Goddard, *Human Efficiency and Levels of Intelligence* (Princeton, N.J.: Princeton University Press, 1920), p. 95.

172 "In a democracy . . .": ibid., p. 126.

172 "there is a sufficiently large group . . .": ibid., p. 128.

PART III: POLITICS

175   "Bedouin Mother and Child . . .": *National Geographic*, June 1917, p. 552.

175   "This device is at a disadvantage . . .": ibid., p. 557.

175   "Motherhood in the Philippines . . .": ibid., p. 562.

177   "the minds of children": George Stocking, Jr., *Victorian Anthropology* (New York: Free Press, 1987), pp. 225–26.

5. ACCENTS OF MENACE

180   "idleness, treachery . . .": Shane White, *Somewhat More Independent: The End of Slavery in New York City, 1770–1810* (Athens: University of Georgia Press, 1991), p. 71.

181   "jailbirds, professional murderers . . .": Barbara Miller Solomon, *Ancestors and Immigrants: A Changing New England Tradition* (Chicago: University of Chicago Press, 1956), p. 88.

181   "Wide open and unguarded . . .": ibid., p. 82.

181   "present the evidence . . .": Robert Rydell, *All the World's a Fair: Visions of Empire at American International Expositions, 1876–1916* (Chicago: University of Chicago Press, 1984), p. 226.

182   "statistical facts for 1914 . . .": ibid.

182   "droves of squalid men . . .": James Bryce, *The American Commonwealth* [1893] (New York: Macmillan, 1905), vol. II, p. 99.

184   "Is it any wonder . . .": Oscar Handlin, ed., *Immigration as a Factor in American History* (Englewood Cliffs, N.J.: Prentice-Hall, 1959), p. 106.

184   "The great mass of people . . .": Thomas O'Connor, *The Boston Irish: A Political History* (Boston: Back Bay, 1995), pp. 122–23.

184   "Bread, meat und coal . . .": Melvin Holli, *Reform in Detroit: Hazen S. Pingree and Urban Politics* (New York: Oxford University Press, 1969), p. 148.

184   ". . . We soon discovered . . .": Jane Addams, *Twenty Years at Hull House* [1910] (New York: Signet, 1960), p. 222.

185   "The Alderman . . ."; "Primitive people . . .": Jane Addams, "Why the Ward Boss Rules," in Bruce Stave, ed., *Urban Bosses, Machines, and Progressive Reformers* (Lexington, Mass.: D. C. Heath, 1972), pp. 10, 11.

185   "Mister, your saloon . . .": Lincoln Steffens, *The Shame of the Cities* [1904] (New York: Hill and Wang, 1957), p. 23.

186   "Ward politics is built . . .": Robert Woods, *Americans in Process* [1902], in Handlin, ed., *Immigration as a Factor*, p. 107.

186   "Irish Catholic despotism . . .": Alexander Callow, Jr., *American Urban History* (New York: Oxford University Press, 1973), p. 236.

186   "common sewer . . .": ibid.

186   "find that the Irish . . .": Steffens, *Shame of the Cities*, pp. 2–3.

187   "prosimian bulk of bone . . .": Howard Chudacoff, *The Evolution of American Urban Society* (Englewood Cliffs, N.J.: Prentice-Hall, 1981), p. 141.

188   "illiterates, full of superstition . . .": Zane Miller, *Boss Cox's Cincinnati: Urban Politics in the Progressive Era* (Chicago: University of Chicago Press, 1968), p. 65.

188   "The clouds are beginning . . .": Blaine A. Brownell and Warren E. Stickle, eds., *Bosses and Reformers: Urban Politics in America, 1880–1920* (Boston: Houghton Mifflin, 1973), p. 173.

189   "There's got to be . . .": Chudacoff, *Evolution of American Urban Society*, p. 161.

189   "nationalizing influence . . .": Elmer Cornwell, "Bosses, Machines, and Ethnic Groups," in Brownell and Stickle, eds., *Bosses and Reformers*, pp. 10–11.

190   "If universal suffrage . . .": James Russell Lowell, *Essays, Poems, and Letters* (New York: Odyssey Press, 1948), p. 147.

190   "ethnological animal show": Rogers Smith, *Civic Ideals: Conflicting Visions of Citizenship in U.S. History* (New Haven: Yale University Press, 1997), p. 362.

191   "Is it the gentleman's idea . . .": *Congressional Record*, 68th Cong., 1st sess., vol. 65, pt. 6, (1924) p. 5648.

191   "constitutionally incapable . . .": Dale T. Knobel, *Paddy and the Republic: Ethnicity and Nationality in Antebellum America* (Middletown, Conn.: Wesleyan University Press, 1986), p. 123.

192   "inherited organic imperfection . . .": ibid., p. 90.

192   "it is impossible to name . . .": George M. Fredrickson, *The Inner Civil War: Northern Intellectuals and the Crisis of the Union* (New York: Harper & Row, 1965), p. 115.

192   "all the qualities . . ."; "to the Celtic mind . . .": *Atlantic Monthly*, May 1866, pp. 574, 575.

192   "A Celt . . . lacks the solidity . . .": ibid., March 1896, pp. 294–95.

192   "cupidity nor brutality . . .": Solomon, *Ancestors and Immigrants*, p. 155.

193   "the qualities which go . . .": *Atlantic Monthly*, June 1896, p. 828.

193   "If there be any truth . . .": John Swinton, *The New Issue: The Chinese-American Question* (New York: American News Company, 1870), p. 7.

193   "liberty is a conception . . .": ibid., pp. 11, 12.

193   "The safety of republican institutions . . .": *Congressional Record*, 44th Cong., 2nd sess., vol. 5, p. 3, 1877, p. 2004.

194   "vast hive from which . . .": ibid., p. 2005.

195   "Is a person of the Mongolian race . . .": *In re Ah Yup*, 1 Fed Cas 223 at 224.

196   "neither expected nor desired . . .": *In re Dow*, 213 Fed 355 at 365.

196   "These Slovacks . . ."; "races most alien . . .": *North American Review*, Jan. 1891, pp. 30–31, 32.

197   "do not promise . . .": ibid., p. 35.

197   ". . . our immigration changing . . .": ibid., May 1891, p. 608.

197   "these degraded races . . .": Solomon, *Ancestors and Immigrants*, pp. 144–45.

198   "Public opinion . . .": *Immigration Restriction League Constitution* (Boston, 1894).

198   "elements undesirable . . ." . . . "pollute the Yankee blood": Solomon, *Ancestors and Immigrants*, pp. 108, 109.

198   "to spoil their breed . . .": ibid., p. 110.

198   "brownish"; "the vigorous Anglo-Saxon . . .": ibid., pp. 126, 141.

199   "purity of race . . .": ibid., p. 112.

199   "classified by race . . .": ibid., p. 115.

199   ". . . The truth is . . .": ibid., p. 93.

199   "Recent investigations . . .": *Reports of the Immigration Commission: Statements and Recommendations of Societies and Organizations Interested in the Subject of Immigration* (Washington, D.C.: Government Printing Office, 1911), pp. 106–7.

200   "within recent memory . . .": Solomon, *Ancestors and Immigrants*, p. 119.

200   "Up to the present time . . .": ibid., p. 152.

201   "We have admitted the dregs . . .": Benjamin Ringer, *"We the People" and Others: Duality and America's Treatment of Its Racial Minorities* (New York: Tavistock, 1983), p. 801.

201   "looked exactly like Americans . . .": Lawrence Fuchs, *The American Kaleidoscope: Race, Ethnicity, and the Civic Culture* (Middletown, Conn.: Wesleyan University Press, 1990), p. 60.

201   "like the immigrant of 1620 . . .": Mary Antin, *They Who Knock at Our Gates* (Boston: Houghton Mifflin, 1914), pp. 56–57.

202   "I am an ardent Pole . . .": Victor Greene, *American Immigrant Leaders, 1800–1910: Marginality and Identity* (Baltimore: Johns Hopkins University Press, 1987), p. 119.

203   "In the New World . . .": ibid., p. 117.

203   "The hearts we bring . . .": Matthew Frye Jacobson, *Special Sorrows: The Diasporic Imagination of Irish, Polish, and Jewish Immigrants in the United States* (Cambridge, Mass.: Harvard University Press, 1995), p. 10.

203   "There are thousands . . .": Werner Sollors, *Beyond Ethnicity: Consent and Descent in American Culture* (New York: Oxford University Press, 1986), p. 87.

204   "As the good wife . . .": Greene, *American Immigrant Leaders*, p. 74.

204   "what a stirring and a seething . . .": Israel Zangwill, *The Melting Pot* [1908] (New York: Macmillan, 1914), pp. 184–85.

205   "I was born, I have lived . . .": Mary Antin, *The Promised Land* [1912] (New York: Penguin, 1997), p. 1.

205   "We did not want to be 'greenhorns' . . .": ibid., p. 146.

206   "our hateful homemade . . .": ibid., p. 148.

206   "With our despised . . .": ibid., p. 149.

206   "We had to . . . be dressed . . .": ibid.

206   "In after years . . .": ibid., p. 156.

206   "thoughts and conduct . . .": ibid., p. 157.

207   "Think, every time you pass . . .": ibid., pp. 144–45.

207   "blessed guide to man . . .": ibid., p. 181.

207   "America is the youngest . . .": ibid., p. 286.

207   "The restrictionists could afford . . .": Werner Sollors, "Introduction" to ibid., p. xxxv.

208   "an irritating habit": ibid., p. xxxvii.

208   "the doctrines of liberty and equality . . .": Antin, *They Who Knock*, pp. 6–7.

208   "Strip the alien down . . .": ibid., p. 10.

208   "What have the experts . . .": ibid., pp. 9–10.

208   "By all means register . . .": ibid., p. 11.

208   "Our brains, our wealth . . .": ibid., p. 66.

208   "Not the immigrant . . .": ibid., p. 95.

209   "I cannot escape . . .": Abraham Cahan, *The Rise of David Levinsky: A Novel* [1917] (New York: Harper Brothers, 1960), p. 530.

210   "a transmutation . . . of Jews . . .": Horace Kallen, "Democracy Versus the Melting-Pot" [1915], in Horace Kallen, *Culture and Democracy in the United States* (New York: Liveright, 1924), p. 79.

210   "In 1776 all men . . .": ibid., p. 69.

210   "The first immigrants . . .": ibid., p. 98.

211   "All the while the immigrant . . .": ibid., p. 115.

211   "People may change . . .": ibid., p. 122.

211   "the wop changes into . . .": ibid., p. 106.

212   "In these days of ready-made garments . . .": ibid., p. 84.

212   "The selfhood which is inalienable . . .": ibid., p. 123.

212   "vanity blind them . . .": ibid., p. 125.

213   "Democracy involves not . . .": Lynn Duminil, *The Modern Temper* (New York: Hill and Wang, 1996), p. 166.

213   "Aid us in Ireland . . .": Thomas Brown, "The Origins and Character of Irish-

American Nationalism," in Lawrence McCaffrey, ed., *Irish Nationalism and the American Contribution* (New York: Arno Press, 1976), p. 334.

214   "feels foreign and misunderstood . . .": Jacobson, *Special Sorrows*, p. 18.

215   "the avenging wolfhound . . .": ibid., p. 15.

215   "I cannot feel that America . . .": Jeremiah O'Donovan Rossa, *Rossa's Recollections, 1838–1898* (Mariner's Harbor, N.Y.: O'Donovan Rossa, 1898), p. 262.

215   "One should know . . .": Him Mark Lai, Genny Lim, and Judy Yung, eds., *Island: Poetry and History of Chinese Immigrants on Angel Island, 1910–1940* (San Francisco: HOC DOI, 1980), p. 88.

216   "in a world of unrealities . . .": Matthew Frye Jacobson, *Whiteness of a Different Color: European Immigrants and the Alchemy of Race* (Cambridge, Mass.: Harvard University Press, 1998), p. 49.

217   "If there comes a day . . .": Lai, Lim, and Young, *Island,* p. 84.

218   "beaten men . . .": Francis Amasa Walker, "Restriction of Immigration," *Atlantic Monthly*, June 1896, p. 828.

218   "ethnological animal show": Smith, Civic Ideals, p. 192.

6. CHILDREN OF BARBARISM

221   "It is time . . .": Stuart Creighton Miller, *"Benevolent Assimilation": The American Conquest of the Philippines, 1899–1903* (New Haven: Yale University Press, 1982), p. 126.

222   "is not enough . . .": Henry Cabot Lodge, "Interview with President McKinley," in Daniel Schirmer and Stephen Rosskamm Shalom, eds., *The Philippines Reader: A History of Colonialism, Neocolonialism, Dictatorship, and Resistance* (Cambridge: South End Press, 1987), pp. 21–22.

222   "Our largest trade . . .": H. W. Brands, *Bound to Empire: The United States and the Philippines* (New York: Oxford University Press, 1992), p. 32.

222   "that there are two . . .": Mark Twain, "To the Person Sitting in Darkness" [1901], in Mark Twain, *Tales, Speeches, Essays, and Sketches* (New York: Penguin, 1994), p. 271.

222   "How dare any man . . .": Miller, *"Benevolent Assimilation,"* p. 126.

222   "Many of [the Philippine] people . . .": Theodore Roosevelt, "The Strenuous Life" [1899], in Theodore Roosevelt, *The Strenuous Life* (New York: Review of Reviews, 1910), p. 19.

223   "In the long run . . .": Walter LaFeber, *The American Search for Opportunity, 1865–1913*, vol. II in *The Cambridge History of American Foreign Relations* (Cambridge: Cambridge University Press, 1993), p. 188.

224   "We had not pondered . . .": D. Michael Shafer, ed., *The Legacy: The Vietnam War in the American Imagination* (Boston: Beacon Press, 1990), p. 11.

225   "the admission . . .": Christopher Lasch, "The Anti-Imperialist as Racist," in Thomas Paterson, ed., *American Imperialism and Anti-Imperialism* (New York: Crowell, 1973), p. 115.

226   "The Philippines are ours forever . . .": Albert Beveridge, "Our Philippine Policy," in Schirmer and Shalom, eds., *Philippines Reader*, p. 23.

226   "the jack-fools . . .": Thomas Dyer, *Theodore Roosevelt and the Idea of Race* (Baton Rouge, La.: LSU Press, 1980), p. 140.

226   "Only the exceptional . . .": Archibald Roosevelt, ed., *Theodore Roosevelt on Race, Riots, Reds, and Crime* (West Sayville, N.Y.: Probe, 1968), p. 87.

226   "It will be hard . . .": Beveridge, "Our Philippine Policy," p. 25.

227   "God has not been preparing . . .": ibid., p. 26.

227   "in a hopeless condition . . .": Mae Ngai, "Illegal Aliens and Alien Citizens: U.S. Immigration Policy and Racial Formation, 1924–1945," unpublished Ph.D. dissertation, Columbia University, 1998, chap. 5.

227   "Our little brown brothers . . .": Miller, *"Benevolent Assimilation,"* p. 134.

227   "disabused [Americans] of any impression . . .": Ngai, "Illegal Aliens," chap. 5.

228   "insane and wicked . . .": Miller, *"Benevolent Assimilation,"* p. 104.

228   "the closest, hardest fight . . .": E. Berkeley Tompkins, *Anti-Imperialism in the United States: The Great Debate, 1890–1920* (Philadelphia: University of Pennsylvania Press, 1970), p. 194.

229   ". . . Republican, Democrat, Socialist . . .": Daniel Schirmer, *Republic or Empire?: American Resistance to the Philippine War* (Cambridge, Mass.: Schenckman, 1972), p. 18.

229   "an inundation of Mongolians": Lasch, "Anti-Imperialist as Racist," p. 115.

229   "making a market . . .": Ray Ginger, *The Bending Cross: A Biography of Eugene Victor Debs* (New Brunswick, N.J.: Rutgers University Press, 1949), p. 203.

229   "any more colored men . . .": Richard Welch, Jr., "Anti-Imperialists and Imperialists Compared: Racism and Economic Expansion," in Paterson, ed., *American Imperialism and Anti-Imperialism*, p. 62.

230   "The sudden departure . . .": Robert L. Beisner, *Twelve Against Empire: The Anti-Imperialists, 1898–1900* (New York: McGraw-Hill, 1968), p. 76.

230   "brutal piracy . . .": *Boston Evening Transcript,* March 1, 1899.

230   "The hearts of men . . .": Jim Zwick, ed., *Mark Twain's Weapons of Satire: Anti-Imperialist Writings on the Philippine-American War* (Syracuse, N.Y.: Syracuse University Press, 1992), p. 65.

231   "Much as we abhor . . .": Schirmer and Shalom, eds., *Philippines Reader*, pp. 30–31 (emphasis added).

232   "they will not only . . .": Lasch, "Anti-Imperialist as Racist," p. 115.

232   "No matter whether . . .": ibid.

232   "understand and realize . . .": ibid., p. 114.

232   "Today we are . . .": Brands, *Bound to Empire*, pp. 29–30.

233   "How can we endure . . .": Gavan Daws, *Shoal of Time: A History of the Hawaiian Islands* (Honolulu: University of Hawaii Press, 1968), p. 290.

233   "You ought to see . . .": LaFeber, *Search for Opportunity*, pp. 154–55.

233   "not merely the white citizens . . .": Reginald Horsman, *Race and Manifest Destiny: The Origins of American Racial Anglo-Saxonism* (Cambridge, Mass.: Harvard University Press, 1982), p. 276.

234   "Tis not more . . .": Finley Peter Dunne, *Mr. Dooley in Peace and War* (Boston: Small, Maynard, 1899), pp. 43, 44.

235   "Shall great public issues . . .": Rubin Weston, *Racism in U.S. Imperialism: The Influence of Racial Assumptions on American Foreign Policy, 1893–1946* (Columbia: University of South Carolina Press, 1972), p. 62.

235   "great victory proves anything . . .": Tompkins, *Anti-Imperialism*, p. 105.

236   "all white persons . . ."; "very like ours": Weston, *Racism in U.S. Imperialism*, p. 72.

236   "The Asiatic has had . . .": Gary Okihiro, *Margins and Mainstreams: Asians in American History and Culture* (Seattle: University of Washington Press, 1994), pp. 155–56.

237   "Why[,] those people" . . . ". . . new methods of doing things": Louis Perez, Jr., *Cuba: Between Reform and Revolution* (New York: Oxford University Press, 1995), pp. 180–81.

238   "responsible for the welfare . . .": ibid., p. 184.

238   "mass of ignorant . . .": ibid., p. 182.

238   "the right to intervene . . .": Paterson, *Major Problems*, p. 328.

238   "the welfare of the Cuban people . . .": Perez, Jr., *Cuba*, p. 187.

239   "require the restraining influence . . .": ibid.

239   "Once the United States . . .": Matthew Frye Jacobson, *Special Sorrows: The Diasporic Imagination of Irish, Polish, and Jewish Immigrants in the United States* (Cambridge, Mass.: Harvard University Press, 1995), p. 143.

239   "the civil rights . . .": Benjamin Ringer, *"We the People" and Others: Duality and America's Treatment of Its Racial Minorities* (New York: Tavistock, 1983), p. 949.

239   "I have not thought . . .": ibid., p. 952.

240   "citizens of the United States . . .": ibid., pp. 954–55.

240   "citizens of Porto Rico . . .": ibid., p. 957.

240   "illiterate . . .": ibid., pp. 968–69.

241   "an incongruous . . ." . . . "Political mixing . . .": ibid., pp. 1001–2.

241   "I think we have enough . . .": Weston, *Racism in U.S. Imperialism*, pp. 202–3.

241   "a system of government . . .": ibid., p. 213.

241   "the United States would at least . . .": Brands, *Bound to Empire*, p. 45.

242   "I have studied attentively . . .": Miller, *"Benevolent Assimilation,"* p. 42.

242   "far superior . . .": Brands, *Bound to Empire*, p. 46.

242   "There must be no joint occupation . . .": ibid., p. 47.

242   "just itching . . .": Miller, *"Benevolent Assimilation,"* p. 176.

243   " 'crushing blows' . . .": ibid., p. 74.

243   "It is not civilized . . .": ibid., p. 211.

243   "Last night one of our boys . . .": ibid., p. 88.

244   "this shooting of human beings . . .": ibid., p. 188.

244   "all persons . . ."; "ten years of age": ibid., p. 220.

244   "Samar to Be Made . . .": ibid., p. 230.

244   "The only good Filipino . . .": ibid., p. 180.

244   "the most ample liberty . . .": Brands, *Bound to Empire*, p. 51.

245   "The war on the part . . .": ibid., p. 56.

245   "are not capable . . .": Marshall Everett, ed., *Exciting Experiences in Our Wars with Spain and the Filipinos* (Chicago: Book Publisher's Union, 1899), pp. 385–86.

245   "I am afraid . . .": Brands, *Bound to Empire*, p. 58.

245   "secure the confidence . . .": ibid., p. 54.

246   "what the Filipinos needed . . .": ibid., p. 64.

246   "a whole people . . ."; "We must have . . .": ibid., p. 68.

246   "Ye-es . . .": Miller, *"Benevolent Assimilation,"* p. 157.

246   "It was never . . ." . . . "desirable to place . . .": Brands, *Bound to Empire*, p. 114.

247   "all, absolutely all . . .": ibid., p. 52.

248   "It is a sorry . . .": Willard B. Gatewood, Jr., *Black Americans and the "White Man's Burden," 1898–1903* (Urbana: University of Illinois Press, 1975), p. 180.

248   "Is it part . . .": Jacobson, *Special Sorrows*, p. 207.

248   "The closer the North . . .": Gatewood, Jr., *Black Americans*, p. 111.

249   "in the great act . . .": ibid., p. 102.

249   "Will the Negro . . .": ibid., p. 222.

250   "black natives . . ."; "The color line . . .": ibid., p. 154.

250   "enough to make . . .": ibid., p. 282.

250   "We would rather . . .": ibid., p. 219.

250   "diabolical outrage . . .": ibid., p. 232.

250   "enlightened civilization . . .": ibid., p. 196.

250   "With the government . . .": ibid., p. 185.

251   "We insist . . .": ibid., p. 240.

251   "The whites have begun . . .": ibid., p. 282.

251   "The poor whites . . .": Willard B. Gatewood, Jr., *"Smoked Yankees" and the Struggle for Empire: Letters from Negro Soldiers, 1898–1902* (Urbana: University of Illinois Press, 1971), p. 257.

251   "I have mingled . . ." . . . "We don't want . . .": ibid., pp. 279–81.

252   "the best opportunities . . .": ibid., p. 316.

252   "It is without honor . . .": Gatewood, Jr., *Black Americans*, p. 287.

252   "Fagen was a traitor . . .": ibid., p. 289.

253   "When I read of these atrocities . . .": Jacobson, *Special Sorrows*, p. 175.

253   "Those miserable foreigners . . .": ibid., p. 183.

253   "Said Samuel Green . . .": ibid., p. 194.

254   "understanding what . . .": ibid., p. 179.

254   "Today the Filipinos . . .": ibid., p. 177.

254   *Dziennik Chicagoski* decried: ibid., p. 195.

255   "the Filipinos are defending . . .": ibid., pp. 201–2.

255   "For us Poles . . .": ibid., p. 176.

256   "American citizenship is to be diluted . . .": ibid., p. 182.

256   "our acquisitions . . .": ibid., p. 183.

256   "so savage and confused . . .": ibid., p. 196.

256   " 'The Philippine vote' . . .": ibid., p. 183.

257   "Pile on the Black Man's Burden . . .": Gatewood, Jr., *Black Americans*, p. 184.

257   "The 'White Man's Burden' . . .": Jacobson, *Special Sorrows*, p. 181.

258   four of the judges: Brands, *Bound to Empire*, p. 77.

258   "barbarous and semi-barbarous peoples . . .": LaFeber, *Search for Opportunity*, p. 195.

258   "Our position is explicitly . . .": Weston, *Racism in U.S. Imperialism*, pp. 212–13.

258   "The Government of Santo Domingo . . .": ibid., p. 228.

258   "to help the Haitian people . . .": ibid., p. 218.

258   "the white men sent . . .": ibid., p. 220.

259   "the troops apparently . . .": ibid., pp. 220–21.

259   "by alleging a desire . . .": Gatewood, Jr., *Black Americans*, p. 174.

259   "Mr. Wilson could not find time . . .": Weston, *Racism in U.S. Imperialism*, p. 222.

CONCLUSION

264   "by the sheer genius . . . ": Anders Stephenson, *Manifest Destiny: American Expansionism and the Empire of Right* (New York: Hill and Wang, 1995), p. 117.

264   "blindly, unintentionally . . .": Michael Sherry, *In the Shadow of War: The United States Since the 1930s* (New Haven: Yale University Press, 1995), p. 57.

Bibliographic Essay

1. EXPORT MARKETS

This chapter seeks to revive an economic or economistic model for the study of U.S. foreign policy, which has fallen into relative disuse in recent years as scholars have turned their attention to matters of culture and ideology. The time has come for some fruitful integration. The classic formulations along economic lines include William Appleman Williams, ed., *The Tragedy of American Diplomacy* (New York: Dell, 1959), *From Colony to Empire: Essays in the History of American Foreign Relations* (New York: John Wiley and Sons, 1972), and *The Contours of American History* (Cleveland: World Publishing, 1961). This line of thinking has been most thoroughly developed in Williams's wake by Walter LaFeber in *The New Empire: An Interpretation of American Expansion, 1860–1898* (Ithaca, N.Y.: American Historical Association/Cornell University Press, 1963), and *The American Search for Opportunity, 1865–1913*, vol. II in *The Cambridge History of American Foreign Relations* (Cambridge: Cambridge University Press, 1993). Charles Campbell, *The Transformation of American Foreign Relations, 1865–1900* (New York: Harper & Row, 1976), and Emily Rosenberg, *Spreading the American Dream: American Economic and Cultural Expansion, 1890–1945* (New York: Hill and Wang, 1982), are also tremendously useful. Martin Sklar, *The Corporate Reconstruction of American Capitalism, 1890–1916* (Cambridge: Cambridge University Press, 1988), conveys much about the perceived economic imperatives of the period, which is valuable in assessing the trajectory of U.S. policy abroad; William Becker, *The Dynamics of Business-Government Relations: Industry and Exports, 1893–1921* (Chicago: University of Chicago Press, 1982) is excellent on the economic actualities. E. J. Hobsbawm, *The Age of Empire* (New York: Vintage Books, 1987), sets the global scene; Stephen Skowronek, *Building a New American State: The*

Expansion of National Administrative Capacities, 1877–1920 (New York: Cambridge University Press, 1982), offers the best account of the American state and its functions during this expansive period. Thomas Paterson, *Major Problems in American Foreign Policy: Documents and Essays* (Lexington, Mass.: D. C. Heath, 1978), is an excellent introductory source for students.

Richard Drinnon, *Facing West: The Metaphysics of Indian-Hating and Empire Building* (Minneapolis: University of Minnesota Press, 1980), is a convincing analysis of the continuities of U.S. encounter and expansionism, from European settlement to Vietnam. Valuable treatments of China as the new "Far West" include Michael Hunt, *The Making of a Special Relationship: The United States and China to 1914* (New York: Columbia University Press, 1983), and *Frontier Defense and the Open Door: Manchuria in Chinese-American Relations, 1895–1911* (New Haven: Yale University Press, 1973); Marilyn Blatt Young, *The Rhetoric of Empire: American China Policy, 1895–1901* (Cambridge, Mass.: Harvard University Press, 1968); Thomas McCormick, *China Market: America's Quest for Informal Empire, 1893–1901* (Chicago: Quadrangle, 1967); James Lorence, *Organized Business and the Myth of the China Market: The American Asiatic Association, 1898–1937* in *Transactions of the American Philosophical Society*, vol. 71, pt. 4 (1981). Shu-Lun Pan, *The Trade of the United States with China* (New York: China Trade Bureau, 1924); Charles S. Campbell, Jr., *Special Business Interests and the Open Door Policy* [1951] (Hamden, Conn.: Archon Books, 1968); and A. Whitney Griswold, *The Far Eastern Policy of the United States* (New York: Harcourt, Brace, & Company, 1938), all contain much that is still useful. On U.S. attitudes toward and ideas about China, see also Warren Cohen, *America's Response to China: An Interpretive History of Sino-American Relations* (New York: Alfred A. Knopf, 1971); Paul A. Varg, *The Making of a Myth: The United States and China, 1897–1912* (East Lansing: Michigan State University Press, 1968), and *Missionaries, Chinese, and Diplomats: The American Protestant Missionary Movement in China, 1890–1952* (Princeton, N.J.: Princeton University Press, 1958); Stuart Creighton Miller, *The Unwelcome Immigrant: The American Image of the Chinese, 1785–1882* (Berkeley: University of California Press, 1969); James Thompson, Peter Stanley, and John Curtis Perry, *Sentimental Imperialists: The American Experience in East Asia* (New York: Harper & Row, 1981); John King Fairbank, *The United States and China* (Cambridge, Mass.: Harvard University Press, 1979); and Akira Iriye, *Across the Pacific: An Inner History of American–East Asian Relations* (New York: Harcourt, Brace & World, 1967).

Walter LaFeber, *Inevitable Revolutions: The United States in Central America* (New York: Norton, 1983), represents a good starting point for U.S. interventionism in Latin America. See also David Healy, *Drive to Hegemony: The United States in the Caribbean, 1898–1917* (Madison: University of Wisconsin Press, 1988). Good general histories include Hector Perez-Brignoli, *A Brief History of Central America* (Berkeley: University of California Press, 1989), and Tulio Halperin Donghi, *The Contemporary History of Latin America* (Durham, N.C.: Duke University Press, 1993). Treatments of particular countries and specific aspects of U.S. involvement in the region include Louis Perez, Jr., *Cuba: Between Reform and Revolution* (New York: Oxford University Press, 1995); José Trías Monge, *Puerto Rico: The Trials of the Oldest Colony in the World* (New Haven: Yale University Press, 1997); Stephen Randall, *Colombia and the United States: Hegemony and Independence* (Athens: University of Georgia Press, 1992); Walter LaFeber, *The Panama Canal: The Crisis in Historical Perspective* (New York: Oxford University Press, 1978); Lester Langley and Thomas Schoonover, *The Banana Men: American Mercenaries and Entrepreneurs in Central America, 1880–1930* (Lexington: University Press of Kentucky, 1995); John M. Hart, *Revolutionary Mexico: The Coming and Process of the Mexican Revolution* (Berkeley: University of California Press, 1987); Friedrich Katz, *The Secret War in Mexico: Europe, the United States, and the Mexican Revolution* (Chicago: University of Chicago Press, 1981); and Daniel Nugent, *Rural Revolt in Mexico: U.S. Intervention and the Domain of Subaltern Politics* (Durham, N.C.: Duke University Press, 1998).

Frederick Pike, *The United States and Latin America: Myths and Stereotypes of Civilization and Nature* (Austin: University of Texas Press, 1992), is an excellent compendium on the racialist baggage that white American policy-makers brought to U.S.–Latin American relations. Frances Aparicio and Susana Chavez-Sliverman, eds., *Tropicalizations: Transcultural Representations of Latinidad* (Hanover, N.H.: University Press of New England, 1997), is also quite suggestive on themes of race, "difference," and international encounter. The longer history of race, expansion, and civic incorporation is nicely handled in Benjamin Ringer, *"We the People" and Others: Duality and America's Treatment of Its Racial Minorities* (New York: Tavistock, 1983); Anders Stephanson, *Manifest Destiny: American Expansion and the Empire of Right* (New York: Hill and Wang, 1995); and Reginald Horsman, *Race and Manifest Destiny: The Origins of American Racial Anglo-Saxonism* (Cambridge, Mass.: Harvard University Press, 1982). On racialized notions of "civilization," see also Robert Berkhofer, *The White Man's Indian: Images of the American Indian from Columbus to the Present* (New York: Vintage, 1978); Roy Harvey Pearce, *Savagism and Civilization: A Study of the Indian and the American Mind* [1953] (Berkeley: University of California Press, 1988); Gail Bederman, *Manliness and Civilization: A Cultural History of Gender and Race in the United States, 1880–1917* (Chicago: University of Chicago Press, 1995); George Stocking, Jr., *Victorian Anthropology* (New York: Free Press, 1987); and Robert Rydell, *All the World's a Fair: Visions of Empire at American International Expositions, 1876–1916* (Chicago: University of Chicago Press, 1984). Two quite disparate but useful interpretations of the technological and economic dimensions of "civilization" are William T. Hagan, "Private Property, the Indian's Door to Civilization," *Ethnohistory*, Spring 1956, pp. 126–37, and Michael Adas, *Machines as the Measure of Man: Science, Technology, and Ideologies of Western Dominance* (Ithaca, N.Y.: Cornell University Press, 1989).

Though this chapter self-consciously harks back to William Appleman Williams and the economic approach to U.S. empire, here and elsewhere I have benefited greatly from the cultural turn in the scholarship on U.S. foreign relations and international relations generally. The foundational texts for this latter body of scholarship include Michael Hunt, *Ideology and U.S. Foreign Policy* (New Haven: Yale University Press, 1987); Amy Kaplan and Donald Pease, eds., *Cultures of United States Imperialism* (Durham, N.C.: Duke University Press, 1993); Michael Hogan and Thomas Paterson, eds., *Explaining the History of American Foreign Relations* (Cambridge: Cambridge University Press, 1991); Edward Said, *Orientalism* (New York: Vintage, 1978), and *Culture and Imperialism* (New York: Vintage, 1993); Anne McClintock, *Imperial Leather: Race, Gender, and Sexuality in the Colonial Context* (New York: Routledge, 1995); Gilbert Joseph, Catherine Legrand, and Ricardo Salvatore, eds., *Close Encounters of Empire: Writing the Cultural History of U.S.–Latin American Relations* (Durham, N.C.: Duke University Press, 1998); and Anne McClintock, Aamir Mufti, and Ella Shohut, eds., *Dangerous Liaisons: Gender, Nation, and Post-Colonial Perspectives* (Minneapolis: University of Minnesota Press, 1997). See also the bibliographies for chapters 3, 4, and 6 below.

2. LABOR MARKETS

Among the best general studies of the dynamic relationship between capitalism and migration are John Bodnar, *The Transplanted: A History of Immigrants in Urban America* (Bloomington: Indiana University Press, 1985); David Montgomery, *The Fall of the House of Labor: The Workplace, the State, and American Labor Activism, 1865–1925* (Cambridge: Cambridge University Press, 1987); Philip Taylor, *The Distant Magnet: European Emigration to the U.S.A.* (New York: Harper & Row, 1971); Roger Daniels, *Coming to America: A History of Immigration and Ethnicity in American Life* (New York: HarperCollins, 1990); Ronald Takaki, *Strangers from a Different Shore* (New York: Penguin, 1989); Lucie Cheng and Edna Bonacich, eds., *Labor Immigration Under Capitalism: Asian Workers in the United States Before World War II* (Berkeley: University of California Press, 1984); Dirk Hoerder, ed., *American Labor and Immigration History, 1877–1920s: Recent European Research* (Urbana: University of Illinois Press, 1983); and Mark Wyman, *Round Trip to America: The Immigrants Return to Europe, 1880–1930* (Ithaca, N.Y.: Cornell University Press, 1993). Oscar Handlin, *The Uprooted* (Boston: Little, Brown, 1951), is still evocative, and Handlin's *Immigration as a Factor in American History* (Englewood Cliffs, N.J.: Prentice-Hall, 1959) remains a very good introduction for students. Stephen Thernstrom, et al., *The Harvard Encyclopedia of American Ethnic Groups* (Cambridge, Mass.: Belknap Press of Harvard University Press, 1980), is a fabulous resource on specific groups and topics.

The literature on immigrants, work, and American labor is of course voluminous. Gwendolyn Mink, *Old Labor and New Immigrants in American Political Development: Union, Party, and State, 1875–1920* (Ithaca, N.Y.: Cornell University Press, 1986), is an excellent account of labor relations and emergent nativism in the period of mass immigration. On working-class consciousness and the genesis of American radicalism in the period, see Philip Foner, *The Workingmen's Party of the United States: A History of the First Marxist Party in the Americas* (Minneapolis: MEP Publications, 1984); David Roediger, *The Wages of Whiteness: Race and the Making of the American Working Class* (London, New York: Verso, 1991); Mari Jo Buhle, *Women and American Socialism 1870–1920* (Urbana: University of Illinois Press, 1981); James Green, *The World of the Worker: Labor in the Twentieth Century* (New York: Hill and Wang, 1980); Ray Ginger, *Altgeld's America: Chicago from 1892–1905* (New York: Harper & Brothers, 1958); Melvyn Dubofsky, *We Shall Be All: A History of the Industrial Workers of the World* (Chicago: Quadrangle, 1969); David Montgomery, *Workers' Control in America: Studies in Work, Technology, and Labor Struggles* (New York: Cambridge University Press, 1979), and *The Fall of the House of Labor;* and Herbert Gutman, *Work, Culture and Society in Industrializing America: Essays in Working-Class and Social History* (New York: Alfred A. Knopf, 1976). The theme of immigration and the American labor movement is also nicely rendered in Norma Fain Pratt, *Morris Hillquit: A Political History of an American Jewish Socialist* (Westport, Conn.: Greenwood Press, 1979); Terence Powderly, *The Path I Trod* (New York: Columbia University Press, 1940); and Irving Howe, *The World of Our Fathers* (New York: Harcourt Brace Jovanovich, 1976). Gary Gerstle, *Working-Class Americanism: The Politics of Labor in a Textile City, 1914–1960* (New York: Cambridge University Press, 1989), treats a later period, but is extremely useful regarding immigrant political orientations in the United States. Philip Foner's multivolume *History of the Labor Movement in the United States* (New York: International Publishers, 1979) is of course a standard.

On various aspects of the history of immigration, work, and American labor, the following list represents a sampling of important topics and scholarly approaches: John Bodnar, *Immigration and Industrialization: Ethnicity in an American Mill Town* (Pittsburgh: University of Pittsburgh Press, 1977); Sucheng Chan, *Asian Americans: An Interpretive History* (Boston: Twayne, 1991), and *This Bittersweet Soil: The Chinese in California Agriculture, 1860–1910* (Berkeley: University of California Press, 1986); James Barret, "Americanization from the Bottom Up: Immigration and the Remaking of the Working Class in the United States, 1880–1930," *Journal of American His-*

tory, Dec. 1992; David Emmons, *The Butte Irish: Class and Ethnicity in an American Mining Town, 1875–1925* (Urbana: University of Illinois Press, 1989); Dirk Hoerder, ed., *"Struggle a Hard Battle": Essays on Working-Class Immigrants* (DeKalb: Northern Illinois University Press, 1986); Neil Foley, *The White Scourge: Mexicans, Blacks, and Poor Whites in Texas Cotton Culture* (Berkeley: University of California Press, 1997); Mario Garcia, *Desert Immigrants: The Mexicans of El Paso, 1880–1920* (New Haven: Yale University Press, 1981); Yuji Ichioka, *The Issei: The World of First Generation Japanese Immigrants, 1885–1924* (New York: Free Press, 1988); Nancy Green, *Ready-to-Wear and Ready-to-Work: A Century of Industry and Immigrants in Paris and New York* (Durham, N.C.: Duke University Press, 1997); Moses Rischin, *The Promised City: New York's Jews, 1870–1914* (New York: Harper & Row, 1962); Ronald Sanders, *The Downtown Jews: Portrait of an Immigrant Generation* (New York: Dover, 1969); Thomas Kessner, *The Golden Door: Italian and Jewish Immigrant Mobility in New York City, 1880–1915* (New York: Oxford University Press, 1977); Humbert Nelli, *The Italians in Chicago, 1880–1930* (New York: Oxford University Press, 1970); Elizabeth Ewen, *Immigrant Women in the Land of Dollars: Life and Culture on the Lower East Side, 1890–1925* (New York: Monthly Review Press, 1985); Daniel Walkowitz, *Worker City, Company Town: Iron and Cotton-Worker Protest in Troy and Cohoes, New York, 1855–84* (Urbana: University of Illinois Press, 1978); Roy Rosenzweig, *Eight Hours for What We Will: Workers and Leisure in an Industrial City, 1870–1920* (Cambridge: Cambridge University Press, 1983); Donald Miller and Richard Sharpless, *The Kingdom of Coal: Work, Enterprise, and Ethnic Communities in the Mine Fields* (Philadelphia: University of Pennsylvania Press, 1985); Ardis Cameron, *Radicals of the Worst Sort: Laboring Women in Lawrence, Massachusetts, 1860–1912* (Urbana: University of Illinois Press, 1993); Alice Kessler-Harris, *Out to Work: A History of Wage-Earning Women in the United States* (New York: Oxford University Press, 1982); Judith Smith, *Family Connections: A History of Italian and Jewish Immigrant Lives in Providence, Rhode Island, 1900–1940* (Albany: State University of New York Press, 1985); Ewa Morawska, *For Bread with Butter* (Cambridge: Cambridge University Press, 1985); Josef Barton, *Peasants and Strangers: Italians, Rumanians, and Slovaks in an American City, 1890–1950* (Cambridge, Mass.: Harvard University Press, 1975); Victor Greene, *The Slavic Community on Strike* (South Bend, Ind.: Notre Dame University Press, 1968); John Bodnar, *Workers' World: Kinship, Community, and Protest in an Industrial Society* (Baltimore, Md.: Johns Hopkins University Press, 1982); Virginia Yans-McLaughlin, *Family and Community: Italian Immigrants in Buffalo, 1880–1930* (Ithaca, N.Y.: Cornell University Press, 1982); John Bodnar, Roger Simon, and Michael Weber, *Lives of Their Own* (Urbana: University of Illinois Press, 1982); Donna Gabaccia, *From Sicily to Elizabeth Street* (Albany: State University of New York Press, 1983), and *Militants and Migrants: Rural Sicilians Become American*

Workers (New Brunswick, N.J.: Rutgers University Press, 1988); John Higham, *Send These to Me: Jews and Other Immigrants in Urban America* [1975] (Baltimore, Md.: Johns Hopkins University Press, 1984); and Olivier Zunz, *The Changing Face of Inequality: Urbanization, Industrial Development, and Immigrants in Detroit, 1880–1920* (Chicago: University of Chicago Press, 1982). Gary Gerstle, "Liberty, Coercion, and the Making of Americans," *Journal of American History*, Sept. 1997, is a breathtaking bibliographic essay on the subject.

For competing but useful analyses of the anti-Chinese movement, see especially Elmer Sandemeyer, *The Anti-Chinese Movement in California* (Urbana: University of Illinois Press, 1973); Alexander Saxton, *The Indispensable Enemy: Labor and the Anti-Chinese Movement in California* (Berkeley: University of California Press, 1971); Shih-Shan Henry Tsai, *The Chinese Experience in America* (Bloomington: Indiana University Press, 1986); and Stuart Creighton Miller, *The Unwelcome Immigrant: The American Image of the Chinese, 1785–1882* (Berkeley: University of California Press, 1969). Roger Daniels, *The Politics of Prejudice: The Anti-Japanese Movement in California and the Struggle for Japanese Exclusion* (New York: Atheneum, 1977), is an excellent account of racial politics in the wake of Chinese Exclusion, and of the centrality of race to late-nineteenth-century U.S. political culture. On antiradicalism and immigration, William Preston, Jr., *Aliens and Dissenters: Federal Suppression of Radicals, 1903–1933* (New York: Harper & Row, 1963), remains important, as does Richard Slotkin, *The Fatal Environment: The Myth of the Frontier in the Age of Industrialization, 1800–1890* (Middletown, Conn.: Wesleyan University Press, 1985).

3. PARABLES OF PROGRESS

Recent years have seen a torrent of conceptually innovative works on the politics and the implications of various genres of travel writing and other narratives of world diversity and "difference." Edward Said, *Orientalism* (New York: Pantheon, 1978), and *Culture and Imperialism* (New York: Vintage, 1993) are touchstones. Other important contributions include Mary Louise Pratt, *Imperial Eyes: Travel Writing and Transculturation* (New York: Routledge, 1992); David Spurr, *The Rhetoric of Empire: Colonial Discourse in Journalism, Travel Writing, and Imperial Administration* (Durham, N.C.: Duke University Press, 1993); Marianna Torgovnik, *Gone Primitive: Savage Intellects, Modern Lives* (Chicago: University of Chicago Press, 1990); Nicholas Thomas, *Colonialism's Culture: Anthropology, Travel, and Government* (Princeton, N.J.: Princeton University Press, 1994); Catherine Lutz and Jane Collins, *Reading National Geographic* (Chicago: University of Chicago Press, 1993); Jan Nederveen Pieterse, *White on Black: Images of Africa and Blacks in Western Popular Culture* (New Haven: Yale University Press, 1992); Timothy Mitchell, *Colonizing Egypt* (Berkeley:

University of California Press, 1988); Nicholas Mirzoeff, *Bodyscape: Art, Modernity and the Ideal Figure* (New York: Routledge, 1995); and Eric Cheyfitz, *The Poetics of Imperialism: Translation and Colonization from "The Tempest" to "Tarzan"* (New York: Oxford University Press, 1991).

Related works that are also helpful in matters of interpreting these genres include Henry Louis Gates, Jr., ed. *"Race," Writing, and Difference* (Chicago: University of Chicago Press, 1985); Malek Alloula, *The Colonial Harem* (Minneapolis: University of Minnesota Press, 1986); H. Alan Cairns, *Prelude to Imperialism: British Reactions to Central African Society, 1840–1890* (London: Routledge and Kegan Paul, 1965); James Clifford, *The Predicament of Culture: Twentieth-Century Ethnography, Literature, and Art* (Cambridge, Mass.: Harvard University Press, 1988); Jacques Derrida, *Writing and Difference* (Chicago: University of Chicago Press, 1978); Stanley Diamond, *In Search of the Primitive: A Critique of Civilization* (New Brunswick, N.J.: Rutgers University Press, 1974); Julia Kristeva, *About Chinese Women* (New York: Urizen, 1977); Edward Said, *Covering Islam: How the Media and the Experts Determine How We See the Rest of the World* (London: Routledge and Kegan Paul, 1981); Michael Taussig, *Shamanism, Colonialism, and the Wild Man: A Study in Terror and Healing* (Chicago: University of Chicago Press, 1987); and Frank McLynn, *Hearts of Darkness: The European Exploration of Africa* (New York: Carroll and Graff, 1992).

On the trope of the "noble savage," see Robert Berkhofer, *The White Man's Indian: Images of the American Indian from Columbus to the Present* (New York: Vintage, 1978); Gail Bederman, *Manliness and Civilization: A Cultural History of Gender and Race in the United States, 1880–1917* (Chicago: University of Chicago Press, 1995); George Stocking, Jr., *Victorian Anthropology* (New York: Free Press, 1987); and Curtis Hinsley, "Zunis and Brahmins," in George Stocking, Jr., ed., *Romantic Motives: Essays on Anthropological Sensibility* (Madison: University of Wisconsin Press, 1989).

4. THEORIES OF DEVELOPMENT

The writings of George Stocking, Jr., continue to dominate the field of the history of anthropology, and indeed the general study of evolutionism and evolutionist thought. See especially George Stocking, Jr., *Victorian Anthropology* (New York: Free Press, 1987); *After Tylor: British Social Anthropology, 1888–1951* (Madison: University of Wisconsin Press, 1995); *Race, Culture, and Evolution: Essays in the History of Anthropology* (Chicago: University of Chicago Press, 1968); as well as Stocking's edited volumes, *Romantic Motives: Essays on Anthropological Sensibility* (Madison: University of Wisconsin Press, 1989); *Bones, Bodies, and Behavior: Essays on Biological Anthropology* (Madison: University of Wisconsin Press, 1988); *The Ethnographer's Magic and Other Essays in the History of Anthropology* (Madison: University of Wisconsin

Press, 1992); and *A Franz Boas Reader: The Shaping of American Anthropology, 1883–1911* (Chicago: University of Chicago Press, 1974).

In Stocking's wake, a number of scholars have added to this tapestry of evolutionist thought from various theoretical perspectives. See Adam Kuper, *The Invention of Primitive Society: Transformation of an Illusion* (New York: Routledge, 1988), and *The Chosen Primate: Human Nature and Cultural Diversity* (Cambridge, Mass.: Harvard University Press, 1994); Nicholas Thomas, *Colonialism's Culture: Anthropology, Travel, and Government* (Princeton, N.J.: Princeton University Press, 1994); Donna Haraway, *Primate Visions: Gender, Race, and Nature in the World of Modern Science* (New York: Routledge, 1989); Johannes Fabian, *Time and the Other: How Anthropology Makes Its Object* (New York: Columbia University Press, 1983); Curtis Hinsley, *The Smithsonian and the American Indian: Making a Moral Anthropology in Victorian America* (Washington, D.C.: Smithsonian, 1981); Elizabeth Edwards, ed., *Anthropology and Photography, 1860–1920* (New Haven: Yale University Press, 1992); and Melissa Banta and Curtis Hinsley, *From Site to Sight: Anthropology, Photography, and the Power of Imagery* (Cambridge, Mass.: Peabody Museum, 1986). Classic formulations in Richard Hofstadter, *Social Darwinism in American Thought* [1944] (Boston: Beacon Press, 1955), remain useful, as do many of the general principles presented in Robert Bannister, *Social Darwinism: Science and Myth in Anglo-American Social Thought* (Philadelphia: Temple University Press, 1979); and Carl N. Degler, *In Search of Human Nature: The Decline and Revival of Darwinism in American Social Thought* (New York: Oxford University Press, 1991).

The history of the eugenics movement has received much fruitful attention in recent years, particularly in Daniel Kevles, *In the Name of Eugenics: Genetics and the Uses of Human Heredity* (Berkeley: University of California Press, 1985); Kenneth Ludmerer, *Genetics and American Society: A Historical Appraisal* (Baltimore, Md.: Johns Hopkins University Press, 1972); and Allan Chase, *The Legacy of Malthus: The Social Cost of the New Scientific Racism* [1975] (Urbana: University of Illinois Press, 1980). Elazar Barkan, *The Retreat of Scientific Racism: Changing Conceptions of Race in Britain and the United States Between the World Wars* (Cambridge: Cambridge University Press, 1992), contains much that is illuminating; and Stefan Kuhl, *The Nazi Connection: Eugenics, American Racism, and German National Socialism* (New York: Oxford University Press, 1994), contains a fully explosive account of the trans-Atlantic intellectual currents of genetic and eugenic thinking in the first part of the twentieth century. The recent re-emergence of eugenic thinking in the form of Richard Herrnstein and Charles Murray, *The Bell Curve* (New York: Free Press, 1994), has provoked a number of thoughtful responses. See, for example, Garland Allen, "Eugenics Comes to America," in Russell Jacoby and Naomi Glauberman, eds., *The Bell Curve Debate: History, Documents, Opinions* (New York: Times Books, 1995).

On mind, intelligence, and the ranking of peoples, see Stephen Jay Gould, *The Mismeasure of Man* (New York: Norton, 1981), and *Ever Since Darwin: Reflections in Natural History* (New York: Norton, 1977); Leon Kamin, "The Pioneers of IQ Testing," in Russell Jacoby and Naomi Glauberman eds., *The Bell Curve Debate: History, Documents, Opinions* (New York: Times Books, 1995); and R. C. Lewontin, Steven Rose, and Leon Kamin, "IQ: The Rank Ordering of the World," in Sandra Harding, ed., *The "Racial" Economy of Science: Toward a Democratic Future* (Bloomington: Indiana University Press, 1993). Robert Rydell, *All the World's a Fair: Visions of Empire at American International Expositions, 1876–1916* (Chicago: University of Chicago Press, 1984), is an invaluable discussion of the dissemination and popularization of both eugenic thought and the sciences of intelligence at world's fairs in the early twentieth century.

5. ACCENTS OF MENACE

Fine general introductions to immigrant politics and the phenomenon of the urban machine can be found in Bruce Stave, ed., *Urban Bosses, Machines, and Progressive Reformers* (Lexington, Mass.: D. C. Heath, 1972); Howard Chudacoff, *The Evolution of American Urban Society* (Englewood Cliffs, N.J.: Prentice-Hall, 1981); Alexander Callow, Jr., *American Urban History* (New York: Oxford University Press, 1973); and Blaine A. Brownell and Warren E. Stickle, eds., *Bosses and Reformers: Urban Politics in America, 1880–1920* (Boston: Houghton Mifflin, 1973). The following are especially good treatments of the local variations: Amy Bridges, *A City in the Republic: Antebellum New York and the Origins of Machine Politics* (New York: Cambridge University Press, 1984); Thomas O'Connor, *The Boston Irish: A Political History* (Boston: Back Bay, 1995); Seymour Mandelbaum, *Boss Tweed's New York* (New York: John Wiley and Sons, 1965); Melvin Holli, *Reform in Detroit: Hazen S. Pingree and Urban Politics* (New York: Oxford University Press, 1969); Zane Miller, *Boss Cox's Cincinnati: Urban Politics in the Progressive Era* (Chicago: University of Chicago Press, 1968); Lyle W. Dorsett, *The Pendergast Machine* (New York: Oxford University Press, 1968); Walton Bean, *Boss Ruef's San Francisco: The Story of the Union Labor Party, Big Business, and the Graft Prosecution* (Berkeley: University of California Press, 1952); and Francis G. Couvares, *The Remaking of Pittsburgh: Class and Culture in an Industrializing City, 1877–1919* (Albany: State University of New York Press, 1984). Paul Kleppner, *The Cross of Culture: A Social Analysis of Midwestern Politics, 1850–1900* (New York: Free Press, 1970), is an insightful treatment of the cultural dimensions of urban ethnic politics. Though focusing on a later period, Milton L. Rakove, *Don't Make No Waves—Don't Back No Losers: An Insider's Analysis of the Daley Machine* (Bloomington: Indiana University Press, 1975), offers a good street-level view of how machines function.

Any investigation of U.S. conceptions of citizenship and the fitness of the immigrant must still take as its starting point John Higham, *Strangers in the Land: Patterns of American Nativism, 1860–1925* [1955] (New York: Atheneum, 1978), and Barbara Miller Solomon, *Ancestors and Immigrants: A Changing New England Tradition* (Chicago: University of Chicago Press, 1956). Rogers Smith, *Civic Ideals: Conflicting Visions of Citizenship in U.S. History* (New Haven: Yale University Press, 1997), is an expansive and careful analysis of the legal discourses surrounding citizenship. Other useful treatments include Dale Knobel, *"America for the Americans": The Nativist Movement in the United States* (New York: Twayne, n.d. [c. 1996]); Michael LeMay, *From Open Door to Dutch Door: An Analysis of U.S. Immigration Policy Since 1820* (New York: Praeger, 1987); Lawrence Fuchs, *The American Kaleidoscope: Race, Ethnicity, and the Civic Culture* (Middletown, Conn.: Wesleyan University Press, 1990); Lucy Salyer, *Laws Harsh as Tigers: Chinese Immigrants and the Shaping of Modern Immigration Law* (Chapel Hill: University of North Carolina Press, 1995); Robert Lee, *Orientals: Asian Americans in Popular Culture* (Philadelphia: Temple University Press, 1999); Ian Haney-Lopez, *White by Law: The Legal Construction of Race* (New York: New York University Press, 1996); and Matthew Frye Jacobson, *Whiteness of a Different Color: European Immigrants and the Alchemy of Race* (Cambridge, Mass.: Harvard University Press, 1998). Though treating a later period, Mae Ngai, "Illegal Aliens and Alien Citizens: U.S. Immigration Policy and Racial Formation, 1924–1945," unpublished Ph.D. dissertation, Columbia University, 1998, provides a fresh and thoughtful interpretation and some very important general propositions regarding the structures governing citizenship. Louise Newman, *White Women's Rights: The Racial Origins of American Feminism* (New York: Oxford University Press, 1998), and Aileen Kraditor, *The Political Ideas of the Women's Suffrage Movement* (New York: Columbia University Press, 1968), are both useful on the intersection of race and gender in Progressive Era debates over citizenship and the franchise.

The classic literature on republicanism is extremely important in understanding the bedrock U.S. conceptions of citizenship and its imperatives. See especially Gordon S. Wood, *The Creation of the American Republic, 1776–1787* (Chapel Hill: University of North Carolina Press, 1969), and *The Radicalism of the American Revolution* (New York: Alfred A. Knopf, 1991); and Bernard Bailyn, *The Ideological Origins of the American Revolution* (Cambridge, Mass.: Belknap Press of Harvard University Press, 1967). Two works that dovetail nicely with these but do take up questions of race overtly are Ronald Takaki, *Iron Cages: Race and Culture in Nineteenth-Century America* (Seattle: University of Washington Press, 1979), and Benjamin Ringer, *"We the People" and Others: Duality and America's Treatment of Its Racial Minorities* (New York: Tavistock, 1983).

Among the most complete and thoughtful treatments of the immigrant voice in U.S. culture is Werner Sollors, *Beyond Ethnicity: Consent and Descent in American*

Culture (New York: Oxford University Press, 1986). See also Marc Schell and Werner Sollors, eds., *Multilingnal America* (New York: New York University Press, 1998), and Robert Park, *The Immigrant Press and Its Control* (New York: Harper and Brothers, 1922). Robert Di Pietro and Edward Ifkovic, eds., *Ethnic Perspectives in American Literature: Selected Essays on the European Contribution* (New York: MLA, 1983), provides compact sketches of various national and ethnic literary traditions. Various ethnic political traditions are captured in John Higham, ed., *Ethnic Leadership in America* (Baltimore, Md.: Johns Hopkins University Press, 1978), and Victor Greene, *American Immigrant Leaders, 1800–1910: Marginality and Identity* (Baltimore, Md.: Johns Hopkins University Press, 1987). David Gutierrez, *Walls and Mirrors: Mexican Americans, Mexican Immigrants, and the Politics of Ethnicity* (Berkeley: University of California Press, 1995), offers a rich analysis of immigrant political sensibilities and voices. On immigrant nationalisms, see Matthew Frye Jacobson, *Special Sorrows: The Diasporic Imagination of Irish, Polish, and Jewish Immigrants in the United States* (Cambridge, Mass.: Harvard University Press, 1995); Kerby A. Miller, *Emigrants and Exiles: Ireland and the Irish Exodus to North America* (New York: Oxford University Press, 1985); Thomas N. Brown, *Irish-American Nationalism, 1870–1890* (Westport, Conn.: Greenwood Press, 1980); James Paul Rodechko, *Patrick Ford and His Search for America: A Case Study of Irish-American Journalism* (New York: Arno, 1976); Michael Hunt, *The Making of a Special Relationship: The United States and China to 1914* (New York: Columbia University Press, 1983); and Victor Greene, *For God and Country: The Rise of Polish and Lithuanian Ethnic Consciousness in America, 1860–1910* (Madison: University of Wisconsin Press, 1975). Susanne Klingenstein, *Jews in the American Academy: The Dynamics of Intellectual Assimilation* (New Haven: Yale University Press, 1991), is a very solid case study of the intellectual history of assimilation.

6. CHILDREN OF BARBARISM

Good general treatments of imperialism and race in the texture of American political thought at the turn of the century include Richard Hofstadter, *Social Darwinism in American Thought* [1944] (Boston: Beacon Press, 1955); Thomas Dyer, *Theodore Roosevelt and the Idea of Race* (Baton Rouge, La.: LSU Press, 1980); David Healy, *U.S. Expansionism: The Imperialist Urge in the 1890s* (Madison: University of Wisconsin Press, 1970); Kaplan and Pease, eds., *Cultures of United States Imperialism;* and Thomas Gossett, *Race: The History of an Idea in America* [1963] (New York: Schocken, 1965). On the specifics of various interventions abroad, in addition to those cited in the bibliography for chapter 1 above, see Oscar Campomanes, "Filipino-American Post-Coloniality and the U.S.-Philippines War of 1898 to 1910s," (unpublished

Ph.D. dissertation, Brown University, 1999); Reynaldo Ileto, *Payson and Revolution: Popular Movements in the Philippines, 1840–1910* (Quezon City, 1979); Stuart Creighton Miller, *"Benevolent Assimilation": The American Conquest of the Philippines, 1899–1903* (New Haven: Yale University Press, 1982); Vincente Rafael, *Discrepant Histories: Translocal Essays on Filipino Cultures* (Philadelphia: Temple University Press, 1995); H. W. Brands, *Bound to Empire: The United States and the Philippines* (New York: Oxford University Press, 1992); Richard Welch, *Response to Imperialism: The United States and the Philippine-American War, 1899–1902* (Chapel Hill: University of North Carolina Press, 1979); Ernest May, *Imperial Democracy: The Emergence of America as a Great Power* (New York: Harper & Row, 1961); Philip S. Foner, *The Spanish-Cuban-American War and the Birth of American Imperialism, 1895–1902* (New York: Monthly Review Press, 1972); Jeffrey Belknap and Raul Fernandez, *José Martí's "Our America": From National to Hemispheric Cultural Studies* (Durham, N.C.: Duke University Press, 1998); Louis Perez, Jr., *Cuba: Between Reform and Revolution* (New York: Oxford University Press, 1995); Kelvin Santiago-Valles, *"Subject People" and Colonial Discourses: Economic Transformation and Social Disorder in Puerto Rico, 1898–1947* (Albany: State University of New York Press, 1994); Gavan Daws, *Shoal of Time: A History of the Hawaiian Islands* (Honolulu: University of Hawaii Press, 1968); Liliuokalani, *Hawaii's Story by Hawaii's Queen* [1898] (Rutland, Vt.: Tuttle, 1964); and Rubin Weston, *Racism in U.S. Imperialism: The Influence of Racial Assumptions on American Foreign Policy, 1893–1946* (Columbia: University of South Carolina Press, 1972). *Radical History Review*, Winter 1999, devoted an entire issue to the U.S. interventions of 1898 and 1899. Gary Okihiro, *Margins and Mainstreams: Asians in American History and Culture* (Seattle: University of Washington Press, 1994), and Lisa Lowe, *Immigrant Acts: On Asian American Cultural Politics* (Durham, N.C.: Duke University Press, 1996), are particularly insightful analyses of the ways in which Asian American history and the figure of the Asian American illuminate the dynamic relationship between global politics and U.S. domestic political culture.

On various brands of anti-imperialism in the United States, see Daniel Schirmer, *Republic or Empire?: American Resistance to the Philippine War* (Cambridge, Mass.: Schenckman, 1972); Robert L. Beisner, *Twelve Against Empire: The Anti-Imperialists, 1898–1900* (New York: McGraw-Hill, 1968); E. Berkeley Tompkins, *Anti-Imperialism in the United States: The Great Debate, 1890–1920* (Philadelphia: University of Pennsylvania Press, 1970); Jim Zwick, ed., *Mark Twain's Weapons of Satire: Anti-Imperialist Writings on the Philippine-American War* (Syracuse, N.Y.: Syracuse University Press, 1992); Matthew Frye Jacobson, *Special Sorrows: The Diasporic Imagination of Irish, Polish, and Jewish Immigrants in the United States* (Cambridge, Mass.: Harvard University Press, 1995); David Noel Doyle, *Irish Americans: Native Rights and National Empires: The Structure, Divisions, and Attitudes of the Catholic Mi-*

nority in the Decade of Expansion, 1890–1901 (New York: Arno Press, 1976); Christopher Lasch, "The Anti-Imperialist as Racist," in Thomas Paterson, ed., *American Imperialism and Anti-Imperialism* (New York: Crowell, 1973); Richard Welch, "Twelve Anti-Imperialists and Anti-Imperialists Compared," in ibid.; Willard B. Gatewood, Jr., *Black Americans and the "White Man's Burden," 1898–1903* (Urbana: University of Illinois Press, 1975); and Gatewood, Jr., ed., *"Smoked Yankees" and the Struggle for Empire: Letters from Negro Soldiers, 1898–1902* (Urbana: University of Illinois Press, 1971).

Index